GCSE
Geography

There's been a seismic shift in GCSE Geography, and the latest Grade 9-1 courses are tougher than ever. Luckily, this CGP book has it all covered...

It's packed with brilliant study notes, clear diagrams and cracking case studies — plus plenty of exam-style practice to test how much you've *really* learned.

We've also included top advice for the decision-making and fieldwork questions, so there won't be any earth-shattering shocks on the day.

--- How to access your free Online Edition ---

This book includes a free Online Edition to read on your PC, Mac or tablet.
You'll just need to go to **cgpbooks.co.uk/extras** and enter this code:

3777 0734 0778 3374

By the way, this code only works for one person. If somebody else has used this book before you, they might have already claimed the Online Edition.

Complete
Revision & Practice
Everything you need to pass the exams!

Contents

Published by CGP

Contributors:
Sophie Anderson, Paddy Gannon, Jack Gillett, Meg Gillett, Barbara Melbourne, Helen Nurton, Sophie Watkins

Editors:
Ellen Burton, Chris McGarry, Liam Neilson, Claire Plowman, David Ryan

Proofreading:
Karen Wells

ISBN: 978 1 78294 625 0

With thanks to Ana Pungartnik for the copyright research.

Printed by Bell & Bain Ltd, Glasgow.
Clipart from Corel®

Based on the classic CGP style created by Richard Parsons.

Natural Hazards

You often see <u>natural hazards</u> on the <u>news</u> — but that's <u>not</u> an excuse to watch telly instead of revising.

A **Natural Hazard** is a **Threat** to **People or Property**

1) A natural hazard is a <u>natural process</u> which <u>could</u> cause <u>death</u>, <u>injury</u> or <u>disruption</u> to humans, or <u>destroy property</u> and possessions.

2) A <u>natural disaster</u> is a natural hazard that has actually <u>happened</u>.

3) Extreme events which do not pose <u>any</u> threat to human activity are <u>not</u> counted as hazards (e.g. a <u>drought</u> in an <u>uninhabited</u> desert or an <u>avalanche</u> in <u>Antarctica</u>).

There are **Two Main Types** of **Natural Hazard**

Most natural hazards can be divided up into <u>two main categories</u>:

1 Geological Hazards

Geological hazards are caused by <u>land</u> and <u>tectonic</u> (see next page) processes.

Examples of geological hazards include <u>volcanoes</u> and <u>earthquakes</u> (see p.4-7), <u>landslides</u> and <u>avalanches</u>.

2 Meteorological Hazards

Meteorological hazards are caused by <u>weather</u> and <u>climate</u>.

Examples of meteorological hazards include <u>tropical storms</u> (p.17-22), other <u>extreme weather</u> (p.16) including heatwaves and cold spells, and <u>climate change</u> (p.35-42).

Different **Factors** Affect the **Hazard Risk** from Natural Hazards

<u>Hazard risk</u> is the <u>probability</u> (chance) that a natural hazard <u>occurs</u>. There are several <u>factors</u> affecting hazard risk:

Vulnerability

1) The <u>more people</u> that are <u>in areas exposed</u> to <u>natural hazards</u>, the <u>greater</u> the <u>probability</u> they will be <u>affected</u> by a natural hazard — so the <u>hazard risk</u> is <u>higher</u>.

2) For example, an area with high population density on a <u>flood plain</u> (like <u>Bangladesh</u>) is very vulnerable to <u>flooding</u> caused by extreme weather, and a city at the base of a <u>volcano</u> (like <u>Naples</u>, Italy) is very vulnerable to <u>volcanic eruptions</u>.

Capacity To Cope

1) Natural hazards have to <u>affect human activities</u> to count as a <u>hazard</u>. The <u>better</u> a population can <u>cope</u> with an extreme event, the <u>lower</u> the <u>threat</u>.

2) For example, <u>developed countries</u> are <u>better</u> able to <u>cope</u> with <u>flooding</u> because they can afford to build <u>flood defences</u>, <u>evacuate</u> people in a disaster and <u>repair</u> damage afterwards.

Nature of Natural Hazards

1) <u>Type</u> — the <u>hazard risk</u> from <u>some</u> hazards is <u>greater</u> than <u>others</u>.
E.g. <u>tropical storms</u> can be <u>predicted</u> and monitored, giving people time to <u>evacuate to safety</u>. But <u>earthquakes</u> happen <u>very suddenly</u>, with no warning, so it's <u>much harder</u> to protect people.

2) <u>Frequency</u> — some natural hazards occur <u>more often</u> than <u>others</u>, <u>increasing</u> the <u>hazard risk</u>.

3) <u>Magnitude</u> — <u>more severe</u> natural hazards cause <u>greater effects</u> than <u>less severe</u> natural hazards.
E.g. a <u>magnitude 9.0</u> earthquake struck Japan in 2011 and <u>killed</u> over <u>15 000 people</u>. When a <u>6.3 magnitude</u> earthquake struck L'Aquila, Italy, around <u>300 people died</u>.

Natural hazards are extreme events that pose a threat to people

If you can get your head around the definitions on this page it will set you up well for the rest of the topic. Remember, not all hazards were created equal — the risk from natural hazards is affected by a range of factors.

Structure of the Earth

The Earth's surface is made of huge floating plates that are constantly moving...

The Earth has a Layered Structure

1) At the centre of the Earth is the core:

> The core is a ball of solid (inner) and liquid (outer) iron and nickel.
> The temperature inside the core ranges from 4400-6000 °C.

2) Around the core is the mantle, which is made up of silicon-based rocks:

- The part of the mantle nearest the core is quite rigid.
- The layer above this, called the asthenosphere, can flow.
- And the very, very top bit of the mantle is rigid.
- The temperature of the mantle is between 1000 and 3700 °C.

3) The solid outer layer of the Earth is called the crust. There are two types:

- Continental crust is thicker and less dense.
- Oceanic crust is thinner and more dense.

4) The crust is divided into slabs called tectonic plates.

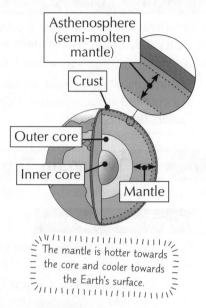

Asthenosphere (semi-molten mantle)

Crust

Outer core

Inner core

Mantle

The mantle is hotter towards the core and cooler towards the Earth's surface.

Tectonic Plates Move due to Convection Currents in the Mantle

1) The tectonic plates float on the mantle. Radioactive decay of some elements in the mantle and core, e.g. uranium, generates a lot of heat. When lower parts of the asthenosphere heat up they become less dense and slowly rise.

2) As they move towards the top of the mantle they cool down, become more dense, then slowly sink.

3) These circular movements are called CONVECTION CURRENTS — they cause tectonic plates to move.

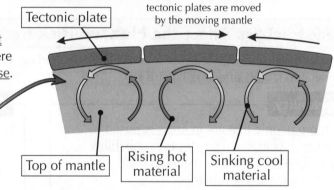

Tectonic plate

tectonic plates are moved by the moving mantle

Top of mantle

Rising hot material

Sinking cool material

Plate Margins are where Tectonic Plates Meet

The places where plates meet are called plate margins or plate boundaries:

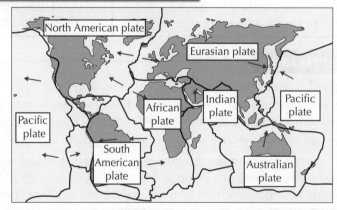

North American plate

Eurasian plate

Indian plate

Pacific plate

African plate

Pacific plate

South American plate

Australian plate

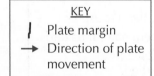

KEY

| Plate margin
→ Direction of plate movement

Earth's structure = core, then mantle, then crust on the outside

Make sure you understand the Earth's structure and what tectonic plates are. Spend some time getting convection currents clear in your head as well. Oh, and don't forget about plate margins too. Sorted? Then move on...

Plate Margins

Tectonic plate margins are where plates meet. How the plates meet is all to do with the direction they're moving in.

There are Different Types of Plate Margins

1 Destructive (Convergent) Margins

- Destructive margins are where two plates are moving towards each other.

- Where an oceanic plate meets a continental plate, the denser oceanic plate is forced down into the mantle and destroyed. This often creates volcanoes and ocean trenches (very deep sections of the ocean floor where the oceanic plate goes down).

- EXAMPLE: the Pacific plate is being forced under the Eurasian plate along the east coast of Japan.

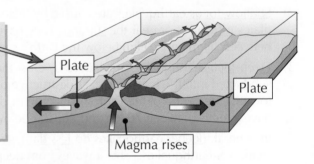

Continental plate

Volcano

Ocean trench

Oceanic plate

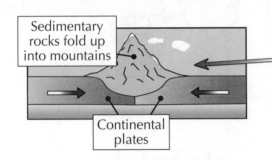

Sedimentary rocks fold up into mountains

Continental plates

2 Collision Plate Margins

Collision plate margins are a type of convergent margin.

- In collision plate margins, both plates are made from continental crust and move towards each other.

- Neither plate is forced down into the mantle — instead both plates are folded and forced upwards, creating fold mountains.

- EXAMPLE: the Eurasian and Indian plates are colliding to form the Himalayas.

3 Constructive (Divergent) Margins

- Constructive margins are where two plates are moving away from each other.

- Magma (molten rock) rises from the mantle to fill the gap and cools, creating new crust.

- EXAMPLE: the Eurasian plate and the North American plate are moving apart at the mid-Atlantic Ridge.

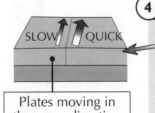

Plate

Plate

Magma rises

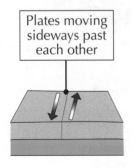

Plates moving sideways past each other

Plates moving in the same direction at different speeds

SLOW   QUICK

4 Conservative Margins

- Conservative margins are where two plates are moving sideways past each other, or are moving in the same direction but at different speeds.

- Crust isn't created or destroyed.

- EXAMPLE: the Pacific plate is moving past the North American plate on the west coast of the USA, e.g. at the San Andreas fault.

REVISION TIP

Make sure you understand the differences between each margin

Each margin has different characteristics — the direction the plates move in affects what happens there. Practise sketching and labelling the diagrams on this page to learn how tectonic plates move.

Earthquake Hazards

Earthquakes happen more often than you think. Obviously there are the big ones that cause loads of damage and make the headlines on the news, but there are also lots of weak earthquakes every year that hardly anyone notices.

Earthquakes Occur at All Types of Plate Margin

1) Earthquakes are caused by the tension that builds up at all types of plate margin:

> Destructive margins — tension builds up when one plate gets stuck as it's moving down past the other into the mantle.

> Constructive margins — tension builds along cracks within the plates as they move away from each other.

> Collision margins — tension builds as the plates are pushed together.

> Conservative margins — tension builds up when plates that are grinding past each other get stuck.

2) The plates eventually jerk past each other, sending out shock waves (vibrations). These vibrations are the earthquake.

3) Earthquakes are measured using the moment magnitude scale, which measures the energy released by an earthquake. You may still see some references to the Richter scale (which also measures the energy released) but it's no longer used by scientists.

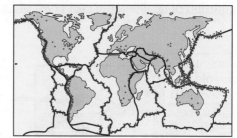

KEY
:::: Earthquakes
| Plate margin

Earthquakes Occur at Various Depths

1) The focus of an earthquake is the point in the Earth where the earthquake starts. This can be at the Earth's surface, or anywhere up to 700 km below the surface.

2) Shallow-focus earthquakes are caused by tectonic plates moving at or near the surface. They have a focus between 0 km and 70 km below the Earth's surface.

3) Deep-focus earthquakes are caused by crust that has previously been subducted into the mantle (e.g. at destructive plate margins) moving towards the centre of the Earth, heating up or decomposing. They have a focus between 70 km and 700 km below the Earth's surface.

4) In general, deeper earthquakes do less damage at the surface than shallower earthquakes. Shock waves from deeper earthquakes have to travel through more rock to reach the surface, which reduces their power (and the amount of shaking) when they reach the surface.

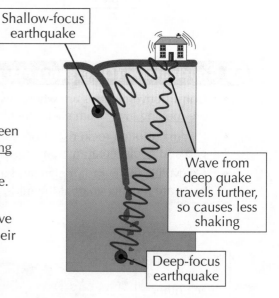

Shallow-focus earthquake

Wave from deep quake travels further, so causes less shaking

Deep-focus earthquake

Earthquakes can Cause Tsunamis

1) Tsunamis are a series of enormous waves caused when huge amounts of water get displaced.

2) Underwater earthquakes cause the seabed to move, which displaces water. Waves spread out from the epicentre of the earthquake (the point on the Earth's surface that's straight above the focus).

3) The depth of an earthquake affects the size of a tsunami — shallow-focus earthquakes displace more water because they're closer to the Earth's surface. This increases the size of a tsunami.

4) The waves travel very fast in deep water so they can hit the shore without much warning. This means they can cause a high death toll.

Shallow earthquakes usually do the most damage

I'd better say this now... don't be put off by maps like the one at the top of the page — you won't ever have to draw them in your exam. But you should know where earthquakes happen and why, so have another read of this page.

Volcanic Hazards

Volcanoes usually look like mountains... until they <u>explode</u> and throw <u>molten rock</u> everywhere.

Volcanoes are Found at Destructive and Constructive Plate Margins

1) At <u>destructive plate margins</u> the <u>oceanic plate</u> goes <u>under</u> the <u>continental plate</u> because it's <u>more dense</u>.

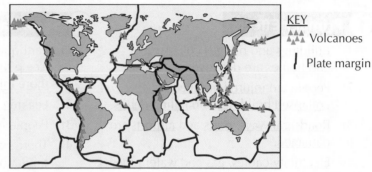

- The <u>oceanic plate</u> moves down into the <u>mantle</u>, where it's <u>melted</u> and <u>destroyed</u>.
- A <u>pool</u> of <u>magma</u> forms.
- The <u>magma rises</u> through <u>cracks</u> in the crust called <u>vents</u>.
- The magma <u>erupts</u> onto the surface (where it's called <u>lava</u>) forming a <u>volcano</u>.

2) At <u>constructive margins</u> the magma <u>rises up</u> into the <u>gap</u> created by the plates moving apart, forming a <u>volcano</u>.

3) When a volcano erupts, it emits <u>lava</u> and <u>gases</u>. Some volcanoes emit <u>lots</u> of <u>ash</u>, which can <u>cover land</u>, <u>block out</u> the <u>sun</u> and form <u>pyroclastic flows</u> (<u>super-heated</u> currents of <u>gas</u>, <u>ash</u> and <u>rock</u>).

Hotspots are Found Away From Plate Margins

Some volcanoes form in the <u>middle</u> of tectonic plates over <u>hotspots</u>:

1) They occur where a <u>plume</u> of <u>hot magma</u> from the <u>mantle</u> moves towards the <u>surface</u>, causing an unusually large <u>flow of heat</u> from the mantle to the crust.

2) Sometimes the magma can <u>break through</u> the crust and reach the <u>surface</u>. When this happens, there is an <u>eruption</u> and a <u>volcano</u> forms.

3) Hotspots remain <u>stationary</u> over time, but the <u>crust moves above them</u>. This can create <u>chains</u> of <u>volcanic islands</u>, e.g. <u>Hawaii</u> is a chain of volcanic islands in the middle of the <u>Pacific plate</u>.

There are Different Types of Volcano

1) <u>Composite volcanoes</u> (E.g. Mount Fuji in Japan)

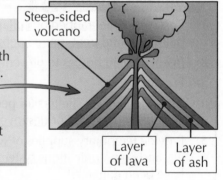

- Occur at <u>destructive plate margins</u> (see p.3).
- Subducted <u>oceanic crust</u> contains lots of <u>water</u>. The water <u>reacts</u> with <u>magma</u> and creates <u>gases</u>, which cause the subducted crust to <u>erupt</u>.
- They have <u>explosive eruptions</u> that start with <u>ashy explosions</u> that deposit a <u>layer of ash</u>.
- They erupt <u>andesitic lava</u> that has a <u>high silica content</u> which makes it <u>thick</u> and <u>sticky</u>. The lava <u>can't flow far</u> so forms a <u>steep-sided cone</u>.

2) <u>Shield volcanoes</u> (E.g. Mauna Loa on the Hawaiian islands)

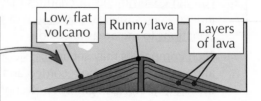

- Occur at <u>hotspots</u> or <u>constructive plate margins</u> (see p.3).
- They are <u>not very explosive</u> and are made up of <u>only lava</u>.
- They erupt <u>basaltic lava</u>, which has a <u>low silica content</u> and is <u>runny</u>. It flows <u>quickly</u> and spreads over a <u>wide area</u>, forming a <u>low, gentle-sided</u> volcano.

Volcanoes only occur in some parts of the world

Make sure you can describe the global pattern of volcanic activity, and remember that not all volcanoes are on plate margins. Examiners love asking about hotspots, so make sure you understand how they work as well.

Earthquakes — Effects and Responses

Earthquakes have a load of really serious effects, as well as being pretty exciting to learn about.

Earthquakes have Primary and Secondary Effects...

The primary effects of an earthquake are the immediate impacts of the ground shaking.
The secondary effects happen later on, often as a result of the primary effects.

1 Primary Effects

1) Buildings and bridges collapse, and homes are destroyed.
2) People are injured or killed by collapsed buildings and falling debris.
3) Roads, railways, ports and airports are damaged.
4) Electricity cables, gas and water pipes and communications networks are damaged, cutting off supplies.

Roads can buckle and crack.

2 Secondary Effects

1) Earthquakes can trigger landslides and tsunamis (see p.4) — these destroy more buildings and cause more injuries and deaths.
2) Leaking gas can be ignited, starting fires.
3) People are left homeless and could die, e.g. from cold.
4) There's a shortage of clean water and a lack of proper sanitation — this makes it easier for diseases to spread.
5) Due to blocked or destroyed roads, aid and emergency vehicles can't get through, and trade is difficult.
6) Businesses are damaged or destroyed, causing unemployment and lost income, and tourists can be put off visiting the area.
7) Repairs and reconstruction can be very expensive, so can weaken a country's economy.

...Which Trigger Immediate and Long-Term Responses

Some effects of earthquakes have to be dealt with immediately to stop further loss of life, injuries or damage to property. Others are dealt with in the longer term:

Immediate Responses

1) Rescue people trapped by collapsed buildings, and treat injured people.
2) Recover dead bodies to prevent spread of disease.
3) Put out fires.
4) Set up temporary shelters for people whose homes have been damaged or destroyed.
5) Provide temporary supplies of water, food, electricity, gas and communications systems if regular supplies have been damaged.
6) Foreign governments or charities may send aid workers, supplies, equipment or financial donations to the areas affected.
7) Tech companies may set up disaster response tools, allowing damage to be recorded and people to confirm their safety, e.g. Google Crisis Response™ service.

Long-Term Responses

1) Re-house people who lost their homes.
2) Repair or rebuild damaged buildings, roads, railways and bridges.
3) Reconnect broken electricity, water, gas and communications connections.
4) If necessary, improve building regulations so that buildings are more resistant to damage from earthquakes.
5) Set up initiatives to help economic recovery, e.g. by promoting tourism.

Primary effects are ones caused directly by the ground shaking

Secondary effects are the ones that happen later on. Earthquakes cause various nasty impacts and you should be clear on which are primary and which are secondary. It's a good idea to learn a few of each for the exams.

Volcanoes — Effects and Responses

People living near a volcano can be <u>seriously affected</u> if it erupts — and <u>not</u> all the effects happen <u>straight away</u>. If an eruption does occur, there are lots of ways that people <u>respond</u> to try and help those affected.

Volcanic Eruptions also have Primary and Secondary Effects...

1 Primary Effects

1) <u>Buildings</u> and <u>roads</u> are <u>destroyed</u> by <u>lava flows</u> and <u>pyroclastic flows</u>. <u>Buildings</u> may also <u>collapse</u> if <u>enough ash falls on them</u>.
2) <u>People</u> and <u>animals</u> are <u>injured</u> or <u>killed</u> by <u>pyroclastic flows</u>, <u>lava flows</u> and <u>falling rocks</u>.
3) <u>Crops</u> are <u>damaged</u> and <u>water supplies</u> are <u>contaminated</u> when <u>ash</u> falls on them.
4) <u>People</u>, <u>animals</u> and <u>plants</u> are <u>suffocated</u> by <u>volcanic gases</u>.

Montserrat's capital city had to be abandoned after an eruption.

2 Secondary Effects

1) <u>Mudflows</u> (also called <u>lahars</u>) form when <u>volcanic material mixes</u> with <u>water</u>, e.g. from <u>heavy rainfall</u> or <u>snow melt</u>. Mudflows and <u>landslides</u> cause more <u>destruction</u>, <u>death</u> and <u>injury</u>.
2) <u>Flooding</u> can be caused by <u>hot</u> rock, ash and gas <u>melting ice</u> and <u>snow</u> on the volcano. Rock and ash can <u>clog up rivers</u> and <u>dams</u>, making <u>flooding worse</u>.
3) <u>Transport networks</u> are blocked or destroyed so <u>aid</u> and <u>emergency vehicles can't get through</u>, and <u>trade</u> is <u>difficult</u>.
4) People are left <u>homeless</u>. <u>Damaged</u> or <u>destroyed</u> businesses cause <u>unemployment</u> and loss of income.
5) <u>Tourism</u> can be <u>disrupted</u> straight after an eruption — but often it can <u>increase afterwards</u> with tourists interested in seeing volcanoes.
6) <u>Ash</u> makes fields <u>more fertile</u> once it's broken down.
7) <u>Recovering</u> after an eruption can take a <u>very long time</u> and cost a <u>huge amount</u> of money, weakening a country's economy.

...Which also lead to Immediate and Long-Term Responses

Immediate Responses

1) <u>Evacuate</u> people before the eruption, if it was <u>predicted</u>, or evacuate <u>as soon as possible</u> after the eruption starts.
2) Provide <u>food</u>, <u>drink</u> and <u>shelter</u> for evacuated people.
3) Treat people <u>injured</u> by the eruption, e.g. from falling debris or ash inhalation.
4) <u>Rescue</u> anyone cut off by <u>damage</u> to <u>roads</u> or <u>bridges</u>.
5) Provide temporary supplies of <u>electricity</u>, <u>gas</u> and <u>communications</u> systems if regular supplies have been <u>damaged</u>.
6) <u>Foreign governments</u> or <u>charities</u> may send <u>aid workers</u>, <u>supplies</u>, <u>equipment</u> or <u>financial donations</u> to the areas affected.
7) <u>Tech companies</u> may set up <u>disaster response tools</u> allowing damage to be <u>recorded</u> and people to <u>confirm</u> their <u>safety</u>, e.g. Google Crisis Response™ service.

Long-Term Responses

1) <u>Repair</u> and <u>rebuild</u> if possible, or <u>resettle</u> affected people elsewhere.
2) <u>Repair</u> and <u>reconnect</u> <u>infrastructure</u> (<u>roads</u>, <u>rail</u>, <u>power lines</u> and <u>communication networks</u> etc.).
3) <u>Improve</u>, <u>repair</u> and <u>update</u> monitoring and evacuation plans.
4) <u>Boost the economy</u> if possible, e.g. by attracting <u>tourists</u> to see the volcano and its effects.

EXAM TIP

Immediate responses are those that happen straight away

Make sure you read the questions in the exam carefully — it's no good writing all about treating injured people and providing emergency aid if the question asks you for the long-term responses.

Living with Tectonic Hazards

Plenty of people live in areas affected by tectonic hazards because most of the time the hazards keep pretty quiet.

Lots of People Live in Areas at Risk from Tectonic Hazards

There are a few reasons why people choose to live close to volcanoes or in areas vulnerable to earthquakes:

1) They've always lived there — moving away may mean leaving friends and family.

2) They're employed in the area. If people move they would have to find new jobs.

3) They're confident of support from their government after an earthquake or volcanic eruption, e.g. to help rebuild houses.

4) Some people think that severe earthquakes or eruptions won't happen again in the area.

5) The soil around volcanoes is fertile because it's full of minerals from volcanic ash and lava. This makes it good for growing crops, which attracts farmers.

6) Volcanoes are tourist attractions — loads of tourists visit volcanoes so lots of people live around volcanoes to work in the tourist industry.

Management can Reduce the Effects of Tectonic Hazards

Management strategies can reduce the number of people killed, injured, made homeless or made unemployed.

Monitoring

1) Networks of seismometers and lasers monitor earth movements, and can be used in early warning systems to give a small but vital amount of warning before a large earthquake occurs.

2) Scientists can monitor the tell-tale signs that come before a volcanic eruption. Things such as tiny earthquakes, escaping gas, and changes in the shape of the volcano (e.g. bulges in the land where magma has built up under it) all mean an eruption is likely.

Prediction

1) Earthquakes cannot be reliably predicted, but by monitoring the movement of tectonic plates scientists can forecast which areas should be prepared for one to occur.

2) Volcanic eruptions can be predicted if the volcano is well-monitored. Predicting when a volcano is going to erupt gives people time to evacuate — this reduces the number of injuries and deaths.

Protection

1) Buildings can be designed to withstand earthquakes, e.g. by using materials like reinforced concrete or building special foundations that absorb an earthquake's energy.

2) Existing buildings and bridges can be strengthened (e.g. by wrapping pillars in steel frames) so they're less likely to collapse under the weight of falling ash or due to shaking from an earthquake.

3) Automatic shut-off switches can be fitted that turn off gas and electricity supplies to prevent fires if an earthquake is detected by a monitoring system.

Planning

1) Future developments can be planned to avoid the areas most at risk from tectonic hazards.

2) Emergency services can train and prepare for disasters, e.g. by practising rescuing people from collapsed buildings or setting up shelters. This will reduce the number of people killed.

3) People can be educated so that they know what to do if an earthquake or eruption happens.

4) Governments can plan evacuation routes to get people out of dangerous areas quickly and safely in case of an earthquake or volcanic eruption. This reduces the number of people killed or injured by things like fires, pyroclastic flows or mudflows.

5) Emergency supplies like blankets, clean water and food can be stockpiled. If a natural hazard is predicted the stockpiles can be moved close to areas likely to be affected.

Predicting a volcanic eruption gives people time to evacuate

Make sure you know how monitoring, prediction, protection and planning can reduce the risks from earthquakes and volcanoes. It's easy to get them muddled up, so try writing out a few points for each.

Tectonic Hazards

And you thought I'd forgotten all about the real-world examples.

Some Countries are **More Prepared** than Others

1) Preparedness for tectonic hazards is different in countries of contrasting wealth and development.
2) Japan (a developed country) and Pakistan (a developing country) have a long history of earthquakes, and both countries have different levels of preparedness.

	Japan	Pakistan
Prediction	• The Japan Meteorological Agency (JMA) and local governments monitor seismic activity all over the country. • If an earthquake is detected, people are warned immediately.	• Up until recently, there wasn't extensive monitoring of seismic activity in Pakistan. • This means earthquakes could strike without warning.
Preparation	• Strict building laws help prevent major damage during an earthquake. • Buildings are reinforced with steel frames to prevent them from collapsing. • High-rise buildings have deep foundations with shock absorbers to reduce vibrations and shaking in the building. • Japan has early warning systems to alert residents to earthquakes and tsunamis. • High-speed 'bullet' trains automatically brake in the event of an earthquake to stop them derailing. • Automatic alarms stop mechanical equipment to alert workers and prevent injuries.	• As a developing country, Pakistan doesn't have access to the same building materials or technologies as Japan. • Many buildings are constructed using wood and cement, which are easily destroyed during earthquakes. • Up until recently, building laws didn't include measures of protection against earthquake damage. Even now, they're often ignored when constructing new buildings. • Poor communication networks make it difficult to alert the population.
Long-Term Planning	• Japan's population is educated on being prepared for earthquakes, e.g. Disaster Prevention Day is an annual nationwide drill to practise evacuations in the event of an earthquake. • Schools carry out drills to teach children what to do if there's an earthquake. • People living in coastal communities practise getting to higher ground or emergency bunkers in the event of a tsunami.	• There are lots of poor, remote settlements in Pakistan that have no education programme for teaching people what to do if there's an earthquake. • Planning evacuations is difficult because there are very few roads and poor communications.

Recent Earthquakes have tested their Preparedness

Japan

1) On 11th March 2011, a powerful earthquake struck north-east Japan.
2) It measured 9.0 on the moment magnitude scale and triggered a tsunami that overwhelmed the coast and inland areas.
3) Japanese scientists had predicted a smaller earthquake to hit the north of the country, but an earthquake of this magnitude was unexpected.
4) It was caused by the sudden movement of the Pacific plate under the North American plate — the two plates meet at a destructive margin.

Pakistan

1) On 8th October 2005, Kashmir, Pakistan was struck by a major earthquake.
2) It measured 7.6 on the moment magnitude scale, causing landslides, rockfalls and huge amounts of destruction.
3) Although scientists monitor seismic activity in the area, the earthquake was unpredicted.
4) It was caused by the release of pressure that had built up along the collision plate margin between the Eurasian and Indian plates.

Tectonic Hazards

Both Earthquakes had Major Impacts

See page 6 for more on primary and secondary impacts.

Primary Impacts

- Thousands of buildings were damaged.
- The earthquake caused severe liquefaction (where waterlogged soil behaves like a liquid). This caused many buildings to tilt and sink into the ground.
- More than 15 000 people died, mostly by drowning.

- The Pakistan earthquake caused around 80 000 deaths, mostly from collapsed buildings.
- Tens of thousands of people were injured.
- Hundreds of thousands of buildings were damaged or destroyed, including whole villages.
- Around 3 million people were made homeless.
- Water pipelines and electricity lines were broken, cutting off supply.

Secondary Impacts

- The earthquake triggered a tsunami which killed thousands of people.
- Hundreds of thousands of buildings were completely destroyed. Over 230 000 people were made homeless.
- The tsunami cut off the power supplies to the Fukushima nuclear power plant, causing a meltdown.
- Road and rail networks suffered severe damage, e.g. 325 km of railway tracks were washed away.

- Landslides buried buildings and people. They also blocked access roads and cut off telephone lines.
- Diarrhoea and other diseases spread due to lack of clean water.
- Freezing winter conditions shortly after the earthquake caused more casualties and meant rescue and rebuilding operations were difficult.

Short-Term Relief was Slow to Reach People in Pakistan

Short-Term Relief

- International aid and search and rescue teams were brought in.
- Rescue workers and soldiers were sent to help deal with the aftermath.
- Transport and communications were restored a couple of weeks after the earthquake.
- Power supplies were restored in the weeks following the earthquake.

- The Pakistani army was initially slow to respond to the disaster.
- Help from India was refused because of political tensions between Pakistan and India.
- Help didn't reach many areas for days or weeks, and many people had to be rescued by hand without any equipment or help from emergency services.
- Tents, blankets and medical supplies were distributed, although it took up to a month for them to reach most areas.

Long-Term Planning in Japan was Very Effective

Effects of Long-Term Planning

- The Japanese authorities gave an advance warning of the earthquake and the tsunami, which gave people time to evacuate and get to higher ground.
- Despite very strong shaking in Tokyo, not a single building collapsed thanks to buildings designed to prevent earthquake damage.
- Nobody died on the bullet train network because of the automatic braking systems.

- Fault lines in the Himalayas were poorly monitored, which meant the Pakistan earthquake was unpredicted.
- The absence of building laws meant buildings weren't reinforced and were extremely vulnerable to damage from earthquake shaking.
- Most buildings had been constructed using poor quality materials, e.g. cement made from sand which crumbled during the earthquake.

The effects of tectonic hazards are not as severe in wealthy areas

The amount of damage an earthquake does, and the number of people that get hurt, are different in different parts of the world. Learn as many facts and figures as you can for a tectonic hazard in a rich and poor country.

Worked Exam Questions

Exam questions are the best way to practise what you've learnt. After all, they're exactly what you'll have to do on the big day — so work through this worked example very carefully.

1   Study **Figure 1**, which shows the Earth's tectonic plates and the distribution of volcanoes.

1.1   Describe the global distribution of volcanoes.

Volcanoes are most commonly found along destructive plate margins, but they also occur at constructive plate margins. Some are also found away from plate margins, e.g. in Hawaii.

[2]

Figure 1

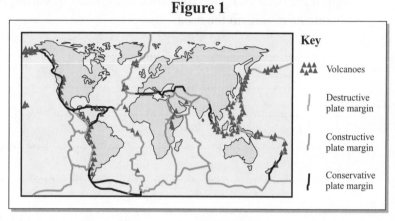

Key

▲▲▲   Volcanoes

| Destructive plate margin

| Constructive plate margin

| Conservative plate margin

1.2   Outline **one** reason for this distribution.

Volcanoes are found at constructive margins because as the plates pull apart, a gap forms between them. Magma rises into this gap and erupts at the surface, forming volcanoes.

[2]

[Total 4 marks]

2   **Figure 2** shows the effects of two tectonic hazards in different parts of the world. Hazard A occurred in a developing country and Hazard B in a developed country.

2.1   Outline **one** possible reason why Hazard B killed fewer people than Hazard A in the first 24 hours after the event.

Hazard B occurred in a developed country, which would have had more money available to evacuate people from the area, so fewer people would have been killed as the hazard struck.

[2]

Figure 2

	Hazard A	Hazard B
Number of deaths in first 24 hours after event	9084	208
Number of deaths in first 30 days after event	19 790	221
Cost of rebuilding (US $)	4 billion	16 billion

2.2   Explain why the number of deaths **after** the first 24 hours might have increased more significantly in the area affected by Hazard A than Hazard B.

There may not have been money to repair roads and transport systems in the area affected by Hazard A because it has a lower income than the country in which Hazard B occurred. This would have made it difficult for aid and medical care to reach those affected. It may also have taken longer to repair damaged water and sewage systems after Hazard A, causing disease to spread and increasing the death toll.

[4]

[Total 6 marks]

Exam Questions

1   **Figure 1** shows Yokohama, a city in Japan. Yokohama is close to Mount Fuji, an active volcano, and is also prone to earthquakes.

Figure 1

1.1   Explain how buildings and other structures shown in **Figure 1** might have been designed to reduce the effects of earthquakes or volcanic eruptions in the area.

....

....

....

....

....

[4]

1.2   Outline **one** other way in which the effects of tectonic hazards in Yokohama could be reduced.

....

....

[2]

[Total 6 marks]

2   Study **Figure 2**, which shows some of the effects of a volcanic eruption in Montserrat in 1997, and **Figure 3**, which shows some of the effects of an earthquake in Nepal in 2015.

Figure 2   **Figure 3**

2.1   Using **Figure 2** or **Figure 3** and your own knowledge, outline **two** primary effects of **either** volcanic eruptions **or** earthquakes. Tick the circle of the hazard you have chosen.

Volcanic eruptions   ◯   Earthquakes   ◯

Effect 1:..

....

Effect 2:..

....

[Total 2 marks]

Revision Summary

You've made it to the end of <u>Section 1</u> — the perfect time to put your <u>knowledge</u> to the <u>test</u>.

- Try these questions and <u>tick off each one</u> when you <u>get it right</u>.
- When you've done <u>all the questions</u> for a topic and are <u>completely happy</u> with it, tick off the topic.

Natural Hazards (p.1) ☑

1) What is a natural hazard? ☑
2) Give five examples of natural hazards. ☑

Structure of the Earth (p.2-3) ☑

3) Describe the Earth's structure. ☑
4) What is the mantle? ☑
5) Why do tectonic plates move? ☑
6) What are the places where tectonic plates meet called? ☑
7) Name the type of plate margin where two plates are moving away from each other. ☑
8) Name the type of plate margin where two plates are moving sideways against each other. ☑

Tectonic Hazards (p.4-5) ☑

9) What causes earthquakes? ☑
10) What is a shallow-focus earthquake? ☑
11) Describe how tsunamis are caused. ☑
12) How do volcanoes form at destructive (convergent) plate margins? ☑
13) What is a hot spot? ☑
14) Name the type of margin that composite volcanoes occur at. ☑
15) Describe the features of shield volcanoes. ☑

Effects of Tectonic Hazards (p.6-8) ☑

16) Give two primary effects of an earthquake. ☑
17) Give two examples of long-term responses to earthquakes. ☑
18) Give two secondary effects of a volcanic eruption. ☑
19) What could be done immediately after a volcanic eruption to reduce the impact? ☑
20) Why do people live in areas vulnerable to tectonic hazards? ☑
21) Describe how scientists can try to predict earthquakes. ☑
22) How can buildings be protected against earthquake damage? ☑
23) Describe one way that governments can plan for tectonic hazards. ☑

Tectonic Hazards — Examples (p.9-10) ☑

For one developed and one developing country that you have studied:

24) Compare the level of preparation for tectonic hazards. ☑
25) Compare the secondary impacts of tectonic hazards that occurred in each of the countries. ☑
26) Compare the response to the hazard that occurred. ☑
27) Compare the effectiveness of the long-term planning for tectonic hazards in each of the countries. ☑

Section 2 — Weather Hazards

Global Atmospheric Circulation

There's an overall movement of air between the equator and the poles that affects the Earth's climate.

Winds Transfer Heat from the Equator to the Poles

1) The Sun heats the Earth's surface unevenly — insolation (the solar radiation that reaches the Earth's surface) is greater at the equator than the poles.

2) The differences in temperature cause differences in air pressure (see below).

3) Winds blow FROM the areas of high pressure TO the areas of low pressure, transferring heat away from the equator.

4) Winds are part of global atmospheric circulation loops (called cells). These loops have warm rising air which creates a low pressure belt, and cool falling air which creates a high pressure belt.

5) There are three cells in each hemisphere — the Hadley, Ferrel and Polar cells.

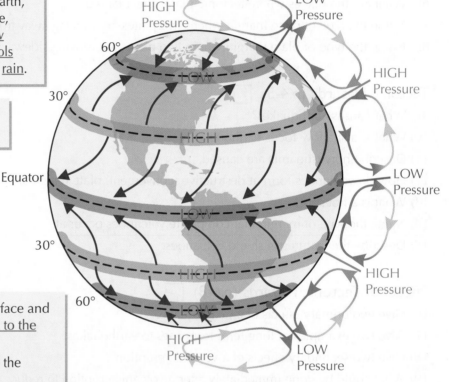

1) At the equator the Sun warms the Earth, which transfers heat to the air above, causing it to rise. This creates a low pressure belt. As the air rises, it cools and condenses forming clouds and rain.

2) The cool, dry air moves out to 30° north and south of the equator.

3) At 30° north and south of the equator, the cool air sinks, creating a high pressure belt with cloudless skies and very low rainfall.

4) The cool air reaches the ground surface and moves as surface winds either back to the equator or towards the poles:
   - Surface winds blowing towards the equator are called trade winds.
   - They blow from the SE in the southern hemisphere and from the NE in the northern hemisphere. At the equator, these trade winds meet and are heated by the sun. This causes them to rise and form clouds.
   - Surface winds blowing towards the poles are called westerlies. They blow from the NW in the southern hemisphere and from the SW in the northern hemisphere.

5) At 60° north and south of the equator, the warmer surface winds meet colder air from the poles. The warmer air is less dense than the cold air so it is forced to rise, creating low pressure and frontal rain (rain that forms where the warm and cold air masses meet).

6) Some of the air moves back towards the equator, and the rest moves towards the poles.

7) At the poles the cool air sinks, creating high pressure. The high pressure air is drawn back towards the equator as surface winds.

Global Atmospheric Circulation

Heat is also Transferred by Ocean Currents

1) Ocean currents are large scale movements of water that transfer heat energy from warmer to cooler regions.

2) Surface currents are caused by winds and help transfer heat away from the Equator, e.g. the Gulf Stream brings warm water from the Caribbean and keeps Western Europe warmer than it would otherwise be.

3) There are also deep ocean currents driven by differences in water density.

4) When water freezes at the poles, the surrounding water gets saltier, increasing its density.

5) As it gets denser, it sinks, causing warmer water to flow in at the surface — creating a current.

6) This warmer water is cooled and sinks, continuing the cycle.

7) This cycle of cooling and sinking moves water in a big loop round the Earth — this is known as the thermohaline circulation.

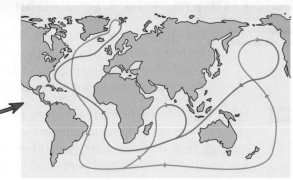

～ deep cold currents   ～ shallow warm

There are Different Climate Zones Around the World

The pressure belts caused by global atmospheric circulation (see previous page) cause variations in climate:

Temperate

A low pressure belt at about 60° N/S caused by rising air from two cells meeting means rainfall is frequent. Located between the tropics and poles, temperate zones have moderate summers and winters.

Arid (Dry)

Sinking air from the Hadley and Ferrel cells meeting causes high pressure. Rainfall is very low for all or most of the year. Temperatures are hot or warm.

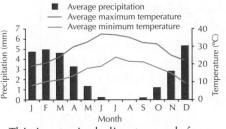

This is a typical climate graph for a location in the arid climate zone.

Polar

Sinking air from the Polar cells creates an area of high pressure at the poles. Temperatures are low all year round and there's very little rainfall.

Tropical

Rising air from the two Hadley cells meeting causes low pressure. Temperatures are hot all the time and rainfall is high.

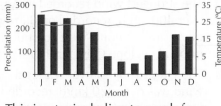

This is a typical climate graph for a location in the tropical climate zone.

Climate graphs show the average precipitation and temperatures for a certain area. Rainfall is shown on a bar chart and temperature is shown on a line graph.

Pressure belts and surface winds are determined by global circulation

Air moves in loops (called cells) from the equator to the poles and back. This gives us surface winds and creates belts of high and low pressure that affect the climate — they're why deserts are so dry and rainforests are so wet.

Extreme Weather

Extreme weather often occurs in areas where atmospheric cells meet.

Global Atmospheric Circulation leads to Extreme Weather in Some Places

Temperature — The equator receives the most energy from the Sun. The poles receive the least. Temperatures can be very high in high pressure areas around 30° N/S. There are few clouds due to the sinking air, so there is little to block the Sun's energy. In contrast, the temperatures in the polar regions of the Arctic and Antarctica are very low.

Wind — Wind is air moving from areas of high to low pressure. This means that atmospheric circulation causes winds, making some parts of the world windier than others. Winds are weak in high and low pressure belts and strong between pressure belts. When the difference in pressure between high and low pressure areas is large, winds can be extremely strong — e.g. the north coast of Australia.

Precipitation — Precipitation (rain, snow, etc.) occurs when warm, wet air rises and cools, causing water vapour to condense. Air rises in low pressure belts, so precipitation is frequent and often intense in these areas. In high pressure belts where the air sinks, precipitation is extremely low.

Australia's Weather is More Extreme than the UK's

Extreme weather depends where you are — if a normal UK spring's amount of rain fell in the Sahara desert, it would be extremely wet for the Sahara desert. In the same way, Iceland's normal winter temperatures would be extremely cold in the UK.

Australia and the UK are contrasting countries which experience different weather extremes:

Temperature

1) Australia is warmer than the UK — it has hotter summers and milder winters.
2) In Darwin, a city in northern Australia, the average maximum summer temperature is about 33 °C. Temperatures over 40 °C are considered to be extremely hot.
3) In London, the average maximum temperature in summer is about 23 °C. Temperatures over 30 °C are considered extremely hot.

Wind

1) Australia has stronger extreme winds than the UK does, partly because it's affected by tropical storms (see next page).
2) In the UK, gales (winds of over 62 km/h) are rare — most places only have a few days of gales each year.
3) The strongest wind recorded in Australia is over 400 km/h, recorded on Barrow Island off Australia's north-west coast during tropical cyclone Olivia in 1996.
4) The UK's strongest ever sea-level wind was over 220 km/h, recorded in Fraserburgh in Scotland in 1989.

Precipitation

1) Australia has much lower precipitation (rain, snow etc.) than the UK. The average annual rainfall in Australia is 465 mm. In the UK, average annual rainfall is over 1150 mm.
2) Extremely wet years in Australia have over 550 mm of rain. In the UK, annual rainfall in extremely wet years is over 1210 mm.
3) Extremely dry years in Australia have less than 360 mm of rainfall. In the UK, extremely dry years have less than 950 mm of rain.

The UK experiences fewer extreme weather conditions than Australia
Australia and the UK have very different weather conditions. Cover the page and see if you can remember the key facts and figures. Even better if you can compare and contrast these figures too.

Tropical Storms

Tropical storms are <u>intense low pressure</u> weather systems with <u>heavy rain</u> and <u>strong winds</u> that spiral around the <u>centre</u>. They have a few different names (<u>hurricanes</u>, <u>typhoons</u>, and <u>cyclones</u>), but they're all the <u>same thing</u>.

Tropical Storms **Develop** over **Warm Water**

1) Tropical storms develop when the <u>sea temperature</u> is <u>27 °C or higher</u> and when the <u>wind shear</u> (the <u>difference</u> in <u>windspeed</u>) between <u>higher</u> and <u>lower</u> parts of the atmosphere is <u>low</u>.

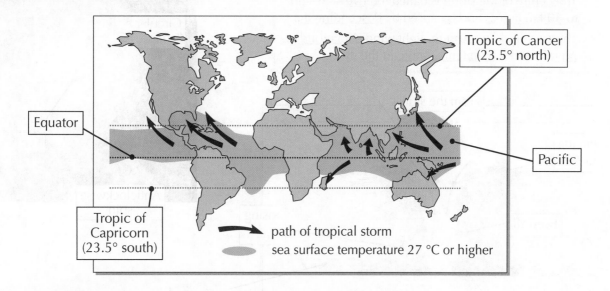

Equator

Tropic of Cancer (23.5° north)

Pacific

Tropic of Capricorn (23.5° south)

path of tropical storm

sea surface temperature 27 °C or higher

2) <u>Warm</u>, <u>moist</u> air <u>rises</u> and <u>condensation</u> occurs. This releases huge amounts of <u>energy</u>, which makes the storms <u>powerful</u>. The <u>rising air</u> creates an area of <u>low pressure</u>, which increases <u>surface winds</u>.

3) Tropical storms <u>move towards the west</u> because of the <u>easterly winds</u> near the equator.

4) The Earth's <u>rotation</u> deflects the paths of the winds, which causes the storms to <u>spin</u>.

5) The storm <u>gets stronger</u> due to <u>energy</u> from the warm <u>water</u>, so <u>wind speeds increase</u>. They <u>lose strength</u> when they move over <u>land</u> or <u>cooler water</u> because the energy supply from the warm water is <u>cut off</u>.

6) Most tropical storms occur between <u>5°</u> and <u>30°</u> north and south of the equator — any further from the equator and the water <u>isn't warm enough</u>. The <u>majority</u> of storms occur in the <u>northern hemisphere</u> (especially over the <u>Pacific</u>), in <u>late summer</u> and <u>autumn</u>, when sea temperatures are <u>highest</u>.

EXAM TIP

Tropical storms form at low latitudes — between 5° and 30° N & S

Since even the top scientists haven't worked it out yet, you don't need to know exactly how tropical storms form, but you might be asked to outline the main steps in their formation in the exam.

Tropical Storms

Tropical storms have a <u>distinctive shape</u> and <u>structure</u>. This makes them quite easy to spot on <u>satellite images</u>...

Learn the **Features** and **Structure** of a Tropical Storm

Tropical storms are <u>circular</u> in shape, <u>hundreds of kilometres wide</u> and usually last <u>7-14 days</u>. They spin <u>anticlockwise</u> in the <u>northern</u> hemisphere, and <u>clockwise</u> in the <u>southern</u> hemisphere.

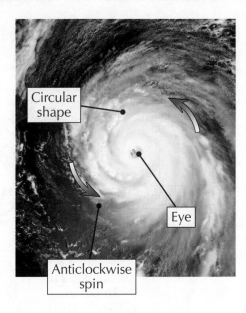

The <u>centre</u> of the storm is called the <u>eye</u> — it's up to <u>50 km across</u> and is caused by <u>descending air</u>. There's very <u>low pressure</u>, <u>light winds</u>, <u>no clouds</u>, <u>no rain</u> and a <u>high temperature</u> in the eye.

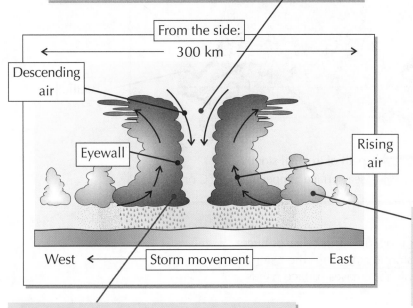

From the side:

300 km

Descending air

Eyewall

Rising air

West ← Storm movement — East

Towards the <u>edges</u> of the storm the <u>wind speed falls</u>, the <u>clouds</u> become <u>smaller</u> and more <u>scattered</u>, the <u>rain</u> becomes <u>less intense</u> and the <u>temperature increases</u>.

The eye is surrounded by the <u>eyewall</u>, where there's <u>spiralling rising air</u>, very <u>strong winds</u> (around 160 km per hour), <u>storm clouds</u>, <u>torrential rain</u> and a <u>low temperature</u>.

Circular shape

Eye

Anticlockwise spin

Climate Change May **Affect** Tropical Storms

1) <u>Global temperatures</u> are expected to <u>rise</u> as a result of climate change. This means that <u>more</u> of the world's oceans could be <u>above 27 °C</u>, so <u>more places</u> in the world may experience tropical storms.

2) Oceans will <u>stay</u> at 27 °C or higher for <u>more of the year</u> — so the <u>number</u> of tropical storms each year could <u>increase</u>.

3) Higher temperatures also mean tropical storms will be <u>stronger</u>, meaning they could cause <u>more damage</u>.

Rising temperatures mean warmer oceans, which might mean more storms

Climate change could mean that tropical storms occur over a larger area, and their strength and frequency may increase too. You should learn the features and structure of a tropical storm, so you won't be fazed by anything the examiners throw at you. Try testing yourself by sketching out the diagram above — remember the labels.

Tropical Storms — Effects and Responses

When tropical storms hit land, they can have serious impacts on people and the environment.

Tropical Storms have Primary and Secondary Effects...

The primary effects of a tropical storm are the immediate impacts of strong winds, high rainfall and storm surges. The secondary effects are the effects that happen later on.

Storm surges are large rises in sea level caused by the low pressure and high winds of a storm.

1 Primary Effects

1) Tropical storms can release trillions of litres of water per day as rain. Heavy rain makes hills unstable, causing landslides, which can damage infrastructure and buildings. Sediment may be deposited in lakes and rivers, killing fish and other wildlife.

2) Rivers and coastal areas flood as a result of storm surges and strong winds driving large waves onto the shore. People may drown in the strong currents and coastal habitats can be eroded and destroyed.

3) Flooding also causes sewage to overflow. The sewage often contaminates water supplies.

4) Windspeeds in a tropical storm can reach 250 km/h — people can be injured or killed by debris that's blown around and buildings are often destroyed.

5) Roads, railways, ports and other infrastructure can be damaged or destroyed. Supplies of electricity may be cut off if cables are damaged.

2 Secondary Effects

1) People are left homeless, which can cause distress, poverty and ill health or death due to lack of shelter.

2) There's a shortage of clean water and a lack of proper sanitation — this makes it easier for diseases to spread.

3) Roads are blocked or destroyed so aid and emergency vehicles can't get through.

4) Businesses are damaged or destroyed, causing unemployment.

5) There can be shortages of food if crops are damaged, livestock are killed or supply lines are blocked.

...Which Trigger Immediate and Long-Term Responses

Immediate responses happen when a storm is forecast to hit a populated area, while it is happening, and immediately afterwards.

Long-term responses are to do with restoring the area to the condition it was before the storm struck, and reducing the impact of future storms.

Immediate Responses

1) Evacuate people before the storm arrives.

2) Rescue people who have been cut off by flooding and treat injured people.

3) Set up temporary shelters for people whose homes have been flooded or damaged.

4) Provide temporary supplies of water, food, electricity, gas and communications systems if regular supplies have been damaged.

5) Recover any dead bodies to prevent the spread of disease.

6) Foreign governments or NGOs may send aid workers, supplies, equipment or financial donations to the area.

Long-Term Responses

1) Repair homes or rehouse people who have been displaced due to damaged buildings.

2) Repair and improve flood defence systems, e.g. levees and flood gates.

3) Improve forecasting techniques to give people more warning in the future.

4) Provide aid, grants or subsidies to residents to repair and strengthen homes.

5) Improve building regulations so more buildings withstand hurricanes, or change planning rules so homes can't be built in the most risky areas.

Tropical storms release trillions of litres of rain, which causes flooding

You need to be able to describe some of the primary and secondary effects of tropical storms, so get revising. Remember, the impacts of storms can be felt for a long time, so many responses have to be long-term.

Tropical Storms — Preparation

Preparation is important in reducing the impacts of tropical storms.

Some **Countries** are More **Vulnerable** than **Others**

Countries can be vulnerable to the effects of tropical storms for different reasons.

1 Physical Vulnerability

1) Low-lying coastlines are vulnerable to storm surge flooding as well as large waves caused by the high winds.
2) Areas in the path of tropical storms are hit more frequently.
3) Steep hillsides may increase the risk of landslides.

2 Economic Vulnerability

Poorer countries are economically vulnerable because:
1) Many people depend on agriculture which is often badly affected — this leads to a loss of livelihoods.
2) People may not have insurance to cover the costs of repairing damage caused by storms.

However, the economic impact is often greater in richer countries as the buildings and infrastructure (roads, rail, bridges etc.) damaged are worth a lot of money.

3 Social Vulnerability

Poorer countries are often more socially vulnerable because:
1) Buildings are poorer quality so more easily damaged.
2) Health care isn't as good so they struggle to treat all the casualties.
3) There is little money for flood defences or training emergency teams.
4) It's harder to rescue people because of poor infrastructure.

There are **Many Strategies** to **Prepare** for **Tropical Storms**

Forecasting

1) When and where tropical storms will hit land can be predicted.
2) Scientists can use weather forecasting and satellite technology to monitor cyclones. Computer models are then used to calculate a predicted path for the storm.
3) The cyclone's magnitude can be monitored by measuring its windspeeds.
4) Predicting where and when a tropical storm is going to happen gives people time to evacuate and protect their homes and businesses, e.g. by boarding up windows.

> Tropical storms are classified using the Saffir-Simpson Scale, which is based on windspeed. Category 5 is the strongest (winds over 250 km/h) and 1 is the weakest (winds of 120-150 km/h).

Evacuation

1) Warning strategies are used to alert people to a tropical storm. An alert will give people enough time to leave their homes and get to a safe place.
2) Governments can plan evacuation routes to get people away from storms quickly. In Florida, evacuation routes are signposted all along the coast.
3) Successful evacuations can reduce the number of deaths and injuries.
4) Emergency services can train and prepare for disasters, e.g. by practising rescuing people from flooded areas with helicopters. This reduces the number of people killed.

Defences

1) Defences (e.g. sea walls) can be built along the coast to prevent damage from storm surges. Buildings can also be designed to withstand a storm surge, e.g. they can be put on stilts so they're safe from floodwater.
2) This will reduce the number of buildings destroyed, so fewer people will be killed, injured, made homeless and made unemployed.

Richer countries are often more prepared for storms than poorer countries

Richer countries are better able to forecast tropical storms and have money to invest in more effective defences. People in these countries are often less badly affected when tropical storms hit than people in poorer countries.

Tropical Storms — Hurricane Katrina

It's time to put all that <u>theory</u> into <u>practice</u> with a couple of <u>case studies</u>.

Hurricane Katrina struck Mississippi and Louisiana, USA, in August 2005

<u>Hurricane Katrina</u>, a tropical storm, struck the <u>south-east USA</u> on <u>29th August 2005</u>:

1 Preparation

1) The USA has a sophisticated <u>monitoring system</u> to <u>predict</u> if (and where) a tropical storm will hit.

2) The <u>National Hurricane Centre</u> (<u>NHC</u>) in Florida tracks and predicts tropical storms using <u>satellite images</u> and <u>planes</u> that collect weather data on approaching storms.

3) The NHC issued a <u>hurricane warning</u> on <u>26th August</u> for Louisiana, Mississippi and Alabama. It continued to <u>track</u> the storm, <u>updating</u> the <u>government</u> on where and when it would hit.

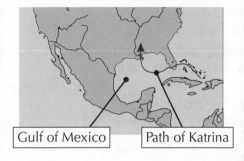

Gulf of Mexico | Path of Katrina

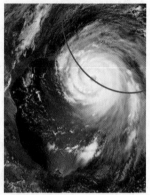

> Tropical storms cause storm surges as strong winds push water towards the shore, causing the water level to rise. If the storm surge coincides with a high tide, flood defences can easily be breached.

2 Causes of Hurricane Katrina

1) Louisiana and Mississippi are in the <u>Gulf of Mexico</u>, where sea temperatures are often <u>27 °C or warmer</u> — this means tropical storms can <u>form</u>.

2) A storm <u>formed</u> 200 miles south-east of the <u>Bahamas</u> on the <u>23rd August</u>. It moved <u>north-west</u> over the southern tip of <u>Florida</u> into the <u>Gulf of Mexico</u>.

3) As it travelled over the <u>warm water</u> of the Gulf of Mexico it became <u>even stronger</u> — it was <u>Category 3</u> at landfall.

4) It struck land on the <u>morning</u> of the <u>29th</u> bringing winds of around <u>200 km/h</u> and <u>200-250 mm</u> rainfall in <u>Louisiana</u> and a <u>storm surge</u> of up to <u>8.5 m</u> in <u>Mississippi</u>.

3 Consequences of Hurricane Katrina

1) More than <u>1800 people</u> were <u>killed</u> and <u>hundreds of thousands</u> of people were made <u>homeless</u>.

2) Large areas were <u>flooded</u>, including <u>80%</u> of <u>New Orleans</u>.

3) <u>Coastal habitats</u> were <u>damaged</u> and <u>water supplies</u> were <u>polluted</u> with sewage and chemicals.

4) The total cost of the damage as estimated at <u>$150 billion</u>.

5) <u>Rescue</u> and <u>recovery</u> efforts were <u>hampered</u> by <u>disagreements</u> between <u>national</u>, <u>state</u> and <u>local officials</u>.

4 Responses to Hurricane Katrina

1) <u>70-80%</u> of New Orleans residents were <u>evacuated before</u> the hurricane <u>reached land</u>.

2) <u>Mississippi</u> and <u>Louisiana</u> declared <u>states of emergency</u>, — they set up <u>control centres</u> and <u>stockpiled supplies</u>.

3) The <u>coastguard</u>, <u>police</u>, <u>fire service</u> and <u>army</u> rescued over <u>50 000 people</u>.

4) The US Army recommended that buildings be <u>rebuilt on stilts</u> or <u>not rebuilt at all</u> in <u>very low-lying areas</u>.

5) <u>Repaired</u> and <u>improved</u> flood defences for New Orleans costing <u>14.5 billion dollars</u> were completed in <u>2013</u>.

The facts on Katrina make for grim reading

You don't have to learn about Katrina if you've studied another tropical storm in class — just check you know about the preparation, causes, consequences and responses. Try jotting down a list of points for each of the four boxes.

Tropical Storms — Cyclone Nargis

Cyclone Nargis caused lots of <u>damage</u>, and also led to <u>a lot of deaths</u>.

Cyclone Nargis hit Myanmar in May 2008

Cyclone Nargis hit the <u>Irrawady Delta</u> on the coast of Myanmar on <u>2nd May 2008</u>:

1 Preparation

1) Myanmar doesn't have a <u>dedicated monitoring centre</u> for tropical cyclones.
2) There were no <u>emergency preparation plans</u>, no <u>evacuation plans</u> and the country didn't have an <u>early warning system</u>.
3) However, Indian weather agencies did <u>warn</u> the government of Myanmar that Cyclone Nargis was likely to hit the country <u>48 hours before</u> it did.

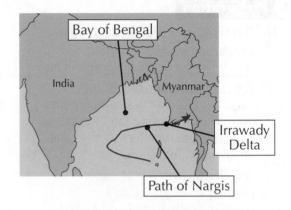

2 Causes of Cyclone Nargis

1) Myanmar is in the <u>Bay of Bengal</u>, a <u>source area</u> of tropical storms.
2) A storm formed during the last week of <u>April</u> and <u>strengthened</u> as it <u>approached the coast</u> — it was classified as a <u>Category 4</u> storm at landfall.
3) On <u>May 2nd</u> it hit the coast of Myanmar with wind speeds of around <u>215 km/h</u> and a <u>storm surge</u> of <u>5 m</u> (<u>storm waves</u> added another <u>2 m</u> on top of this).

Many houses were destroyed

3 Consequences of Cyclone Nargis

1) The <u>Irrawaddy delta</u> in Myanmar was the <u>hardest hit</u> area — a large proportion of it is <u>only just above sea level</u> and 14 000 km² of land was <u>flooded</u>.
2) <u>38 000 hectares</u> of mangrove forests were <u>destroyed</u>.
3) More than <u>140 000 people</u> were <u>killed</u>.
4) <u>450 000 houses</u> were <u>destroyed</u> and <u>350 000</u> were <u>damaged</u>.
5) Around <u>65% of rice paddies</u> in the Irrawaddy delta were <u>damaged</u>, which led to a loss of <u>livelihoods</u>.
6) A lot of people suffered from <u>diseases</u> caused by <u>poor sanitary conditions</u> and <u>contaminated water</u>.

4 Responses to Cyclone Nargis

1) <u>Warnings</u> were issued on the <u>TV</u> and <u>radio</u>, but they <u>didn't reach</u> people in poor rural communities. This meant more people were <u>killed</u> because they didn't know <u>what to do</u> or <u>where to evacuate to</u>.
2) The government of Myanmar initially <u>refused</u> to accept <u>foreign aid</u> and wouldn't allow <u>aid workers</u> into the country.
3) Some of the <u>aid</u> sent by other countries was <u>seized</u> by the military, which <u>delayed its delivery</u> to the people who needed it.
4) The delays in accepting <u>international aid</u> increased the number of <u>deaths</u> because <u>help</u> for some people <u>came too late</u>.

The slow response to Cyclone Nargis made the consequences worse

You might have used different case studies in class. Whatever case studies you choose, if you learn the specific effects and responses, you'll find you've also learned some of the general info from page 19.

Worked Exam Questions

These exam questions are similar to the type you'll get in the exam — except they've got the answers written in for you already. Have a look to see the sorts of things you should be writing.

1   Study **Figure 1**, a photograph of Slidell, Louisiana after Hurricane Katrina in 2005.

Figure 1

1.1   Give two primary effects of the tropical storm shown in **Figure 1**.

Effect 1: Buildings were destroyed.

Effect 2: Roads were damaged.

[2]

1.2   Outline **two** immediate responses that could help reduce the effects of an event such as that shown in **Figure 1**.

Response 1:

Evacuate people before the storm arrives.

Response 2: Set up temporary shelters for people whose homes have been flooded or damaged.

[2]

1.3   Outline **two** long-term responses that could help reduce the effects of an event such as that shown in **Figure 1**.

Response 1: Repair homes or rehouse people who have been displaced due to damaged buildings.

Response 2: Repair and improve flood defence systems, e.g. levees and floodgates.

[2]

[Total 6 marks]

2   Study **Figure 2**, a graph showing global temperature change between 1960 and 2015.

Figure 2

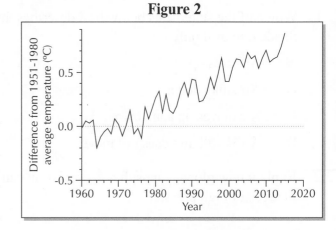

2.1   Suggest how the distribution of tropical storms could change in the future if the trend in temperature change shown in **Figure 2** continues.

Tropical storms only form in areas where the

sea temperature is 27 °C or higher.

The graph shows an average global

temperature increase of 0.5 °C over 50 years.

This may have caused ocean temperatures to increase. If the warming continues, larger areas of ocean

will be 27 °C or warmer. This means the area affected by tropical storms will increase in size,

with areas at higher latitudes affected.

[Total 4 marks]

Exam Questions

1 Study **Figure 1**, a forecast map showing the predicted path of a hurricane over Cuba, approaching Miami, Florida.

Figure 1

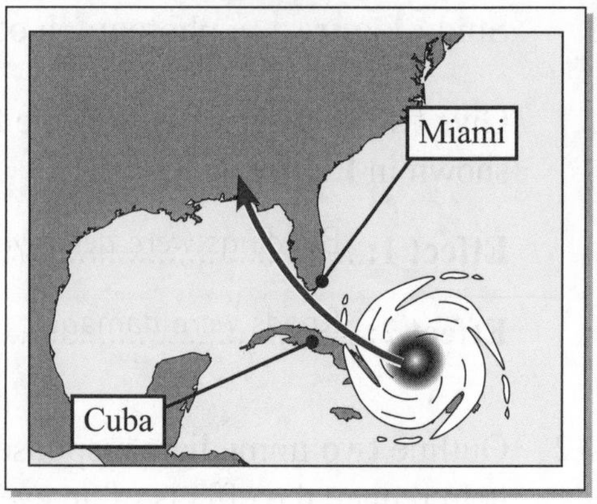

1.1 Explain how this prediction could help to reduce the effects of the storm in Miami.

....

....

....

....
[2]

1.2 Using an example of a tropical storm that you have studied, discuss how immediate and long-term responses helped to reduce its effects.

....

....

....

....

....

....
[6]
[Total 8 marks]

2 Global atmospheric circulation leads to areas of alternating high and low pressure in different parts of the world.

2.1 Which of the statements below best describes the movement of air at the equator?
Shade **one** oval only.

A   Air rises up.   ⬭

B   Air sinks down.   ⬭

C   Air moves up and down.   ⬭

D   Air is still and does not move.   ⬭
[1]

2.2 Explain how global atmospheric circulation can cause extremely high temperatures in areas of high pressure.

....

....

....
[2]
[Total 3 marks]

El Niño and La Niña

El Niño and La Niña are climatic events that happen in the Pacific Ocean.
They can cause some quite worrisome weather conditions.

El Niño Events are when **Air** and **Ocean Currents** Change

1) Air currents in the atmosphere and water currents in the ocean usually flow one way in the Pacific Ocean.

2) Every few years, they weaken or reverse — this is an El Niño event. Sometimes they get stronger
— this is a La Niña event. Both cause changes in weather patterns in surrounding areas.

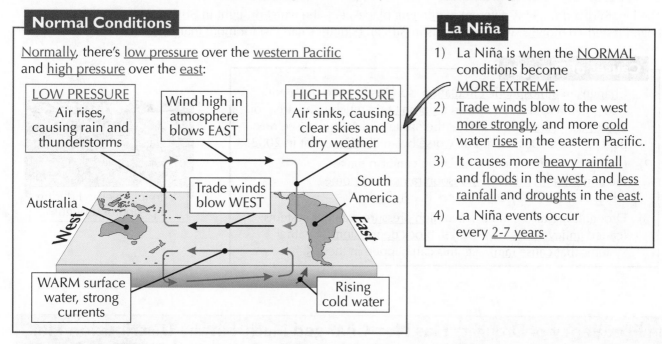

Normal Conditions

Normally, there's low pressure over the western Pacific
and high pressure over the east:

| LOW PRESSURE |
Air rises, causing rain and thunderstorms

Wind high in atmosphere blows EAST

HIGH PRESSURE
Air sinks, causing clear skies and dry weather

Trade winds blow WEST

Australia

South America

West

East

WARM surface water, strong currents

Rising cold water

La Niña

1) La Niña is when the NORMAL conditions become MORE EXTREME.

2) Trade winds blow to the west more strongly, and more cold water rises in the eastern Pacific.

3) It causes more heavy rainfall and floods in the west, and less rainfall and droughts in the east.

4) La Niña events occur every 2-7 years.

El Niño Events

1) In an El Niño event, pressure rises in the western Pacific and falls in the east.

2) This causes the trade winds (which normally blow from east to west) to weaken or reverse direction.

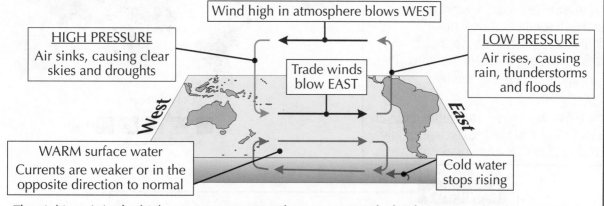

Wind high in atmosphere blows WEST

HIGH PRESSURE
Air sinks, causing clear skies and droughts

Trade winds blow EAST

LOW PRESSURE
Air rises, causing rain, thunderstorms and floods

West

East

WARM surface water
Currents are weaker or in the opposite direction to normal

Cold water stops rising

3) The sinking air in the high pressure area over the western Pacific leads to unusually dry weather.
This can cause drought — there can be much less rainfall in areas like eastern Australia.

4) The rising air in the low pressure area over the eastern Pacific leads to unusually wet weather.
This can cause serious floods in places that don't normally get much rain, e.g. Peru.

5) El Niño events occur every 3-4 years on average, and last for 9 to 12 months.

Make sure you know the difference between El Niño and La Niña

El Niño occurs when trade winds reverse direction or weaken, whereas La Niña happens when trade winds blow
West more strongly. You will also need to know the extreme weather conditions that are caused by them.

Drought

You <u>already</u> know a couple of causes of drought from the previous page — time to go into a bit <u>more detail</u>...

Drought is when Conditions are Drier than Normal

1) A <u>drought</u> is a <u>long period</u> (weeks, months or years) when <u>rainfall</u> is <u>below average</u>.

2) <u>Water supplies</u>, e.g. lakes and rivers, become <u>depleted</u> during a drought because <u>people keep using them</u> but they <u>aren't replenished</u> by rainfall. Also, droughts are often accompanied by <u>high temperatures</u>, which <u>increase</u> the <u>rate of evaporation</u>, so water supplies are <u>depleted faster</u>.

3) The <u>length</u> of a drought is <u>different</u> in <u>different places</u>, e.g. the <u>worst drought</u> in <u>Britain</u> since records began lasted <u>16 months</u>, whilst droughts in <u>African countries</u> can last for <u>more than a decade</u>.

Causes of Drought

1) <u>Changes</u> in <u>atmospheric circulation</u>, such as El Niño or La Niña (see previous page), can mean it <u>doesn't rain much</u> in an area for <u>months</u> or <u>years</u>. For example, the drought in <u>Australia</u> (see next page) in the 2000s was made <u>worse</u> by an <u>El Niño</u> event in <u>2002</u>.

2) Changes in atmospheric circulation can also make the <u>annual rains fail</u> (e.g. <u>monsoon rains don't come</u> when they normally do in places like <u>India</u>).

3) Droughts are also caused when <u>high pressure</u> weather systems (called <u>anticyclones</u> — see p.29) <u>block depressions</u> (weather systems that <u>cause rain</u>), e.g. this can happen in the <u>UK</u>.

A drying riverbed during a period of drought.

The Frequency of Droughts Has Not Changed Much, but the Distribution Has

Distribution

1) The <u>map</u> on the right shows the <u>distribution</u> of <u>severe droughts</u> around the <u>world</u>.

2) Areas <u>most at risk</u> from drought are <u>central</u> and <u>southern Africa</u>, the <u>Middle East</u>, <u>Australia</u>, <u>eastern South America</u> and parts of <u>North America</u>.

3) The locations affected by drought <u>vary</u> over <u>time</u>.

4) Since 1950, there have been <u>more droughts</u> in <u>Africa</u>, <u>Asia</u> and the <u>Mediterranean</u> and <u>fewer droughts</u> in the <u>Americas</u> and <u>Russia</u>.

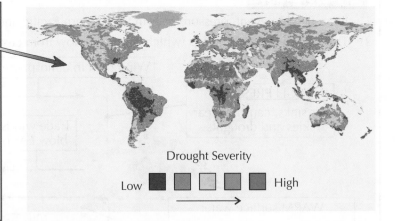

Drought Severity

Low ▮ ▮ ▮ ▮ ▮ High

Frequency

1) Globally, the <u>frequency</u> of droughts has <u>varied</u> from year to year but <u>overall</u> has <u>not changed</u> much since 1950.

2) Some scientists have <u>suggested</u> that droughts might become <u>more frequent</u> and <u>more severe</u> in future due to <u>climate change</u>.

Future climate change could affect the frequency and distribution of droughts

You won't be expected to recreate the map above in the exam, but you might need to describe the pattern of global drought distribution. Make sure you understand all of this information before you move on to the case study.

Drought — Australia

Australia experienced a drought between 2001 and 2009. This had a massive impact on its inhabitants.

There was a Drought in Australia in the Early 21st Century

1) South-east Australia suffered from a severe, long-term drought from roughly 2001 to 2009, although scientists don't agree on exactly when it started and finished. It's known as the Millennium Drought or the "Big Dry".

2) The worst-hit area was the Murray-Darling Basin, an important agricultural region.

1 Causes of the Millennium Drought in Australia

1) There were several factors that may have contributed to the Millennium Drought:

2) Australia has a naturally low rainfall due to global atmospheric circulation (see p.14). The 30° S high pressure belt passes through Australia, causing low precipitation.

3) El Niño events (see page 25) in 2002-2003, 2004-2005 and 2006-2007 led to especially low rainfall totals in south-east Australia.

4) Scientists think that climate change may be increasing global temperatures and changing rainfall patterns. So climate change may have contributed to the Millennium Drought:

- Temperatures in Australia were higher than normal during this period, resulting in more water evaporating than normal.

- Weather fronts that normally bring rain to south-east Australia moved further south, away from Australia, causing annual rainfall totals to be lower.

2 Consequences of the Millennium Drought in Australia

1) Water levels in lakes and rivers (particularly the Murray and Darling) fell, so water supplies ran low.

2) The largest impacts were on farming:

- Crop yields fell, and crops that rely on irrigation (watering) were particularly badly affected, e.g. rice production fell to just 2% of pre-drought totals. This increased food prices.

- Livestock died — the number of sheep in Australia fell by around 8 million during 2002-2003.

- Farmers' incomes fell, and over 100 000 people employed in farming lost their jobs.

3) The drought caused vegetation loss and soil erosion, and rivers and lakes suffered from outbreaks of toxic algae.

4) Dust storms caused by the drought affected inland Australia and some coastal cities.

5) The drought conditions were perfect for wildfires. Over 30 000 km² of land burned, and hundreds of houses were destroyed. 8 people were killed.

3 Responses to the Millennium Drought in Australia

1) Water conservation measures were introduced. E.g. the 3 million people who rely on the River Murray for their water supply had their allocation reduced.

2) Cities such as Sydney built desalination plants that can turn sea water into drinking water.

3) The Australian government provided more than 23 000 rural families and 1500 small businesses with income support to help them survive.

4) The government is also investing in improving drought forecasts so farmers can prepare better, improving irrigation schemes and developing drought-resistant crops.

Australia's drought had a huge impact on rural and farming communities

The farming industry suffered a lot during the drought — crops yields fell and livestock died, which reduced farmers' incomes. However, the government's responses to the drought have helped these communities to recover.

UK Climate

You may think it <u>rains</u> a lot in the <u>UK</u>. Well, now's your chance to find out <u>why</u>.

The **UK** has a **Mild Climate** — **Cool, Wet Winters** and **Warm, Wet Summers**

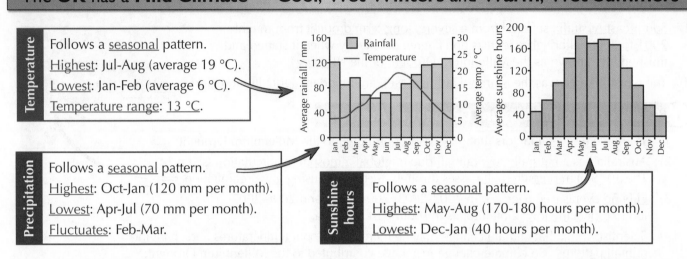

Temperature

Follows a <u>seasonal</u> pattern.
<u>Highest</u>: Jul-Aug (average 19 °C).
<u>Lowest</u>: Jan-Feb (average 6 °C).
<u>Temperature range</u>: <u>13 °C</u>.

Precipitation

Follows a <u>seasonal</u> pattern.
<u>Highest</u>: Oct-Jan (120 mm per month).
<u>Lowest</u>: Apr-Jul (70 mm per month).
<u>Fluctuates</u>: Feb-Mar.

Sunshine hours

Follows a <u>seasonal</u> pattern.
<u>Highest</u>: May-Aug (170-180 hours per month).
<u>Lowest</u>: Dec-Jan (40 hours per month).

Continentality, the **North Atlantic Drift** and **Air Masses** Affect UK **Weather**

The <u>climate</u> of the UK is different to most other countries at a <u>similar latitude</u>.
This is down to <u>three</u> main reasons:

Continentality

1) The UK is made up of <u>islands</u> so it is surrounded by the <u>sea</u>.
2) Areas <u>near</u> the sea are <u>warmer</u> than inland areas in <u>winter</u> because the <u>sea stores</u> up <u>heat</u> and <u>warms the land</u>.
3) Areas <u>near</u> the sea are <u>cooler</u> in <u>summer</u> because the <u>sea</u> takes a <u>long time</u> to <u>heat up</u> and so <u>cools the land down</u>.
4) This means that the UK is <u>milder</u> in <u>winter</u> and <u>cooler</u> in <u>summer</u> than countries on the <u>continent</u>, e.g. Germany.

The North Atlantic Drift

1) The North Atlantic Drift is an <u>ocean current</u> that brings <u>warm water</u> from the <u>Caribbean</u> across the <u>Atlantic</u> to the <u>west coast</u> of the UK.
2) This keeps the west coast of the UK <u>warmer</u> than other countries at <u>similar latitudes</u>.

The North Atlantic Drift is part of the Gulf Stream (see p.15).

Air Masses

1) Air masses are <u>large volumes of air</u> with roughly the same <u>temperature</u> and <u>water</u> content.
2) They're classified by the <u>region</u> they <u>form over</u>:
   - <u>Arctic</u> or <u>Polar</u> air masses form at <u>high latitudes</u> (so they're <u>cooler</u>).
   - <u>Tropical</u> air masses form at <u>low latitudes</u> (so they're <u>warmer</u>).
   - <u>Maritime</u> air masses form over <u>oceans</u>, i.e. the Atlantic (so they're <u>wetter</u>).
   - <u>Continental</u> air masses form over <u>land</u>, i.e. mainland Europe (so they're <u>drier</u>).
3) The UK is affected by <u>five different air masses</u> — each bringing different <u>weather</u>.

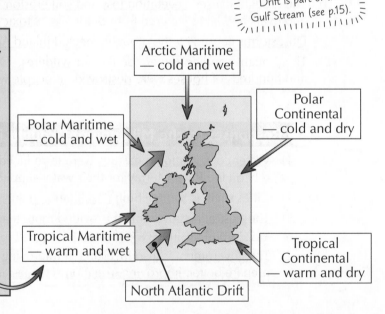

Arctic Maritime — cold and wet

Polar Continental — cold and dry

Polar Maritime — cold and wet

Tropical Maritime — warm and wet

Tropical Continental — warm and dry

North Atlantic Drift

Climate conditions vary in different parts of the UK

Although the UK's climate is mild overall, air masses have different impacts on different parts of the country. In general, the South East of the UK tends to be warmer and drier, while the North West is colder and wetter.

UK Extreme Weather

On the whole, UK weather isn't that extreme, but it has its <u>moments</u>.

The **Weather** in the **UK** can be **Extreme**

1) When <u>two different</u> air masses <u>interact</u> it can cause <u>extreme</u> weather.
2) Very <u>wet</u> and <u>windy</u> weather is caused by <u>depressions</u> (<u>colliding</u> air masses and <u>low pressure</u>).
3) Very <u>hot</u> or very <u>cold</u> weather is the result of <u>anticyclones</u> (<u>stable</u> air masses with <u>high pressure</u>).

Depressions Form when **Warm Air Meets Cold Air**

Depressions form over the <u>Atlantic ocean</u>, then move <u>east</u> over the UK. Here's how they <u>form</u>:

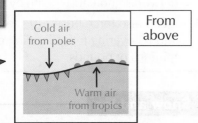

1) <u>Warm</u>, <u>moist</u> air from the tropics collides with <u>cold</u>, <u>dry</u> air from the poles.
2) The <u>warm</u> air is <u>less dense</u> so it is forced to <u>rise</u> above the cold air.
3) <u>Condensation</u> occurs as the warm air rises, causing <u>rain clouds</u> to develop.
4) Rising air also causes <u>low pressure</u> at the Earth's surface.
5) So <u>winds</u> blow <u>into</u> the depression in a <u>spiral</u> (winds always blow <u>from</u> areas of high pressure <u>to</u> areas of low pressure).

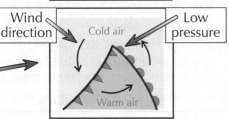

> 1) The <u>heaviest rain</u> caused by depressions is often in the <u>autumn</u> because the <u>sea temperatures</u> in the <u>Atlantic</u> are at their <u>warmest</u> (they've been heated by the sun all summer). <u>Lots of</u> water <u>evaporates</u> forming <u>thick</u>, <u>towering clouds</u>, which can fall as <u>rain</u>, <u>sleet</u>, <u>hail</u> or <u>snow</u>.
> 2) <u>Strong winds</u> are caused when there is a <u>big difference</u> in <u>temperature</u> between the two air masses. The difference in temperature causes a <u>steep pressure gradient</u> (warmer air has a lower pressure), so the air <u>rushes in</u> to fill the area of <u>lower</u> pressure.

Anticyclones can cause **Very Hot** or **Very Cold** Weather

Anticyclones also form over the <u>Atlantic ocean</u> and move <u>east</u> over the UK.

1) Anticyclones form where <u>air</u> is <u>falling</u>, creating <u>high pressure</u> and <u>light winds</u> blowing <u>outwards</u>.
2) Falling air gets <u>warmer</u> so <u>no clouds</u> are formed, giving <u>clear skies</u> and <u>no rain</u> for <u>days</u> or even <u>weeks</u>.
3) In <u>summer</u>, anticyclones cause <u>long periods</u> of <u>hot</u>, <u>dry</u>, <u>clear</u> weather. There are <u>no clouds</u> to <u>absorb</u> the Sun's heat energy, so <u>more gets through</u> to the Earth's surface causing <u>high temperatures</u>.
4) In <u>winter</u>, anticyclones give <u>long periods</u> of <u>cold</u>, <u>foggy</u> weather. <u>Heat</u> is <u>lost</u> from the Earth's surface at <u>night</u> because there are <u>no clouds</u> to <u>reflect it back</u>. The <u>temperature drops</u> and <u>condensation</u> occurs near the surface, forming <u>fog</u>. (It <u>doesn't heat up</u> much in the <u>day</u> because the <u>Sun is weak</u>.)

> 1) Some anticyclones are described as '<u>blocking</u>'. Blocking anticyclones can sit over the UK and remain there for <u>many days</u>.
> 2) Depressions that would normally travel across Britain are forced around the upper edge of the anticyclone. <u>Extreme weather conditions</u> are likely, e.g. <u>heatwaves</u> in summer and <u>dry</u>, <u>freezing</u> weather in winter.

Extreme weather in the UK is often caused by depressions

Although the UK experiences lots of rain and wind, extreme events are still unusual. However, climate change might increase the frequency of extreme events in the UK, which could have a serious impact on people.

UK Weather Hazards

Weather hazards are quite common in the UK — and it's not just about rain, either...

The UK Experiences Lots of Different Weather Hazards

Rain

1) Too much rain in too short a time can cause flooding, which can damage homes and possessions, disrupt transport networks and cause death by drowning.

2) It can also force businesses to close, and recovering from flooding can cost millions of pounds.

Wind

1) Strong winds (gales) can damage properties and cause disruption to transport.

2) Uprooted trees and debris can injure or kill people.

3) Forests can be damaged when trees are blown over.

4) Winds are strongest in coastal areas of the UK, particularly the west coast, and in upland areas.

Snow and Ice

1) Snow and ice can cause injuries due to slipping and deaths due to the cold.

2) Schools and businesses can be forced to shut, and major disruption to road, rail and air travel can occur causing economic impacts.

3) Cold snaps can damage crops and other plants.

Thunderstorms

1) Heavy rain, lightning and strong winds occur in thunderstorms.

2) They are most common in summer in the south and east of the UK.

3) Lightning can occasionally cause death and can cause fires that damage property or the environment.

Hailstorms

Hailstorms make driving very dangerous and can damage property and destroy crops.

Heat Waves

1) Sometimes the UK can have long periods of hot weather. This can cause deaths from heat exhaustion or breathing difficulties as pollution builds up in the air.

2) Disruption to transport from rails buckling or roads melting can cause economic impacts — but the tourism industry may benefit from the better weather.

Drought

1) Drought is a lack of precipitation (i.e. not enough rain or snow).

2) Water supplies can run low during a drought, causing economic impacts such as crop failures. Rules to conserve water (like banning hosepipe use) have to be introduced.

Weather in the UK is Becoming More Extreme

1) Temperatures have become more extreme in recent years — December 2010 was the coldest for over 100 years, with severe snow and ice causing several deaths, and school and road closures. But just four months later, April 2011 was the warmest April on record.

2) It's raining more — more rainfall records have been broken in 2010-2014 than in any decade on record, even after only half a decade. 2013 was one of the wettest years on record, and December 2015 was the wettest month ever recorded.

3) Major flooding occurs often — e.g. there was major flooding caused by storms and high rainfall in the Somerset Levels during the winter of 2013-2014, in west Wales in 2012, in Cumbria in 2005, 2009 and 2015-2016 (along with large parts of northern England and parts of Scotland).

The UK has lots of different weather hazards

The weather hazards affecting the UK might not seem as bad as volcanoes, earthquakes or hurricanes, but the effects on people can still be pretty severe — and there's some evidence that weather is getting worse.

UK Heat Wave

Now the UK might not be as <u>warm</u> as we'd all like it to be, but having a little extra <u>heat</u> isn't always a good thing...

A **Heat Wave** is when Conditions are **Hotter than Normal**

1) A <u>heat wave</u> is a <u>long period</u> (days or weeks) during which the <u>temperature</u> is much <u>higher</u> than <u>normal</u>.

2) The <u>conditions</u> of a <u>heat wave</u> are <u>different</u> in <u>different places</u>, e.g. the conditions considered a heat wave in the <u>UK</u> would be much <u>cooler</u> than in a country like <u>Spain</u>, where higher temperatures are <u>expected</u>.

3) Heat waves are <u>caused</u> when <u>anticyclones</u> (see p.29) stay in the <u>same place</u> for some time.

4) Anticyclones can last for a long period of time, leading to a <u>heat wave</u>, like the <u>European Heat Wave</u> that affected the UK (and much of Europe) in <u>August 2003</u>.

1 Causes of the 2003 Heat Wave

1) An <u>anticyclone</u> was situated over <u>western Europe</u> for most of <u>August</u>.

2) Air moves <u>clockwise</u> around an anticyclone, so <u>hot</u>, <u>dry air</u> from the <u>centre of the continent</u> was brought to <u>western Europe</u>. This meant temperatures in the UK were <u>higher</u> than normal and rainfall was <u>lower</u> than normal.

3) The anticyclone <u>blocked low pressure systems</u> that would normally bring <u>cooler, rainier</u> conditions from the Atlantic Ocean.

2 UK Consequences of the 2003 Heat Wave

1) People suffered from <u>heat stroke</u>, <u>dehydration</u>, <u>sunburn</u> and <u>breathing problems</u> caused by <u>air pollution</u>. Some people <u>drowned</u> when cooling off in <u>rivers</u>, <u>lakes</u> and <u>pools</u>.

2) Around <u>2000</u> people <u>died</u> in the UK from causes linked to the heatwave.

3) <u>20 people</u> were <u>injured</u> when they were struck by <u>lightning</u> during thunderstorms caused by the heat wave.

4) <u>Water levels fell</u> in <u>reservoirs</u>, which threatened <u>water supplies</u> to houses and businesses.

5) <u>Livestock died</u> due to the heat, and <u>crop yields</u> were <u>lower</u> due to the lack of water.

6) <u>Trains</u> were disrupted by <u>rails buckling</u> in the heat and some <u>roads melted</u>, which caused <u>delays</u>.

Water levels in Haweswater reservoir dropped severely during the heatwave.

3 UK Responses to the 2003 Heat Wave

1) The <u>NHS</u> and the <u>media</u> gave <u>guidance</u> to the public on how to survive the heat wave — e.g. <u>drink</u> lots of <u>water</u>, have <u>cool baths</u> and <u>showers</u>, <u>block</u> out <u>sunlight</u> to keep rooms <u>cool</u>, etc.

2) <u>Limitations</u> were placed on water use, e.g. some parts of the UK had <u>hose pipe bans</u>.

3) A <u>speed limit</u> was imposed on <u>trains</u> because of the risk of <u>rails buckling</u>. Some rails were <u>painted white</u> to <u>reflect heat</u> and keep them <u>cooler</u>.

4) The UK created a '<u>heat wave plan</u>' to minimise the <u>consequences</u> of <u>future</u> heat waves.

The 2003 heat wave caused lots of problems in the UK

REVISION TIP

Seriously hot weather causes serious disruption, and so do other weather hazards. You may have studied a different extreme weather event in class — whatever example you learn, make sure you know the causes and impacts, as well as strategies to reduce the risk of that particular event in the UK.

Worked Exam Questions

Time for a few exam-style questions to test what you know. The first page has the answers already filled in to help you understand how to answer exam questions effectively. It's over to you for the second page though.

---

1 Study **Figure 1**, a photograph of a weather hazard experienced in the UK.

1.1 Outline **two** possible effects of the weather hazard shown in **Figure 1**.

Figure 1

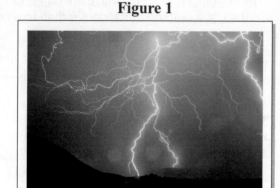

Effect 1: Lightning can cause fires that damage property or the environment.

Effect 2: Thunderstorms can cause flooding due to torrential rain.

[2]

1.2 Suggest two possible effects of heat waves in the UK.

Effect 1: People can experience health problems such as heat exhaustion.

Effect 2: Transport can be disrupted due to rails buckling or roads melting.

[2]

[Total 4 marks]

---

2 **Figure 2** shows normal atmospheric and oceanic circulation patterns in the South Pacific Ocean.

Figure 2

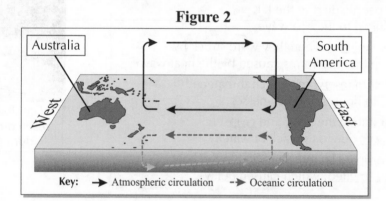

Key: → Atmospheric circulation ⇢ Oceanic circulation

2.1 Describe how the circulation patterns shown in **Figure 2** change during an El Niño event.

During an El Niño event, normal atmospheric circulation is reversed, so air rises in the eastern

Pacific and falls in the west. This causes wind direction to reverse. Oceanic circulation also reverses

direction or becomes weaker, and cold water stops rising in the east.

[4]

2.2 Explain how El Niño events can cause droughts in some areas.

During an El Niño event, there is sinking air in the high pressure area over the western Pacific.

This leads to unusually dry weather, which can cause droughts.

[2]

[Total 6 marks]

Exam Questions

1 Study **Figure 1**, which gives information about the weather conditions in a town in southern England during the first two weeks of December 2010.

Figure 1

	December 2010													
Day	1	2	3	4	5	6	7	8	9	10	11	12	13	14
Minimum temperature (°C)	−5	−3	−4	0	−1	1	−1	−2	−1	0	−2	−3	1	0
Maximum temperature (°C)	−2	1	−1	2	1	2	3	0	1	2	0	0	2	3
Precipitation (mm)	0	0	1	2	3	3	7	0	0	0	2	1	1	8

1.1 Calculate the range of minimum temperatures shown in **Figure 1**.

....
[1]

1.2 What type of extreme weather event is shown in **Figure 1**? Shade **one** oval only.

A Tropical storm ◯

B Cold snap ◯

C Extremely high precipitation ◯

D Heatwave ◯

[1]

1.3 Explain how an anticyclone may have led to the weather conditions shown in **Figure 1**.

....

....

....

....

....

....
[4]
[Total 6 marks]

2 Answer this question using a case study of **either** a drought **or** a heat wave event.

Chosen weather hazard event:...

Outline the consequences of this weather hazard event and the responses to it.

[Total 8 + 3 SPaG]

Revision Summary

Right, that's Weather Hazards done and dusted — high time for some revision questions.
- Try these questions and tick off each one when you get it right.
- When you've done all the questions for a topic and are completely happy with it, tick off the topic.

Global Atmospheric Circulation and Extreme Weather (p.14-16) ☐

1) How does global atmospheric circulation lead to high and low pressure belts?
2) Describe how ocean currents transfer heat around the Earth.
3) How do high and low pressure belts create climatic zones?
4) How does global atmospheric circulation cause extremes of precipitation in some parts of the world?
5) Compare extreme temperatures in two different countries.

Tropical Storms (p.17-22) ☐

6) What conditions are required for a tropical storm to develop?
7) In what direction does a tropical storm move?
8) What can cause a tropical storm to lose strength?
9) Which way does a tropical storm rotate?
10) Describe two characteristics of the eye of a tropical storm.
11) What are the extreme weather conditions caused by tropical storms?
12) Why might climate change cause more damaging tropical storms?
13) Describe two primary and two secondary effects of tropical storms.
14) Explain why some countries are more vulnerable to tropical storms than others.
15) How might stronger defences help to reduce the impacts of tropical storms?
16) What were the causes of a tropical storm that you have studied?
17) What were the consequences of a tropical storm that you have studied?

El Niño, La Niña and Drought (p.25-27) ☐

18) What is El Niño?
19) What is La Niña?
20) How does an La Niña event cause wet weather in some places?
21) What is a drought?
22) How has the distribution of droughts varied over time?
23) What were the causes of a drought that you have studied?

UK Climate and Weather Hazards (p.28-31) ☐

24) Describe how continentality influences weather in the UK.
25) a) What is the North Atlantic Drift?
    b) How does it affect the UK's climate?
26) Name two air masses that influence weather in the UK.
27) What is a depression?
28) Explain how depressions can cause extreme weather.
29) What is an anticyclone?
30) List the types of extreme weather that can be experienced in the UK.
31) Give one piece of evidence for the weather becoming more extreme in the UK.

Climate Change — Evidence

We British like to talk about the weather, so global climate change should give us plenty to go on...

The Earth is **Getting Warmer**

Climate change is any significant change in the Earth's climate over a long period. The climate constantly changes, it always has, and it always will.

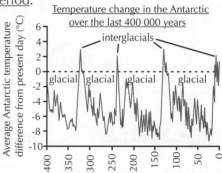

Temperature change in the Antarctic over the last 400 000 years

1) The Quaternary period is the most recent geological time period, spanning from about 2.6 million years ago to the present day.

2) In the period before the Quaternary, the Earth's climate was warmer and quite stable. Then things changed a lot.

The Quaternary period includes the whole of human history.

3) During the Quaternary, global temperature has shifted between cold glacial periods that last for around 100 000 years, and warmer interglacial periods that last for around 10 000 years.

4) The last glacial period ended around 15 000 years ago. Since then the climate has been warming.

5) Global warming is the term used to describe the sharp rise in global temperatures over the last century. It's a type of climate change.

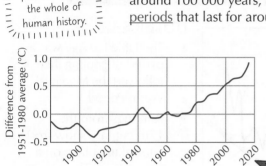

This graph shows the last 400 000 years but the glacial-interglacial cycles have been repeating throughout the Quaternary period — there have been at least 20.

Evidence for **Climate Change** Comes from **Many Sources**

Scientists can work out how the climate has changed over time using a range of methods. For example:

Ice and Sediment Cores

1) Ice sheets are made up of layers of ice — one layer is formed each year.

2) Scientists drill into ice sheets to get long cores of ice.

3) By analysing the gases trapped in the layers of ice, they can tell what the temperature was each year.

4) One ice core from Antarctica shows the temperature changes over the last 400 000 years (see graph above).

5) The remains of organisms found in cores taken from ocean sediments can also be analysed. These can extend the temperature record back at least 5 million years.

6) Data collected from ice cores is very detailed and reliable.

Tree Rings

1) As a tree grows it forms a new ring each year — the tree rings are thicker in warm, wet conditions.

2) Scientists take cores and count the rings to find the age of a tree. The thickness of each ring shows what the climate was like.

3) Tree rings are a reliable source of evidence of climate change for the past 10 000 years.

Diaries and Paintings

1) Historical diaries can show what the climate was like in the past, e.g. by giving the number of days of rain or snow and the dates of harvests (e.g. an early harvest suggests warm weather).

2) Paintings of fairs and markets on frozen rivers show that winters in Europe were regularly much colder 500 years ago than they are now.

3) However, diaries and paintings aren't very reliable, as they just give one person's viewpoint.

Sea Ice Positions

1) Sea ice forms around the poles in winter when ocean temperatures fall below -1.8 °C and melts during the summer when it's warmer.

2) By observing the maximum and minimum extent of sea ice each year, scientists can tell how ocean temperatures are changing.

3) The data is very reliable, but accurate records don't go very far back.

Climate Change — Evidence

Pollen Analysis

1) <u>Pollen</u> from plants gets <u>preserved</u> in <u>sediment</u>, e.g. at the bottom of lakes or in peat bogs.

2) Scientists can <u>identify</u> and <u>date</u> the preserved pollen to show which <u>species</u> were living at that time.

3) Scientists know the <u>conditions</u> that plants live in <u>now</u>, so preserved pollen from <u>similar plants</u> shows that <u>climate conditions</u> were <u>similar</u>.

Temperature Data

1) Since the <u>1850s</u>, global temperatures have been measured accurately using <u>thermometers</u>. This gives a <u>reliable</u> but <u>short-term record</u> of temperature change.

2) However, <u>weather stations</u> are not <u>evenly distributed</u> across the world — data from some areas is <u>patchy</u>.

These **Sources** have been used to **Reconstruct** the **UK's Past Climate**

<u>MEDIEVAL WARM PERIOD</u>

- The Medieval Warm Period was a period of <u>warming</u> between <u>900</u> and <u>1300</u>.

- <u>Harvest records</u> show that England was warm enough to grow <u>large amounts</u> of <u>grapes</u>.

Tree ring data suggests that UK temperatures were almost 1.0 °C warmer during Roman times than today.

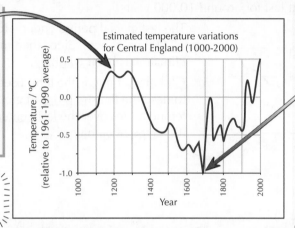

Estimated temperature variations for Central England (1000-2000)

<u>LITTLE ICE AGE</u>

- The Little Ice Age was a period of <u>cooling</u> that <u>followed</u> the Medieval Warm Period.

- Paintings from the <u>17th century</u> show frost <u>fairs</u> taking place on a <u>frozen</u> River Thames.

- <u>Historical records</u> talk about <u>arctic ice</u> reaching as far south as <u>Scotland</u>.

There is Some **Evidence** that **Human Activity** is causing **Climate Change**

<u>Scientists</u> have identified <u>several factors</u> which <u>support</u> the idea that <u>humans</u> are causing <u>global warming</u>.

Declining Arctic Ice

The <u>extent</u> of arctic sea ice in <u>winter</u> has <u>decreased</u> by more than <u>3%</u> each decade over the past <u>35 years</u>.

Global Temperature Rise

Temperatures have <u>increased</u> by nearly <u>1 °C</u> since 1880 and are expected to rise by <u>0.3-4.8 °C</u> between <u>2005</u> and <u>2100</u>. The top <u>ten warmest</u> years since records began have <u>all</u> been <u>since</u> the year <u>2000</u>.

Sea Level Rise and Warming Oceans

Since <u>1901</u> sea levels have risen by almost <u>0.2 m</u>. Scientists have highlighted <u>two factors</u> behind this rise:

- **EUSTATIC SEA LEVEL RISE**

  <u>Warmer</u> temperatures are causing <u>glaciers</u> to <u>shrink</u> and <u>ice sheets</u> to <u>melt</u>, which means that water stored on land as ice <u>returns</u> to the <u>oceans</u>. This causes <u>sea levels</u> to <u>rise</u>.

- **THERMAL EXPANSION**

  Water in the oceans <u>expands</u> as it gets <u>warmer</u> — this is called <u>thermal expansion</u>. Scientists think this accounts for about <u>half</u> of the measured rise in sea levels.

Extreme Weather Events

1) Since <u>1950</u> there has been a <u>higher</u> frequency of <u>heat waves</u> in many areas and fewer <u>cold weather extremes</u>.

2) In the <u>UK</u> the weather has also been much <u>wetter</u> in recent decades (see p.30).

Learn the evidence for climate change

There were no thermometers 2.6 million years ago but scientists can reconstruct climates using the clever methods shown on these pages. Climate change is a hot topic, so make sure you learn this stuff inside out before your exam.

Causes of Climate Change

Climate change goes back long before humans roamed the Earth — this has been caused by natural factors.

There are **Natural Causes** of **Climate Change**

1 Orbital Changes (Milankovitch Cycles)

1) Orbital changes are variations in the way the Earth moves round the Sun.

- Stretch (also called eccentricity) — the path of the Earth's orbit around the Sun changes from an almost perfect circle to an ellipse (an oval) and back again about every 96 000 years.

- Tilt — the Earth's axis is tilted at an angle as it orbits the Sun. This tilt changes over a cycle of about 41 000 years.

- Wobble (also called precession) — the axis of the Earth wobbles like a spinning top on a cycle of about 22 000 years.

2) These cycles affect the amount of solar radiation (energy) the Earth receives. If the Earth receives more energy, it gets warmer.

3) Orbital changes may have caused the glacial and interglacial cycles of the Quaternary period.

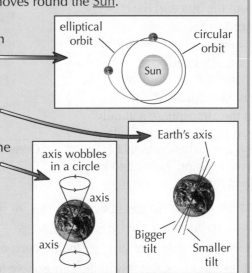

2 Volcanic Activity

1) Major volcanic eruptions eject large quantities of material, e.g. ash, into the atmosphere.

2) Some of these particles reflect the Sun's rays back out to space, so the Earth's surface cools.

3) Volcanic activity may cause short-term changes in climate, e.g. the eruption of Mount Tambora in Indonesia in 1815 led to the 'Year Without a Summer' in 1816.

3 Solar Output (Sunspots)

1) The Sun's output of energy isn't constant — it changes in short cycles of about 11 years, and possibly also in longer cycles of several hundred years.

2) Periods when solar output is reduced may cause the Earth's climate to become cooler.

3) The Maunder Minimum was a period of very low sunspot activity between 1645 and 1715 which coincided with the Little Ice Age (see previous page).

> Sunspots are cooler areas of the Sun's surface that are visible as dark patches. They coincide with an increase in the Sun's energy output.

4 Asteroid Collisions

1) Asteroids hitting the Earth's surface can throw up huge amounts of dust into the atmosphere.

2) These particles prevent the Sun's energy from reaching the Earth's surface so global temperatures fall (possibly for several years).

3) Some scientists believe that an asteroid collision caused a period of global cooling (the Younger Dryas) around 12 000 years ago.

Many natural factors have contributed to historical climate change

It's important to remember that climate change is not a new phenomenon — it's been happening for thousands of years. Examiners love to ask about climate change, so it's important that you understand how each natural factor can lead to climate change. Try jotting down in your own words how each factor can impact global temperatures.

Causes of Climate Change

In the last 150 years or so <u>human activities</u> have begun to have an <u>impact</u> on the Earth's climate.

The **Natural Greenhouse Effect** is **Essential** for Keeping Our Planet **Warm**

1) The <u>temperature</u> of the Earth is a <u>balance</u> between the heat it <u>gets</u> from the <u>Sun</u> and the heat it <u>loses</u> to <u>space</u>.

2) The <u>incoming</u> energy from the Sun is <u>short-wave radiation</u>. The <u>outgoing</u> energy from the Earth is <u>long-wave radiation</u>.

3) <u>Gases</u> in the atmosphere naturally act like an <u>insulating layer</u> — they let short-wave radiation in, but <u>trap</u> long-wave radiation, helping to keep the Earth at the <u>right temperature</u>.

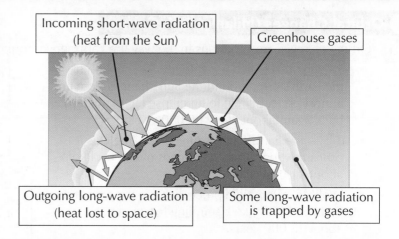

Incoming short-wave radiation (heat from the Sun)

Greenhouse gases

Outgoing long-wave radiation (heat lost to space)

Some long-wave radiation is trapped by gases

4) This is called the <u>greenhouse effect</u> ('cos it's a bit like a greenhouse trapping heat).

5) Gases that trap heat are called <u>greenhouse gases</u> — they include <u>carbon dioxide</u> (CO_2) and <u>methane</u> (CH_4).

6) Some greenhouse gases are <u>stronger</u> than others, e.g. <u>methane</u> absorbs <u>more</u> heat than <u>carbon dioxide</u>.

7) Different greenhouse gases <u>stay</u> in the atmosphere for different lengths of time. For example, methane usually stays in the atmosphere for around <u>10 years</u> after it has been emitted.

8) The <u>longer</u> the gases stay in the atmosphere, the more they'll contribute to <u>warming</u>.

Human Activities are Making the Greenhouse Effect **Stronger**

1) The <u>rate</u> of the recent <u>rise</u> in <u>global temperature</u> (<u>global warming</u>) is <u>unheard of</u>.

2) There's a <u>scientific consensus</u> (general agreement) that <u>human activities</u> are <u>causing</u> global warming by making the <u>greenhouse effect</u> stronger. This is called the <u>enhanced greenhouse effect</u>.

3) <u>Too much</u> greenhouse gas in the atmosphere means <u>too much</u> energy is trapped and the planet <u>warms up</u>.

4) <u>Humans</u> are increasing the <u>concentration</u> of greenhouse gases:

Energy — <u>CO_2</u> is <u>released</u> into the atmosphere when <u>fossil fuels</u> like coal, oil and natural gas are <u>burnt</u>, e.g. in power stations.

Transport — Most <u>cars</u>, <u>lorries</u>, <u>ships</u> and <u>planes</u> run on fossil fuels. <u>Car ownership</u> is rapidly <u>increasing</u> in countries which are <u>developing</u>, e.g. <u>China</u>. This means there are <u>more</u> cars on the <u>roads</u> (especially in <u>urban areas</u>). This increases <u>congestion</u> and greenhouse gas <u>emissions</u> because car engines are running for longer.

Industry — Most industry uses a lot of <u>energy</u> and some <u>industrial processes</u>, e.g. <u>cement production</u>, also release greenhouse gases.

Farming — <u>Farming</u> of <u>livestock</u> produces a lot of <u>methane</u> — cows love to belch... <u>Rice paddies</u> contribute to global warming, because <u>flooded fields</u> emit <u>methane</u>.

Deforestation — <u>Plants remove CO_2</u> from the atmosphere and convert it into <u>organic matter</u> using photosynthesis. When trees and plants are <u>chopped down</u>, they <u>stop taking in CO_2</u>. CO_2 is also <u>released</u> into the atmosphere when trees are <u>burnt</u> as <u>fuel</u> or to make way for <u>agriculture</u>.

REVISION TIP

Global warming is caused by a stronger greenhouse effect

You may have to explain the causes of climate change in your exam — try writing an explanation in your own words of how human activities can cause the greenhouse effect to become stronger.

Global Effects of Climate Change

Whether human or natural factors are to blame, scientists are pretty sure climate change is having an impact...

Climate Change has Environmental, Economic and Social Impacts

Environmental Impacts

1) Temperatures are expected to rise by 0.3-4.8 °C between 2005 and 2100.

2) Warmer temperatures are causing glaciers to shrink and ice sheets like Greenland to melt. The melting of ice on land, especially from the Greenland and Antarctic ice sheets, means that water stored on land as ice returns to the oceans. This causes sea level rise.

3) Sea ice is also shrinking, leading to the loss of polar habitats.

4) Other species are declining due to warming, e.g. some coral reefs are suffering from bleaching due to increasing sea water temperatures.

5) Precipitation patterns are changing — warming is affecting how much rain areas get.

6) The distribution and quantity of some species could change and biodiversity could decrease:

   • Some species are now found in higher latitudes due to warming temperatures.

   • Some habitats are being damaged or destroyed due to climate change
     — species that are specially adapted to these areas may become extinct.

Economic Impacts

1) Climate change means the weather is getting more extreme. This means more money has to be spent on predicting extreme weather events (e.g. floods, droughts and tropical storms), reducing their impacts and rebuilding after them.

2) Rising temperatures are causing areas of permafrost (see p.73) to melt — this can lead to the collapse of buildings, pipelines etc. built on it. However, it's easier to extract natural resources from unfrozen ground.

3) Climate change is affecting farming in different ways around the world:

   • Globally, some crops have suffered from climate change (e.g. maize crops have got smaller due to warming in recent years).

   • But some farmers in high-latitude countries are finding that crops benefit from warmer conditions.

4) Water shortages might affect our ability to generate power — hydroelectric power and thermal power stations require lots of water.

Social Impacts

1) In some places, reduced rainfall means there's an increased threat from wildfires. These can damage homes and also put people's lives at risk.

2) Some areas could become so hot and dry that they're difficult or impossible to inhabit. Low-lying coastal areas could be lost to the sea or flood so often that they also become impossible to inhabit. This could lead to migration and overcrowding in other areas.

3) Some areas are struggling to supply enough water for their residents due to problems with water availability caused by changing rainfall patterns. This can lead to political tensions, especially where rivers cross borders.

4) Lower crop yields could increase malnutrition, ill health and death from starvation, particularly in lower latitudes.

Rising temperatures are affecting rainfall patterns and causing ice sheets to melt

Scientists still don't know what the exact impacts of climate change will be, but some effects are already being seen. Make sure you know how climate change could have environmental, economic and social impacts.

Effects of Climate Change on the UK

The effects of climate change aren't just happening in places far away — the impacts can be felt in the underline{UK} too.

Climate Change in the UK Causes Environmental Impacts...

Climate

1) Temperature will increase. The increase is expected to be greatest in southern England, where the average summer temperature is projected to increase by 3.9 °C by 2080.
2) Winter rainfall is expected to increase by 16% in parts of the western side of the UK.
3) Summer rainfall is expected to decrease by 23% in parts of southern England.

Extreme Events

1) Droughts are expected to be more frequent and intense, especially in southern England.
2) Flooding will become more common due to increased rainfall and sea level rise.

Sea Level Rise

1) Sea level is expected to rise by 12-76 cm by 2095.
2) This will lead to the loss of habitats, e.g. saltmarsh.

Wildlife

Climate change will change the UK's habitats. Some species have already left their original habitats and moved north to areas with lower temperatures (e.g. the comma butterfly). This can upset the balance of natural ecosystems (see p.46) and lead to species extinction.

...Economic Impacts...

Tourism

1) Warmer weather in the UK could boost the tourist industry if more people decide to holiday at home.
2) However, in some areas, it could also lead to a decline, e.g. skiing in the Cairngorms.

Fishing

1) The UK fishing industry could also be affected — more extreme UK weather conditions could put fishing infrastructure (e.g. ports, boats) at risk from storm damage.
2) Fishermen's livelihoods could be affected by changing fish populations and species found in UK waters.

Agriculture

1) Temperature increase and a longer growing season may increase productivity of some crops, e.g. asparagus, onions, courgettes, peas and beans.
2) New crops adapted to warmer climates could be grown in southern England (e.g. soya and grapes), but reduced rainfall and droughts would increase the need for irrigation and water storage schemes.

...and Social Impacts

Water Shortages

Drier summers will affect water availability, particularly in areas of south east England where population density is increasing.

Health

Deaths from cold-related illnesses may decrease, but health services may have to treat more heat-related illnesses, e.g. heat exhaustion.

Floods

Flooding from increased rainfall and sea level rise might damage homes and businesses, especially those on estuaries (e.g. in cities such as Hull, Cardiff, Portsmouth and London) and low lying areas near the coast (e.g. large areas of Norfolk).

REVISION TIP

Many impacts on the UK are the same as other places

If you concentrate on learning the specific details of the environmental, economic and social impacts of climate change in the UK, you'll find you've also learned some of the information on page 39.

Climate Change Projections

You should now be an expert in the causes and evidence for climate change — so it's time to find out all about how our current understanding of climate change can be used to predict future changes to the climate.

Data about **Climate Change** can be used to **Make Predictions**

1) Physical processes, e.g. atmospheric circulation and the effect of volcanic eruptions on the climate, can be modelled on computers.

2) Human activity, e.g. growth of industry or development of clean energy, can also be modelled using data that's been collected about greenhouse gas emissions.

3) Scientists can use these models to work out how the climate would be affected under certain scenarios, e.g. what would happen if there was a volcanic eruption in 20 years' time and there were still high levels of greenhouse gas emissions.

4) The Intergovernmental Panel on Climate Change (IPCC) is an international group of scientists that uses models to predict how the climate might change and the consequences of any changes.

5) The IPCC have chosen four "Representative Concentration Pathways" (RCPs) — possible scenarios covering the best to the worst possible outcomes.

6) The IPCC uses projection graphs to show the predicted changes in temperature and sea level by 2100.

7) Lines for the best and worst scenarios are plotted on the graphs. All other outcomes fall between these lines.

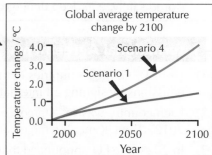

SCENARIO 1 — Minimum Emissions

This is the best outcome, in which levels of greenhouse gases peak, then reduce (i.e. greenhouse gas emissions are significantly reduced).

SCENARIOS 2 & 3 — Stabilising Scenarios

These are scenarios in which greenhouse gas levels continue to increase, but eventually level off (after steps are taken to reduce emissions).

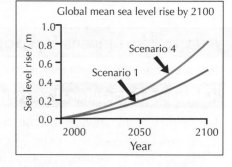

SCENARIO 4 — Maximum Emissions

This is the worst outcome, in which the rate of production of emissions continues to increase and greenhouse gas levels end up very high.

You might be asked to use and interpret projection graphs in your exam.

There is Lots of **Uncertainty** about **Future Climate Change**

It's difficult to predict the impacts of changes in climate because there's so much uncertainty.

1) EMISSIONS — we don't actually know how emissions will change, i.e. which scenario is most accurate.
   - Predictions have to take into account things like population increase and economic development.
   - It's hard to know how global population will change in the future (i.e. whether it'll keep growing at the rate it is today) or how much development will take place in the future.

2) COMPLEXITY — we don't know what exact climate changes each scenario will cause.
   - There are lots of natural processes that we don't fully understand, which makes it difficult to predict what will change. We don't know how these natural factors could have an impact on climate change.

3) MANAGEMENT — we don't know what attempts there will be to manage the amount of greenhouse gases in the atmosphere, or how successful they'll be.

No-one can accurately predict the future of climate change

Some people think that the rate of greenhouse gas emissions will continue to rise, leading to climate change and sea level rises. Others think that emissions will lessen in the future, which will reduce long-term global warming.

Managing Climate Change

You've just seen the <u>effects</u> of climate change — some of them are pretty <u>worrying</u>. People have come up with a variety of ways of <u>reducing</u> the <u>causes</u> of climate change and <u>adapting</u> to the changes to minimise disruption though.

Mitigation Strategies aim to Reduce the Causes of Climate Change

Various strategies aim to <u>reduce</u> the <u>causes</u> of climate change, by <u>reducing</u> the concentration of <u>greenhouse gases</u> in the atmosphere:

Planting Trees

Planting trees <u>increases</u> the amount of <u>carbon dioxide</u> that is <u>absorbed</u> from the atmosphere through photosynthesis.

Carbon Capture

1) <u>Carbon Capture and Storage</u> (<u>CCS</u>) is a new technology designed to reduce climate change by <u>reducing emissions</u> from <u>fossil fuel</u> burning <u>power stations</u>.

2) CCS involves <u>capturing CO$_2$</u> and <u>transporting it</u> to places where it can be stored safely, e.g. deep underground.

Alternative Energy Production

1) <u>Replacing</u> fossil fuels with nuclear power and renewable energy can help reduce climate change by <u>reducing</u> greenhouse gas emissions from <u>power stations</u>.

2) In the UK, more <u>offshore wind farms</u> are being built, several <u>wave</u> and <u>tidal power projects</u> are planned, and new <u>nuclear power plants</u> are also being planned.

International Agreements

1) From 1997, <u>most countries</u> in the world agreed to <u>monitor</u> and <u>cut greenhouse gas emissions</u> by signing an <u>international agreement</u> called the <u>Kyoto Protocol</u>.

2) Each country was set a <u>target</u>, e.g. the <u>UK</u> agreed to reduce emissions by <u>12.5%</u> by 2012. The UK met the target, actually reducing emissions by an average of <u>22%</u>.

3) In 2021, the <u>EU</u> announced that it had cut its emissions by <u>20%</u> from their 1990 levels.

Adaptation Means Responding to Changes Caused by Climate Change

Here are some of the ways that people are <u>adjusting</u> to the effects of <u>climate change</u>:

Changing Agricultural Systems

Changing <u>rainfall patterns</u> and <u>higher temperatures</u> will affect the <u>productivity</u> of existing systems.

1) It may be necessary to plant <u>new crop types</u> that are more <u>suitable</u> to the <u>new climate conditions</u> in an area, e.g. soya, peaches and grapes may be grown in southern England.

2) In some regions, <u>biotechnology</u> is being used to create <u>new crop varieties</u> which are <u>more resistant</u> to extreme weather events, e.g. drought resistant millet is being grown in Kenya.

Managing Water Supply

<u>Dry areas</u> are predicted to get <u>drier</u>, leading to more <u>water shortages</u> — so people need to use water resources more <u>efficiently</u>.

1) <u>Water meters</u> can be installed in people's homes to <u>discourage</u> them from using a lot of water.

2) <u>Rainwater</u> can be <u>collected</u> and <u>waste water</u> can be <u>recycled</u> to make more water available.

Coping with Rising Sea Levels

<u>Sea levels</u> are predicted to <u>rise</u> by up to 82 cm by 2100, which would <u>flood</u> many <u>islands</u> and <u>coastal areas</u>.

1) <u>Physical defences</u> such as <u>flood barriers</u> are being built and better <u>flood warning systems</u> are being put in place. E.g. the <u>Thames Barrier</u> in London can be closed to prevent sea water flooding the city.

2) In areas that can't afford expensive flood defences, e.g. Bangladesh, people are <u>building</u> their <u>houses</u> on top of <u>earth embankments</u> and building raised <u>flood shelters</u> to use in emergencies.

It's possible to reduce the causes and effects of climate change

Make sure you get the difference between mitigation and adaptation — don't let the examiners catch you out. Mitigation means reducing the risk, and adaptation means adjusting to extreme events.

Worked Exam Questions

Working through exam questions is a great way of testing what you've learned and practising for the exam.
This worked example will give you an idea of the kind of answers examiners are looking for.

---

1 Study **Figure 1**, which shows data on sea level rise between 1900 and 2100.

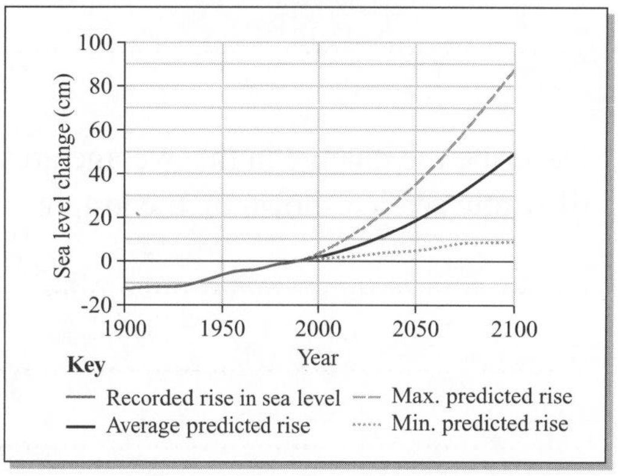

1.1 What is the average predicted rise in sea level between 2050 and 2100?

.... 30 .... cm

[1]

Figure 1

Key
— Recorded rise in sea level   -- Max. predicted rise
— Average predicted rise   ...... Min. predicted rise

1.2 Suggest **one** way in which the rise in sea level might affect the environment.

Low-lying and coastal areas may be flooded more regularly.

[1]

1.3 Apart from sea level rise, outline **two** possible environmental effects of climate change.

Effect 1: Warmer temperatures may cause glaciers to shrink and ice sheets like Greenland to melt, leading to the loss of polar habitats.

Effect 2: Some species that are adapted to particular climates may decline if they don't adapt to the changing climate.

[2]

[Total 4 marks]

---

2 Study **Figure 2**, a photograph of a coal-fired power plant in South Africa.

2.1 Explain what impact this activity may have on climate change.

Burning coal releases carbon dioxide into the atmosphere, so coal-fired power plants increase the concentration of greenhouse gases in the atmosphere. Greenhouse gases absorb outgoing heat, so less is lost to space — this is called the greenhouse effect. Increasing the amount of greenhouse gases in the atmosphere enhances the greenhouse effect. This means that more heat is trapped and the planet warms up, leading to climate change.

Figure 2

[4]

2.2 Explain how **one** other human activity may contribute to climate change.

Farming of livestock produces a lot of methane, which is a greenhouse gas that contributes to climate change.

[2]

[Total 6 marks]

Exam Questions

1   Study **Figure 1**, which shows the average area of sea ice in the Arctic in September between 1979 and 2016.

Figure 1

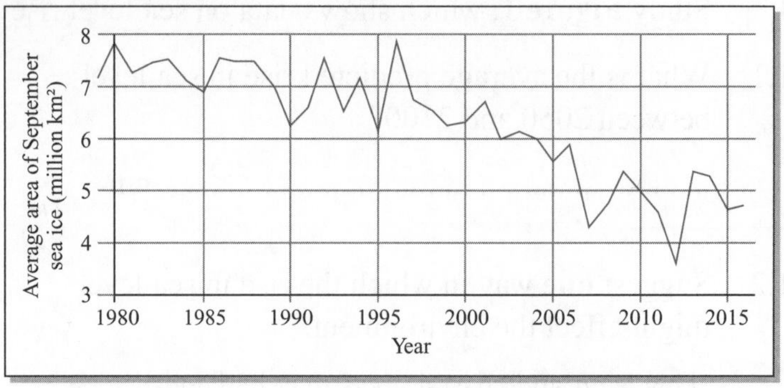

1.1   How much did the area of sea ice decrease by between 1980 and 2015?

....
[1]

1.2   Describe the change in the average area of Arctic sea ice shown by the graph.

....

....

....

....
[3]

[Total 4 marks]

2   Study **Figure 2**, a graph showing temperature changes during the Quaternary period.

Figure 2

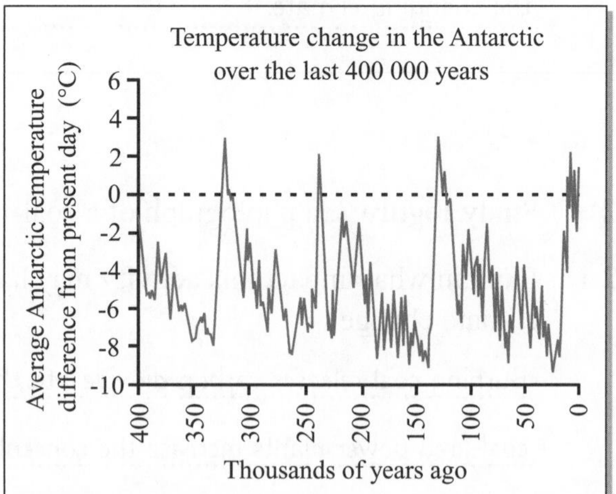

2.1   The temperature changes shown in **Figure 2** were worked out from ice core records. Explain how ice cores provide evidence for past climate change.

....

....

....

....
[2]

2.2   Explain **two** possible causes of the changes in temperature between 400 000 and 100 000 years ago shown in **Figure 2**.

Cause 1: ....

....

....

Cause 2: ....

....

....
[4]

[Total 6 marks]

Revision Summary

Well done for reaching the end of <u>Section 3</u>. Here are some revision questions to test your knowledge.
- Try these questions and <u>tick off each one</u> when you <u>get it right</u>.
- When you've done <u>all the questions</u> for a topic and are <u>completely happy</u> with it, tick off the topic.

Evidence for Climate Change (p.35-36) ☑

1) What is the Quaternary period?
2) Describe how climate has changed from the beginning of the Quaternary period to the present day.
3) Why are ice cores a useful source of information about past climate?
4) Describe how diary entries and paintings can give evidence of climate change.
5) How do sea ice positions provide evidence for climate change?
6) Why might data provided by weather stations be unreliable as a record of global climate?
7) How do harvest records show that past climate in the UK was different to today?
8) Give three pieces of evidence for human activity causing climate change.

Causes of Climate Change (p.37-38) ☑

9) a) What are orbital changes?
   b) How do they affect the Earth's climate?
10) Describe how volcanic activity might cause climate change.
11) How might solar output affect the Earth's climate?
12) How might asteroid collisions cause climate change?
13) What is the natural greenhouse effect?
14) Name two greenhouse gases.
15) What is the enhanced greenhouse effect?
16) Give three ways that human activities increase the concentration
    of greenhouse gases in the atmosphere.

Effects of Climate Change (p.39-40) ☑

17) What effect might increasing temperatures have on polar habitats?
18) How might species distribution be affected by climate change?
19) Outline the possible global economic impacts of extreme weather.
20) Give one possible social impact of sea level rise.
21) Give one way that climate change might have an impact on health.
22) Give one possible environmental impact of sea level rise in the UK.
23) How might climate change affect tourism in the UK?
24) Outline the possible economic impacts of climate change on agriculture in the UK.
25) How might the UK fishing industry be affected by climate change?
26) Describe one social impact of climate change in the UK.

Climate Change Projections and Management (p.41-42) ☑

27) How do scientists make projections about future climate change?
28) Give three reasons why it is difficult to predict the impacts of climate change.
29) How might alternative energy production reduce the causes of climate change?
30) Name one international agreement that aims to mitigate the effects of climate change.
31) Describe what adaptation strategies are.
32) Give three possible adaptation strategies in the management of climate change.

Ecosystems

Welcome to a lovely new topic — get ready to learn all about ecosystems.

An **Ecosystem** Includes all the **Living** and **Non-Living Parts** in an **Area**

1) An ecosystem is a unit that includes all the biotic (living) parts (e.g. plants and animals) and the abiotic (non-living) parts (e.g. soil and climate) in an area.

2) The organisms in ecosystems can be classed as producers, consumers or decomposers.

3) A producer is an organism that uses sunlight energy to produce food.

4) A consumer is an organism that gets its energy by eating other organisms — it eats producers or other consumers.

5) A food chain shows what eats what. A food web shows lots of food chains and how they overlap.

6) A decomposer is an organism that gets its energy by breaking down dead material, e.g. dead producers, dead consumers or fallen leaves. Bacteria and fungi are decomposers.

7) When dead material is decomposed, nutrients are released into the soil. The nutrients are then taken up from the soil by plants. The plants may be eaten by consumers. When the plants or consumers die, the nutrients are returned to the soil. This transfer of nutrients is called nutrient cycling.

Example of a small scale ecosystem

- A hedgerow ecosystem includes the plants that make up the hedgerow, the organisms that live in it and feed on it, the soil in the area and the rainfall and sunshine it receives.

- The producers include hawthorn bushes and blackberry bushes.

- The consumers include thrushes, ladybirds, spiders, greenfly, sparrows and sparrowhawks.

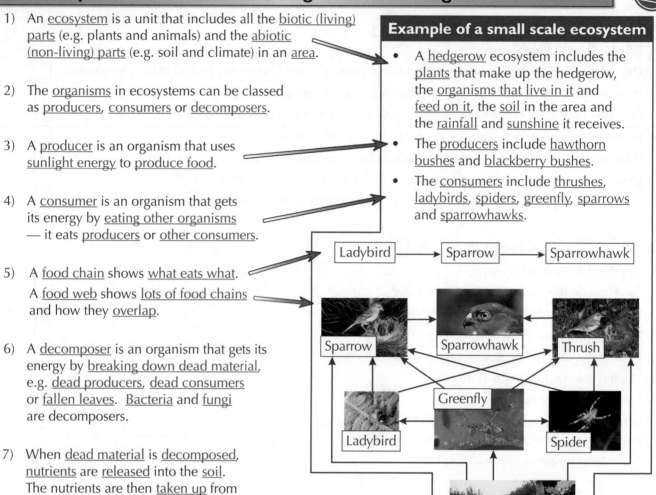

Ladybird → Sparrow → Sparrowhawk

Bushes with berries

A **Change** to **One Part** of an **Ecosystem** has an **Impact** on **Other Parts**

Some parts of an ecosystem depend on the others, e.g. consumers depend on producers for a source of food and some depend on them for a habitat (a place to live). So, if one part changes it affects all the other parts that depend on it. Here are two hedgerow examples:

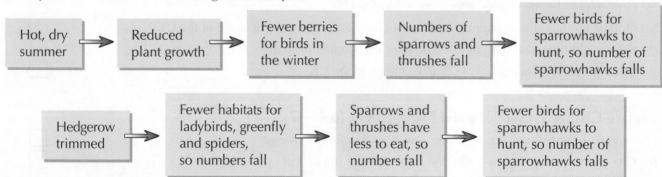

Hot, dry summer → Reduced plant growth → Fewer berries for birds in the winter → Numbers of sparrows and thrushes fall → Fewer birds for sparrowhawks to hunt, so number of sparrowhawks falls

Hedgerow trimmed → Fewer habitats for ladybirds, greenfly and spiders, so numbers fall → Sparrows and thrushes have less to eat, so numbers fall → Fewer birds for sparrowhawks to hunt, so number of sparrowhawks falls

Food webs show multiple interlinked food chains

You may be asked how a change in an ecosystem affects the other parts. To help you figure out the answer, draw a food web for the ecosystem so you can easily see what will have more food, less food, no habitat and so on.

Global Ecosystems

There are loads of different ecosystems in the world. Time for a whistle-stop tour...

You Need to Know the **Global Distribution** of **Major Biomes**

1) Biomes are large-scale, global ecosystems with distinctive vegetation.

2) The climate in an area determines what type of biome forms. So different parts of the world have different biomes because they have different climates.

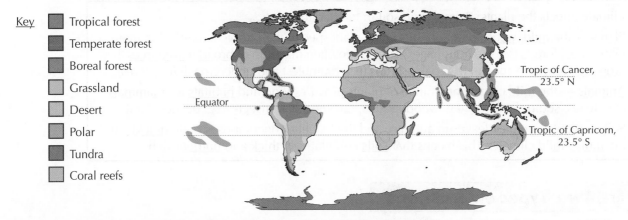

Key
- Tropical forest
- Temperate forest
- Boreal forest
- Grassland
- Desert
- Polar
- Tundra
- Coral reefs

Tropic of Cancer, 23.5° N

Equator

Tropic of Capricorn, 23.5° S

Biome **Distribution** is Affected by **Local Factors**

Climate (i.e. temperature, rainfall and sunshine hours) is the main factor influencing biome distribution, but there are other factors that alter distribution at a smaller scale:

Altitude is the height above sea level.

1) Altitude — higher altitudes are colder, so fewer plants grow there, which also limits the number of animal species. This means there's not much organic matter, so soils are thin or non-existent.

2) Rock type — some rock types are easily weathered (see p.92) to form soils, and different rock types contain different minerals. This affects how nutrient-rich the soil is. Some rocks are also permeable (water can flow through them) and others are impermeable (they don't let water through).

3) Soil type — more nutrient-rich soils can support more plants. The acidity and drainage of soils also varies, affecting the plants that can grow. E.g. peat soils are very acidic, so only acid-tolerant plants such as conifers can grow, and clay soils are sticky, so water can't flow through very easily.

4) Drainage — if drainage is poor, soil gets waterlogged and only plants adapted to wet conditions can grow there. Very wet areas may be home to aquatic species of plants and animals.

Boreal Forests Have a **Cold, Dry Climate**

The boreal biome is also called the taiga.

Climate

1) Boreal forests have short summers and long winters. In winter, average temperatures are below −20 °C and can drop much lower. In summer, average temperatures are about 10 °C.

2) Precipitation is low — generally less than 500 mm per year. A lot of this falls as snow.

3) Boreal forests get lots of daylight during the summer months, but little or none during the winter. Skies tend to be clear, so during daylight hours there's plenty of sunshine.

See pages 79-80 for more about the characteristics of the taiga.

Characteristics

The climate affects the plants, animals and soil in boreal forests:

1) Plants — most trees are evergreen, so they can grow whenever there's enough light. Coniferous trees such as pine and fir are common, as are low-growing mosses and lichen.

2) Animals — there are relatively few animal species in boreal forests compared to e.g. tropical forests, because there is less food available and animals need to be adapted to the cold climate to survive. Animals that do live there include black bears, wolves, elk and eagles.

3) Soil — the cool, dry climate means that needles from the trees decompose slowly, so soils are quite thin, nutrient-poor and acidic. In some areas the ground is frozen for most of the year.

Global Ecosystems

Temperate Forests Have a Mild, Wet Climate

Climate

1) Temperate forests have <u>four</u> distinct <u>seasons</u>. The <u>summers</u> are <u>warm</u> and the <u>winters</u> are <u>cool</u>.
2) <u>Rainfall</u> is very <u>high</u> (up to 1500 mm per year) and there's <u>rain all year</u> round.
3) Days are <u>shorter</u> in winter and <u>longer</u> in summer — the <u>hours</u> of <u>sunshine vary</u> through the year.

Characteristics

The climate affects the <u>plants</u>, <u>animals</u> and <u>soil</u> in temperate forests:

1) <u>Plants</u> — the <u>mild</u>, <u>wet climate</u> supports <u>fewer</u> plant species than tropical forests, but <u>more</u> than boreal forests (see previous page). Forests are often made up of <u>broad-leaved trees</u> that <u>drop their leaves</u> in autumn (e.g. oak), <u>shrubs</u> (e.g. brambles) and <u>undergrowth</u> (e.g. ferns).
2) <u>Animals</u> — the <u>mild</u> climate and range of <u>plants</u> provides <u>food</u> and <u>habitats</u> for <u>mammals</u> (e.g. foxes, squirrels), <u>birds</u> (e.g. woodpeckers, cuckoos) and <u>insects</u> (e.g. beetles, moths).
3) <u>Soil</u> — plants lose their leaves in <u>autumn</u>, and the leaf litter decomposes quite <u>quickly</u> in the <u>moist</u>, <u>mild</u> climate. This means that <u>soils</u> are relatively <u>thick</u> and <u>nutrient-rich</u>.

There are Two Types of Grassland

Climate

1) <u>Tropical</u> grasslands have quite <u>low rainfall</u> (800-900 mm per year) and <u>distinct wet and dry seasons</u>. Temperatures are <u>highest</u> (around 35 °C) just <u>before</u> the wet season and <u>lowest</u> (about 15 °C) just <u>after</u> it. They are found around the <u>equator</u>, so they get <u>lots of sunshine</u> all year round.
2) <u>Temperate</u> grasslands have <u>hot summers</u> (up to 40 °C) and <u>cold winters</u> (down to −40 °C). They receive <u>250-500 mm</u> precipitation each year, mostly in the <u>late spring</u> and <u>early summer</u>. Because they're <u>further</u> from the <u>equator</u>, the amount of <u>light</u> they receive <u>varies</u> through the year.

Characteristics

Rainfall is <u>too low</u> to support many <u>trees</u> in <u>tropical</u> or <u>temperate</u> grasslands, which affects <u>animals</u> and <u>soil</u>:

1) <u>Tropical</u> grasslands consist mostly of <u>grass</u>, <u>scrub</u> and <u>small plants</u>, with a few <u>scattered trees</u>, e.g. acacia. They are home to lots of <u>insects</u>, including <u>grasshoppers</u>, <u>beetles</u> and <u>termites</u>. Larger animals include <u>lions</u>, <u>elephants</u>, <u>giraffes</u>, <u>zebras</u> and <u>antelope</u>. Grass <u>dies back</u> during the <u>dry</u> season, forming a <u>thin</u>, <u>nutrient-rich soil</u>, but nutrients are <u>washed out</u> of the soil during the wet season.
2) <u>Temperate</u> grasslands are also dominated by <u>grasses</u> and <u>small plants</u>, and have very <u>few trees</u>. They are home to <u>fewer</u> animal species than tropical grasslands — mammals include <u>bison</u> and <u>wild horses</u>, and rodents such as <u>mole rats</u>. <u>High temperatures</u> in summer mean that decomposition is <u>fast</u>, so soils are relatively <u>thick</u> and <u>nutrient-rich</u>.

Coral Reefs Support a Large Number of Animals

See pages 61-62 for more on coral reefs.

Climate

1) <u>Coral reefs</u> are most common in <u>warm</u> areas that receive lots of <u>sunlight</u>.
2) They grow best in <u>shallow</u>, <u>clear</u>, <u>salty</u> water.

Characteristics

1) <u>Plants</u> — coral reefs form underwater, so <u>few plants</u> grow there. Tiny <u>algae</u> (plant-like organisms) live <u>inside</u> the tissue of corals. The algae and the coral <u>depend</u> on each other for <u>nutrients</u>.
2) <u>Animals</u> — coral itself is an <u>animal</u> — it's a bit like a <u>sea anemone</u>, but some species create a <u>hard outer coating</u> for protection. Around <u>25% of all marine species</u> live in coral reefs, including <u>fish</u>, <u>molluscs</u>, <u>sea snakes</u>, <u>turtles</u> and <u>shrimps</u>. Many fish have <u>flat bodies</u> so they can easily swim through and hide in <u>small gaps</u> in the coral.

The climate in an area determines the type of ecosystem found there

Make sure you're clear on where each biome is found, what they're like and the factors that affect their distribution.

Role of the Biosphere

The <u>biosphere</u> is basically the <u>world's life support</u> and has several <u>really important</u> jobs to do.

The Biosphere Helps to **Regulate** the **Gases** in the **Atmosphere...**

1) The biosphere helps to <u>control</u> the proportion of different <u>gases</u> in the atmosphere:

- <u>Plants</u> take in <u>carbon dioxide</u> (CO_2) and give out <u>oxygen</u> during <u>photosynthesis</u>.
- <u>Animals</u> take in <u>oxygen</u> from the air and give out <u>carbon dioxide</u> when they breathe.

2) Maintaining the <u>balance</u> of gases in the atmosphere is <u>important</u> because:

- Most <u>living organisms</u> need <u>oxygen</u> to survive.
- <u>Increased</u> levels of <u>CO_2</u> lead to <u>global warming</u> (see p.35).
- <u>Increased</u> levels of <u>CO_2</u> can also make the <u>oceans acidic</u>, <u>affecting</u> the <u>organisms</u> that live there.
- Some CO_2 is needed to keep the Earth <u>warm enough</u> to support life.

> Forests are essential in maintaining the balance of gases because they take in huge amounts of CO_2 and release huge amounts of oxygen.

... to Keep **Soil Healthy...**

The biosphere is important for maintaining <u>soil nutrients</u> and <u>structure</u>:

- <u>Plant roots</u> and <u>animals</u> (e.g. earthworms) spread nutrients through the soil — this helps to maintain <u>soil structure</u> and <u>fertility</u>, which allows plants to <u>grow</u>.
- The <u>roots</u> of vegetation also <u>hold</u> the soil together — without this, the soil can be <u>eroded</u> by wind and rain.
- Vegetation <u>intercepts</u> (catches) rainfall before it reaches the ground. This helps to prevent <u>leaching</u> — where <u>nutrients</u> in the soil are <u>washed downwards</u> out of reach of <u>plants</u>.

> The nutrient cycle is the way that nutrients move through an ecosystem. For more on nutrient cycles, see p.53.

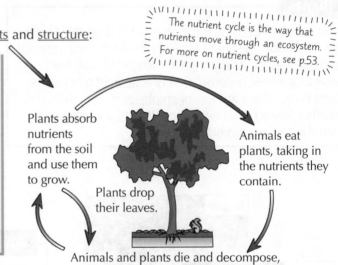

Plants absorb nutrients from the soil and use them to grow.

Plants drop their leaves.

Animals eat plants, taking in the nutrients they contain.

Animals and plants die and decompose, returning nutrients to the soil.

... and to **Regulate** the **Water Cycle**

1) The <u>water cycle</u> (also called the <u>hydrological cycle</u>) is the movement of water between the <u>land</u>, bodies of <u>water</u> (e.g. lakes, rivers, the sea) and the <u>atmosphere</u>. It looks a bit like this.

2) The biosphere is an important <u>control</u> on the water cycle:

- Water is <u>taken up</u> by plants, so <u>less</u> reaches rivers. This helps to prevent <u>flooding</u> and <u>soil erosion</u>.
- Plants also help to <u>regulate</u> the <u>global water cycle</u> by <u>storing</u> water and releasing it into the atmosphere <u>slowly</u>. Large areas of <u>forest</u>, e.g. the Amazon rainforest, can reduce the <u>risk</u> of <u>drought</u> and <u>flooding</u> in areas a long way away.

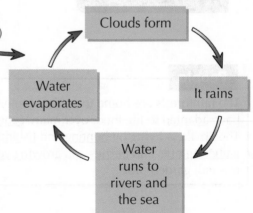

Clouds form

It rains

Water runs to rivers and the sea

Water evaporates

The biosphere is important in sustaining life on Earth

So, the biosphere is pretty important for keeping the Earth ticking over comfortably, as it turns out. Make sure you understand all the ways that the biosphere regulates the Earth's systems, then head on over to the next page.

Tropical Rainforests

Let's have an in-depth look at <u>tropical rainforests</u>...

Tropical Rainforests are Hot and Wet All Year Round

Climate

- The climate is <u>the same all year</u> round — there are <u>no definite seasons</u>.
- It's <u>hot</u> (the temperature is generally between <u>20-28 °C</u> and only varies by a few degrees over the year). This is because near the <u>equator</u>, the <u>sun is overhead</u> all year round.
- <u>Rainfall</u> is very high, around 2000 mm per year. It <u>rains every day</u>, usually in the <u>afternoon</u>.

Soil

The soil <u>isn't very fertile</u> as heavy rain <u>washes nutrients away</u>. There are nutrients at the <u>surface</u> due to decayed leaf fall, but this layer is <u>very thin</u> as decay is <u>fast</u> in the <u>warm</u>, <u>moist</u> conditions.

Plants

Most trees are <u>evergreen</u> (i.e. they don't <u>drop</u> their <u>leaves</u> in a particular <u>season</u>) to take advantage of the <u>continual growing season</u>. Many trees are really <u>tall</u> and the vegetation cover is <u>dense</u> — very <u>little light</u> reaches the forest floor. There are lots of <u>epiphytes</u> (plants that grow on other living plants and take <u>nutrients</u> and <u>moisture</u> from the air), e.g. orchids and ferns.

Jaguar

Toucan

Animals

Rainforests are believed to contain <u>more animal species</u> than any other ecosystem. Gorillas, jaguars, anacondas, tree frogs and sloths are all <u>examples</u> of rainforest animals. There are also loads of species of <u>insects</u> and <u>birds</u>. Many animals are <u>brightly coloured</u> and make a lot of <u>noise</u>.

People

The rainforests are home to many people, who have <u>adapted</u> to life there over many <u>generations</u>. They make a living by <u>hunting</u> and <u>fishing</u>, <u>gathering nuts</u> and <u>berries</u> and <u>growing vegetables</u> in small garden plots.

Rainforests are hot and wet with dense vegetation

Make sure you know the characteristics of the rainforest ecosystem — it'll help with the next few pages as well as getting you easy marks in the exam. Cover the page and scribble down what you know to check you've got it all.

Tropical Rainforests — Biodiversity

All the parts in ecosystems are linked together, so if one part changes it can have major consequences.
Tropical rainforests are no exception — especially because biodiversity is so high.

Rainforests are Interdependent Ecosystems

All the parts of the rainforest (climate, water, soils, plants, animals and people) are dependent
on one another — if any one of them changes, everything else is affected. For example:

1) The warm and wet climate means that dead plant material is decomposed quickly by fungi and bacteria on
the forest floor. This makes the surface soil high in nutrients, meaning plants can grow quickly and easily.

2) Plants pass on their nutrients when they are eaten by animals. The dense vegetation provides
lots of food, so animal populations are high. Many plant and animal species have formed
symbiotic relationships (where they each depend on the other for survival). For example:

> Agouti (a rodent) are one of the only animals who can crack open the hard seed pod of the Brazil nut to
> eat the nut inside. Sometimes, the agouti bury the nuts — these can sprout into new seedlings.
> If the agouti became extinct, the Brazil nut trees would decline and so could all the other animals who
> live in or feed on the Brazil nut trees. People who sell Brazil nuts to make a living may also be affected.

3) Changes to the rainforest ecosystem, such as people reducing tree cover by
deforestation (see p.55), can have knock-on effects on the whole ecosystem.
For example, by reducing the amount of CO_2 being absorbed from the
atmosphere, adding to the greenhouse effect and changing the climate (see p.38).

4) Trees also intercept and take up lots of water, and release it back into the atmosphere,
providing moisture for further rainfall. Deforestation means the climate may change, and
the risk of drought increases, affecting the plants and animals that live in the ecosystem.

Rainforests Have Very High Biodiversity

1) Biodiversity is the variety of organisms living in a particular area — both plants and animals.
2) Rainforests have extremely high biodiversity — they contain around 50% of the world's plant,
animal and insect species, and may contain around half of all life on Earth. This is because:

- The rainforest biome has been around for a very long time (10s of millions
of years) without the climate changing very much, so there has been
lots of time for plants and animals to evolve to form new species.
- The layered structure of the rainforest provides lots of different habitats — plants
and animals adapt to become highly specialised to their particular environment
and food source (their 'ecological niche') so lots of different species develop.
- Rainforests are stable environments — it's hot and wet all year round.
They are also very productive (the plants grow quickly and all year round,
producing lots of biomass) because of the high rate of nutrient cycling (see p.53).
This means that plants and animals don't have to cope with changing conditions
and there is always plenty to eat — so they are able to specialise (see above).

Interdependence means everything affects everything else

To revise interdependence try thinking of a scenario that might happen, e.g. it gets hotter, then draw
a flow diagram showing how that change impacts the plants, animals, people etc. in the rainforest.
If you follow each step logically you should be able to figure out what might happen to each part.

Tropical Rainforests — Adaptations

You may be wondering how <u>plants</u> and <u>animals</u> are able to <u>survive</u> in this <u>hot</u>, <u>steamy</u> environment...

Plants and Animals have Adapted to the Physical Conditions

<u>Plants</u> in the rainforest are <u>adapted</u> to cope with the <u>high rainfall</u>, <u>high temperatures</u> and competition for <u>light</u>:

1) <u>Tall trees</u> competing for sunlight have big roots called <u>buttress roots</u> to <u>support</u> their trunks.

2) Plants have <u>thick</u>, <u>waxy leaves</u> with <u>pointed tips</u>. The pointed tips (called <u>drip-tips</u>) channel the water to a point so it <u>runs off</u> — that way the <u>weight</u> of the <u>water doesn't damage</u> the plant, and there's no standing water for <u>fungi</u> and <u>bacteria</u> to grow in. The waxy coating of the leaves also helps <u>repel</u> the rain.

3) Many trees have <u>smooth</u>, <u>thin bark</u> as there is no need to <u>protect</u> the trunk from cold temperatures. The smooth surface also allows water to <u>run off easily</u>.

4) The rainforest has <u>four distinct layers</u> of plants with different adaptations. For example, plants in the highest layer (<u>emergents</u>) <u>only</u> have branches at their <u>crown</u> (where <u>most light</u> reaches them), and plants in the <u>undercanopy</u> have <u>large leaves</u> to absorb as <u>much light</u> as possible.

5) <u>Climbing plants</u>, such as lianas, <u>use</u> the <u>tree trunks</u> to <u>climb</u> up to the sunlight.

6) Plants <u>drop</u> their <u>leaves</u> gradually throughout the year, meaning they can go on growing <u>all year round</u>.

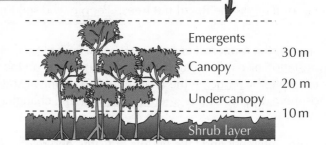

Emergents — 30 m
Canopy — 20 m
Undercanopy — 10 m
Shrub layer

<u>Animals</u> are <u>adapted</u> in different ways so that they can <u>find food</u> and <u>escape predators</u>:

1) Many animals spend their <u>entire lives</u> high up in the <u>canopy</u>. They have <u>strong limbs</u> so that they can spend all day <u>climbing</u> and <u>leaping</u> from tree to tree, e.g. howler monkeys.

2) Some animals have <u>flaps of skin</u> that enable them to <u>glide</u> between trees, e.g. flying squirrels. Others have <u>suction cups</u> for <u>climbing</u>, e.g. red-eyed tree frogs.

3) Some <u>birds</u> have <u>short</u>, <u>pointy wings</u> so that they can easily <u>manoeuvre</u> between the <u>dense</u> tangle of branches in the trees, e.g. the harpy eagle has a short wingspan.

4) Some animals are <u>camouflaged</u>, e.g. leaf-tailed geckos look like leaves so they can <u>hide</u> from <u>predators</u>.

5) Many animals are <u>nocturnal</u> (active at <u>night</u>), e.g. sloths. They <u>sleep</u> through the day and <u>feed</u> at night when it's <u>cooler</u> — this helps them to <u>save energy</u>.

6) Some animals are adapted to the <u>low light levels</u> on the rainforest floor, e.g. anteaters have a sharp sense of <u>smell</u> and <u>hearing</u>, so they can <u>detect predators</u> without seeing them.

7) Many rainforests animals can <u>swim</u>, e.g. jaguars. This allows them to cross <u>river channels</u>.

EXAM TIP

Adaptations help animals and plants to thrive in the hot, wet conditions

You may be given a picture of a plant or animal in the exam and asked to describe how it's adapted to its environment. Don't panic if you have no idea what species it is — just think about the conditions in the rainforest and how the features shown in the picture might be adaptations to help it survive.

Tropical Rainforests — Nutrient Cycling

The warm, moist conditions combined with the nutrient cycle give rainforest soils distinct characteristics.

Nutrients are Cycled Quickly in Tropical Rainforests

1) The nutrient cycle is the way that nutrients move through an ecosystem.

2) Nutrients are stored in three ways in the ecosystem:

- living organisms (biomass),
- dead organic material, e.g. fallen leaves (litter),
- the soil.

3) In the cycle, nutrients are transferred between these three stores.

4) The store and transfer of nutrients in different ecosystems can be shown as flow diagrams. The size of the circles and arrows is proportional to the amount of nutrients.

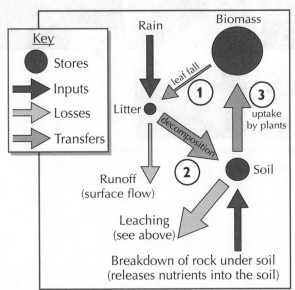

5) In tropical rainforests most nutrients are stored as biomass and the transfer of nutrients is very rapid. This is because:

1) Trees are evergreen, so dead leaves and other material fall all year round.

2) The warm, moist climate means that fungi and bacteria decompose the dead organic matter quickly. The nutrients released are soluble (they dissolve in water) and are soaked up by the soil.

3) Dense vegetation and rapid plant growth mean that nutrients are rapidly taken up by plants' roots.

Rainforest Soils are Low in Nutrients

Soils in tropical rainforests are often very deep but they only have a very thin fertile layer and are generally nutrient poor. This is a result of the combination of high temperatures and high rainfall:

1) The hot, wet climate means that chemical weathering is rapid. This means there is usually a deep layer of soil — the bedrock can be up to 30 m below the surface.

2) The constant supply of dead leaves and twigs falling onto the soil surface, forms a thick leaf layer.

3) This is quickly broken down (see above) to form humus, which then gets mixed with the soil.

4) The layer of humus is thin because the high density, fast-growing plants quickly absorb the nutrients.

5) Nutrients are also leached (washed downwards) through the soil by the heavy rainfall, making the soil nutrient poor.

6) Trees and other vegetation have roots close to the surface, where the nutrients are — there are lots of roots in the humus layer.

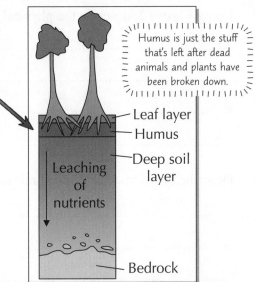

Humus is just the stuff that's left after dead animals and plants have been broken down.

Leaf layer
Humus
Deep soil layer
Leaching of nutrients
Bedrock

Take the time to understand how nutrients are cycled in rainforests

Make sure you know the characteristics of rainforest soils and how nutrients are cycled. Cover the page and write down all the facts you can remember. Then take another look at the page and fill in any gaps before you move on.

Exam Questions

Here are a few practice questions. If you can't answer one of them, head back to the page for another look.

1   Study **Figure 1**, which shows part of a food web for a coastal ecosystem.

Figure 1

1.1   Which of the organisms in the food web shown in **Figure 1** is a producer? Shade **one** oval only.

    A   Sea otter   ⬭

    B   Crab   ⬭

    C   Sea snail   ⬭

    D   Seaweed   ⬭

[1]

1.2   Give **one** example of a consumer from the food chain shown in **Figure 1**.

....
[1]

1.3   Describe how nutrients are cycled in a land-based ecosystem.

....

....

....

....
[4]

[Total 6 marks]

2   Study **Figure 2**, a diagram showing layers of vegetation in a tropical rainforest.

2.1   Using **Figure 2**, describe the physical conditions in the layers labelled A and B.

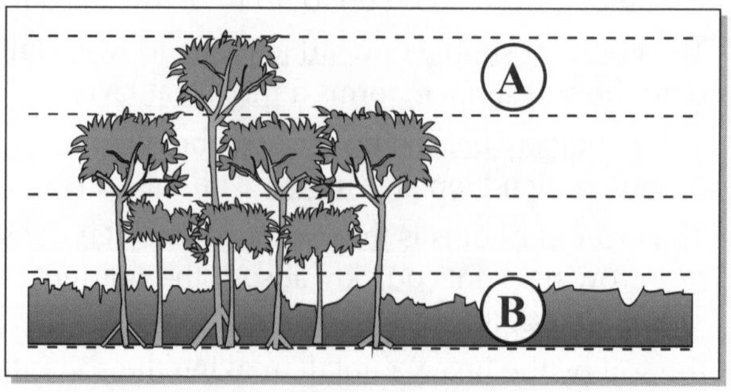

    A:...

    ....

    B:...

    ....
[2]

Figure 2

2.2   Describe the climate of tropical rainforests.

....

....

....
[3]

[Total 5 marks]

Tropical Rainforests — Human Impacts

Tropical rainforests are really <u>important</u>, but trees are being removed from them on a <u>huge scale</u>.

Tropical Rainforests **Provide** Lots of **Goods** and **Services**

<u>High biodiversity</u> (the range of <u>plants</u> and <u>animals</u> found there) means rainforests are a <u>rich source</u> of <u>goods</u>:

- Many <u>products</u>, including <u>rubber</u>, <u>coffee</u>, <u>chocolate</u> and <u>medicines</u>, are sourced from the rainforest. Undiscovered species might give us <u>new medicines</u> and other <u>new products</u>.

- <u>Hardwoods</u>, e.g. mahogany, are widely used for furniture and building. <u>Logging</u> of hardwoods can contribute a huge amount to a country's <u>economy</u>.

- Rainforests provide opportunities for <u>farming</u> and <u>mining</u> if the vegetation is cleared. This provides lots of <u>jobs</u> and <u>income</u> in many rainforest areas.

Rainforests also provide <u>services</u> through their impact on the <u>global climate</u> and <u>local environment</u>:

- They are home to the <u>highest diversity</u> of animal and plant species on the planet.

- Rainforest <u>plants</u> absorb around <u>0.7 billion tonnes of carbon dioxide</u> (CO_2) from the atmosphere each year, which helps to <u>reduce</u> climate change (see p.38).

- Rainfall is <u>intercepted</u> by the <u>high density</u> of <u>vegetation</u> — this <u>reduces</u> the risk of local <u>flooding</u> because the movement of water to rivers is <u>slowed down</u>.

- Rainforests have an important role in the <u>regulation</u> of the <u>global water cycle</u> (see p.49) — the high density of trees means <u>lots</u> of water can be <u>stored</u> and then <u>slowly released</u> into the atmosphere.

> Rainforests also directly provide services for people, e.g. tourists visit to see the plants and animals.

Deforestation is the **Main Threat** to **Tropical Rainforests**

There are <u>lots of reasons</u> why tropical rainforests are chopped down:

<u>Population pressure</u> — as the population in the area <u>increases</u>, <u>trees</u> are <u>cleared</u> to <u>make land</u> for <u>new settlements</u>. Trees are also used as fuel for <u>cooking</u> or to burn to make <u>charcoal</u>.

<u>Mineral resources</u> — <u>minerals</u> (e.g. gold, copper and iron ore) are often found in tropical rainforests. <u>Explosives</u> are sometimes used to clear earth or <u>deep pits</u> are <u>dug</u> to reach the deposits.

<u>Energy development</u> — many tropical rainforests have <u>large rivers</u>. Building dams to generate hydro-electric power (HEP) <u>floods large areas</u> of forest.

<u>Commercial hardwood logging</u> — trees are <u>felled</u> to make <u>furniture</u> and for <u>construction</u>. <u>Road building</u> for logging also requires more <u>tree clearance</u>.

<u>Commercial farming</u> — forest is cleared to make space for <u>cattle grazing</u>, or for huge <u>palm oil</u> or <u>soya plantations</u>.

<u>Subsistence farming</u> — forest is cleared so farmers can grow food for <u>themselves</u> and their <u>families</u>.

<u>Demand for biofuels</u> — biofuels are <u>fuels</u> made from <u>plants</u>. Growing the <u>crops</u> needed to make biofuels takes up <u>large amounts of land</u> — trees have to be cut down to <u>make space</u> for them.

Deforestation can bring wealth into an area

Tropical rainforests are a major source of goods and services, so are vulnerable to human exploitation. Cover the page and see if you can remember all of the reasons why rainforests are being chopped down.

Tropical Rainforests — Human Impacts

Human activity is having all kinds of impacts on tropical rainforests — some <u>good</u>, some <u>bad</u>.

Human Activity in the Rainforest has **Economic** Impacts...

1) A lot of <u>money</u> is <u>made</u> from <u>selling timber</u>, <u>mining</u> and <u>commercial farming</u>.

2) However, in the <u>long term</u>, deforestation can destroy the <u>resources</u> that countries depend on, e.g. <u>timber</u>, and reduce the attractiveness of the area to <u>tourists</u>. The <u>livelihoods</u> of some <u>local people</u> may also be <u>destroyed</u> — deforestation can cause the <u>loss</u> of the <u>animals</u> and <u>plants</u> that they <u>rely on to make a living</u>.

...as well as Big Impacts on the **Environment**

Logging
- With <u>no trees</u> to <u>hold</u> the <u>soil together</u>, heavy rain <u>washes away the soil</u> (<u>soil erosion</u>). Eroded soil can enter <u>rivers</u>, silting up habitats that <u>fish</u> use for breeding.
- The removal of trees <u>interrupts</u> the <u>water cycle</u> — this can lead to some areas becoming very <u>dry</u> with an <u>increased</u> risk of <u>wildfires</u>, while other areas become more likely to <u>flood</u>.
- <u>Deforestation</u> means <u>more</u> CO_2 in the <u>atmosphere</u>, which adds to the <u>greenhouse effect</u>.

Agriculture
- Land is often cleared using <u>slash-and-burn</u> techniques. <u>Burning</u> vegetation <u>produces CO_2</u>, which adds to the <u>greenhouse effect</u>.
- Without <u>trees</u> to <u>intercept rainfall</u>, <u>more water reaches</u> the <u>soil</u>. <u>Nutrients</u> are <u>washed away</u>, so <u>soil fertility</u> is <u>reduced</u> — rainforest soils usually lose their fertility in <u>3-5 years</u>.
- Artificial <u>fertilisers</u> added to improve soil fertility are washed into <u>streams</u>, <u>threatening wildlife</u>.

Mineral Extraction
- <u>Mining</u> of precious metals, e.g. gold, often requires <u>heavy machinery</u> and the <u>removal</u> of <u>trees</u>.
- <u>Toxic chemicals</u> used to extract and purify the metals are <u>washed</u> into streams and rivers, <u>killing wildlife</u> and <u>polluting</u> people's drinking water.
- There can also be <u>conflict</u> with local people over <u>rights</u> to the land.

Tourism
- Tourists may <u>scare wildlife</u>, e.g. causing nesting birds to abandon their young.
- They may also <u>damage vegetation</u> and leave behind lots of <u>litter</u>.
- If tourism is unregulated, a <u>lack</u> of <u>infrastructure</u>, e.g. sewers, can lead to <u>pollution</u> of <u>waterways</u>. In order to <u>build</u> infrastructure (e.g. roads and airports), vegetation must be <u>cleared</u>.

Climate Change is an **Indirect Threat** to Tropical Rainforests

Tropical rainforests also face <u>indirect threats</u> — things that <u>don't</u> involve deliberately <u>chopping down</u> trees but still lead to <u>damage</u> to the ecosystem. One of the main indirect threats is <u>climate change</u> (see pages 39-40):

- Climate change can severely impact tropical rainforests. In some areas <u>temperature</u> is <u>increasing</u> and <u>rainfall</u> is <u>decreasing</u>, which leads to <u>drought</u>.
- Droughts lead to <u>ecosystem stress</u> — plants and animals living in tropical rainforests are adapted to <u>moist conditions</u>, so many species die in dry weather. <u>Frequent</u> or <u>long periods</u> of drought could lead to <u>extinction</u> of some species.
- <u>Drought</u> can also lead to <u>forest fires</u>, which can <u>destroy</u> large areas of forest.

Deforestation has economic and environmental impacts

Human exploitation of the rainforest is a big issue, which makes it very popular with examiners. So make sure you properly understand both the positive and negative impacts of deforestation.

Deforestation

The Amazon is the largest rainforest on Earth, but it's shrinking fast due to deforestation.

Case Study — Deforestation is a Problem in the Amazon

1) The Amazon is the largest rainforest on Earth — covering an area of around 8 million km², including parts of Brazil, Peru, Colombia, Venezuela, Ecuador, Bolivia, Guyana, Suriname and French Guiana.

2) Since 1978, over 750 000 km² (more than three times the size of the UK) has been destroyed by deforestation.

3) There are lots of causes — for example, between 2000 and 2005:

- 65-70% was caused by commercial (cattle) ranching.

- 20-25% was caused by small-scale subsistence farming — many farmers have been settled by the Brazilian government along the Trans-Amazonian Highway.

- 5-10% was caused by other commercial farming — mostly soy farming, but rice, corn and sugar cane are also grown.

- 2-3% was caused by logging, including lots of illegal logging. New roads have opened up areas of the forest that were previously too hard to get to.

- 1-2% was caused by other activities such as mineral extraction (e.g. gold mining), road building, energy development and building new settlements.

4) Population growth and migration to the area is also putting pressure on the Amazon rainforest, especially as the Brazilian government offers land in the rainforest to poor people from overcrowded cities.

5) There are many more small-scale subsistence farmers now, and people who have no land or whose land has become unproductive are opening up more areas of the forest.

Amazon Rainforest — South America

Deforestation in the Amazon has Many Impacts

Environmental

1) The Amazon stores around 100 billion tonnes of carbon — deforestation will release some of this as carbon dioxide, which causes global warming.

2) Brazil is losing 55 million tons of topsoil every year because of soil erosion caused by soy farming.

Economic

1) Economic development has brought wealth to countries that were very poor.

2) Farming makes a lot of money for countries in the rainforest, e.g. in 2008, Brazil made $6.9 billion from trading cattle. It is also the world's second biggest exporter of soy beans.

3) The mining industry creates jobs for loads of people, e.g. the Buenaventura mining company in Peru employs over 3100 people.

4) Logging contributes a huge amount to Brazil's economy.

5) Local Brazilian rubber tappers who extract natural rubber from rubber trees have lost their livelihoods as trees have been cut down.

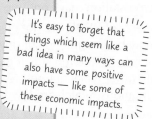

It's easy to forget that things which seem like a bad idea in many ways can also have some positive impacts — like some of these economic impacts.

The Amazon rainforest is being rapidly deforested

If you've learned the information from the previous couple of pages, there shouldn't be anything too surprising here. But make sure you also learn plenty of case study facts — it's possible that you'll need them in the exam.

Tropical Rainforests — Conservation

Some countries are managing to <u>turn off</u> the chainsaws and are even <u>joining together</u> to protect the world's rainforests.

The **Rate** of Deforestation **Varies Globally**

1) The <u>rate</u> of rainforest deforestation is <u>very high</u> — roughly 130 000 km² per year.

2) Deforestation rates are <u>rising</u> in some areas, e.g. Borneo and Nigeria. This is largely a result of:

- <u>Poverty</u> — <u>population growth</u> and <u>poverty</u> mean there are many <u>more</u> small-scale <u>subsistence</u> farmers, e.g. in Borneo, and <u>greater</u> use of <u>fuel wood</u> (as other fuels are expensive), e.g. in Nigeria.
- <u>Foreign debt</u> — there is a huge <u>market</u> for goods from tropical rainforests, so it's an easy way for <u>poor countries</u> to make money to <u>pay back</u> the <u>debt</u> they owe to richer countries.
- <u>Economic development</u> — <u>road</u> and <u>rail</u> projects to promote development <u>open up</u> areas of the rainforest to <u>logging</u>, <u>mining</u> and <u>farming</u>, e.g. Borneo has huge palm plantations for biofuels.

3) However, some areas, e.g. Costa Rica and Brazil, are <u>reducing</u> deforestation rates as a result of:

- <u>Government policies</u> — e.g. the Costa Rican government has invested in <u>ecotourism</u> (see next page) and pays landowners to <u>reforest</u> areas. Now, forest cover is <u>increasing</u>.
- <u>International condemnation</u> — puts pressure on companies by <u>naming</u> and <u>shaming</u> those that are <u>involved</u> in deforestation. Many companies have <u>pledged zero-deforestation</u> as a result.
- <u>Monitoring systems</u> — e.g. Global Forest Watch (GFW) provides <u>satellite data</u> to <u>track forest loss</u>. This means authorities can act more <u>quickly</u> to <u>stop illegal logging</u> etc.

REDD and **CITES** are **Global Actions** to **Protect Tropical Rainforests**

1) The threats to tropical rainforests involve the <u>whole world</u> — the <u>goods</u> from rainforests are <u>traded internationally</u> and all countries contribute to <u>climate change</u>.

2) This means that <u>global actions</u> are needed to try to <u>protect</u> rainforest <u>plants</u> and <u>animals</u>. For example:

	REDD	CITES
Overview	<u>REDD</u> (Reduced Emissions from Deforestation and forest Degradation) is a scheme that aims to <u>reward</u> forest owners in poorer countries for <u>keeping forests</u> instead of cutting them down.	<u>CITES</u> (Convention on International Trade in Endangered Species of Wild Fauna and Flora) is an agreement to tightly control <u>trade</u> in <u>wild animals</u> and <u>plants</u>.
Advantages	• Deals with the <u>cause</u> of <u>climate change</u> as well as <u>direct impacts</u> of <u>deforestation</u>. • The forest is <u>protected</u> so remains a <u>habitat</u> for species — <u>biodiversity</u> is not lost. • <u>Everyone</u> benefits from reducing emissions and it's a relatively <u>cheap</u> option for doing so.	• The issue is tackled at a <u>global</u> level, which means the trade of <u>endangered species</u> is controlled <u>all over the world</u> and not just in a handful of countries. • Raises <u>awareness</u> of <u>threats</u> to biodiversity through <u>education</u>.
Disadvantages	• Deforestation may <u>continue</u> in <u>another area</u>. • Aspects of REDD are <u>not clear</u>, meaning that it may be possible to <u>cut down</u> rainforests, but still <u>receive</u> the <u>rewards</u> if they are <u>replaced</u> with <u>other types</u> of forest, e.g. with <u>palm oil plantations</u>, which are <u>low</u> in <u>biodiversity</u>. • <u>Preventing</u> activities, e.g. <u>agriculture</u> and <u>mining</u>, may affect <u>local communities</u> who <u>depend</u> on the <u>income</u> from them.	• Although <u>individual species</u> are protected from <u>poaching</u>, it doesn't protect their <u>habitat</u> — they could still go extinct, e.g. due to the impacts of <u>climate change</u>. • Some rules are <u>unclear</u>, e.g. on the trade of ivory. • <u>Not all</u> countries are <u>members</u> — some countries even <u>promote</u> the trade of materials from <u>endangered species</u>.

Some areas are experiencing higher rates of deforestation than others

Many countries are experiencing deforestation, but only some are trying to stop it. Make sure you know about some strategies being used to reduce deforestation, and their advantages and disadvantages, before moving on.

Tropical Rainforests — Sustainable Management

The Amazon may be having a rough time (see page 57), but here are a few ways people are trying to help.

People are Trying to Use and Manage the Amazon Sustainably

1) Some management strategies aim to use the Amazon rainforest in a way that's sustainable — that is, allowing people today to get the things that they need, without stopping people in the future getting what they need.

2) Here are some of the ways they're doing it:

Sustainable Forestry

1) Sustainable forestry balances the removal of trees to sell with the conservation of the forest as a whole. It can involve selective logging, where only some trees are felled so that the forest is able to regenerate or planting new trees to replace the ones that were cut down.

2) International agreements try to reduce illegal logging, and promote wood from sustainably managed forests. For example, the Forest Stewardship Council® (FSC) is an organisation that marks sustainably sourced timber products with its logo so that consumers can choose sustainable products.

3) Precious Woods Amazon is a logging company operating in Brazil. They place limits on the number of trees that can be cut down, to make sure the forest can regenerate. They also use a variety of species, so that no species is over-exploited. They are FSC®-certified.

Community Programmes

1) Natütama is an organisation in Puerto Nariño in Colombia that is working with the local community to protect river species, e.g. the Amazon river dolphin.

2) It employs local people to teach other people in the community how they can protect endangered river animals and their habitats.

3) Local fishermen collect information about the number and distribution of species, and report any illegal hunting or fishing that is taking place.

4) The team also organise clean-up days to remove litter from the local rivers.

Ecotourism

1) Ecotourism is tourism that minimises damage to the environment and benefits the local people.

2) Yachana Lodge is an ecotourism project in Ecuador, in a remote area of the Amazon rainforest where local people rely on subsistence farming to provide a living.

3) It employs local people, giving them a more reliable income and a better quality of life.

4) It also encourages the conservation of the rainforest so that visitors continue to want to visit.

5) Tourists visit in small groups so that harm to the environment is minimised, and take part in activities to raise awareness of conservation issues.

6) Tourists have to pay entrance fees — this brings in more money for rainforest conservation. Profits are invested in education projects to promote conservation in the local community.

Sustainable Farming

Sustainable farming techniques protect the soil so that the land remains productive — there is no need to clear new land every few years. Techniques used in the Amazon include:

- Agro-forestry — trees and crops are planted at the same time, so that the tree roots bind the soil and the leaves protect it from heavy rain.

- Green manure — plants which add nutrients to the soil as they grow are planted to maintain soil fertility.

Conservation

1) National parks and nature reserves have been set up within the Amazon, e.g. Mamirauá. In these areas damaging activities, e.g. logging, are restricted. However, a lack of funds can make it difficult to police the restrictions.

2) As a result, funds have been set up which overseas governments and businesses can invest in. The money is paid to the countries involved in exchange for rainforest conservation. Norway has paid $1 billion into Brazil's Amazon Fund to be used for conservation.

Tropical Rainforests — Sustainable Management

Reducing Debt

1) Some of the Amazon rainforest is in <u>less wealthy countries</u>, e.g. Peru, Guyana and Bolivia.

2) Less wealthy countries often <u>borrow money</u> from <u>wealthier countries</u> or <u>organisations</u>
   (e.g. the World Bank) to fund <u>development schemes</u> or <u>cope with emergencies</u> like floods.

3) This <u>money</u> has to be <u>paid back</u> with <u>interest</u>.

4) These countries often <u>allow logging</u>, <u>farming</u> and <u>mining</u> in rainforests to <u>make money</u> to <u>pay back the debt</u>.

5) So <u>reducing debt</u> means countries <u>don't have to do this</u> and the rainforests can be <u>conserved for the future</u>.

6) Debt can be <u>cancelled</u> by countries or organisations. A <u>conservation swap</u> is where part of a country's
   debt is paid off in exchange for a guarantee that the <u>money is spent on conservation</u>.
   In <u>2008</u> the USA reduced Peru's debt by <u>$25 million</u> in exchange for <u>rainforest conservation</u>.

Biosphere Reserves

1) A <u>biosphere reserve</u> is an <u>internationally</u> recognised <u>protected</u> area
   that aims to combine <u>conservation</u> and <u>sustainable use</u>.

2) The <u>Central Amazon Conservation Complex (CACC)</u> in <u>Brazil</u> is the <u>largest protected area</u>
   in the rainforest, covering around <u>60 000 km²</u>. It's home to <u>loads</u> of different species of
   plants and animals, e.g. <u>black caimans</u> and <u>river dolphins</u>.

3) Access to the CACC is <u>restricted</u>, and there are strict <u>limits</u> on <u>hunting</u>, <u>logging</u> and <u>fishing</u>.

4) <u>Scientific research</u> projects and <u>environmental education</u> activities are
   encouraged to make people more <u>aware</u> of <u>conservation issues</u>.

Achieving **Sustainable Forest Management** is a **Challenge**

1) <u>Sustainable forestry methods</u> such as selective logging and replanting (see previous page) reduce
   the impacts of deforestation but there are lots of <u>challenges</u> involved in making them <u>successful</u>:

Economic

1) The <u>economic benefits</u> of sustainable management
   are only seen in the <u>long-term</u> — this affects
   <u>poorer</u> countries who need income <u>immediately</u>.

2) Sustainable forestry is usually <u>more expensive</u>,
   so it can be <u>difficult</u> to persuade <u>private</u>
   <u>companies</u> to adopt <u>sustainable</u> methods.

3) Many sustainable forestry schemes are <u>funded</u> by
   <u>government departments</u> and <u>NGOs</u> (see p.190).
   If the <u>priorities</u> of these organisations
   <u>change</u>, <u>funding</u> could <u>stop</u> quite quickly.

Environmental

1) If trees are <u>replanted</u>, the new forest
   may not resemble the <u>natural</u> forest
   — the <u>trees</u> are <u>replaced</u> but the
   entire <u>ecosystem</u> may <u>not</u> be <u>restored</u>.

2) Trees that are <u>replanted</u> for <u>logging</u> in
   the future can be very <u>slow growing</u>
   — companies may <u>chop down</u> more
   <u>natural forest</u> whilst they are waiting
   for the <u>new</u> trees to <u>mature</u>.

3) Even <u>selective logging</u> can <u>damage</u>
   lots of trees in the process of
   <u>removing</u> the <u>target trees</u>.

Social

1) Sustainable forest management generally provides
   <u>fewer jobs</u> for <u>local people</u> than conventional forestry,
   so many locals <u>won't</u> see the <u>benefits</u>. Some may turn to illegal logging, which is <u>difficult</u> to police.

2) If the <u>population</u> of a forest area <u>increases</u>, the <u>demand</u> for <u>wood</u> and <u>land</u> from the forest <u>increases</u>.
   Sustainable forestry is <u>unlikely</u> to provide enough resources to match the <u>increasing demand</u>.

2) The best way to <u>protect</u> tropical rainforests may be to encourage <u>alternative</u> ways of making a <u>living</u> from the
   rainforest that <u>don't</u> involve <u>large-scale deforestation</u>, such as ecotourism or alternative farming (previous page).

There are many barriers to achieving sustainable forest management

This may seem like a lot of information, but you don't have to learn every detail — think about how each strategy
enables people to manage the rainforests sustainably, and the challenges involved in making them successful.

Coral Reefs

If tropical rainforests just weren't wet enough for you, you've got a treat in store. It's time for coral reefs.

Coral Reefs are Found Between 30° North and South of the Equator

Coral can form barrier reefs (reefs that run parallel to a coastline, but are not attached to it) or fringing reefs (reefs that lie very close to the shore). Here is where some of the major coral reefs in the world are found:

Florida Reef

The Florida Reef is a barrier reef that lies off the coast of Florida in the southeastern USA. The reef runs parallel with the east coast of Florida, then extends westward, forming the Florida Keys (a chain of islands).

Red Sea Reef

The Red Sea is a narrow body of water between northern Africa and Saudi Arabia. Much of the coastline is edged with fringing coral reefs. There are numerous ridges and islands of coral further from shore.

Great Barrier Reef

The Great Barrier Reef is located off the northeast coast of Australia, in the Coral Sea. It is the world's largest coral reef and is made up of around 2900 smaller reefs and 900 islands.

Tropic of Cancer, 23.5° N

Equator

Tropic of Capricorn, 23.5° S

Mesoamerican Reef

The Mesoamerican Reef is a barrier reef located in the Caribbean Sea, to the east of the Yucatan Peninsula. It lies off the coast of southern Mexico, Belize, Guatemala and Honduras.

Andros Coral Reef

The Andros Reef lies to the east of Andros Island, the biggest island in the Bahamas — a chain of islands in the Atlantic Ocean, just east of Florida. It is part of a larger reef system that surrounds much of the Bahamas.

New Caledonia Barrier Reef

This barrier reef is located in the southwestern Pacific Ocean, about 1500 km east of Australia. The reef surrounds a chain of islands, including New Caledonia, the Loyalty Islands and the Bélep Islands. It is the second-largest double barrier reef in the world — it consists of two reefs parallel to each other.

Nutrients are Cycled Between Water, Algae and Marine Animals

1) The nutrient cycle in a coral reef looks a bit like this.

2) Some coral polyps feed off passing plankton and small fish, absorbing nutrients from them.

3) Most coral polyps have tiny algae living inside their tissues — these algae use light from the sun and nutrients in the coral's waste to create more nutrients, some of which are passed back to the coral.

4) Marine animals, such as fish, turtles and crustaceans (e.g. crabs) feed on the coral, on algae and on other animals and acquire their nutrients.

5) When they die, nutrients return to the sea bed or to the water, providing nutrients for marine creatures.

Algae use sunlight and nutrients in the water to create more nutrients.

Coral and other sea creatures feed off the algae, taking in the nutrients they contain.

Animals die and decompose, returning nutrients to the sea bed and water.

Nutrients can also be added to the reef ecosystem by runoff from the land, e.g. when runoff carries eroded soil containing fertilisers. Reefs are naturally nutrient-poor. Adding extra nutrients can cause too much algae to grow, killing the coral.

Coral reefs are only found near the equator

This page gives you some useful background to the case study that's coming up next, so make sure you understand it.

Coral Reefs — Sustainable Management

CASE STUDY

The Great Barrier Reef is <u>the largest</u> coral reef in the world, and one of the most <u>biodiverse</u>.

The **Different Parts** of the Great Barrier Reef are **Interdependent**

All the parts of the Great Barrier Reef (climate, water, soils, plants, animals and humans) are <u>dependent</u> on one another — if any <u>one</u> of them <u>changes</u>, <u>everything</u> else is <u>affected</u>. For example:

1) <u>Fish</u> rely on coral for <u>shelter</u> and <u>food</u> — they eat the <u>coral</u> itself and the <u>algae</u> that live in it.

2) The Great Barrier Reef <u>slows down waves</u> as they approach the shore, <u>decreasing</u> their <u>energy</u> before they hit land. This provides a <u>low-energy environment</u> where <u>mangrove forests</u> and <u>seagrass meadows</u> can grow.

3) The seagrass and the <u>roots</u> of the mangroves <u>trap sediment</u> that would otherwise be transported into the reef. This helps to keep the water <u>clear</u> and <u>nutrient-poor</u>, providing the conditions coral needs to <u>grow</u>.

The Reef is **Important** for **Humans** and the **Planet**

1) The Great Barrier Reef is the <u>largest coral reef system</u> in the world and is <u>valuable</u> to <u>people</u>:

- It is very important for <u>Australia's economy</u>. <u>Tourism</u> is the major source of employment and income on the reef — around <u>2 million tourists</u> visit the reef <u>every year</u>.
- By <u>slowing waves</u> and <u>decreasing wave energy</u>, the Great Barrier Reef helps to <u>protect coastal communities</u> from high waves generated by <u>tropical storms</u> and <u>decreases coastal erosion</u> and <u>flooding</u>.
- The Great Barrier Reef is home to lots of <u>marine creatures</u> that scientists don't know much about. Research suggests that some of these creatures might give us <u>new medicines</u> to treat diseases.

2) It's also very <u>important</u> for the <u>Earth</u>:

- Coral absorbs <u>dissolved carbon dioxide</u> (CO_2) from the seawater and uses it to build its hard outer case. This means it <u>stores carbon</u> that might otherwise be released into the <u>atmosphere</u>, so it helps to <u>reduce the greenhouse effect</u> (see p.38) and <u>global climate change</u>.
- The <u>algae</u>, <u>seagrasses</u> and <u>mangroves</u> that depend on coral <u>photosynthesise</u>, <u>removing CO_2</u> from the atmosphere and <u>adding oxygen</u>. This also helps to limit the <u>greenhouse effect</u>.

Biodiversity is **Threatened** by **Human Activity**

The Great Barrier Reef is very biodiverse — it is home to around 6000 species.

The Great Barrier Reef is a <u>fragile ecosystem</u> — this means it can easily be <u>damaged</u> by <u>human activity</u> and can't easily <u>adapt to change</u>. There are lots of <u>management plans</u> in place to allow the reef to be used <u>sustainably</u> in order to <u>protect biodiversity</u>. For example:

1) The reef is easily damaged by <u>pollution</u> caused by, e.g. <u>runoff</u> from <u>farmland</u>, pollution by <u>boats</u> and <u>disposal of sewage</u>. The <u>Reef Water Quality Protection Plan 2013</u> aims to <u>limit pollutants</u> running off the <u>land</u> into the <u>reef</u>.

2) <u>Coastal developments</u> can damage or destroy <u>mangrove forests</u>, increasing the amount of <u>nutrients</u> and <u>sediment</u> that are added to the reef ecosystem. Companies using the reef pay an <u>Environmental Management Charge</u> (EMC). This money funds <u>research</u>, <u>education</u> and <u>management</u> of the reef.

3) <u>People</u> can <u>disturb wildlife</u>, e.g. by disturbing <u>nesting sea birds</u>. Much of the reef is managed by the <u>Great Barrier Reef Marine Park Authority</u> (GBRMPA) — they try to make sure that the reef is used in a <u>sustainable way</u>, e.g. by restricting <u>human activities</u> in <u>vulnerable areas</u>.

4) <u>Global warming</u> may cause <u>sea temperatures</u> to <u>rise</u>. If water temperature increases <u>above</u> about 29 °C, the coral <u>can't</u> provide enough <u>nutrients</u> to support the <u>algae</u> that live in it. <u>Tourist operators</u> and <u>tourists</u> are <u>encouraged to help monitor</u> the reef, e.g. reporting on the extent of <u>coral bleaching</u>.

The Great Barrier Reef is increasingly under threat

Reefs around the world are facing lots of pressures. You might be asked about them in the exam, so get learning...

Worked Exam Questions

Make sure you pay attention to this page — it will show you how to answer exam questions to get the highest marks. When you've read it through, have a go at the questions on the next page on your own.

1   Study **Figure 1**, a series of maps showing the extent of deforestation in an area of tropical rainforest in developing country between 1966 and 2016.

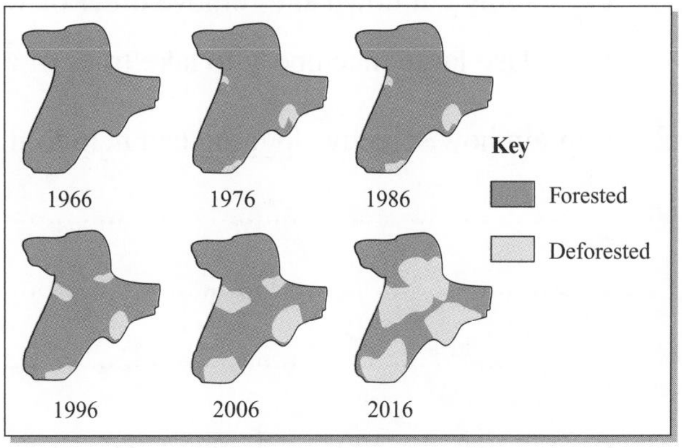

1.1   Outline **two** possible causes of deforestation in the area shown in **Figure 1**.

Figure 1

Key
- Forested
- Deforested

1966   1976   1986
1996   2006   2016

Cause 1: As the population in the area increases, trees are cleared to make land for new settlements.

Cause 2: The forest may be cleared for commercial farming, such as cattle grazing, palm oil or soya plantations.

[2]

1.2   Outline **one** positive economic impact of deforestation.

Logging, mining and farming create jobs.

[1]

1.3   Outline **one** environmental impact of deforestation.

Without a tree canopy to intercept rainfall and tree roots to absorb it, more water reaches the soil. This reduces soil fertility as nutrients in the soil are washed away, out of reach of plants.

[2]

1.4   Explain how climate change is an indirect threat to tropical rainforests.

In some areas, climate change is causing temperature to increase and rainfall decrease. Plants and animals adapted to moist conditions may die due to the dry weather. Frequent or long periods of drought could lead to extinction of some species. Drought can also lead to forest fires, which can destroy large areas of forest.

[4]

1.5   Explain how reducing the debt of the country shown in **Figure 1** might help to reduce deforestation there.

The country may be allowing logging, farming and mining in its rainforests to make money to pay its debts. Reducing the debt would mean the country wouldn't have to do this, so the rainforest would be conserved for the future.

[2]

[Total 11 marks]

Exam Questions

1   Sustainable forest management can be used to conserve tropical rainforests.

1.1   Which of the following best describes a way of managing tropical rainforests sustainably?

    A   Remove all trees in an area.   ◯

    B   Replant deforested areas with a single tree species.   ◯

    C   Only cut down and remove older or weaker trees.   ◯

    D   Use large machinery to take trees of a single species.   ◯

[1]

1.2   Explain how selective logging can help to make tropical rainforest use more sustainable.

....

....

....

[3]

1.3   Explain why it can be a challenge to make sustainable forest management schemes successful.

....

....

....

....

[4]

1.4   For a tropical rainforest that you have studied, assess the extent to which deforestation
benefits the people who live there.

[9 + 3 SPaG]

[Total 20 marks]

2   Coral reefs are found between 30° north and south of the equator, close to the coast.

2.1   Explain why coral reefs are found in this location.

....

....

....

[3]

2.2   Explain two ways in which biodiversity is being threatened by human activity
in a named coral reef.

1:..

....

2:..

....

[4]

[Total 7 marks]

Revision Summary

That's <u>Section 4</u> sorted. Time for some quick revision questions — you'll find the answers in the section.
- Try these questions and <u>tick off each one</u> when you <u>get it right</u>.
- When you've done <u>all the questions</u> for a topic and are <u>completely happy</u> with it, tick off the topic.

Global Ecosystems (p.46-48) ☑
1) What is an ecosystem?
2) Give two abiotic features of ecosystems.
3) Describe the role of decomposers in ecosystems.
4) What is a biome?
5) Where are temperate forests found?
6) Give two local factors that can affect biome distribution.
7) Describe the climate of temperate grasslands.

Role of the Biosphere (p.49) ☑
8) How does the biosphere regulate the composition of the atmosphere?
9) Describe one way in which the biosphere helps to keep soil healthy.
10) Sketch the water cycle.

Tropical Rainforests (p.50-60) ☑
11) Describe the types of plants typically found in tropical rainforests.
12) Give an example of an interdependent relationship in the tropical rainforest ecosystem.
13) Why are nutrients cycled quickly in tropical rainforests?
14) Why is the humus layer thin in rainforest soils?
15) Describe three ways that plants are adapted to living in tropical rainforests.
16) What is biodiversity?
17) Why does the layered structure of tropical rainforests increase biodiversity there?
18) Why is it important to protect tropical rainforests?
19) What are the effects of mineral extraction on tropical rainforests?
20) Describe the environmental impacts of deforestation in one named rainforest.
21) Give two reasons why the rate of deforestation of tropical rainforests is decreasing in some areas.
22) a) Describe the purpose of REDD and give one advantage of using it as a method of conservation.
    b) Describe CITES and give one disadvantage of using it as a method of conservation.
23) What is ecotourism?
24) Explain how community programmes can be used in the sustainable management of rainforests.
25) Suggest three challenges to the success of sustainable forestry schemes.

Coral Reefs (p.61-62) ☑
26) Where are coral reefs found?
27) Name two major coral reefs.
28) Describe how nutrients are cycled in coral reefs.
29) Give one example of interdependence in coral reefs.
30) Why is the Great Barrier Reef important for people?
31) What is meant by the term 'fragile ecosystem'?

Hot Deserts

Hot deserts are <u>hot</u> and also very <u>dry</u>. This affects the <u>plants</u> and <u>animals</u> that can live there.

Hot Deserts Are Found in Hot, Dry Climates

See page 47 for the distribution of hot desert ecosystems.

Climate

There's very <u>little rainfall</u> — <u>less than 250 mm</u> per year. <u>When</u> it rains also <u>varies a lot</u> — it might only rain <u>once</u> every two or three years. <u>Temperatures</u> are <u>extreme</u> — they range from very <u>hot</u> in the <u>day</u> (e.g. 45 °C) to very <u>cold</u> at <u>night</u> (e.g. 5 °C).

Soil

It's usually <u>shallow</u> with a <u>coarse</u>, <u>gravelly texture</u>. There's <u>hardly any leaf fall</u> so the soil <u>isn't very fertile</u>. Lack of <u>rainfall</u> and <u>plant material</u> mean the soil is often <u>dry</u>.

Plants

Plant growth is pretty <u>sparse</u> due to the <u>lack of rainfall</u>. Plants that do grow include <u>cacti</u> and <u>thornbushes</u>. The plants are usually quite <u>short</u> (e.g. low shrubs or short woody trees) though cacti can grow fairly tall. Many plants have a <u>short life cycle</u>, only appearing when it <u>rains</u> (see next page).

Animals

1) Hot deserts contain animals <u>adapted</u> to survive in the <u>harsh</u> environment. There are lots of <u>lizards</u>, <u>snakes</u>, <u>insects</u> and <u>scorpions</u>.
2) <u>Mammals</u> tend to be <u>small</u> and <u>nocturnal</u>, e.g. kangaroo rats. Most <u>birds leave</u> the desert during the harshest conditions but some, e.g. roadrunners, can live there <u>all year round</u>.

People

1) <u>Many</u> people living in the desert grow a few <u>crops</u> where there are natural springs or wells to supply water, usually in the desert <u>fringes</u>.
2) Indigenous people are often <u>nomadic</u> — they <u>travel</u> all the time in search of food and water for their <u>herds</u>, which are mostly goats and sheep.

Hot Deserts are Fragile, Interdependent Ecosystems

The <u>biotic</u> (living) components of hot deserts (plants, animals and people) and the <u>abiotic</u> (non-living) components (climate, water, soils) are <u>closely related</u> — if <u>one</u> of them <u>changes</u>, <u>the others</u> are <u>affected</u>.

1) <u>Plants</u> gain their <u>nutrients</u> from the <u>soil</u>, and <u>provide nutrients</u> and <u>water</u> to the <u>animals</u> that eat them. In turn, animals spread <u>seeds</u> through their <u>dung</u>, helping the plants to <u>reproduce</u>.

2) The hot and dry <u>climate</u> affects the soil in deserts. Soils are salty due to <u>high evaporation</u>, and relatively low in nutrients because there is little <u>decomposition</u> of dead plant material by <u>fungi</u> and <u>bacteria</u>. This means that plants <u>struggle to grow</u>.

3) The <u>sparse</u> vegetation <u>limits</u> the amount of <u>food</u> available, so the desert can only support <u>low-density</u> populations of <u>animals</u>.

4) <u>Water</u> supplies in deserts can be extremely <u>scarce</u>. Rainfall is <u>very low</u>, and the coarse desert soil means that any rain that does fall <u>quickly drains away</u>. <u>Animals</u> and <u>people</u> have to find ways of <u>coping</u>, e.g. by <u>constantly moving</u> to new places, or digging <u>deep wells</u>.

5) <u>People</u> have to <u>irrigate</u> (artificially water) the land in order to be able to <u>grow crops</u>. Drawing <u>unsustainable</u> amounts of water from wells <u>lowers the level</u> of water underground — <u>reducing</u> the amount available to other plants. Some <u>plant species</u> and the <u>animals</u> that <u>depend</u> on them can struggle to survive as a result.

6) <u>Changes</u> to components of the ecosystem, such as allowing cattle to <u>overgraze</u> vegetation, can have <u>knock-on effects</u> on the <u>whole ecosystem</u>, e.g. by causing <u>soil erosion</u>. Without plant roots to <u>stabilise</u> the soil, the wind can <u>blow</u> fine sand/soil particles away. Soil erosion can lead to clouds of <u>dust</u> in the atmosphere, which can change the <u>climate</u> of deserts — <u>reducing rainfall</u>, making them even <u>drier</u>.

REVISION TIP

Hot deserts have shallow soils and sparse vegetation

You don't have to learn these examples of interdependence, if there are others that you have studied. Just make sure you can say what might happen to the other parts of the ecosystem if something changes.

Hot Deserts — Biodiversity

Plants and animals in the desert need to have characteristics that make them well-suited to the harsh environment.

Plants and Animals are Adapted to the Hot, Dry Conditions

Desert plants have adaptations to help them cope with the high temperatures and limited supply of water.

1) Plant roots are either extremely long to reach very deep water supplies, or spread out very wide near the surface to catch as much water as possible when it rains.
2) Many plants, e.g. cacti, are succulents. They have large, fleshy stems for storing water and thick waxy skin to reduce water loss (water loss from plants is called transpiration). Some also have sharp spines and toxins to stop animals stealing water from their stems.
3) Some plants have small leaves or spines — this gives them a low surface area, reducing transpiration.
4) The seeds of some plants only germinate when it rains — the plants grow, flower and release seeds in just a few weeks, which makes sure they only grow when there's enough water to survive.

Desert animals are also adapted to cope with the hot, dry conditions.

1) Being nocturnal means that animals can stay cool in burrows during the day or sit still in the shade whilst it's hottest, e.g. fennec foxes. Desert animals also often have long limbs or ears, providing a large surface area to lose heat from.
2) Lizards and snakes are able to tolerate high body temperatures, e.g. desert iguanas can survive temperatures up to 42 °C.
3) Some bigger animals store large amounts of fat which they can break down into water when needed, e.g. camels' humps.

Fennec foxes

Lizard

4) Some animals get all the water they need from what they eat, e.g. cactus mice get water from cactus fruits and insects, and most desert animals minimise water loss from sweat and urine.
5) Adaptations to cope with the sand are common. For example, camels keep sand out of their eyes and nose during sand storms by having triple eyelids, long eyelashes and being able to close their nostrils. They also have large, flat feet so that they don't sink into the sand.

Biodiversity is Higher in Areas with Water

1) Hot deserts have relatively low biodiversity (compared with tropical rainforests). Small areas around ephemeral (temporary) ponds or rivers or along the desert margins have the highest levels of biodiversity, and contain a high proportion of species that are endemic (unique) to the desert.
2) Areas with water also have the highest density of human populations. Human development threatens biodiversity by increasing desertification (see p.70) and by over-using or contaminating water supplies.
3) Development around the desert margins also means that habitats are being divided up by roads. This is threatening animals that migrate over large distances to find food and water, e.g. desert bighorn sheep.
4) Global warming is generally making hot deserts hotter and drier. This is forcing some species, e.g. lizards, to move to cooler areas to cope with the rising temperatures. However, species that are already at the limits of their environment don't have anywhere else to go, so are at risk of decline or extinction.
5) Low biodiversity and pressure from development and climate change mean that deserts contain many biodiversity hotspots — places where there are a high proportion of endemic species that are threatened with extinction.

Biodiversity in hot deserts is low and many species are threatened
Desert plant and animal adaptations are mostly about getting enough water and surviving the extreme temperatures. Keep this in mind if you get asked about an organism you don't recognise in the exam.

Development in Hot Deserts

It's time to learn about the <u>economic opportunities</u> in a real desert...

There are Lots of **Development Opportunities** in the **Sahara**

The <u>Sahara</u> is Earth's <u>largest</u> desert — it's almost the size of the United States. It stretches across parts of <u>many countries</u> in <u>north Africa</u>. Opportunities for <u>economic development</u> in the Sahara include:

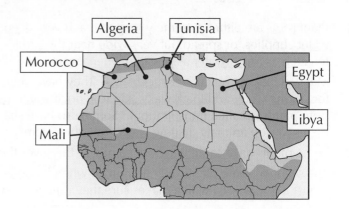

1) <u>Mineral resources</u> — <u>Morocco</u> is now the world's <u>largest exporter</u> of <u>phosphate</u> (which is used in fertilisers, cleaning products, batteries etc.).

2) <u>Oil and gas</u> — <u>Algeria</u> is a leader in <u>oil exploration</u> and <u>extraction</u> in the Sahara Desert. <u>60%</u> of its <u>income</u> comes from the oil and gas industry. It has many oil fields, including <u>Hassi Messaoud</u>, and the industry employs over <u>40 000 people</u>.

3) <u>Solar energy</u> — 12 or more hours of bright sunshine and <u>cloudless skies</u> every day are ideal for generating <u>solar power</u>. <u>Tunisia</u> has been expanding its solar energy infrastructure and has plans to supply <u>electricity</u> to millions of homes in Tunisia and Western Europe.

4) <u>Tourism</u> — many people are fascinated by <u>remote</u> and <u>exotic</u> desert locations. Sandboarding, carting and cross-desert treks are popular <u>tourist activities</u> in the Sahara, e.g. <u>camel trekking</u> in <u>Morocco</u>. Tourism in the Sahara itself remains on a <u>small scale</u>, though many people visit <u>cities</u> on the <u>outskirts</u>, e.g. <u>Marrakech</u>.

5) <u>Farming</u> — water is essential for plant growth so commercial agriculture in the Sahara is only possible where there is enough <u>irrigation water</u> — e.g. the <u>Aswan Dam</u> provides a year-round water supply in <u>Egypt</u>.

The Sahara isn't just sand — there's economic development too

You might need to write about a desert case study in the exam. If you've studied a different one in class, that's fine — just make sure you learn plenty of facts and figures about whichever desert you choose.

Development in Hot Deserts

There may be lots of <u>opportunities</u> in hot deserts but they come with some pretty tough <u>challenges</u> too.

The **Extreme Climate** and **Inaccessibility** Make **Development Challenging**

1) The harsh conditions mean that the Sahara's <u>population</u> is only about <u>2 million</u>. Most people live in small <u>fertile</u> areas, where <u>water</u> from a spring or well is used to <u>irrigate</u> the ground so that crops, e.g. dates, can be grown. Others are <u>nomadic</u>, constantly searching for <u>fresh grazing</u> for their herds of goats, sheep and camels.

2) <u>Development</u> in the Sahara is <u>challenging</u> — trying to <u>locate</u> and <u>exploit</u> resources in the <u>hot</u>, <u>dry</u> and <u>remote desert</u> is difficult:

Extreme Temperatures

1) Due to the lack of <u>cloud cover</u>, daily temperatures can <u>range</u> from over <u>40 °C</u> during the day to <u>below freezing</u> at night. Exposure to high temperatures can cause <u>illness</u> or <u>death</u>, and <u>healthcare</u> may be a <u>long distance</u> away.

2) The hot season is often <u>too hot</u> for <u>tourists</u> so employment in the tourism industry can be <u>seasonal</u>.

Inaccessibility

1) The Sahara is <u>huge</u> — people and materials have to travel <u>long distances</u> — often by <u>air</u>, which is <u>expensive</u>.

2) It's difficult to provide <u>services</u>, e.g. medical care, to <u>remote regions</u>, making it hard for them to develop.

3) <u>Expensive pipelines</u> have to be built to transport <u>oil</u> and <u>gas</u> from remote areas.

4) It takes <u>5 days</u> by <u>truck</u> to transport <u>salt</u> from salt mines in <u>Mali</u> out of the desert.

Water Supply

1) The Sahara has very <u>low annual rainfall</u> (less than 70 mm in places). Rainfall is <u>unpredictable</u> and most <u>rivers</u> only flow during <u>part</u> of the year.

2) Providing enough water for <u>workers</u>, <u>industry</u> or <u>irrigation</u> is extremely hard.

3) <u>Deep boreholes</u> are used to extract water <u>stored</u> naturally <u>under the Sahara</u> but this <u>isn't sustainable</u> because the supply isn't being replenished.

4) Some desert resources are so <u>valuable</u> that <u>new developments</u> find ways of supplying the water they need, e.g. the phosphate mines in <u>Morocco</u> pipe water from a <u>dam</u> in <u>central Morocco</u>.

The Sahara is very hot, inaccessible and lacking water

Don't worry if you've studied a different hot desert environment. As long as you know the opportunities and challenges for development and you've got some good, specific examples from that place, you'll be sorted.

Desertification

Like most places, deserts have their problems and desertification is a big one, but there are ways to manage it too.

Desertification is Caused by Human and Physical Factors

1) Desertification is the degradation of land so that it becomes more desert-like — it becomes drier and less productive. A third of the world's land surface is at risk of desertification, particularly at the margins of deserts.

2) Soil erosion is a key part of desertification. Soil that is exposed (not covered by plants) is easily removed by wind or water. Nutrients in the soil (e.g. from fallen leaves and dead plants) are lost, making soil unproductive. Eventually the ground becomes sandy, dusty, stony or just bare rock.

3) The main causes of desertification are:

Climate Change

1) Rainfall — climate change is expected to reduce rainfall in areas that are already quite dry. Less rain means that less water is available for plant growth, so plants die. Plant roots hold the soil together. If the plants die, the soil is easily eroded.

2) Temperatures — global temperatures are expected to increase. Higher temperatures mean that more water evaporates from the land and from plants. This makes soils drier and means that plants die (so their roots no longer hold the soil together).

Human Activities

1) Removal of fuel wood — many people in arid (dry) areas rely on wood for fuel for cooking. Removal of trees leaves the soil exposed so it is more easily eroded.

2) Overgrazing — too many cattle or sheep eat the plants faster than they can re-grow. This leads to more soil erosion because the plants no longer hold the soil together. Trampling by animals also erodes the soil.

3) Over-cultivation — if crops are planted in the same area continually, all the nutrients in the soil get used up. This means that plants can no longer be grown in those soils and, without plants, soil erosion increases.

4) Population growth — this puts pressure on the land, leading to more deforestation (for firewood), more overgrazing and more over-cultivation.

The Risk of Desertification can be Reduced

There are lots of different strategies for reducing the risk of desertification, for example:

1) WATER MANAGEMENT — growing crops that don't need much water (e.g. millet, sorghum or olives) can reduce water use. Using drip irrigation on crops instead of surface irrigation means that the soil isn't eroded by lots of water being added all in one go.

2) TREE PLANTING — trees can be planted to act as windbreaks to protect soil from wind erosion. Trees can also be used to stabilise the sand to prevent the desert from encroaching on farm land. Growing trees in amongst crops protects the crops (and soil) by providing shade, which reduces temperatures and evaporation rates.

3) SOIL MANAGEMENT — leaving areas of land to rest in between grazing or planting lets them recover their nutrients. Rotating crops that use different nutrients from the soil means that the same nutrients don't keep being removed. Compost can be used to add extra nutrients to the soil.

4) APPROPRIATE TECHNOLOGY — this involves using cheap, sustainable and easily available materials that are easy for local people to maintain. For example, sand fences (barriers to trap windblown sand) or terraces can be constructed to stabilise the soil and reduce erosion. The rate of deforestation can be reduced by using solar cookers, which use the sun's energy to heat food. They are cheap and easy to make, and don't require fuel wood to work.

Desertification is when productive land turns into desert

There's a lot to learn here — but the key thing is that the loss of plants means that the soil is more easily eroded, making it less fertile and so less able to support plants. Management strategies aim to reverse this process.

Worked Exam Questions

Here's a typical exam question with the answers filled in to help. They won't be there on the real exam though, so you'd better learn how to answer them yourself...

1   Study **Figure 1**, a photograph of a water source in Libya.

Figure 1

1.1   Using **Figure 1**, describe where biodiversity in hot deserts is highest.

Biodiversity is highest around water sources, such as the

oasis shown in Figure 1.

[1]

1.2   Explain why biodiversity in hot desert environments is particularly vulnerable to human activity.

Most species of plants and animals live near water sources, and this is also where human populations

are highest. Human activity in these areas is therefore likely to have a negative effect on biodiversity.

If water sources are used up (e.g. for irrigation) or contaminated (e.g. by livestock), there is no

water available for plants and animals, so they may die. Also, human activities are thought to be

contributing to climate change. Climate change may make some desert environments hotter and

drier, so species that are adapted to particular conditions may move or die out.

[4]

[Total 5 marks]

2   Study **Figure 2**, a map of a hot desert region showing some of the sources of income in different locations.

Figure 2

2.1   Using **Figure 2**, describe the economic opportunities at location A.

Economic opportunities

at location A may

include mining and

commercial farming.

There are mineral

resources to the north of the settlement, which could encourage mining companies to extract them

for export. The settlement is also situated on the river, so there is water for irrigation, creating

opportunities for commercial farming, e.g. to the south of the settlement.

[Total 3 marks]

Exam Questions

1   Study **Figure 1**, a diagram showing interdependence in a hot desert environment.

1.1   Using **Figure 1**, describe and explain the interdependence between the climate and the soil in a hot desert environment.

Figure 1

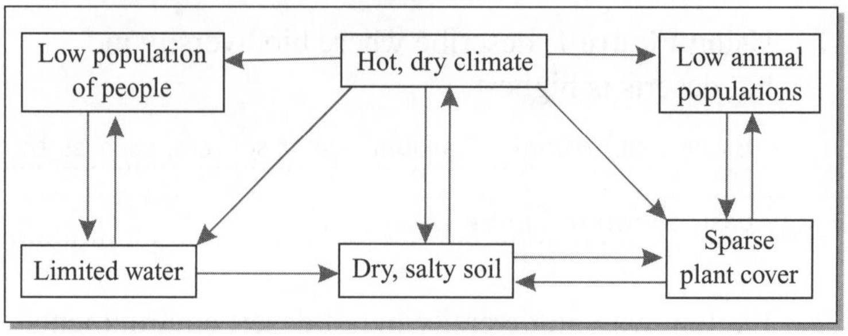

| Low population of people | ← | Hot, dry climate | → | Low animal populations |

Dry, salty soil

Limited water

Sparse plant cover

....

....

....

....

....

[3]

1.2   Using **Figure 1**, outline **two** ways that water extraction for crop irrigation may affect hot desert environments.

1:...

....

2:...

....

[2]

[Total 5 marks]

2   Study **Figure 2**, a photograph of an area of hot desert in Morocco.

2.1   Suggest how human activity may contribute to desertification in areas on the fringes of hot deserts.

Figure 2

....

....

....

....

....

....

....

....

....

[Total 6 marks]

Cold Environments — Tundra and Polar

It's time for a foray into the <u>ice cold</u> world of <u>tundra</u> and <u>polar environments</u>...

Tundra and Polar Environments are found in Cold Climates

Climate

1) Polar areas are very cold, temperatures are <u>never</u> normally above 10 °C. Winters are <u>normally</u> below <u>−40 °C</u> and can reach <u>−90 °C</u>.

2) Tundra areas are also <u>cold</u> — temperatures in the <u>warmest</u> month are a maximum of only <u>10 °C</u>, and winters can reach around <u>−50 °C</u>.

3) Rainfall (and snowfall) is <u>low</u> — no more than <u>100 mm</u> a year in <u>polar</u> areas and <u>380 mm</u> or less in <u>tundra</u> areas (mainly in the summer).

4) There are <u>clearly defined</u> seasons — <u>cold summers</u> and <u>even colder winters</u>.

Soil

1) Polar environments are <u>covered by ice sheets</u>, so there is <u>no soil</u> exposed and <u>few</u> plants or animals.

2) Soil in <u>tundra</u> environments is <u>thin</u> and <u>acidic</u> and <u>not very fertile</u>.

3) There is normally a layer of <u>permanently frozen ground</u> called <u>permafrost</u> beneath the thin soil — the permafrost layer contains large amounts of trapped greenhouse gas.

Plants

1) There are <u>very few</u> plants in polar areas — some <u>lichens</u> and <u>mosses</u> are found on rocks, and there are a few <u>grasses</u> on the <u>coast</u> of Antarctica where it's <u>warmer</u>.

2) Plants grow <u>slowly</u> and <u>don't</u> grow <u>very tall</u> — <u>grasses</u> are the most common plants. Further north, only <u>mosses</u> and <u>lichens</u> can survive.

3) Some <u>small</u>, <u>short</u> trees grow in <u>warmer</u>, <u>sheltered</u> areas.

Animals

1) There are <u>relatively few</u> different species of animals compared with <u>other ecosystems</u>.

2) <u>Polar bears</u>, penguins and marine mammals like <u>whales</u>, <u>seals</u> and <u>walrus</u> are examples of animals found in <u>polar regions</u>. <u>Lemmings</u>, Arctic <u>hares</u>, <u>wolves</u> and <u>reindeer</u> are all animals that live in <u>tundra</u> areas.

People

1) Polar environments are <u>almost uninhabited</u>. A few <u>scientists</u> live on <u>Antarctica</u> for short periods. Some <u>indigenous</u> people live in <u>Arctic</u> areas.

2) Tundra environments are home to many people, including <u>indigenous peoples</u>, and <u>oil</u> and <u>gas workers</u> in larger towns.

Cold Environments are Fragile, Interdependent Ecosystems

The <u>biotic</u> (living) components of cold environments (plants, animals and people) and the <u>abiotic</u> (non-living) components (climate, soils, permafrost) are <u>closely related</u> — if <u>one</u> of them <u>changes</u>, <u>the others</u> are <u>affected</u>.

1) <u>Plants</u> gain their <u>nutrients</u> from the <u>soil</u>, and <u>provide nutrients</u> to the animals that eat them. In turn, animals spread <u>seeds</u> through their <u>dung</u>, helping the plants to <u>reproduce</u>.

2) <u>Plant cover</u> is <u>low</u> — the cold climate causes plants to <u>grow slowly</u> and also to <u>decompose very slowly</u>. This means that the soil is relatively <u>low in nutrients</u> — further <u>reducing</u> the ability of plants to <u>grow</u>.

3) <u>Herbivores</u> like reindeer that rely on plants like <u>mosses</u> to survive must migrate to areas where plants are <u>able to grow</u> to find food. <u>Carnivores</u> like wolves have to <u>follow</u> the <u>herbivores</u>.

4) In <u>summer</u>, when the tundra has greater <u>plant cover</u>, the surface plants <u>absorb heat</u> from the sun, and prevent the permafrost below from <u>thawing</u>. The permafrost provides <u>water</u> for plants.

5) Changes to components of the ecosystem, such as vehicles <u>damaging plant cover</u>, can have <u>knock-on effects</u> on the <u>whole ecosystem</u>, e.g. by causing permafrost to <u>melt</u>. Melting permafrost can <u>flood land</u>, preventing plants from growing. It also <u>releases</u> trapped <u>greenhouse gases</u> — leading to increased <u>global warming</u>, and changes to the <u>climate</u> of cold environments, threatening <u>plants and animals</u>.

REVISION TIP

Cold environments are often frozen, but they're not lifeless

Knowing the characteristics of cold environments will help you understand how the components are related, so make sure you're clear on the details then draw a diagram showing all the connections.

Cold Environments — Biodiversity

Cold environments are <u>difficult</u> to <u>survive</u> in — even well-equipped polar explorers can get it <u>wrong</u>. Plants and animals have some <u>clever adaptations</u> to help them <u>survive</u> in the harsh conditions.

The **Plants** and **Animals** have **Adapted** to the **Cold, Dry Climate**

<u>Plants</u> in tundra environments have <u>adapted</u> to survive the <u>extreme cold</u> and <u>strong winds</u>. They must also adapt to the <u>dry winter</u> conditions when all moisture is <u>frozen</u>, and <u>wet summer</u> conditions when the <u>top layer</u> of soil <u>thaws</u> and the ground becomes <u>boggy</u> and <u>waterlogged</u>.

1) Most plants become <u>dormant</u> (stop trying to grow) to survive the <u>cold</u>, <u>dark winters</u>.

2) Plants are <u>small</u> and <u>round-shaped</u> to provide protection from the <u>wind</u>.

3) Most plants have <u>shallow roots</u> because of the layer of <u>permafrost</u> beneath the soil layer.

4) Leaves are generally <u>small</u> to limit the amount of <u>moisture lost</u> through <u>transpiration</u>.

5) The warmer, wetter summer is <u>very short</u>, so most plants have adapted to have a <u>growing season</u> of just <u>50-60 days</u>.

6) Many plants use <u>underground runners</u> or <u>bulbs</u> instead of <u>seeds</u> to <u>reproduce</u> because the growing season is so <u>short</u>.

Tundra vegetation

<u>Animals</u> in cold environments have also <u>adapted</u> to the cold, dry, snowy conditions:

1) Animals in cold environments tend to be <u>well-insulated</u> — they might have a <u>thick fur coat</u> like polar bears or a <u>layer of blubber</u> like seals. This reduces the amount of <u>energy</u> they have to use to keep <u>warm</u>.

2) Some animals <u>hibernate</u> to conserve energy and survive the <u>winter</u>, e.g. Arctic <u>ground squirrels</u> hibernate for 7-8 months of the year and can survive even if their <u>body temperature drops</u> below freezing.

3) Animals that <u>don't hibernate</u> have adapted to survive on the <u>limited food</u> sources available in winter. For example, <u>reindeer</u> have adapted to eat <u>lichens</u> in winter.

4) Many birds <u>migrate</u> to <u>warmer</u> areas during <u>winter</u> — for example, <u>Arctic terns</u> live in the <u>Arctic</u> during the <u>northern</u> hemisphere summer, then fly to the <u>Antarctic</u> for the <u>southern</u> hemisphere summer.

5) Many animals have <u>white coats</u> in <u>winter</u> for <u>camouflage</u> — this helps predators to <u>sneak up</u> on prey, and prey to <u>hide</u> in the snow. E.g. <u>Arctic hares</u> are <u>white</u> so they are harder for predators to <u>spot</u> in the <u>snow</u>.

An Arctic tern

A camouflaged Arctic hare

Cold Environments have **Low Biodiversity**

1) Cold environments have very <u>low biodiversity</u> (particularly <u>Antarctica</u>) — there are <u>fewer species</u> of plants and animals in cold environments than most other environments.

2) <u>Low biodiversity</u> means when the population of one species <u>changes</u> it can affect the population of <u>dependent species</u> — e.g. <u>changes</u> in the number of <u>lemmings</u> affects the number of <u>Arctic foxes</u> (their predators).

3) <u>Global warming</u> is causing some species to move <u>towards</u> the poles, where it is <u>cooler</u>, to cope with <u>temperature rises</u> elsewhere. Species already adapted to polar environments <u>can't</u> go anywhere colder, so are at <u>risk</u> of <u>decline</u> or <u>extinction</u> if <u>climate change</u> causes the polar areas to <u>warm up</u>.

Arctic hares have white coats because they're adapted to wintry conditions

Cold environments have low biodiversity because it's such a struggle to survive there. Learning how the few species of animals and plants that do live there have adapted to the harsh conditions will set you up nicely for the exam.

Cold Environments — Human Impacts

No surprises here — you've learnt about the <u>characteristics</u> of polar environments, so now it's time to hear about all the <u>negative things</u> people are doing to them (and some of the positive things too).

Human Activities Impact Polar Ecosystems

Tourism

1) <u>Tourism</u> occurs in <u>both</u> the <u>Arctic</u> and <u>Antarctica</u>.

2) It <u>increases shipping</u> and <u>air travel</u>, leading to <u>water</u> and <u>air</u> pollution. There is also a <u>risk</u> of <u>boats grounding</u>, which can cause <u>oil spills</u>.

3) Tourists can <u>disturb breeding colonies</u> of <u>birds</u> and <u>seals</u>. <u>Trampling</u> damages fragile <u>vegetation</u> and <u>erodes</u> the landscape, leaving paths.

4) <u>Litter</u> and <u>waste disposal</u> damages <u>habitats</u> and can <u>harm wildlife</u>, especially because <u>decomposition</u> rates in the cold environments are so <u>slow</u>.

5) In Antarctica, there is concern over the introduction of <u>non-native species</u>, which could alter <u>food webs</u>, changing the ecosystem <u>irreversibly</u>.

Fishing

1) <u>Commercial</u> fishing takes place in <u>both</u> the <u>Arctic</u> and <u>Antarctic</u> oceans.

2) <u>Over-fishing threatens</u> many species, e.g. in Antartica the <u>Patagonian Toothfish</u> has been fished to near <u>extinction</u>.

3) <u>Reduced fish populations</u> have <u>knock-on effects</u> on other species in the <u>food chain</u>, e.g. the <u>larger fish</u> and <u>birds</u> that <u>eat</u> them.

4) Other species can also be affected, e.g. <u>albatrosses</u> and <u>petrels</u> get <u>caught</u> in the fishing lines and <u>drown</u>.

Indigenous People

1) There are <u>no permanent inhabitants</u> in <u>Antarctica</u> and the <u>Arctic</u> only has a population of about <u>4 million</u>, including the <u>Inuit</u> of Greenland and Canada.

2) Traditional indigenous people rely on <u>reindeer herding</u>, or <u>fishing</u> and <u>hunting</u> to support themselves — but they only take what they <u>need</u> and don't upset the <u>balance</u> of the <u>ecosystem</u>.

3) Many indigenous people now live in <u>modern towns</u> and <u>cities</u>, e.g. Anchorage in Canada — this impacts the environment through <u>waste disposal</u>, <u>air</u> and <u>noise pollution from vehicles</u>, and <u>heat</u> from buildings, which can <u>melt permafrost</u>.

Scientific Research

1) <u>Scientists</u> use polar environments for important <u>research</u>, e.g. on global climate change. This has a <u>positive</u> impact on <u>global environmental management</u>, and on management of <u>polar ecosystems</u>.

2) In the past, some scientists working in Antarctica <u>dumped rubbish</u> in the sea and <u>abandoned</u> broken equipment. This polluted the <u>land</u> and <u>sea</u>, damaging habitats and posing a <u>risk</u> to <u>wildlife</u>.

3) <u>Research stations</u> and <u>ships</u> produce <u>chemical</u> and <u>sewage pollution</u>. However, research organisations try to <u>limit</u> this.

> There are mineral reserves in Antarctica too but they're not allowed to be extracted (see p.78). (see p.78)

Mineral Extraction

1) The <u>Arctic</u> has large <u>gas</u> and <u>oil reserves</u>, e.g. at Prudhoe Bay in Alaska, as well as other <u>mineral deposits</u>, e.g. uranium and phosphate are mined in Arctic Russia.

2) <u>Drilling</u> for gas and oil is <u>risky</u> — oil spills are <u>difficult</u> to <u>clean up</u> and can <u>harm habitats</u> and <u>kill wildlife</u>.

3) <u>Pipelines</u> also have to be built to <u>transport</u> the oil and gas — these can <u>melt</u> the <u>permafrost</u> below and <u>interrupt</u> the <u>migration routes</u> of caribou herds.

4) The <u>extraction</u> of <u>metals</u> from mined rocks produces lots of <u>pollution</u>, damaging <u>ecosystems</u> in the surrounding area.

Whaling

1) <u>Whaling</u> was a <u>big industry</u> in <u>both</u> the <u>Arctic</u> and <u>Antarctic</u> during the last <u>two centuries</u>.

2) Many species of whale were hunted to <u>near extinction</u>, e.g. Blue, Fin and Minke whales.

3) Whales are very <u>slow breeders</u>, so it takes a <u>long time</u> for their populations to <u>recover</u>.

4) Whaling has mostly <u>stopped</u>, but <u>some</u> countries, e.g. Japan, still <u>hunt whales</u> in polar areas.

The exploitation of resources has negative impacts on cold environments

Cover the page and write down all six activities that are affecting polar ecosystems. Then see how many details about the impacts of each activity you can add. Bonus points for any examples you remember.

Development in Cold Environments

Alaska is one example of a <u>cold environment</u> where the extreme climate creates <u>challenges</u> for <u>development</u>.

There are **Development Opportunities** in **Alaska...**

Alaska is a <u>cold environment</u> that's part of the <u>USA</u>.
The <u>northern</u> parts of Alaska are inside the <u>Arctic circle</u>.
<u>Opportunities</u> for economic development include:

1) <u>Oil and gas</u> — <u>over half</u> Alaska's income comes from the <u>oil and gas industry</u>. Most oil fields are around <u>Prudhoe Bay</u>, and the <u>Trans-Alaska oil pipeline</u> links the oil fields with <u>Valdez</u>, from where the oil can be <u>shipped</u> to customers.

2) <u>Mineral resources</u> — gold, silver, iron ore and copper are mined, particularly in the <u>Tintina gold belt</u>. It contributed <u>$2.2 billion</u> to Alaska's GDP in 2013.

3) <u>Fishing</u> — salmon, crab and pollock are fished. Fishing employs over <u>65 000</u> people and contributes over <u>$5bn</u> to Alaska's economy.

4) <u>Tourism</u> — tourists are attracted by Alaska's <u>wilderness scenery</u>. Around <u>2 million tourists</u> visit Alaska each year, bringing in <u>money</u> and creating opportunities for <u>employment</u>.

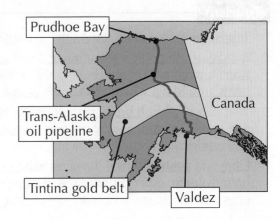

Prudhoe Bay

Canada

Trans-Alaska oil pipeline

Tintina gold belt

Valdez

...but there are also **Challenges to Development**

1) Alaska's state <u>population</u> is one of the <u>smallest</u> in the US, despite being the <u>largest state</u> by <u>area</u>. Most people live in the <u>south</u> and <u>southeast</u> of the state, near the <u>coast</u>, where it is <u>warmer</u> and <u>less remote</u>.

2) <u>Development</u> in Alaska can present <u>challenges</u> — getting <u>access</u> to resources and finding a <u>workforce</u> to exploit them, as well as providing <u>buildings</u>, <u>infrastructure</u> and protection from the <u>extreme weather</u>.

Extreme Temperature

1) It's <u>really cold</u> — in <u>Prudhoe Bay</u> the mean annual temperature is around <u>–9 °C</u>. Extreme weather such as <u>snow</u> and <u>strong winds</u> are common. <u>Exposure</u> to the extreme cold can cause <u>injury or death</u>, and <u>healthcare</u> may be a <u>long distance</u> away.

2) As well as extreme temperature and weather, Alaska is subject to <u>extremes</u> in the amount of <u>daylight</u> it gets — in winter, it can be <u>dark</u> nearly <u>all the time</u>.

Inaccessibility

1) Alaska is a <u>long way</u> from the rest of the US. Some areas are <u>extremely remote</u>, and the <u>mountainous terrain</u> makes access <u>difficult</u> and <u>expensive</u>.

2) In <u>winter</u>, the only way to get to some towns is via <u>air</u> or <u>dangerous ice roads</u>. In <u>summer</u>, there are <u>no roads</u> to some towns because the ground is <u>too soft</u>.

3) The population of Alaska is <u>small</u> and <u>scattered</u> — people in <u>small towns</u> may be a long way from <u>employment opportunities</u> or <u>services</u>.

Buildings and Infrastructure

1) <u>Providing buildings</u> and <u>infrastructure</u> that can cope with the <u>ground</u> and <u>weather</u> conditions is <u>difficult</u> and <u>expensive</u>.

2) Most <u>construction work</u> can only take place in <u>summer</u>, when the days are <u>longer</u> and temperatures are <u>warmer</u>.

3) The <u>value</u> of some resources means that people find ways to <u>overcome the challenges</u>, e.g. some parts of the <u>Trans-Alaska</u> oil pipeline are raised on <u>stilts</u>, to prevent it <u>melting the permafrost</u>, which would make the ground <u>unstable</u>.

Cold environments have opportunities, but exploiting them can be difficult

Cold environments can be full of challenges — it's what happens when you combine beautiful, frozen wildernesses with useful economic development opportunities. You might be asked about them in the exam, so get learning...

Cold Environments — Sustainable Management

Cold environments are <u>fragile</u> areas that need to be <u>protected</u> from damage by <u>sustainable management</u>.

Cold Environments are **Valuable Wilderness Areas** worth **Conserving**

<u>Wilderness</u> areas are wild, natural environments that haven't been changed significantly by people. They are mainly <u>undeveloped</u>, <u>uninhabited</u> and <u>undisturbed</u>. <u>Large parts</u> of cold environments are wilderness areas.

Wilderness areas are <u>important</u> and worth <u>protecting</u> for the future because:

1) They provide <u>habitats</u> for <u>organisms</u>, so help to protect <u>biodiversity</u>.
2) Scientists can <u>study wild plants</u> and <u>animals</u> in their <u>natural habitats</u>.
3) They are <u>natural ecosystems</u> that are useful to <u>compare</u> to <u>managed</u> ecosystems.
4) They are the <u>last remaining</u> areas that <u>haven't</u> been <u>altered</u> by human activity.

Cold Environments are **Fragile** and Take a **Long Time** to **Recover**

Cold environments are very <u>fragile</u> — if they are <u>interfered</u> with, it can take a <u>long time</u> for them to return to their <u>original state</u>.

1) Plant <u>growth</u> is very <u>slow</u> — if plants are <u>damaged</u> (e.g. by vehicle tyres) they take a <u>long time</u> to regrow.
2) Species are <u>highly specialised</u> so find it difficult to <u>adapt to change</u> — e.g. polar bears are adapted to hunt on ice and their numbers are <u>decreasing</u> as sea ice melts <u>earlier</u> each year.

Strategies are Needed to **Balance** Economic Development with **Conservation**

There are lots of <u>different strategies</u> that can help balance <u>conservation</u> with <u>economic development</u>:

Use of Technology

1) Development can cause <u>problems</u> that can be <u>solved</u> by <u>modern technology</u>. E.g. heated buildings can <u>melt permafrost</u>, leading to <u>subsidence</u> which may cause <u>roads</u> and <u>buildings</u> to <u>collapse</u> and <u>pipes to crack</u>.
2) Modern <u>construction methods</u> can minimise environmental impacts, for example <u>elevating buildings</u> on piles or building on <u>gravel beds</u> can prevent buildings <u>warming the ground</u>.

International Agreements

1) Some cold environments are protected by <u>international agreements</u>, e.g. Antarctica.
2) The <u>Antarctic Treaty</u> (see next page) aims to <u>protect</u> the Antarctic ecosystem — it has now been signed by <u>53 countries</u>.

Role of Governments

1) If development is allowed <u>without regulation</u>, it can cause <u>damage</u> to the environment. E.g. <u>mineral</u> and <u>energy mining</u> can cause ground and water <u>pollution</u> and logging activities <u>destroy habitats</u>.
2) Governments can make <u>laws</u> to <u>protect</u> cold environments, such as the <u>1964 Wilderness Act</u> that designated <u>wilderness areas</u> and <u>protected</u> them from development, including large parts of <u>Alaska</u>.

Conservation Groups

1) Conservation groups <u>pressure governments</u> to <u>protect</u> cold environments that are <u>at risk</u> or have been <u>damaged</u>.
2) E.g. the <u>World Wild Fund for Nature</u> and <u>Greenpeace</u> encourage <u>sustainable management</u> of cold environments and argue for <u>governments</u> to prevent actions that would cause <u>damage</u>.

EXAM TIP

Development can cause damage that takes a very long time to recover

Balancing the benefits of economic development against the need to protect cold environments from being damaged could well come up in your exam. To ace a question on this topic, you need to make sure you know both sides of the argument and be ready to write about a few strategies that can be used.

Managing Cold Environments

Here are some <u>examples</u> of <u>sustainable management</u> in both the <u>Arctic</u> and the <u>Antarctic</u>.

Tourism is Being Managed Sustainably on Svalbard

1) <u>Svalbard</u> is a group of islands in the <u>Arctic Circle</u>, north of Norway, that is <u>promoting sustainable tourism</u>.

2) Over <u>60%</u> of Svalbard is <u>protected</u>. For example, there are <u>strict limits</u> on the use of off-road <u>motorised vehicles</u>, and tour operators and visitors have to get <u>permission</u> to <u>visit</u> the <u>nature reserves</u>.

3) Different zones have <u>different levels</u> of <u>protection</u> — <u>nature reserves</u> allow <u>very little access</u>, while <u>tourism areas</u> have <u>fewer regulations</u>.

4) Here's an <u>example</u> of how tourism is being managed <u>sustainably</u> in one part of Svalbard:

Ny-Ålesund

<u>Ny-Ålesund</u> is the most <u>northerly</u> settlement in the world and is run by a company called <u>Kings Bay AS</u>. The population is mostly made up of <u>scientific researchers</u>. The company and researchers have taken actions to <u>limit</u> the <u>impact</u> of tourism on the area. For example:

- <u>Cruise ships</u> are required to <u>tell passengers</u> about the <u>rules</u> visitors have to follow, e.g. not <u>disturbing nesting birds</u> or leaving <u>litter</u>.

- Visitors have to stick to the <u>1.5 km path</u> around the settlement and there are lots of <u>boards</u> with <u>environmental information</u>, to make tourists <u>aware</u> of the issues.

- The ships are only allowed to <u>remain anchored</u> for a <u>few hours</u> — this reduces the amount of <u>pollution</u> from e.g. diesel fumes entering the <u>local environment</u>.

5) More recently there has been a <u>ban</u> on the <u>most polluting fuels</u> used by cruise ships — this means that the bigger cruise ships are now <u>unable</u> to visit <u>Ny-Ålesund</u>, as well as some other areas around Svalbard.

The Antarctic Treaty is an Example of Global Sustainable Management

1) The <u>Antarctic Treaty</u> is an <u>agreement</u> made by <u>twelve countries</u> in 1959 about how to <u>sustainably manage</u> Antarctica's ecosystems.

2) The <u>environmental protocol</u> (which came into force in 1998) sets out <u>6 basic principles</u> for <u>human activity</u>:

- no <u>mineral exploitation</u> is allowed
- <u>plants</u> and <u>animals</u> must be <u>conserved</u>
- <u>areas</u> of the <u>environment</u> must be <u>protected</u>
- there are <u>rules</u> for <u>waste disposal</u> and <u>waste</u> must be <u>minimised</u>
- there are <u>regulations</u> for the <u>discharge</u> of <u>sewage</u> from vessels
- <u>activities</u> must have an <u>Environmental Impact Assessment</u> before they are able to go ahead

3) There are <u>strict rules</u> about the introduction of <u>non-native species</u> so that ecosystems aren't <u>disturbed</u>, e.g. visitors have to wear <u>disinfected overboots</u> when they land and aren't allowed to <u>eat</u>, <u>drink</u> or <u>wee</u> whilst ashore.

4) There are also globally agreed <u>rules</u> amongst <u>tour operators</u> — only <u>100 visitors</u> are allowed to land at any one time and <u>cruise ships</u> of over <u>500 passengers</u> are <u>prevented</u> from stopping.

5) There have been <u>no major problems</u> with the <u>treaty</u> and some people think it should be <u>extended</u> to cover the <u>ocean</u> surrounding Antarctica so that there is <u>more protection</u> for <u>marine life</u>, e.g. whales and fish.

Tourism is being managed in many cold environments to protect ecosystems

Sustainable management is one of those topics that examiners love asking about, so it's worth having a couple of case studies up your sleeve for the exam. And remember, sustainable management occurs at a range of different scales.

Taiga Forests

Taiga forests are <u>found</u> just <u>south</u> of the <u>tundra zone</u> in Russia, Scandinavia and Canada, where it is <u>warm</u> and <u>wet</u> enough for trees to grow. It's still <u>pretty cold</u> and <u>dry</u> though, so animals and plants have had to <u>adapt</u>.

Taiga Forests are Interdependent Ecosystems

<u>All</u> the parts of taiga forests (climate, soils, water, plants, animals and people) are <u>dependent</u> on one another — if any one of them <u>changes</u>, <u>everything</u> else is <u>affected</u>. For example:

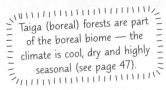
Taiga (boreal) forests are part of the boreal biome — the climate is cool, dry and highly seasonal (see page 47).

1) The <u>cold climate</u> in taiga forests has a huge influence on all parts of the ecosystem. <u>Decomposition</u> happens very <u>slowly</u>, so nutrients don't easily pass into the soil (see next page).

2) Decomposing pine needles mean that <u>soils</u> in taiga forests also tend to be quite <u>acidic</u>. The acidic and nutrient-poor soil won't support many species of plants, but can support the <u>coniferous trees</u> that are common in this ecosystem.

There's more about interdependence in cold ecosystems on page 73.

3) The trees <u>protect</u> the soil from <u>erosion</u>. If people <u>cut down</u> trees, then the soil becomes <u>exposed</u> and may get <u>blown</u> or <u>washed away</u>, making it difficult for anything new to grow.

4) <u>Animals</u> like moose rely on trees in the taiga to provide <u>food</u>. They prefer to eat broad-leafed trees to conifers, so <u>conifers</u> are more <u>numerous</u> in areas of heavy <u>grazing</u> by moose.

5) Some indigenous <u>people</u> in the taiga <u>herd reindeer</u>, and rely on them for <u>meat</u>, <u>milk</u> and transportation. In return, the reindeer are given some <u>protection</u> from <u>predators</u> such as bears, wolves and lynx.

Plants and Animals are Adapted to the Cool, Dry Climate

1) Taiga forests have a much <u>simpler structure</u> than tropical rainforests — lots of <u>tall trees</u> growing quite <u>close together</u> and not much else.

2) There aren't many plants on the <u>forest floor</u> because the <u>soils</u> are <u>poor</u> and very <u>little light</u> gets through the <u>dense canopy</u>. Plants that do survive include <u>mosses</u> and <u>lichens</u>.

3) Most of the trees are <u>conifers</u>, which are <u>adapted</u> to the cold, dry climate:

- They are <u>evergreen</u> (they don't drop their leaves in a particular season), so they can make best use of the <u>available light</u>.
- They have <u>needles</u> instead of flat leaves — this reduces <u>water loss</u> from strong, cold winds because it reduces the <u>surface area</u>.
- They are <u>cone-shaped</u> — this means that <u>heavy winter snowfall</u> can <u>slide</u> straight off the <u>branches</u> without <u>breaking them</u>. The branches are also quite <u>bendy</u> so they're less likely to snap.

4) <u>Animals</u> in the taiga forest need to find ways to <u>survive</u> the <u>long</u>, <u>cold winters</u>. They also need to be able to find <u>enough food</u> and <u>escape</u> from <u>predators</u>.

- Many of the <u>larger mammals</u>, e.g. caribou, are <u>migratory</u> — they move <u>long distances</u> through the forest in order to <u>find food</u>.
- Many animals are <u>well-insulated</u> against the winter cold, e.g. wolves have <u>thick fur</u>, and birds, e.g. ptarmigan, have <u>thick layers</u> of <u>downy feathers</u>.
- Some animals <u>hibernate</u> to conserve energy and survive the <u>winter</u>, e.g. brown bears and marmots.
- Some animals, e.g. snowshoe hares, have <u>white coats</u> in the <u>winter</u>, so they are <u>camouflaged</u> against the winter <u>snow</u> — this helps them <u>hide</u> from predators. Camouflage also helps predators to <u>sneak up</u> on prey <u>undetected</u>.

REVISION TIP

Most trees are cone-shaped conifers with needles instead of leaves

To help you remember the adaptations of animals in the taiga, think about how you would cope with the cold — put on a coat (thick fur) or stay indoors (hibernate). Go over this page until you've got it all.

Taiga Forests

The cold climate of the taiga forest leads to <u>slow nutrient cycling</u> and <u>lack of biodiversity</u>.

Slow Nutrient Cycling Leads to Slow Plant Growth

1) In taiga forests, <u>few nutrients</u> are added through <u>precipitation</u> or <u>weathering</u>. Quite a lot of the nutrients that are added are <u>lost</u> through <u>runoff</u> and <u>leaching</u>.

2) <u>Most</u> of the nutrients are <u>stored</u> in dead organic material (<u>litter</u>), e.g. the layer of <u>fallen needles</u> on the forest floor.

3) The <u>cold</u>, <u>dry climate</u> means that nutrient cycling is much <u>slower</u> in taiga forests than in tropical rainforests.

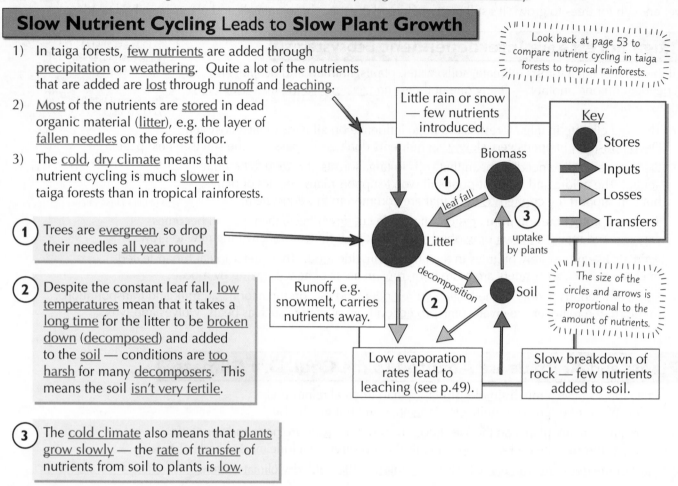

Look back at page 53 to compare nutrient cycling in taiga forests to tropical rainforests.

Little rain or snow — few nutrients introduced.

Biomass

Key
● Stores
➜ Inputs
➜ Losses
➜ Transfers

leaf fall
① Litter
decomposition ②
uptake by plants ③
Soil

The size of the circles and arrows is proportional to the amount of nutrients.

Runoff, e.g. snowmelt, carries nutrients away.

Low evaporation rates lead to leaching (see p.49).

Slow breakdown of rock — few nutrients added to soil.

1) Trees are <u>evergreen</u>, so drop their needles <u>all year round</u>.

2) Despite the constant leaf fall, <u>low temperatures</u> mean that it takes a <u>long time</u> for the litter to be <u>broken down</u> (<u>decomposed</u>) and added to the <u>soil</u> — conditions are <u>too harsh</u> for many <u>decomposers</u>. This means the soil <u>isn't very fertile</u>.

3) The <u>cold climate</u> also means that <u>plants grow slowly</u> — the <u>rate</u> of <u>transfer</u> of nutrients from soil to plants is <u>low</u>.

Taiga Forests have Low Biodiversity

Taiga forests have much <u>lower</u> biodiversity than tropical rainforests — many areas of forest contain a <u>single type</u> of tree, e.g. spruce, fir or pine. This is because:

1) The <u>land</u> was much colder and covered by <u>ice</u> until around 15 000 years ago. Species have had relatively <u>little time</u> to <u>adapt</u> to the current climate.

2) The <u>simple structure</u> means there aren't many different <u>habitats</u> — there are <u>fewer ecological niches</u> (see page 51) for organisms to fill, so <u>fewer</u> varieties of <u>species</u>.

3) Taiga forests are much <u>less productive</u> than tropical rainforests (plants grow <u>slowly</u>, so there's less biomass) and <u>nutrients</u> take a long time to be <u>returned</u> to the <u>soil</u> because it's so <u>cold</u>. The <u>growing season</u> is also <u>very short</u> — just a few months in the summer. This means there's <u>not much food</u> available, so there is a constant <u>struggle</u> for <u>survival</u>.

4) Some groups of animals are <u>under-represented</u> — there aren't many <u>amphibians</u> or <u>reptiles</u> because they <u>can't cope</u> with the <u>cold</u> climate (e.g. reptiles can't regulate their own body temperature and depend on the <u>sun</u> to stay warm).

Nutrient cycling is much slower in taiga forests than in tropical rainforests

In comparison, taiga forests are less productive than rainforests — they have slower plant growth and lower biodiversity. Re-read the page and then explain why the biggest store of nutrients is in the leaf litter in taiga forests.

Threats to Taiga Forests

Taiga forests are facing deforestation as well as a whole host of indirect threats.

The **Exploitation** of **Resources** is **Threatening** Taiga Forests

Taiga forests are exploited to make money — trees are deliberately chopped down for wood and paper, in the search for minerals and to satisfy the world's increasing demand for energy.

Logging for softwood — trees are cut down so that they can be made into housing, furniture and matches.

Pulp and paper production — felled trees are mashed into a pulp and used to make paper.

Exploitation of fossil fuels — trees are cleared to extract gas and oil from the ground.

HEP — dams to generate hydroelectric power from rivers in taiga forests flood large areas of land.

Example: Tar sands

1) Tar sand is earth containing a thick, black oil, which can be processed into fossil fuels (e.g. petrol). Tar sands are found underneath taiga forests, e.g. in Canada.

2) Extraction of the tar sands often involves open pit mining or strip mining — digging up the land surface in strips to get to the sands beneath. This causes large-scale deforestation.

Exploitation of minerals — many taiga forests are rich in minerals, e.g. iron ore, gold, copper and silver. Lots of trees are chopped down to make way for mines as well as access roads.

Acid Rain, Fire, Pests and **Disease** are Causing **Loss of Biodiversity**

Acid Precipitation

1) Burning fossil fuels releases gases, such as sulfur dioxide and nitrogen oxides. These dissolve in water in the atmosphere to form acids. When it rains or snows, the acids are deposited on plants and soils.

2) Acid rain damages plants' leaves and makes it harder for them to cope with the cold. It can also make the soils too acidic to support growth and kills organisms in lakes and streams.

Pests & Diseases

1) Pests and diseases cause damage to organisms.

2) Many pests and diseases are specific to one species, e.g. Spruce Bark Beetles attack spruce trees. As there is often a single tree species in a particular area in taiga forests, it's easy for the pests and diseases to spread and multiply — they can do a lot of damage.

3) It is thought that warming caused by climate change is making it easier for pests and disease-causing pathogens to survive — new pests and diseases are arriving and the frequency of attack is increasing.

Forest Fires

1) Wildfires are a natural part of the ecosystem — they allow new growth and regenerate the forest.

2) However, it's thought that climate change is leading to warmer, drier conditions in taiga forests. This is increasing the frequency of fires and making the fire season longer.

3) Forest fires can destroy huge numbers of trees and may change the distribution of species as some species are better at recolonising burnt areas. They may also break forests up into smaller sections, which makes it hard for migratory animals that need a lot of space to find enough food.

The taiga forest is under threat from lots of different factors

Human exploitation is leading to deforestation. On top of this, acid rain, fire, pests and disease are all putting extra pressure on the ecosystem. Make sure you can explain how these pressures are leading to biodiversity loss.

Taiga Forests — Conservation

Taiga forests are under threat but it's not all bad news — here are some ways they can be conserved...

Conservation Methods Include Protected Areas and Sustainable Forestry

1) Taiga forests cover a huge area — a lot of them are inaccessible and very remote.
   However, human activity is expanding into these wilderness areas, particularly in Canada and Russia.

2) The forests can be conserved by setting up protected areas or by controlling the way that they are used.

Method	Overview	Strengths	Challenges
Creating a Wilderness Area	An area that is undisturbed by human activity that is managed with the aim of protecting the landscape.	Has the highest level of protection — most human activity is banned. The area is kept as pristine (untouched by humans) as possible. Usually covers a very large area so large-scale processes can still take place, e.g. animal migrations.	The large, remote areas are hard to police. There is economic pressure on governments from logging, mining and energy companies who want to use the resources. There is pressure from companies and tourists to build roads to allow greater access.
Creating a National Park	An area that is mostly in its natural state that is managed to protect biodiversity and promote recreation.	May be established to protect particular species, e.g. wood bison. Often cover a large area. Unsustainable human activity such as logging and mining is not permitted. There is good access for tourists and recreational users.	National parks must take into account the needs of indigenous communities, who may use the land for hunting etc. Tourism may be required to pay for the conservation, but access roads, infrastructure and pollution from tourists can harm the ecosystem.
Sustainable Forestry	Ways of harvesting the timber from the forest without damaging it in the long-term.	Limits can be placed on the number of trees felled or the size of clear-cut areas to allow the forest to regenerate. Companies may be required to regenerate the area after logging. Selective logging means some trees remain to become part of the new forest.	Some countries struggle to enforce the restrictions, e.g. Russia — lots of illegal logging takes place. There may be a lack of clear management or information about the ecosystem. Different groups may not agree with the rules and restrictions, e.g. indigenous people, loggers, government, environmentalists.

There are Conflicting Views on Managing Taiga Forests

Some people think that taiga forests should be protected. Other people think that the forest and its natural resources should be exploited. You need to know the reasons for each view point.

Protection

1) Taiga forests store lots of carbon — deforestation will release some of this as CO_2, which causes global warming.

2) Some species are only found in taiga forests. Because they are adapted to the conditions, the destruction of the habitat could lead to their extinction.

3) Many indigenous people, e.g. the Sami people of Scandinavia, depend on the forest for their traditional way of life.

Exploitation

1) The demand for resources is increasing — people need the wood, fuel and minerals that the forests provide.

2) Forest industries, e.g. logging and mining, provide a lot of jobs (e.g. forestry and logging employ 25 thousand people in Canada).

3) The exploitation of the forest generates a lot of wealth for the countries involved (e.g. the forestry industry in Sweden is worth nearly US $15 billion each year).

The future of taiga forests is uncertain

There's no agreement on how to manage the taiga forests — some people think that they should be protected, but others think that their natural resources should be exploited. You should be able to make the case for both sides.

Worked Exam Questions

It's not enough just to learn some facts for the exam, you'll also need to know how to put them into a good exam answer. So here are some worked examples to help you on the way.

1   Study **Figure 1**, a diagram showing interdependence in cold environments.

Figure 1

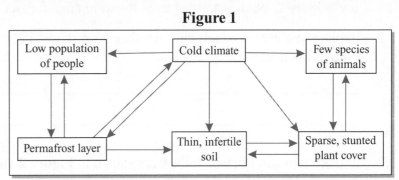

1.1   Using **Figure 1** and your own knowledge, describe how the climate can affect the soil fertility in a cold environment.

The cold climate causes plants to decompose very slowly. This means that the soil is relatively low in nutrients.

[2]

1.2   Explain how damage to the plants in a tundra environment could affect the climate there.

Damaging plant cover can cause permafrost to melt. Melting permafrost can release trapped greenhouse gases. These contribute to global warming, leading to changes in the climate of cold environments.

[3]

1.3   To what extent can the needs of economic development be balanced with the need for conservation in cold environments?

People living in cold environments need to be able to exploit economic opportunities to provide jobs and earn money, e.g. from mining, tourism and mineral extraction. However, cold environments are fragile and often pristine natural ecosystems that are worth conserving and can take a long time to recover. Governments can introduce laws (e.g. the 1964 Wilderness Act in the USA) to protect parts of cold environments from development and regulate potentially damaging economic activities. International agreements can be made between countries to protect uninhabited areas, for example the 1959 Antarctic Treaty limits visitors to Antarctica and prohibits nuclear activities. Technology can be used to prevent or minimise environmental problems caused by development, for example using modern construction methods like elevating buildings on piles or building on gravel beds can prevent buildings warming the ground and melting the permafrost. In conclusion, although any development in cold environments can cause damage, it is possible to use strategies like regulation and modern technology to reduce the damage to an acceptable amount and contain it within a limited area.

[6]

[Total 11 marks]

Exam Questions

1   Study **Figure 1**, a photograph of a snowshoe hare,
      and **Figure 2**, photographs of trees found in taiga forests.

Figure 1

1.1   Explain **one** way in which the snowshoe hare shown in
      Figure 1 is adapted to its habitat.

      ....

      ....
      [2]

1.2   Explain **two** ways in which the trees shown in **Figure 2** are
      adapted to their habitat.

      Figure 2

      1:..

      ....

      2:..

      ....
      [4]
      [Total 6 marks]

2   Study **Figure 3**, a map of a cold environment.

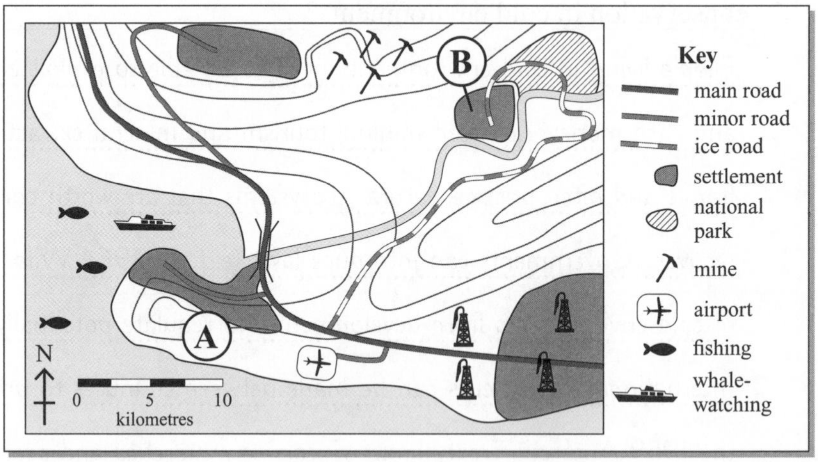

2.1   Using **Figure 3**, describe
      the economic opportunities
      at location A.

      Figure 3

      ....

      ....

      ....

      ....

      ....

      ....

      ....

      ....
      [3]

2.2   Using evidence from **Figure 3**, outline **one** challenge to the economic development of location B.

      ....

      ....

      ....
      [2]
      [Total 5 marks]

Revision Summary

That's just about it for Section 5 — so now's an excellent moment to test your knowledge with some questions.
- Try these questions and tick off each one when you get it right.
- When you've done all the questions for a topic and are completely happy with it, tick off the topic.

Hot Deserts (p.66-70) ☑
1) Describe the climate in hot deserts. ☑
2) What is the soil like in hot deserts? ☑
3) Describe two ways that people cope with the lack of water in hot deserts. ☑
4) Give two adaptations of plants to hot desert environments. ☑
5) Give two adaptations of animals to hot desert environments. ☑
6) Describe one issue related to biodiversity in hot deserts. ☑
7) Describe how inaccessibility can make development challenging in hot desert environments. ☑
8) Explain how tree planting can reduce the risk of desertification. ☑
9) Give one strategy, other than tree planting, that can reduce the risk of desertification. ☑

Cold Environments (p.73-74) ☑
10) Describe the climate of cold environments. ☑
11) How are polar and tundra environments different? ☑
12) Give two adaptations of plants to cold environments. ☑
13) Give two adaptations of animals to cold environments. ☑
14) Describe one issue related to biodiversity in cold environments. ☑

Cold Environments — Development and Management (p.75-78) ☑
15) What are the impacts of fishing on polar ecosystems? ☑
16) What are the impacts of mineral extraction on the Arctic ecosystem? ☑
17) How can inaccessibility make development challenging in a cold environment? ☑
18) a) What is a wilderness area? ☑
    b) Why are these areas worth protecting? ☑
19) Describe a small-scale example of sustainable management in either the Arctic or Antarctica. ☑
20) How is either the Arctic or Antarctica being managed sustainably on a global scale? ☑

Taiga Forests (p.79-80) ☑
21) Give one example of interdependence in the taiga forest ecosystem. ☑
22) True or false: taiga forests have a more complex structure than tropical rainforests. ☑
23) Why do trees in taiga forests have needles rather than leaves? ☑
24) How does hibernation help animals to survive in the taiga forest ecosystem? ☑
25) How does the cold, dry climate affect the rate of nutrient cycling in taiga forests? ☑

Taiga Forests — Threats and Conservation (p.81-83) ☑
26) How does the generation of hydroelectric power (HEP) threaten taiga forests? ☑
27) Name two other human activities that are threatening taiga forests. ☑
28) What is acid rain? ☑
29) How do forest fires threaten the biodiversity of taiga forests? ☑
30) Why do some people want to protect taiga forests? ☑
31) Give one reason why some people want to exploit taiga forests. ☑

The UK Physical Landscape

Ah, the UK landscape. Majestic <u>mountains</u>, cracking <u>coasts</u> and raging <u>rivers</u> — I could go on all day...

The UK has large **Upland** and **Lowland** Areas, and Important **Rivers**

The UK's main <u>upland</u> areas (orange and red on the map below) tend to be in the <u>north</u> and <u>west</u> of the country, and <u>lowland</u> areas (green on the map) to the <u>south</u> and <u>east</u>. You might be asked to <u>identify</u> them on a map.

Grampian Mountains

Part of the <u>Highlands</u> and home to <u>Ben Nevis</u> (the highest mountain in the UK), the Grampians are <u>steep</u>, <u>rocky</u> and <u>sparsely populated</u>.

The Cheshire Plain

An area of <u>low</u>, <u>flat</u> land formed by the <u>deposition</u> of material eroded by <u>glaciers</u> (see p.88).

The land is very <u>fertile</u> and is mainly used for <u>dairy farming</u>.

The climate of UK uplands tends to be cooler and wetter than the lowlands — see p.161.

Snowdonia

Snowdonia is a <u>glaciated</u> <u>upland</u> area formed from <u>rock</u> from extinct volcanoes.

It contains steep <u>mountains</u>, such as Snowdon, and <u>glaciated valleys</u>.

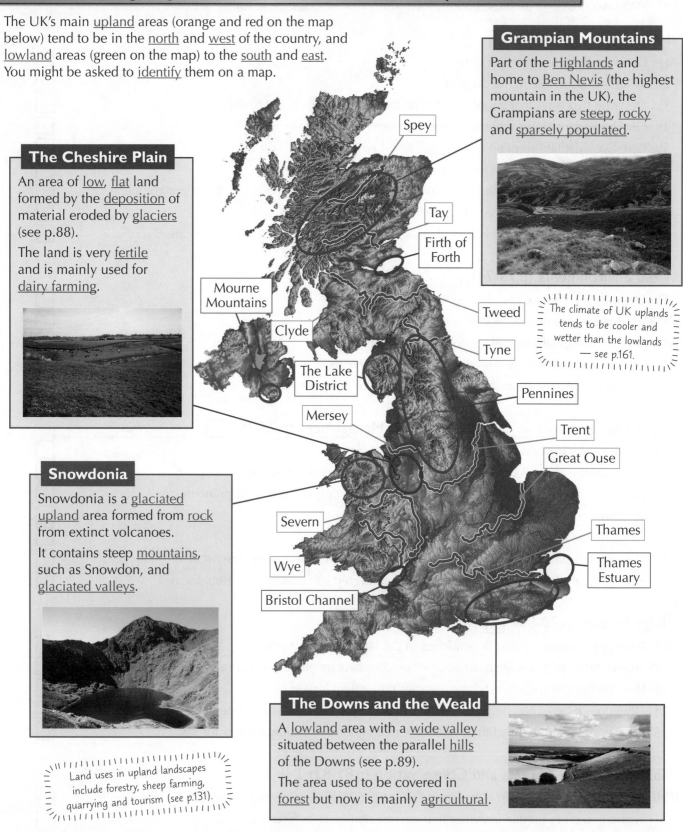

Map labels: Spey, Tay, Firth of Forth, Mourne Mountains, Clyde, Tweed, Tyne, The Lake District, Pennines, Mersey, Trent, Great Ouse, Severn, Thames, Wye, Thames Estuary, Bristol Channel

Land uses in upland landscapes include forestry, sheep farming, quarrying and tourism (see p.131).

The Downs and the Weald

A <u>lowland</u> area with a <u>wide valley</u> situated between the parallel <u>hills</u> of the Downs (see p.89).

The area used to be covered in <u>forest</u> but now is mainly <u>agricultural</u>.

Most uplands are found in the north and west of the UK

This is a lovely introduction to the rest of the UK physical landscapes section. Make sure you've got a grasp of the distribution of the UK's geographical features before you turn over. It'll help you understand the rest of the section.

Rocks and the UK Physical Landscape

There are three types of <u>rock</u> — <u>igneous</u>, <u>sedimentary</u> and <u>metamorphic</u>. They're formed in different ways.

There are **Three Types** of **Rocks**

Rock type depends on <u>how</u> the rock was <u>formed</u>:

1) <u>Igneous</u> — igneous rocks are formed when <u>molten rock</u> (magma) from the mantle <u>cools down</u> and <u>hardens</u>. The rock forms <u>crystals</u> as it cools. Igneous rocks are usually <u>hard</u>, e.g. <u>granite</u>.

2) <u>Sedimentary</u> — sedimentary rocks are formed when layers of <u>sediment</u> are <u>compacted together</u> until they become <u>solid rock</u>. There are <u>two</u> main types in the UK:

- <u>Carboniferous limestone</u> and <u>chalk</u> are formed from <u>tiny shells</u> and <u>skeletons</u> of dead sea creatures. <u>Limestone</u> is quite <u>hard</u>, but <u>chalk</u> is a much <u>softer</u> rock.

- <u>Clays</u> and <u>shales</u> are made from <u>mud</u> and <u>clay minerals</u>. They are very <u>soft</u>.

3) <u>Metamorphic</u> — <u>metamorphic</u> rocks are formed when other rocks (igneous, sedimentary or older metamorphic rocks) are <u>changed</u> by <u>heat</u> and <u>pressure</u>. The new rocks become <u>harder</u> and more <u>compact</u>, e.g. <u>shale</u> becomes <u>slate</u> and, with further pressure and heat, slate becomes <u>schist</u>.

| Geological map of the UK |

HARDER
- Carboniferous limestone
- Slate (and shale)
- Schist and other metamorphic rocks
- Igneous rocks

SOFTER
- Clays and sandstones
- Chalk, mudstones and sandstones

There **Used** to be **More Tectonic Activity** in the UK

There are <u>three</u> main ways that <u>past tectonic processes</u> have shaped the UK <u>landscape</u>:

1 Active Volcanoes

520 million years ago the <u>land</u> that now makes up the UK used to be much <u>closer</u> to a <u>plate margin</u> than it is now. <u>Active volcanoes</u> forced <u>magma</u> through the <u>Earth's crust</u> which cooled to form <u>igneous rocks</u>, e.g. granite.

2 Plate Collisions

1) <u>Plate collisions</u> caused the rocks to be <u>folded</u> and <u>uplifted</u>, forming <u>mountain ranges</u>. Many of these areas remain as <u>uplands</u>, e.g. the Scottish Highlands, the Lake District and north Wales — the igneous granite is <u>hard</u> and <u>more resistant</u> to <u>erosion</u>.

2) The <u>intense heat</u> and <u>pressure</u> caused by <u>plate collisions</u> formed <u>hard metamorphic rocks</u> in northern Scotland and northern Ireland.

3 Plate Movements — UK Position

1) <u>Plate movements</u> meant that 345-280 million years ago Britain was in the <u>tropics</u> and higher sea levels meant it was partly underwater — <u>carboniferous limestone</u> formed in the <u>warm shallow seas</u>. This can be seen in the <u>uplands</u> of the Peak District (northern England), south Wales and south west England.

2) The <u>youngest</u> rocks in the UK are the <u>chalks</u> and <u>clays</u> found in <u>southern England</u>. They formed in <u>shallow seas</u> and <u>swamps</u>. Chalks and clays are <u>softer</u> rocks that are more <u>easily eroded</u> — they form <u>lowland</u> landscapes.

Different areas of the UK are made up of different types of rock

Igneous and metamorphic rocks are mostly found in the north and west of the UK. Softer sedimentary rocks are generally found in the south and east. Tip — thinking of them as <u>SE</u>dimentary rocks might help you remember this.

Rocks and the UK Physical Landscape

Each rock type has different characteristics. The characteristics of each rock type influence the type of landscape that forms. Much of the UK landscape has also been affected by erosion and deposition caused by glaciers.

Different Rock Types Create Different Landscapes

Granite

1) Granite is very resistant and forms upland landscapes.

2) It has lots of joints (cracks) which aren't evenly spread. The parts of the rock where there are more joints wear down faster. Areas that have fewer joints are weathered more slowly than the surrounding rock and stick out at the surface forming tors.

3) Granite is impermeable — it doesn't let water through. This creates moorlands — large areas of waterlogged land and acidic soil, with low-growing vegetation.

Slate and Schist

1) Slate forms in layers creating weak planes in the rock. It is generally very hard and resistant to weathering but it is easily split into thin slabs.

2) Schist has bigger crystals than slate and also splits easily into small flakes.

3) Slate and schist often form rugged, upland landscapes. They are impermeable, which can lead to waterlogged and acidic soils.

Carboniferous Limestone

1) Rainwater slowly eats away at limestone through carbonation weathering (see p.92). Most weathering happens along joints in the rock, creating some spectacular features, e.g. limestone pavements (flat areas with deep weathered cracks), caverns and gorges.

2) Limestone is permeable, so limestone areas also have dry valleys and resurgent rivers (rivers that pop out at the surface when limestone is on top of impermeable rock).

Chalk and Clay

1) Chalk is harder than clay. It forms escarpments (hills) in UK lowlands and cliffs at the coast. One side of the hill is usually steep and the other side is more gentle.

2) Chalk is permeable — water flows through it and emerges as a spring where it meets impermeable rock.

3) Clay is very soft and easily eroded. It forms wide flat valleys in UK lowlands. It is impermeable so water flows over the surface — there are lots of streams, rivers and lakes.

Much of the UK Used to be Covered in Ice

1) During the last glacial period (p.35), ice covered the UK roughly as far south as the line on this map, so glaciated landscapes are mostly found in upland areas in the north-west of the UK.

2) Ice is very powerful, so it was able to erode the landscape, carving out large U-shaped valleys in upland areas such as the Lake District.

3) Glaciers also deposited lots of material as they melted. Landscapes formed by glacial meltwater and deposits extend south of the ice sheets. E.g. large parts of eastern England are covered in till (an unsorted mixture of clay, sand and rocks) deposited by melting glaciers.

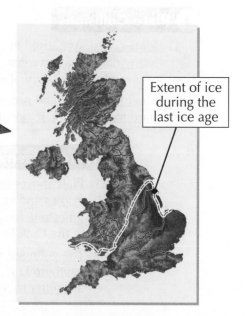

Extent of ice during the last ice age

The UK landscape is influenced by rock type and the action of ice

Some of the most beautiful landscapes in the country have been shaped by powerful glaciers. Many of these areas are popular tourist destinations because of their scenery, e.g. the Lake District (see p.133). Make sure you're fully clued up on how rock types and glaciers have affected the UK's landscape before you move on to the next page.

Landscape Processes — Physical

It might look like nothing's changing, but <u>rocks</u> are constantly being <u>broken down</u>, <u>moved around</u> and <u>dumped</u>.

Physical Processes Alter the Landscape

1) <u>Physical processes</u> are constantly <u>changing</u> the <u>landscape</u> of the UK. They include:

- <u>Weathering</u> — weathering is the <u>breakdown</u> of rock into smaller pieces.
  It can be <u>mechanical</u>, <u>chemical</u> or <u>biological</u> (see page 92).
- <u>Erosion</u> — erosion <u>wears away</u> rock. During the last glacial period, <u>ice</u> eroded the landscape.
  <u>Rivers</u> and the <u>sea</u> now <u>constantly</u> erode the landscape.
- <u>Post-glacial river processes</u> — <u>melting ice</u> at the <u>end</u> of <u>glacial periods</u> made rivers <u>much bigger</u> than
  normal with more <u>power</u> to <u>erode</u> the <u>landscape</u>. The ice also left <u>distinctive landforms</u> when it <u>melted</u>,
  e.g. hanging valleys (little valleys that are left at a higher level than the main valley).
- <u>Slope processes</u> — including <u>mass movements</u>, e.g. rockfalls, slides and slumps (see page 92).

2) Physical process are affected by <u>climate</u>. For example, a <u>cold</u> climate increases the likelihood of
<u>freeze-thaw weathering</u> (see p.108) and a <u>wet climate</u> increases the <u>number</u> of <u>streams</u> and <u>rivers</u>.

Physical Processes Interact to Create Distinctive Upland Landscapes...

<u>Snowdonia</u> is an <u>upland</u> landscape —
the map shows <u>tightly packed contours</u>
and there are lots of <u>rocky crags</u>.

<u>Llyn Idwal</u> is a <u>tarn</u>.
It sits in a corrie
(basin) that was
<u>hollowed out</u> by ice
during glacial times.

<u>Freeze-thaw weathering</u> occurs on
the <u>steep back wall</u> of the corrie.
As the rocks are <u>broken up</u> there are
<u>rock falls</u>, which form <u>scree slopes</u>.

This <u>large U-shaped valley</u> was
<u>eroded</u> by ice — it has a <u>flat
floor</u> and <u>steep sides</u>. The valley
contains a <u>misfit river</u> that looks
<u>too small</u> to have created it.

There is lots of <u>rain</u> in
<u>Snowdonia</u> and the rocks
are mostly <u>impermeable</u>.
This means there are lots
of <u>streams</u> that are <u>eroding</u>
the steep sides of the
corrie and forming <u>gullies</u>.

... and Distinctive Lowland Landscapes

<u>The Downs and the Weald</u> are
a <u>lowland</u> landscape — <u>chalk
escarpments</u> (the Downs) lie
either side of a <u>large flat area</u>
of <u>clay</u> (the Weald). The valley
is <u>flat</u> (the contour lines on the
map are <u>widely spaced</u>).

Large rivers, e.g. the
River Arun, <u>meander</u>
on the <u>impermeable</u>
clay, <u>widening</u> the
valley floor (see p.110).

The UK has a <u>wet climate</u> — heavy rain can
lead to <u>flooding</u>. The overflowing river <u>deposits</u>
<u>silt</u> on the valley floor forming a <u>flood plain</u>.

<u>Dry valleys</u> are found in UK lowland
landscapes. These are valleys with <u>no
streams</u> visible (they flow <u>underground</u>
in the <u>permeable chalk</u>). They formed
during <u>glacial periods</u> when the <u>colder</u>
climate led to more <u>freeze-thaw
weathering</u> and <u>glacial snow melt</u>
meant that <u>streams</u> had much <u>more
water</u> in them than they do today.

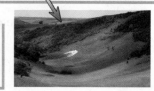

Physical processes combine to create the different landscapes of the UK

You don't need to know the examples on this page off by heart, but they'll help you understand some of the
interactions that can occur between physical processes. Practise identifying the resulting features from maps.

Landscape Processes — Human

The UK is <u>small</u> and there are <u>a lot</u> of <u>people</u> — wherever you go, the <u>actions</u> of people have <u>changed</u> the <u>landscape</u>.

Humans have Changed the Landscape Through Agriculture...

1) People have <u>cleared</u> the land of <u>forest</u> to make space for <u>farming</u>.

2) Over time <u>hedgerows</u> and <u>walls</u> have been put in to mark out <u>fields</u>.

3) Different landscapes are best for <u>different types</u> of farming:

- <u>Arable</u> — <u>flat land</u> with good <u>soil</u>, e.g. east England, is used for arable farming (growing <u>crops</u>).

- <u>Dairy</u> — warm and wet areas, e.g. south west England, are good for <u>dairy farming</u>. There are lots of <u>large</u>, <u>grassy fields</u>.

- <u>Sheep</u> — sheep farming takes place in the <u>harsher</u> conditions in the <u>uplands</u>. Sheep farming has led to a <u>lack of trees</u> on the hills (<u>young trees</u> are <u>eaten</u> or <u>trampled</u> before they get a chance to mature).

4) <u>OS®</u> <u>maps</u> show the influence of agriculture, including <u>field boundaries</u> and <u>drainage ditches</u> (dug to make the land dry enough for farming).

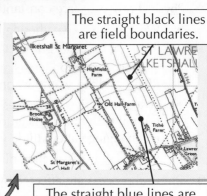

The straight black lines are field boundaries.

The straight blue lines are man-made drainage ditches.

... Forestry...

1) <u>Forestry</u> is the management of areas of <u>woodland</u> — they can be used for <u>timber</u>, <u>recreation</u> or <u>conservation</u>.

2) The UK used to be covered in <u>deciduous woodland</u>, but there is very <u>little</u> natural woodland <u>left</u>.

3) <u>Coniferous</u> (evergreen) forests have been planted for <u>timber</u>. The trees are often planted in <u>straight lines</u> — the forests don't look natural. When areas are <u>felled</u>, the landscape is left <u>bare</u>.

4) In some places, <u>deciduous</u> woodland is being <u>replanted</u> to try to <u>return</u> the area to a more <u>natural state</u>.

5) OS® maps show <u>forestry plantations</u> and areas that are being <u>managed</u>.

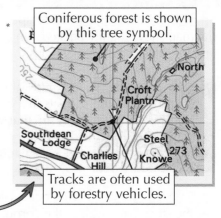

Coniferous forest is shown by this tree symbol.

Tracks are often used by forestry vehicles.

... and Settlement

1) Lots of factors influence <u>where settlements</u> have developed. For example, early settlers needed a <u>water supply</u>, somewhere that could easily be <u>defended</u> or that was <u>sheltered</u> from wind and rain.

2) Other factors such as <u>bridging points</u> over rivers and the <u>availability</u> of <u>resources</u>, e.g. wood for building, also played a part.

3) As settlements grew they further influenced the landscape. For example:

- land was <u>concreted</u> over for <u>roads</u> and <u>buildings</u>, which affected <u>drainage patterns</u>.

- some <u>rivers</u> were diverted through <u>underground channels</u>.

- some river channels were <u>straightened</u> or had <u>embankments</u> built to prevent flooding.

4) Most of the biggest cities are <u>ports</u> and <u>industrial areas</u>, e.g. London, West Midlands, Manchester and Portsmouth. These landscapes are <u>more urban</u> than natural.

5) Look for <u>buildings</u>, <u>railways</u>, <u>canals</u> and <u>embankments</u> to identify settlements on OS® maps.

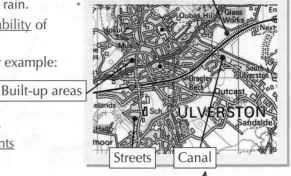

The land has been raised so the railway line is level — the dashed lines show embankments.

Built-up areas

Streets | Canal

Farming, forestry and construction have changed the UK landscape

If you're struggling to remember the different landscape processes, cover the pages and try drawing some mind maps showing both the human and physical processes and how they affect the landscape. When you've written everything you can remember, have a peek at the pages and fill in any gaps you've left.

Exam Questions

Practice questions are a great way of checking what you know now and what you need to go over again.
Work through these questions — the first one has been done for you to help show what the examiners are after.

1   Study **Figure 1**, a map of the UK's upland and lowland areas.

Figure 1

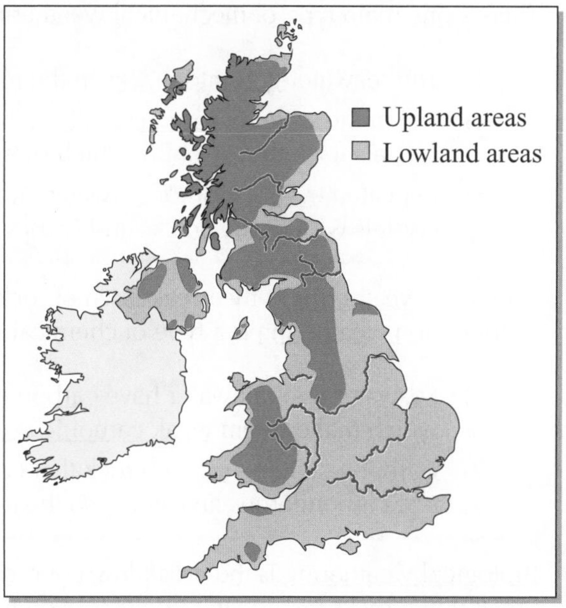

1.1   Describe the physical characteristics of
lowland areas in the UK.

Lowland areas in the UK are generally formed

of relatively soft rocks, e.g. chalk and sandstone.

The landscape is relatively flat, with gently

rolling hills.

[2]

1.2   Explain how past tectonic processes have shaped
the UK landscape.

....

....

....

....

....

[4]

[Total 6 marks]

2   Study **Figure 2**, which shows the distribution
of different rock types in the UK.

Figure 2

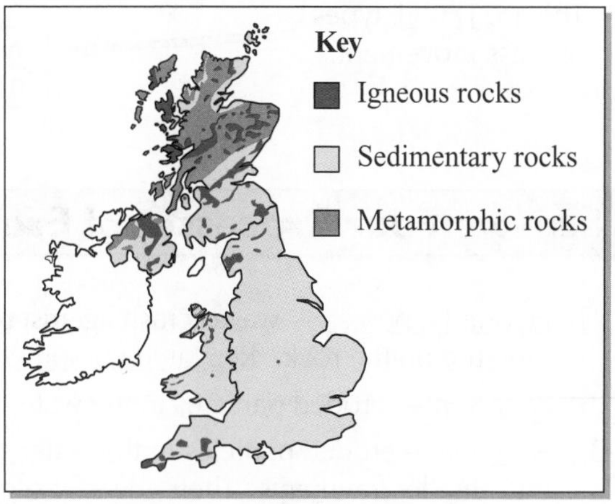

2.1   Give **one** example of a sedimentary rock.

....

[1]

2.2   Define the term 'igneous rock'.

....

[1]

2.3   State **one** characteristic of igneous rock.

....

[1]

2.4   Using **Figure 2**, describe the distribution of igneous rocks in the UK.

....

....

[2]

[Total 5 marks]

Coastal Weathering and Erosion

Weathering is the <u>breakdown</u> of rocks <u>where they are</u>, <u>erosion</u> is when the rocks are broken down and <u>carried away</u> by something, e.g. by seawater.

Rock is Broken Down by Mechanical, Chemical and Biological Weathering

1) <u>Mechanical weathering</u> is the <u>breakdown</u> of rock <u>without changing</u> its <u>chemical composition</u>. There's <u>one</u> main type of mechanical weathering that affects coasts — <u>salt weathering</u>:

> 1) The seawater <u>gets into cracks</u> in the rock.
>
> 2) When the water <u>evaporates</u>, <u>salt crystals</u> form. As the salt crystals form they <u>expand</u>, which puts <u>pressure</u> on the rock.
>
> 3) Repeated <u>evaporation</u> of saltwater and the <u>forming</u> of salt crystals <u>widens</u> the cracks and causes the rock to <u>break up</u>.

2) <u>Chemical weathering</u> is the breakdown of rock by <u>changing</u> its <u>chemical composition</u>. <u>Carbonation weathering</u> is a type of chemical weathering that happens in <u>warm</u> and <u>wet</u> conditions:

> 1) Seawater and rainwater have <u>carbon dioxide</u> dissolved in them, which makes them <u>weak carbonic acids</u>.
>
> 2) Carbonic acid <u>reacts</u> with rock that contains <u>calcium carbonate</u>, e.g. carboniferous limestone, so the <u>rocks</u> are <u>dissolved</u> by the rainwater.

3) <u>Biological weathering</u> is the breakdown of rock by <u>living things</u>, e.g. <u>plant roots</u> break down rocks by <u>growing into cracks</u> on their surface and <u>pushing them apart</u>.

Mass Movement is when Material Falls Down a Slope

Weathering and mass movement are called 'sub-aerial processes'.

1) Mass movement is the <u>shifting</u> of <u>rocks and loose material</u> down a slope, e.g. a cliff. It happens when the force of <u>gravity</u> acting on a slope is <u>greater than</u> the force <u>supporting</u> it.

2) Mass movements cause coasts to <u>retreat rapidly</u>.

3) They're <u>more likely</u> to happen when the material is <u>full of water</u> — it acts as a <u>lubricant</u>, and makes the material <u>heavier</u>.

4) The are <u>THREE</u> types of mass movement.

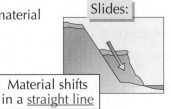

Slides:

Material shifts in a <u>straight line</u>

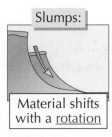

Slumps:

Material shifts with a <u>rotation</u>

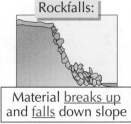

Rockfalls:

Material <u>breaks up</u> and <u>falls</u> down slope

There are Four Processes of Erosion

Hydraulic power is also known as hydraulic action.

1) <u>Hydraulic power</u> — waves crash against rock and <u>compress</u> the <u>air</u> in the cracks. This puts <u>pressure</u> on the rock. <u>Repeated compression</u> widens the cracks and makes bits of rock <u>break off</u>.

2) <u>Abrasion</u> — eroded particles in the water <u>scrape</u> and <u>rub</u> against rock, <u>removing small pieces</u>.

3) <u>Attrition</u> — eroded particles in the water <u>smash into each other</u> and break into <u>smaller fragments</u>. Their <u>edges</u> also get <u>rounded off</u> as they rub together.

4) <u>Solution</u> — dissolved <u>carbon dioxide</u> makes sea water slightly <u>acidic</u>. The acid <u>reacts</u> chemically with some rocks, e.g. <u>chalk</u> and <u>limestone</u>, <u>dissolving</u> them.

REVISION TIP

Practise sketching the three types of mass movement

This page is packed full of information, but it's just about how the coast is worn away and rocks are broken down into smaller pieces. Make sure you can sketch the diagrams without looking at the page.

Coastal Landforms Caused by Erosion

Erosion by waves forms many coastal landforms over long periods of time.

Coastlines can be Concordant or Discordant

1) The geological structure of a coastline influences the formation of erosional landforms.

2) Hard rocks like limestone and chalk are more resistant, so it takes longer for them to be eroded and weathered by physical processes.

3) Softer rocks like clay and sandstone are less resistant, which means they are eroded more quickly.

4) Joints and faults are cracks and weaknesses in the rock. Rocks with lots of joints and faults erode faster.

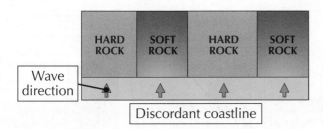

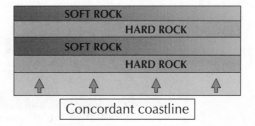

5) Some coastlines are made up of alternating bands of hard and soft rock that are at right angles to the coast — these are called discordant coastlines.

6) On a concordant coastline, the alternating bands of hard and soft rock are parallel to the coast.

7) Erosional landforms like bays and headlands are more common on discordant coastlines because the bands of rock are being eroded at different rates.

8) Concordant coastlines are eroded at the same rate along the coast. This means there are fewer erosional landforms.

The UK's Climate has an Impact on Coastal Erosion and Retreat

1) Temperature in the UK varies with the seasons. Temperatures are coldest in winter, warm through spring, hottest in summer, then cool through autumn.

2) Differences in temperature have an impact on processes along the coast, e.g. mild temperatures increase the rate of salt weathering (see previous page) because water evaporates more quickly.

3) Storms are very frequent in many parts of the UK, especially in winter. The strong winds create high energy, destructive waves which increase erosion of the cliffs. Intense rainfall can cause cliffs to become saturated — this makes mass movement (see previous page) more likely.

4) The prevailing (most common) winds in the UK are mostly warm south westerlies which bring storms from the Atlantic Ocean. The UK's south coast is exposed to these winds.

5) Cold northerly winds are also common, especially on the east coast of the UK.

Destructive Waves Wear Away the Coast

1) The waves that carry out erosional processes are called destructive waves.

2) Destructive waves are high, steep, and have a high frequency (10-14 waves per minute).

3) Their backwash (the movement of the water back down the beach) is more powerful than their swash (the movement of the water up the beach). This means material is removed from the coast.

4) Storms increase the erosional power of destructive waves, which can lead to increased rates of coastal retreat.

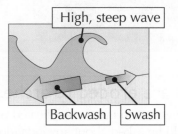

Coastal Landforms Caused by Erosion

Waves Erode Cliffs to Form Wave-cut Platforms

1) Waves cause <u>most erosion</u> at the <u>foot</u> of a cliff (see diagrams below).

2) This forms a <u>wave-cut notch</u>, which is enlarged as <u>erosion</u> continues.

3) The rock above the notch becomes <u>unstable</u> and eventually <u>collapses</u>.

4) The <u>collapsed material</u> is washed away and a <u>new</u> wave-cut notch starts to form.

5) <u>Repeated collapsing</u> results in the <u>cliff retreating</u>.

6) A <u>wave-cut platform</u> is the platform that's <u>left behind</u> as the <u>cliff retreats</u>.

Hard rock cliffs tend to be more vertical, and soft rock cliffs tend to be more sloping.

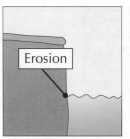
Erosion

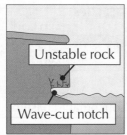
Unstable rock
Wave-cut notch

Collapsed material

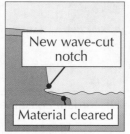
New wave-cut notch
Material cleared

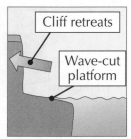
Cliff retreats
Wave-cut platform

Headlands and Bays Form Along Discordant Coastlines

1) <u>Soft</u> rocks or rocks with <u>lots of joints</u> have <u>low resistance</u> to erosion.
<u>Hard</u> rocks with a <u>solid structure</u> have a <u>high resistance</u> to erosion.

2) <u>Headlands</u> and <u>bays</u> form where there are <u>alternating bands</u> of <u>resistant</u> and <u>less resistant</u> rock along a coast.

3) The <u>less resistant</u> rock (e.g. clay) is eroded <u>quickly</u> and this forms a <u>bay</u> — bays have a <u>gentle slope</u>.

4) The <u>resistant</u> rock (e.g. chalk) is eroded more <u>slowly</u> and it's left <u>jutting out</u>, forming a <u>headland</u> — headlands have <u>steep sides</u>.

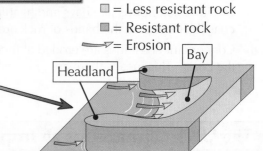
☐ = Less resistant rock
▨ = Resistant rock
⇀ = Erosion
Bay
Headland

Headlands are Eroded to form Caves, Arches and Stacks

1) Headlands are usually made of <u>resistant rocks</u> that have <u>weaknesses</u> like <u>cracks</u>.

2) <u>Waves</u> crash into the headlands and <u>enlarge</u> the cracks — mainly by <u>hydraulic power</u> and <u>abrasion</u>.

3) <u>Repeated erosion</u> and <u>enlargement</u> of the cracks causes a <u>cave</u> to form.

4) Continued erosion <u>deepens</u> the cave until it <u>breaks through</u> the headland — forming an <u>arch</u>, e.g. Durdle Door in Dorset.

5) Erosion continues to wear away the rock <u>supporting</u> the arch, until it eventually <u>collapses</u>.

6) This forms a <u>stack</u> — an <u>isolated rock</u> that's <u>separate</u> from the headland, e.g. Old Harry in Dorset.

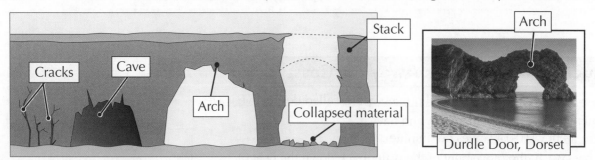
Cracks
Cave
Arch
Stack
Collapsed material
Arch
Durdle Door, Dorset

Caves are eroded to arches, which are eroded to stacks

These might seem quite complicated pages to begin with but take your time to learn how each landform is created. You could be asked about any individual landform in the exam, or about the whole process of formation.

Coastal Transportation and Deposition

The <u>material</u> that's been <u>eroded</u> is <u>moved around</u> the coast and <u>deposited</u> by waves.

Transportation is the Movement of Material

Material is transported <u>along coasts</u> by a process called <u>longshore drift</u>:

1) <u>Waves</u> follow the <u>direction</u> of the <u>prevailing</u> (most common) <u>wind</u>.

2) They usually hit the coast at an <u>oblique angle</u> (any angle that <u>isn't a right angle</u>).

3) The <u>swash</u> carries material <u>up the beach</u>, in the <u>same direction as the waves</u>.

4) The <u>backwash</u> then carries material <u>down the beach</u> at <u>right angles</u>, back towards the sea.

5) Over time, material <u>zigzags</u> along the coast.

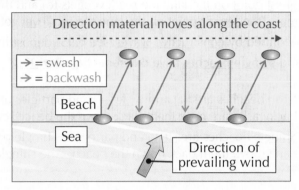

There are <u>four</u> other <u>processes of transportation</u>:

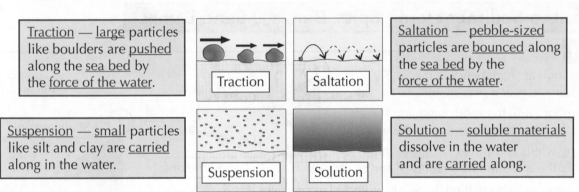

<u>Traction</u> — <u>large</u> particles like boulders are <u>pushed</u> along the <u>sea bed</u> by the <u>force of the water</u>.

Traction Saltation

<u>Saltation</u> — <u>pebble-sized</u> particles are <u>bounced</u> along the <u>sea bed</u> by the <u>force of the water</u>.

<u>Suspension</u> — <u>small</u> particles like silt and clay are <u>carried</u> along in the water.

Suspension Solution

<u>Solution</u> — <u>soluble materials</u> dissolve in the water and are <u>carried</u> along.

Deposition is the Dropping of Material

1) Deposition is when <u>material</u> being <u>carried</u> by the seawater is <u>dropped on the coast</u>. It occurs when water carrying sediment <u>slows down</u> so that it isn't moving <u>fast enough</u> to carry so much sediment.

2) Coasts are <u>built up</u> when the <u>amount of deposition</u> is <u>greater</u> than the <u>amount of erosion</u>.

3) The <u>amount of material</u> that's <u>deposited</u> on an area of coast is <u>increased</u> when:

- There's <u>lots</u> of <u>erosion</u> elsewhere on the coast, so there's <u>lots of material available</u>.
- There's <u>lots</u> of <u>transportation</u> of material <u>into</u> the area.

4) <u>Low energy</u> waves (i.e. <u>slow</u> waves) carry material to the coast but they're <u>not strong enough</u> to take a lot of material away — this means there's <u>lots of deposition</u> and <u>very little erosion</u>.

Waves that <u>deposit more material</u> than they <u>erode</u> are called <u>constructive waves</u>.

1) Constructive waves have a <u>low frequency</u> (6-8 waves per minute).

2) They're <u>low</u> and <u>long</u>.

3) The <u>swash</u> is <u>powerful</u> and it <u>carries material up the coast</u>.

4) The backwash is <u>weaker</u> and it <u>doesn't</u> take a lot of material <u>back down the coast</u>. This means material is <u>deposited</u> on the coast.

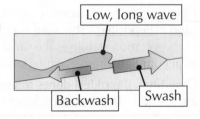

EXAM TIP

The amount of erosion affects the amount of deposition elsewhere

If you're asked to explain coastal processes in the exam, you might find drawing a diagram helps. It doesn't have to be a work of art — just make sure you add labels to it so it's clear what it's showing.

Coastal Landforms Caused by Deposition

Here are some more <u>landforms</u> for you to learn about. This time it's all about <u>deposition</u>.

Beaches are formed by Deposition

1) Beaches are found on coasts <u>between</u> the <u>high water mark</u> (the <u>highest point on the land</u> the <u>sea level</u> gets to) and the <u>low water mark</u> (the <u>lowest point</u> on the land the <u>sea level</u> gets to).

2) They're formed by <u>constructive waves</u> (see p.95) depositing material like <u>sand</u> and <u>shingle</u>.

3) <u>Sand</u> and <u>shingle beaches</u> have different <u>characteristics</u>:

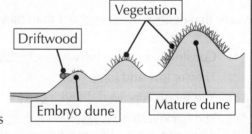

- <u>Sand</u> beaches are <u>flat</u> and <u>wide</u> — sand particles are <u>small</u> and the weak backwash <u>can</u> move them <u>back down</u> the beach, creating a <u>long</u>, <u>gentle slope</u>.

- <u>Shingle</u> beaches are <u>steep</u> and <u>narrow</u> — shingle particles are <u>large</u> and the weak backwash <u>can't</u> move them back down the beach. The shingle particles <u>build up</u> and create a <u>steep slope</u>.

Deposited Sediment forms Spits, Bars and Sand Dunes

Spits

1) Spits form at <u>sharp bends</u> in the coastline, e.g. at a <u>river mouth</u>.

2) <u>Longshore drift</u> transports sand and shingle <u>past</u> the bend and <u>deposits</u> it in the sea.

3) Strong winds and waves can <u>curve</u> the end of the spit (forming a <u>recurved end</u>).

4) The <u>sheltered area</u> behind the spit is <u>protected from waves</u> — lots of material <u>accumulates</u> in this area, which means <u>plants</u> can grow there.

5) <u>Over time</u>, the sheltered area can become a <u>mud flat</u> or a <u>salt marsh</u>.

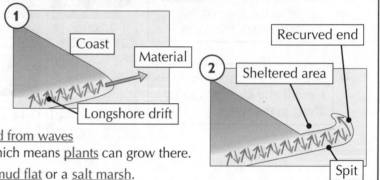

Bars

1) A bar is formed when a spit <u>joins two headlands together</u>.

2) The bar <u>cuts off</u> the bay between the headlands <u>from the sea</u>.

3) This means a <u>lagoon</u> can form <u>behind</u> the bar.

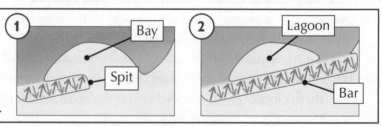

Sand Dunes

1) <u>Sand dunes</u> are formed when <u>sand</u> deposited by <u>longshore drift</u> is moved <u>up</u> the beach by the <u>wind</u>.

2) <u>Obstacles</u> (e.g. driftwood) cause wind speed to <u>decrease</u> so <u>sand</u> is <u>deposited</u>. This sand is <u>colonised</u> by <u>plants</u> and <u>grasses</u>. The vegetation <u>stabilises</u> the sand and encourages more sand to <u>accumulate</u> there, forming small dunes called <u>embryo dunes</u>.

3) Over time, the <u>oldest</u> dunes <u>migrate</u> inland as newer embryo dunes are formed. These <u>mature dunes</u> can reach heights of <u>up to 10 m</u>.

Bars are just spits that join two headlands together

In the exam, you might have to identify coastal landforms caused by deposition on photographs or diagrams. It's not too tricky — just make sure you're familiar with the main features of each landform before the exam.

Identifying Coastal Landforms

Map skills could well come in very useful in your exam so it's worth practising them now.

Identifying **Landforms** Caused by **Erosion**

You might be asked to identify coastal landforms on a map in the exam. The simplest thing they could ask is whether the map is showing erosional or depositional landforms, so here's how to identify a few erosional landforms to get you started:

Caves, Arches and Stacks

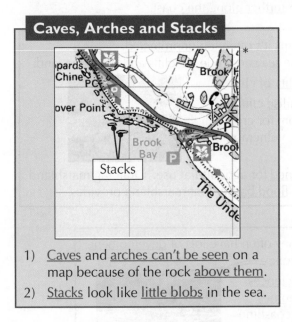

1) Caves and arches can't be seen on a map because of the rock above them.
2) Stacks look like little blobs in the sea.

Cliffs and Wave-cut Platforms

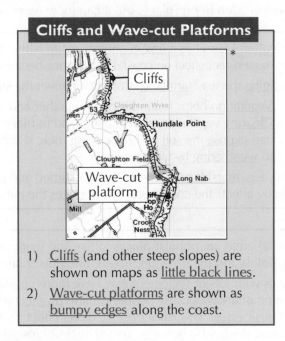

1) Cliffs (and other steep slopes) are shown on maps as little black lines.
2) Wave-cut platforms are shown as bumpy edges along the coast.

Identifying **Landforms** Caused by **Deposition**

Identifying depositional landforms is easy once you know that beaches are shown in yellow on maps. Here's how to identify a couple of depositional landforms:

Beaches

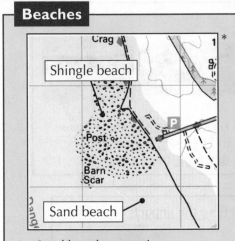

1) Sand beaches are shown on maps as pale yellow.
2) Shingle beaches are shown as white or yellow with speckles.

Spits

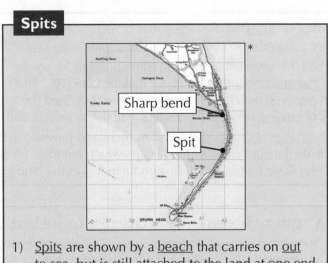

1) Spits are shown by a beach that carries on out to sea, but is still attached to the land at one end.
2) There might also be a sharp bend in the coast that caused it to form (see p.96).

 REVISION TIP

Make sure you can identify each landform on a map

There are some easy marks up for grabs with map questions, so learn this page. Practise looking for landforms on any maps you can get hold of. Don't forget though, caves and arches can't be seen.

Human Activity at the Coast

The way <u>humans use</u> the coast can have an <u>effect</u> on the <u>landscape</u> and it's not always <u>positive</u>...

Human Activities have Direct and Indirect Effects on the Coast

1) <u>Direct effects</u> on the coastline are the <u>immediate result</u> of <u>human activities</u>.
   For example, building <u>coastal defences</u> will <u>prevent erosion</u>.

2) <u>Indirect effects</u> happen as a result of the <u>direct effects</u>. For example, building coastal defences will prevent erosion in <u>one place</u>, but it can increase erosion <u>further along the coast</u>.

Agriculture

1) Agricultural land has a <u>low economic value</u> which means it's often left <u>unprotected</u>. This has a direct effect on coastal landscapes because the sea can <u>erode</u> the cliffs and shape the land.

2) <u>Changing</u> the way <u>farmland</u> is used can affect the <u>stability</u> of cliffs.

   • <u>Vegetation</u> helps to bind the soil together and <u>stabilise</u> clifftops. <u>Clearing</u> vegetation from grazing land to make room for crops can <u>expose</u> the <u>soil</u> and underlying rock, leaving it vulnerable to <u>weathering</u> by wind and rain.

3) Land, e.g. <u>marshland</u>, is sometimes <u>reclaimed</u> and <u>drained</u> for agricultural use. Draining marshland directly affects the coast because it <u>reduces</u> the natural <u>flood barrier</u> that marshland provides.

Development

1) Coastal areas are popular places to <u>live</u> and <u>work</u>, so they often have lots of <u>development</u>, e.g. hotels and <u>infrastructure</u> (roads, rail, power lines etc.).

2) Coasts with lots of <u>settlement</u> may have more <u>coastal defences</u> than other areas because people want to <u>protect</u> their <u>homes</u> and <u>businesses</u>. This has a <u>positive</u> direct effect on the coastline because the land is <u>better protected</u> against erosion.

3) However, an <u>indirect effect</u> of development is the <u>change</u> in the <u>transportation</u> and <u>deposition</u> of material along the coast. Building on coastal lowlands can <u>restrict sediment</u> supply to <u>beaches</u>, making them narrower. Narrow beaches <u>don't protect</u> the coast as well, which means the land is more <u>vulnerable</u> to erosion.

Industry

1) Coastal <u>quarries</u> expose large areas of rock, making them more <u>vulnerable</u> to chemical <u>weathering</u> and <u>erosion</u>.

2) <u>Gravel</u> has been extracted from some <u>beaches</u> for use in the <u>construction industry</u>, e.g. for making concrete. This has <u>removed</u> material from the coast and <u>increased</u> the <u>risk</u> of <u>erosion</u> because there's <u>less</u> material to protect cliffs.

3) <u>Industrial growth</u> at <u>ports</u> has led to increased pressure to build on <u>salt marshes</u>. These areas provide <u>flat land</u> and <u>sheltered water</u>, which are ideal for <u>ports</u> and <u>industry</u>, but are also <u>natural flood barriers</u>. Building on them leaves the land <u>more vulnerable</u> to <u>erosion</u>.

Coastal Management

1) <u>Coastal management</u> is about <u>protecting coastal landscapes</u> from the <u>impacts</u> of <u>erosion</u>.

2) Some <u>management strategies</u> (see p.100) alter <u>sediment movement</u>, which <u>reduces</u> the amount of <u>protective</u> beach material further along the coast — this <u>increases erosion</u>.

3) Coastal defences can also <u>reduce erosion</u>. This has a direct effect on the coast because it <u>prevents</u> the landscape from <u>changing</u>, i.e. <u>retreating</u>.

Learn how human activity has an impact on the coast

It might not seem obvious how human activity affects the coast, but pretty much everything we do does. Read over this page until you're clear how each activity affects the rate of weathering and erosion and the impact this has.

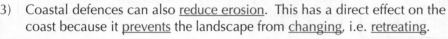

Coastal Flooding

Coastal areas are <u>increasingly at risk</u> from <u>flooding</u> by the sea. This can cause a lot of <u>problems</u> for the <u>environment</u> and the <u>people</u> living there.

Climate Change is Increasing the Risk of Coastal Flooding

<u>Rising sea levels</u> and an increased <u>frequency of storms</u> are making coastal flooding more likely.

Rising Sea Levels

1) <u>Rising sea levels</u> (see p.36) pose a threat to <u>low-lying</u> and <u>coastal areas</u>.

2) An increase in sea levels could cause <u>higher tides</u> that would <u>flood</u> coastal areas <u>more frequently</u>.

3) Higher tides could also remove <u>larger amounts</u> of material from <u>beaches</u>. This could lead to <u>increased erosion</u> of cliffs because there's <u>less material</u> to <u>protect</u> them from the sea.

4) Rising sea levels could <u>expose</u> more of the coastline to <u>erosion</u> — <u>beaches</u> could become <u>narrower</u> as the sea will be able to <u>move further inland</u>.

Storm Frequency

1) <u>Climate change</u> is causing <u>storms</u> to become <u>more frequent</u>.

2) Storms give the sea more <u>erosional power</u> — areas of <u>hard rock</u> will be <u>more vulnerable</u> to erosion and areas of <u>soft rock</u> will erode <u>more quickly</u>.

3) The sea will also have more <u>energy</u> to <u>transport material</u>. <u>High-energy waves</u> can move more material for <u>greater distances</u>, which could lead to some areas being <u>starved</u> of material. This leaves these areas <u>vulnerable</u> to <u>erosion</u> and to <u>flooding</u>.

4) <u>Storm surges</u> (see p.19) could become <u>more frequent</u> and <u>sea level rise</u> could cause surges to <u>reach</u> areas <u>further inland</u>.

There are Threats to People and the Environment

Threats to People

1) <u>Low-lying coastal areas</u> could be <u>permanently flooded</u> or <u>flood</u> so often that they become <u>impossible</u> to inhabit.

2) Coastal <u>industries</u> may be shut down because of <u>damage</u> to <u>equipment</u> and <u>buildings</u>, e.g. <u>fishing boats</u> can be destroyed.

3) There's a risk of damage to <u>infrastructure</u> like <u>roads</u> and <u>rail networks</u>. For example, railway lines in <u>Dawlish</u>, <u>Devon</u> run <u>parallel</u> to the sea and are <u>badly affected</u> by flooding. Storms in 2014 damaged <u>flood defences</u> and parts of the <u>track</u>.

4) There's a <u>booming tourist industry</u> in coastal areas. Flooding and erosion can <u>put people off visiting</u>. Fewer tourists means <u>businesses</u> that <u>rely on tourism</u> may <u>close</u>, leading to a loss of <u>livelihoods</u>.

Waves crashing on to the car park in Barmouth, Wales

Threats to the Environment

1) <u>Ecosystems</u> will be affected because <u>seawater</u> has a <u>high salt content</u>. Increased salt levels due to coastal flooding can <u>damage</u> or <u>kill</u> organisms in an ecosystem. It can also affect <u>agricultural land</u> by reducing <u>soil fertility</u>.

2) The <u>force</u> of floodwater can <u>uproot</u> trees and plants, and <u>standing</u> floodwater drowns some trees and plants.

3) Some <u>conservation areas</u> are threatened by coastal erosion. For example, there are <u>lagoons</u> on the <u>Holderness coast</u> that are protected. The lagoons are separated from the sea by a <u>bar</u>. If this is <u>eroded</u> it will connect the lagoons to the <u>sea</u> and they would be <u>destroyed</u>.

Coastal areas are increasingly threatened by flooding

Coastal flooding can be very disruptive for local residents, and climate change is probably going to increase the frequency and impacts of floods. Make sure you learn the impacts of flooding on people and the environment.

Coastal Management

The <u>aim</u> of coastal management is to <u>protect</u> people and the environment from the <u>impacts</u> of flooding and erosion.

Coastal Defences Include Hard and Soft Engineering

Hard Engineering
<u>Man-made structures</u> built to <u>control the flow</u> of the sea and <u>reduce flooding</u> and <u>erosion</u>.

Soft Engineering
Schemes set up using <u>knowledge</u> of the sea and its <u>processes</u> to <u>reduce the effects of flooding</u> and <u>erosion</u>.

	Defence	What it is	Benefits	Costs
Hard Engineering	**Sea Wall**	A <u>wall</u> made out of a <u>hard material</u> like <u>concrete</u> that <u>reflects waves</u> back to sea.	It <u>prevents erosion</u> of the coast. It also acts as a <u>barrier</u> to <u>prevent flooding</u>.	It creates a <u>strong backwash</u>, which <u>erodes under</u> the wall. Sea walls are <u>very expensive</u> to <u>build</u> and to <u>maintain</u>.
	Gabions	A <u>wall</u> of <u>wire cages</u> filled with <u>rocks</u> usually built at the foot of cliffs.	The gabions <u>absorb wave energy</u> and so <u>reduce erosion</u>. They're <u>cheap</u> and <u>easy to build</u>.	They're <u>ugly</u> to look at and the wire cages can <u>corrode</u> over time.
	Rock Armour	<u>Boulders</u> that are <u>piled up</u> along the coast. (It's also sometimes called <u>rip-rap</u>.)	The boulders <u>absorb wave energy</u> and so <u>reduce erosion</u> and <u>flooding</u>. It's a fairly <u>cheap</u> defence.	Boulders can be <u>moved around</u> by <u>strong waves</u>, so they need to be <u>replaced</u>.
	Groynes ← longshore drift	Wooden or stone <u>fences</u> that are built at <u>right angles</u> to the coast. They <u>trap material</u> transported by <u>longshore drift</u>.	They create <u>wider beaches</u> which <u>slow</u> the <u>waves</u>. This gives greater <u>protection</u> from <u>flooding</u> and <u>erosion</u>. They're a fairly <u>cheap</u> defence.	They <u>starve beaches</u> further down the coast of sand, making them <u>narrower</u>. Narrower beaches <u>don't protect</u> the coast as well, leading to <u>greater erosion</u> and <u>floods</u>.
Soft Engineering	**Beach Nourishment and Reprofiling**	Sand and shingle from <u>elsewhere</u> (e.g. from the <u>seabed</u>) or from <u>lower down</u> the beach that's <u>added</u> to the <u>upper part</u> of beaches.	It creates <u>wider beaches</u> which <u>slow</u> the <u>waves</u>. This gives greater <u>protection</u> from <u>flooding</u> and <u>erosion</u>.	Taking <u>material</u> from the <u>seabed</u> can <u>kill</u> organisms like <u>sponges</u> and <u>corals</u>. It's a <u>very expensive</u> defence. It has to be <u>repeated</u>.
	Dune Regeneration	<u>Creating</u> or <u>restoring sand dunes</u> by either <u>nourishment</u>, or <u>by planting vegetation</u> to <u>stabilise</u> the sand.	Sand dunes provide a <u>barrier</u> between the land and the sea. <u>Wave energy</u> is <u>absorbed</u> which <u>prevents flooding</u> and <u>erosion</u>. Stabilisation is <u>cheap</u>.	The <u>protection</u> is <u>limited</u> to a <u>small area</u>. <u>Nourishment</u> is <u>very expensive</u>.

1) Another option is to <u>do nothing</u> — <u>managed retreat</u> (also called <u>coastal realignment</u>) involves <u>removing current defences</u> and allowing the sea to <u>flood</u> the land behind.

2) Over time the land will become <u>marshland</u>, which then protects the land behind from <u>flooding</u> and <u>erosion</u>.

3) It's a <u>cheap</u> strategy that <u>doesn't need maintaining</u>, but there can be <u>conflicts</u> over which areas to flood.

Management Strategies Need to be Sustainable

1) To be <u>sustainable</u> and avoid <u>conflict</u>, management strategies should <u>control flooding</u> and <u>erosion</u> without causing <u>more problems</u> elsewhere or affecting the <u>people</u> who <u>live</u> and <u>work</u> at the coast.

2) <u>Integrated Coastal Zone Management</u> (<u>ICZM</u>) is a sustainable approach that aims to <u>protect</u> the coast while <u>taking everyone's interests into account</u>.

3) It's also a <u>long-term</u> approach so it can be <u>adapted</u> to any <u>future needs</u> and <u>changes</u> along the coastline.

You might be asked to identify management strategies from a photo
Don't just learn the names of the different engineering strategies — make sure you know exactly what they look like, how they work and a couple of benefits and disadvantages of each one.

UK Coastal Landscape

The Dorset coast has lots of landforms — <u>headlands</u>, <u>bays</u>, <u>arches</u>, <u>stacks</u>, <u>coves</u>, <u>lagoons</u>...

The **Dorset Coast** is a **Popular Tourist Destination** in **Southern England**

1) The <u>Dorset coast</u> is located on the <u>south</u> coast of England.

2) It is called the <u>Jurassic Coast</u> because it has lots of <u>fossils</u> dating from the Jurassic period. Lots of people come to the area to hunt for <u>fossils</u>, and it's an important location for scientists studying <u>geology</u>.

3) It also has a variety of <u>coastal landforms</u>, including <u>sandy beaches</u>, making it a popular tourist destination.

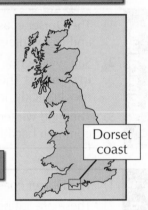

Dorset coast

Geomorphic Processes have Created a **Variety** of Landforms

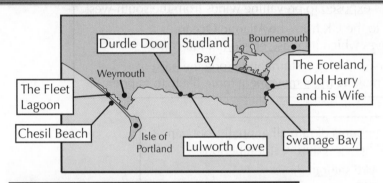

Durdle Door

<u>Durdle Door</u> is a great example of an <u>arch</u> (see page 94). It formed on a <u>hard limestone headland</u>. <u>Erosion</u> by <u>waves</u> opened up a <u>crack</u> in the <u>headland</u>, which became a <u>cave</u> and then developed into an arch. The arch is being gradually broken down by <u>mechanical</u>, <u>chemical</u> and <u>biological weathering</u>.

The Foreland, Old Harry and his Wife

In between two areas of <u>softer</u> rock that have formed <u>bays</u>, there is a <u>headland</u> called <u>The Foreland</u> made from a band of <u>harder rock</u> (chalk). An arch at the end of the headland has collapsed to form a <u>stack</u> called <u>Old Harry</u> and a <u>stump</u> (a collapsed stack) called <u>Old Harry's Wife</u>. <u>Salt</u> and <u>carbonation weathering</u>, along with <u>erosion</u>, are gradually <u>wearing down</u> old Harry and his Wife. The <u>vegetation</u> growing on top also <u>breaks up</u> the rock through biological weathering.

Chesil Beach

<u>Chesil Beach</u> is a <u>tombolo</u> (a type of <u>spit</u> that extends out to an <u>island</u>). It joins the <u>Isle of Portland</u> to the mainland. It has been formed by <u>longshore drift</u>. Behind Chesil Beach is a shallow <u>lagoon</u> called <u>The Fleet Lagoon</u>.

Lulworth Cove

<u>Lulworth Cove</u> is a small bay formed after a gap was eroded in a <u>band of limestone</u>. Behind the limestone is a band of <u>clay</u>. The clay is <u>softer</u>, so it has been <u>eroded</u> and <u>transported</u> away, forming the <u>bay</u>. The <u>limestone cliffs</u> forming the back wall of the bay are vulnerable to <u>mass movement</u>, and sometimes experience small <u>slides</u> and <u>slumps</u>.

Swanage Bay

The cliffs backing Swanage Bay are made of <u>clay</u>, which is a <u>soft</u> rock. Towards the <u>northern</u> end of the bay, the cliffs are covered in <u>vegetation</u>, <u>stabilising</u> them and <u>protecting</u> them from weathering. Elsewhere, the cliffs are <u>not stabilised</u> by vegetation, so <u>wet</u> weather weakens them and can cause <u>slumps</u>. <u>Longshore drift</u> carries material (mainly gravel) from the <u>south</u> to the <u>north</u> of the beach in the bay. Overall, <u>erosion</u> is the <u>dominant</u> process in the bay — the beach has been <u>losing material</u> for decades.

CASE STUDY

UK Coastal Landscape

Climate and Weather influence Physical Processes on the Dorset Coast...

There are several <u>climate</u> and <u>weather</u> factors that affect how <u>weathering</u> and <u>erosion</u> shape the Dorset coast:

Temperature

1) The Dorset coast has <u>warm</u>, <u>dry</u> summers (around 21 °C in July) and <u>mild</u> and <u>wet</u> winters (average minimum temperature in January is about 3 °C).

2) <u>Salt weathering</u> is the dominant form of <u>mechanical</u> weathering, particularly in summer. The warm temperatures cause sea water to evaporate from rocks <u>quickly</u>, leaving a <u>build-up</u> of salt crystals in tiny <u>cracks</u> in the rock.

3) The <u>mild</u> winters mean that <u>freeze-thaw weathering</u> is <u>less common</u> because it's usually <u>not cold enough</u> for ice to form.

Wind

1) The Dorset coast's <u>location</u> means that it's <u>exposed</u> to <u>prevailing winds</u> from the <u>south-west</u>.

2) These prevailing winds can bring <u>storms</u> to the UK from the <u>Atlantic Ocean</u>. Storms bring <u>high energy</u>, <u>destructive</u> waves which <u>increase erosion</u> of the cliffs.

3) <u>Hydraulic power</u> and <u>abrasion</u> both increase during a storm and <u>erode</u> the <u>base</u> of the cliffs. This makes the cliffs <u>unstable</u>, making <u>mass movement</u> more likely to happen.

Rainfall

1) The Dorset coast receives relatively <u>low amounts</u> of rainfall <u>annually</u>, but can experience <u>very wet winters</u>, with rainfall <u>heaviest</u> during <u>storm periods</u>.

2) Soils and rocks become <u>heavier</u> when they're <u>saturated</u>, which can make them more prone to <u>mass movement</u>.

3) In <u>January 2016</u>, <u>intense</u> rainfall combined with <u>high-energy</u> waves during Storm Frank to cause the collapse of cliffs between <u>Burton Bradstock</u> and <u>West Bay</u>.

...and so does Geology

1) The coastline is made from bands of <u>hard rock</u> and <u>soft rock</u>. The rocks have been <u>eroded at different rates</u>, which has created the area's coastal landforms, e.g. <u>Lulworth Cove</u>.

2) <u>Soft rock</u> like sandstone and clay are <u>easily eroded</u> by hydraulic power and abrasion.

Map: Soft — Kimmeridge — Hard — Soft — Soft — Hard; Lulworth Cove; Swanage Bay

Key
- ☐ Clay and sandstone
- ◼ Chalk
- ◼ Limestone
- ◼ Clay

3) The harder <u>chalk</u> and <u>limestone</u> cliffs are <u>weathered</u> and <u>eroded</u> more <u>slowly</u>, meaning that they stick out into the sea as exposed <u>headlands</u>. <u>Chalk</u> and <u>limestone</u> are vulnerable to erosion by <u>solution</u>, where the sea water <u>chemically reacts</u> with the rock, causing it to <u>dissolve</u>.

4) Weathering tends to happen <u>gradually</u> and cause <u>small changes</u>. Erosion can happen more <u>suddenly</u> on a <u>much larger</u> scale. A single storm can cause <u>large amounts</u> of erosion along a big stretch of the coast.

Geology, Climate and Weather can also Interact

1) It's often a <u>combination</u> of <u>climatic</u> and <u>geological</u> factors that affect how erosion and weathering <u>shape</u> the landscape.

2) Lots of <u>rain</u> makes <u>chalk</u> and <u>limestone</u> vulnerable to <u>carbonation weathering</u> because the rain water is <u>slightly acidic</u>.

3) <u>Prolonged heavy rain</u> causes clay to become heavier, <u>softer</u> and more <u>slippery</u>, making <u>mass movement</u> more <u>likely</u>. During the winter, when there is more <u>rainfall</u>, there are often <u>slides</u> and <u>slumps</u> on the clay cliffs.

Mudslides and rock falls near Kimmeridge

UK Coastal Landscape

Coastal Management Strategies are Protecting Cliffs and Beaches

1) Areas of the <u>Dorset coast</u> are being <u>eroded</u>, putting <u>properties</u> and <u>infrastructure</u> at <u>risk</u>. There is also <u>danger</u> to <u>people</u> from <u>landslides</u> and <u>rockfalls</u>.

2) <u>Coastal management strategies</u> have been used to protect the coastline for roughly the last <u>150 years</u>.

3) These management strategies have helped <u>prevent erosion</u> in some areas, but they have <u>impacted the landscape</u> and caused <u>changes</u> to the natural <u>environment</u>.

Groynes

1) <u>Groynes</u> are <u>wooden</u> or <u>stone fences</u> that are built at <u>right angles</u> to the coast.

2) They <u>trap</u> material transported by <u>longshore drift</u>. This creates <u>wider</u> beaches which <u>slow</u> the waves, giving greater protection from <u>erosion</u>.

3) New timber groynes were put in place along <u>Swanage beach</u> in 2005-6. They've helped to stop the <u>loss</u> of beach material.

4) However, by stopping beach material from moving along the coast, they've <u>starved</u> areas further <u>down</u> the coast of sediment, making them <u>narrower</u>. Narrow beaches don't <u>protect</u> the coast as well, so there may be <u>more</u> erosion.

Sea Walls

1) There are <u>concrete sea walls</u> in place along most of <u>Swanage beach</u>.

2) Sea walls <u>reflect waves</u> back out to sea, <u>preventing</u> the <u>erosion</u> of the coast.

3) But they can create a strong <u>backwash</u>, which <u>removes</u> <u>sediment</u> from the beach and can erode <u>under</u> the wall.

4) They also <u>prevent</u> the cliffs from being <u>eroded</u>, so there's no new material to <u>replenish</u> the beach. This will gradually <u>lower</u> the <u>level</u> of the beach.

Beach Replenishment

1) In <u>winter 2005/2006</u>, <u>sand</u> and <u>shingle</u> dredged from the sea bed at <u>Poole Harbour</u> was added to the upper parts of <u>Swanage</u> beach.

2) This has created <u>wider</u> beaches, which slow the waves and help protect <u>cliffs</u> and <u>coastal properties</u> from <u>erosion</u>.

3) However, it cost <u>£5 million</u> to replenish the beach and it will need to be <u>repeated</u> roughly <u>every 20 years</u>.

Industry and Tourism are also Shaping the Landscape

1) A lot of <u>quarrying</u> has taken place along the coast because <u>limestone</u> is a valuable building stone. There are a number of quarries on the <u>Isle of Portland</u> and to the <u>west</u> of <u>Chesil Beach</u>. Quarries <u>expose</u> large areas of rock, making them <u>vulnerable</u> to <u>chemical weathering</u> and <u>erosion</u>.

2) Up until the <u>1960s</u>, <u>gravel</u> was removed from <u>Chesil Beach</u> for use in the construction industry. Material was <u>removed</u> from the beach much <u>more quickly</u> than the sea could <u>replenish</u> it, so this began to <u>damage</u> the landform.

3) The Dorset coast attracts large numbers of tourists every year. Coastal footpaths run along the <u>cliff tops</u>, and are gradually <u>worn down</u> as people repeatedly walk on them. <u>Vegetation</u> along the cliff top may be <u>trampled</u> and <u>worn away</u> by repeated use of the footpaths. This can expose the <u>underlying soil</u> and <u>rock</u> to <u>weathering</u> and <u>erosion</u> by wind and rain.

You might have studied a different coastal landscape in class

You don't have to learn about Dorset if you've studied a different example in class. But before you go on, make sure you know the ins and outs of the landforms, physical processes and human impacts in your chosen area.

Worked Exam Questions

Have a read of these worked answers — they'll give you an idea of what you could write in the exam.

1   Study **Figure 1**, a photograph showing coastal landforms.

Figure 1

1.1   Name the type of landform labelled A in **Figure 1**.

Headland

[1]

1.2   Explain how the landforms shown in **Figure 1** are formed.

Headlands and bays form where there are alternating bands of resistant and less resistant rock along the coast. The less resistant rock is eroded quickly and this forms a bay. The resistant rock is eroded more slowly, forming a headland.

[3]

[Total 4 marks]

2   Study **Figure 2**, a graph showing how the width of a beach varied along its length in the years 2010 and 2015.

Figure 2

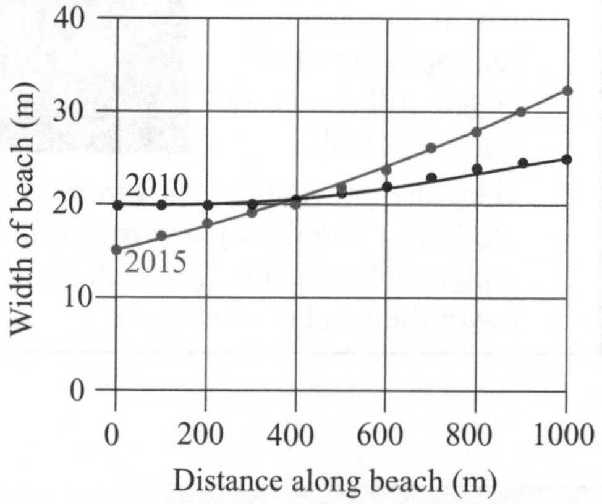

2.1   Name and describe the process of sediment transport that caused these changes in beach width.

The sediment was transported by longshore drift. Waves follow the direction of the prevailing wind, hitting the coast at an oblique angle. The swash carries material up the beach, in the same direction as the waves. The backwash then carries material down the beach at right angles to the beach, back towards the sea. Over time, material zigzags along the coast. The beach becomes narrower where material is transported away and wider where it is deposited.

[4]

2.2   Name the type of wave acting on the stretch of coast shown in **Figure 2**.

Constructive waves

[1]

2.3   Give **two** characteristics of this type of wave.

1: Constructive waves are low frequency.

2: They have a powerful swash.

[2]

[Total 7 marks]

Exam Questions

1   Study **Figure 1**, an Ordnance Survey® map of a coastal area in Devon.

1.1   The end of the spit is marked X on **Figure 1**. Give the six figure grid reference for the end of the spit.

....

[1]

1.2   What is the distance between the end of the spit and Dawlish Warren station at 979786?

> You'll need to use a ruler and the scale at the bottom of Figure 1 to work this out.

.... km

[1]

1.3   Explain how the spit shown in **Figure 1** was formed.

....

....

....

....

[2]

[Total 4 marks]

Figure 1

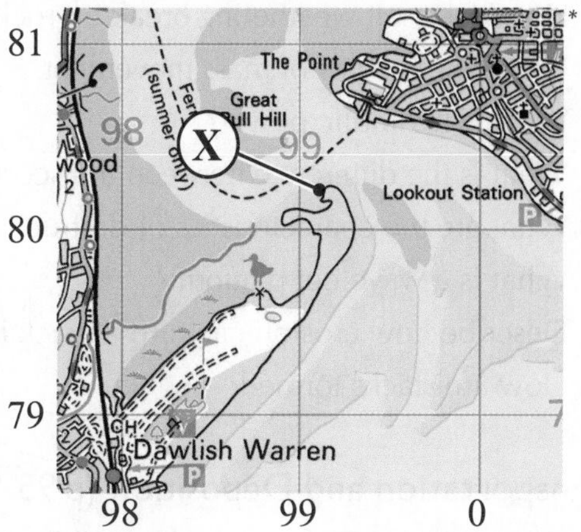

2 centimetres to 1 kilometre (one grid square)

Kilometres

0   1   2

2   Study **Figure 2**, a news article about coastal defences in Cliffall, a UK coastal town.

Figure 2

HOPE FOR CLIFFALL'S COASTLINE

Work is due to start next week on new defences for the Cliffall coastline. The town has been suffering from the effects of coastal erosion over the last few years but it's hoped the new defences will prevent further problems. The scheme will use a combination of defences, including groynes, dune regeneration and beach nourishment. The work will be completed gradually over the next four years, with the groynes the top priority.

2.1   Describe **one** soft engineering strategy mentioned in **Figure 2**.

....

....

[1]

2.2   Give **one** advantage and **one** disadvantage of this soft engineering strategy.

Advantage:...

Disadvantage:...

[2]

[Total 3 marks]

Revision Summary

That wraps up <u>UK Coastal Landscapes</u> — time to test yourself and find out how much you really know.
- Try these questions and <u>tick off each one</u> when you <u>get it right</u>.
- When you've done <u>all the questions</u> for a topic and are <u>completely happy</u> with it, tick off the topic.

Weathering and Erosion (p.92-94) ☑

1) How does salt weathering break up rock? ☑
2) Name three types of mass movement. ☑
3) What is hydraulic power? ☑
4) What is the difference between a discordant and a concordant coastline? ☑
5) What are the characteristics of destructive waves? ☑
6) What is a wave-cut platform? ☑
7) Describe how erosion can turn a crack in a cliff into a cave. ☑
8) How are stacks formed? ☑

Transportation and Deposition (p.95-96) ☑

9) What is the main factor in determining the direction of longshore drift along a coast? ☑
10) Apart from longshore drift, what are the four other processes of transportation? ☑
11) a) When does deposition occur? ☑
    b) What can increase the amount of material that is deposited? ☑
12) What are the characteristics of shingle beaches? ☑
13) Where do spits form? ☑
14) How do bars form? ☑

Identifying Coastal Landforms (p.97) ☑

15) Why can't cracks, caves and arches be seen on a map? ☑
16) What do stacks look like on a map? ☑
17) How are cliffs shown on a map? ☑
18) On maps, what do speckles on top of yellow shading tell you? ☑

Human Activity and Coastal Management (p.98-100) ☑

19) Explain how agriculture can have a direct effect on the coast. ☑
20) How does development affect the coast? ☑
21) Give one effect of coastal management on the coastline. ☑
22) Why does sea level rise increase the risk of coastal flooding? ☑
23) Give two threats of coastal flooding to the environment. ☑
24) What is the difference between hard and soft engineering? Give an example of each. ☑
25) What are the possible disadvantages of using groynes for coastal management? ☑
26) What is managed retreat? ☑

UK Coastal Landscape (p. 101-103) ☑

27) For a UK coastline you have studied, name one erosional landform and one depositional landform. ☑
28) a) For a named coastline, describe the climate of the region. ☑
    b) Explain how geology and climate have influenced the formation of one landform found there. ☑
29) a) For a named UK coastline, explain why coastal management is needed. ☑
    b) Give examples of potential conflicts caused by coastal management along this coastline. ☑

The River Valley

The shape of a river valley and a river's gradient change as the river flows downhill.

A River's **Long Profile** and **Cross Profile Vary** Over its Course

1) The path of a river as it flows downhill is called its course.

2) Rivers have an upper course (closest to the source of the river),
   a middle course and a lower course (closest to the mouth of the river).

3) Rivers form channels and valleys as they flow downhill.

4) They erode the landscape — wear it down, then transport
   the material to somewhere else where it's deposited.

5) The shape of the valley and channel changes along the river depending on
   whether erosion or deposition is having the most impact (is the dominant process).

6) The long profile of a river shows you how the gradient (steepness) changes over the different courses.

7) The cross profile shows you what a cross-section of the river looks like.

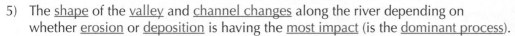

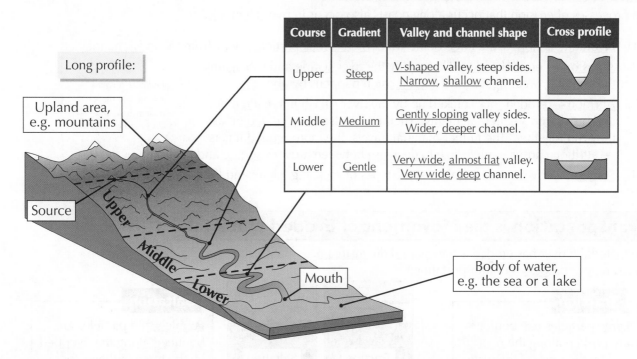

Course	Gradient	Valley and channel shape	Cross profile
Upper	Steep	V-shaped valley, steep sides. Narrow, shallow channel.	
Middle	Medium	Gently sloping valley sides. Wider, deeper channel.	
Lower	Gentle	Very wide, almost flat valley. Very wide, deep channel.	

Vertical and **Lateral Erosion** Change the **Cross Profile** of a River

Erosion can be vertical or lateral — both types happen at the same time,
but one is usually dominant over the other at different points along the river:

There's more on the processes of erosion on the next page.

Vertical erosion

This deepens the river valley (and channel),
making it V-shaped. It's dominant in the
upper course of the river. High turbulence
causes the rough, angular particles to be
scraped along the river bed, causing intense
downwards erosion.

Lateral erosion

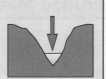

This widens the river valley
(and channel) during the
formation of meanders (see page 110).
It's dominant in the middle and lower courses.

REVISION TIP

Long profile = gradient, cross profile = a cross-section of the river

Try sketching the cross profile diagrams and describing the shape of the valley and channel, just to check
you've got it all memorised. Make sure you learn where vertical and lateral erosion are more dominant.

River Processes

As rivers flow, they erode material, transport it and then deposit it further downstream.

Weathering Helps Shape River Valleys

Weathering breaks down rocks on the valley sides.
Freeze-thaw weathering is a type of mechanical weathering (see p.92):

1) Freeze-thaw weathering happens when the temperature alternates above and below 0 °C (the freezing point of water).

Chemical and biological weathering also affect river valleys.

2) Water gets into rock that has cracks, e.g. granite. When the water freezes it expands, which puts pressure on the rock. When the water thaws it contracts, which releases the pressure on the rock.

3) Repeated freezing and thawing widens the cracks and causes the rock to break up.

There are Four Processes of Erosion

The processes of erosion that occur along coasts also occur in river channels:

1) Hydraulic action — the force of the water breaks rock particles away from the river channel.

2) Abrasion — eroded rocks picked up by the river scrape and rub against the channel, wearing it away. Most erosion happens by abrasion.

The faster a river's flowing, the more erosion happens.

3) Attrition — eroded rocks picked up by the river smash into each other and break into smaller fragments. Their edges also get rounded off as they rub together. The further material travels, the more eroded it gets — attrition causes particle size to decrease between a river's source and its mouth.

4) Solution — river water dissolves some types of rock, e.g. chalk and limestone.

Transportation is the Movement of Eroded Material

The material a river has eroded is transported downstream.
There are four processes of transportation:

Traction
Large particles like boulders are pushed along the river bed by the force of the water.

Suspension
Small particles like silt and clay are carried along by the water.

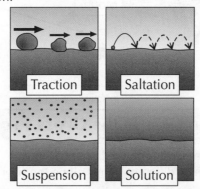

Traction Saltation

Suspension Solution

Saltation
Pebble-sized particles are bounced along the river bed by the force of the water.

Solution
Soluble materials dissolve in the water and are carried along.

Deposition is When a River Drops Eroded Material

Deposition is when a river drops the eroded material it's transporting.

It happens when a river slows down (loses velocity).

There are a few reasons why rivers slow down and deposit material:

1) The volume of water in the river falls.
2) The amount of eroded material in the water increases.
3) The water is shallower, e.g. on the inside of a bend.
4) The river reaches its mouth.

Learn the four processes of erosion and the four processes of transportation

There are lots of very similar names to remember here — try not to confuse saltation, solution and suspension. And yes, solution is both a process of erosion and transportation. Get them fixed in your head before moving on.

River Landforms — Erosion

The <u>processes</u> of erosion on the previous page <u>change the landscape</u> and create <u>distinctive landforms</u>. Now's your chance to find out all about them, starting with <u>waterfalls</u>...

Waterfalls and Gorges are Found in the Upper Course of a River

1) <u>Waterfalls</u> form where a river flows over an area of <u>hard rock</u> followed by an area of <u>softer rock</u>.

2) The <u>softer rock</u> is <u>eroded</u> (by <u>hydraulic action</u> and <u>abrasion</u>) <u>more</u> than the <u>hard rock</u>, creating a 'step' in the river.

3) As water goes over the step it <u>erodes more and more</u> of the softer rock.

4) A <u>steep drop</u> is eventually created, which is called a <u>waterfall</u>.

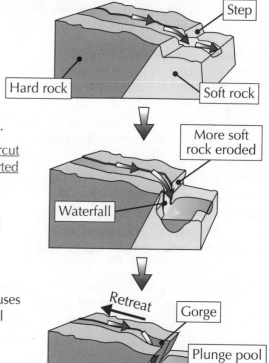

5) The <u>hard rock</u> is eventually <u>undercut</u> by erosion. It becomes <u>unsupported</u> and <u>collapses</u>.

6) The collapsed rocks are <u>swirled around</u> at the foot of the waterfall where they <u>erode</u> the softer rock by <u>abrasion</u> (see previous page). This creates a deep <u>plunge pool</u>.

7) Over time, <u>more undercutting</u> causes <u>more collapses</u>. The waterfall will <u>retreat</u> (move back up the channel), leaving behind a steep-sided <u>gorge</u>.

Some Rivers Wind around Interlocking Spurs

1) In the <u>upper course</u> of a river most of the <u>erosion</u> is <u>vertically downwards</u>. This creates <u>steep-sided</u>, <u>V-shaped valleys</u>.

2) The rivers <u>aren't powerful enough</u> to <u>erode laterally</u> (sideways) — they have to <u>wind around</u> the <u>high hillsides</u> that stick out into their paths on either side.

3) The <u>hillsides that interlock</u> with each other (like a zip if you were looking from above) as the river winds around them are called <u>interlocking spurs</u>.

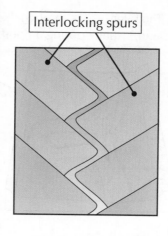

Interlocking spurs along a river in Shropshire

Waterfalls, gorges and interlocking spurs are landforms resulting from erosion

Step over the hard rock and plunge into the pool — that's how I remember how waterfalls are formed. Geography examiners love river landforms (they're a bit weird like that) so make sure you learn how they form.

River Landforms — Erosion and Deposition

When a river's <u>eroding</u> and <u>depositing</u> material, <u>meanders</u> and <u>ox-bow lakes</u> can form.

Meanders are Formed by **Erosion** and **Deposition**

Rivers develop <u>large bends</u> called <u>meanders</u> in their <u>middle</u> and <u>lower courses</u>, in areas where there are both <u>shallow</u> and <u>deep</u> sections in the channel:

1) The <u>current</u> (the flow of the water) is <u>faster</u> on the <u>outside</u> of the bend because the river channel is <u>deeper</u> (there's <u>less friction</u> to <u>slow</u> the water down).

2) So more <u>erosion</u> takes place on the <u>outside</u> of the bend, forming <u>river cliffs</u>.

3) The <u>current</u> is <u>slower</u> on the <u>inside</u> of the bend because the river channel is <u>shallower</u> (there's <u>more friction</u> to <u>slow</u> the water down).

4) So eroded material is <u>deposited</u> on the <u>inside</u> of the bend, forming <u>slip-off slopes</u>.

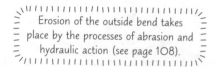

Erosion of the outside bend takes place by the processes of abrasion and hydraulic action (see page 108).

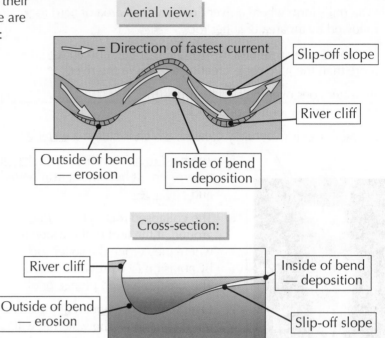

Aerial view:

⇒ = Direction of fastest current

Slip-off slope

River cliff

Outside of bend — erosion

Inside of bend — deposition

Cross-section:

River cliff

Outside of bend — erosion

Inside of bend — deposition

Slip-off slope

Ox-Bow Lakes are Formed from **Meanders**

Meanders get <u>larger</u> over time — they can eventually turn into an <u>ox-bow lake</u>:

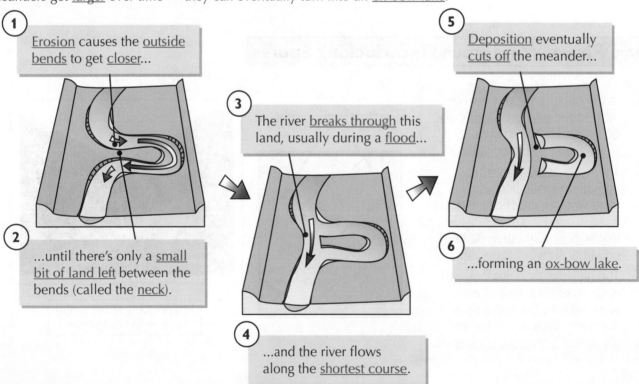

1 <u>Erosion</u> causes the <u>outside bends</u> to get <u>closer</u>...

2 ...until there's only a <u>small bit of land left</u> between the bends (called the <u>neck</u>).

3 The river <u>breaks through</u> this land, usually during a <u>flood</u>...

4 ...and the river flows along the <u>shortest course</u>.

5 <u>Deposition</u> eventually <u>cuts off</u> the meander...

6 ...forming an <u>ox-bow lake</u>.

EXAM TIP

The features of meanders are formed by erosion and deposition

In the exam, don't be afraid to draw diagrams of river landforms — examiners love a good diagram and they can help make your answer clear. Don't spend forever making them into works of art though...

River Landforms — Deposition

When rivers <u>flow fast</u>, they <u>erode</u> the landscape. As they <u>slow down</u>, they make <u>landforms</u> through <u>deposition</u>.

Flood Plains are Flat Areas of Land that Flood

1) The <u>flood plain</u> is the <u>wide valley floor</u> on either side of a river, which regularly <u>floods</u>.

2) When a river <u>floods</u> onto the flood plain, the water <u>slows down</u> and <u>deposits eroded material</u>. This <u>builds up</u> the flood plain.

3) <u>Meanders migrate</u> (move) <u>across</u> the flood plain, making it <u>wider</u>.

4) Meanders also migrate <u>downstream</u>, <u>flattening</u> out the valley floor.

Flood plain

Levees are Natural Embankments

1) Levees are <u>natural embankments</u> (raised bits) along the <u>edges</u> of a <u>river channel</u>.

2) During a flood, <u>eroded material</u> is <u>deposited</u> over the whole flood plain.

3) The <u>heaviest material</u> is <u>deposited closest</u> to the channel, because it gets <u>dropped first</u> when the river <u>slows down</u>.

4) <u>Over time</u>, the <u>deposited material builds up</u>, creating <u>levees</u> along the edges of the channel.

All these landforms are found in the lower course of a river.

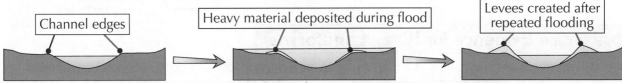

Channel edges

Heavy material deposited during flood

Levees created after repeated flooding

Estuaries and Deltas can Form Where a River Meets the Sea

Deltas

1) Rivers are forced to <u>slow down</u> when they <u>meet the sea</u> or a <u>lake</u>. This causes them to <u>deposit</u> the <u>material</u> that they're carrying.

2) If the <u>sea doesn't wash away</u> the <u>material</u>, it <u>builds up</u> and the <u>channel gets blocked</u>. This forces the channel to <u>split up</u> into lots of <u>smaller rivers</u> called <u>distributaries</u>.

3) Eventually the material <u>builds up so much</u> that <u>low-lying areas of land</u> called <u>deltas</u> are <u>formed</u>.

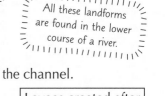

Estuaries

1) <u>Estuaries</u> are found at the <u>mouth</u> of a river, where it meets the <u>sea</u>. The water here is <u>tidal</u> — the river level <u>rises</u> and <u>falls</u> each day.

2) The water <u>floods</u> over the <u>banks</u> of the river carrying the <u>silt</u> and <u>sand</u> onto the valley floor.

3) As the tide reaches its <u>highest point</u>, the water is moving very <u>slowly</u> so the sediment is <u>deposited</u>.

4) Over time, more and more mud builds up, creating large areas of <u>mudflats</u>.

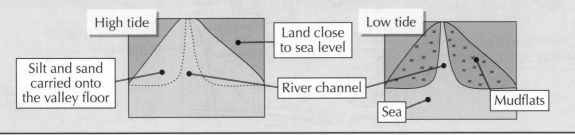

High tide

Silt and sand carried onto the valley floor

Land close to sea level

River channel

Low tide

Sea

Mudflats

Deposition is common in the lower course of a river

As the river slows down in its lower course, material is dropped. This leads to the formation of different landforms. Make sure you know the characteristics of these landforms and you can describe the processes of their formation.

Identifying River Landforms

You can know all the facts about <u>rivers</u>, but if you don't know what their <u>features</u> look like on <u>maps</u> then some of the exam questions could get a wee bit tricky. Here's something I prepared earlier...

Contour Lines Tell you the Direction a River Flows

<u>Contour lines</u> are the <u>orange lines</u> drawn all over maps. They tell you about the <u>height</u> of the land (in metres) by the numbers marked on them, and the <u>steepness</u> of the land by how <u>close together</u> they are (the <u>closer</u> they are, the <u>steeper</u> the slope).

It sounds obvious, but rivers <u>can't</u> flow uphill. Unless gravity's gone screwy, a river flows <u>from higher</u> contour lines <u>to lower</u> ones. Have a look at this map of Cawfell Beck:

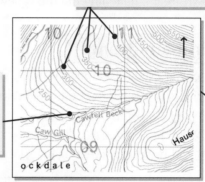

(1) The <u>height values</u> get <u>smaller</u> towards the <u>west</u> (left), so west is <u>downhill</u>.

(2) Cawfell Beck is flowing from <u>east</u> to <u>west</u> (right to left).

(3) A <u>V-shape</u> is formed where the contour lines <u>cross</u> the river. The V-shape is <u>pointing uphill</u> to where the river came from.

Maps contain Evidence for River Landforms

Exam questions might ask you to look at a <u>map</u> and give the <u>evidence</u> for a <u>landform</u>. Remember, different landforms are found in the <u>upper</u> and <u>lower course</u> — you can use this evidence to help you <u>identify</u> them.

Evidence for the Upper Course

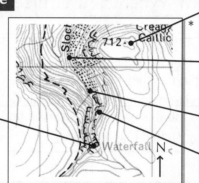

The nearby land is <u>high</u> (712 m).

The river <u>crosses lots</u> of <u>contour lines</u> in a <u>short distance</u>, which means it's <u>steep</u>.

<u>Waterfalls</u> are marked on maps, but the <u>symbol for a cliff</u> (black, blocky lines) and the <u>close contour lines</u> are evidence for an upper-course waterfall.

The river is <u>narrow</u> (a <u>thin</u> blue line).

The <u>contour lines</u> are very <u>close together</u> and the valley floor is narrow. This means the river is in a <u>steep-sided V-shaped</u> valley.

Evidence for the Lower Course

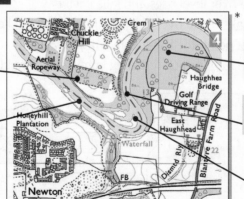

The river meanders across a large flat area (<u>no contours</u>), which is the <u>flood plain</u>.

The nearby land is <u>low</u> (less than 15 m).

The river doesn't <u>cross any contour lines</u> so it's <u>very gently sloping</u>.

The river is <u>wide</u> (a <u>thick</u> blue line).

The river has <u>large meanders</u> and an <u>ox-bow lake</u> may be formed here.

Pay close attention to contour lines, height values and symbols

Map questions can be a goldmine of easy marks — all you have to do is say what you see. You just need to understand what the maps are showing, so read this page carefully, then see if you can remember it all.

UK River Basin

You can see many of the <u>landforms</u> of <u>erosion</u> and <u>deposition</u> from pages 109-111 along the <u>River Eden</u>.

The **River Eden's Landscape Changes** Along its **Course**

1) The River Eden is in <u>north-west England</u>, between the <u>mountains</u> of the <u>Lake District</u> and the <u>Pennines</u>. It's just over <u>140 km long</u> from source to mouth.

2) The River Eden's <u>source</u> is in the Pennine hills in south Cumbria. It flows north-west through <u>Appleby-in-Westmorland</u> and <u>Carlisle</u>. Its mouth is in the <u>Solway Firth</u> at the Scottish border.

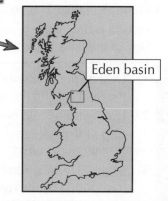

Eden basin

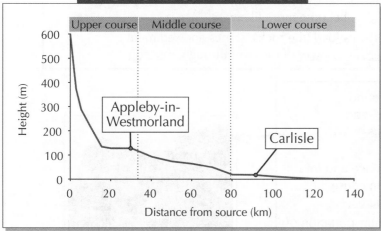

LONG PROFILE OF THE RIVER EDEN

UPPER COURSE

- The <u>source</u> of the Eden is about <u>600 m</u> above sea level in an area of <u>hard</u>, <u>resistant rock</u>.
- The valley is <u>steep-sided</u> due to <u>vertical erosion</u> and the channel has a <u>steep gradient</u>.
- The <u>river channel</u> is <u>narrow</u> and <u>shallow</u> — this means the <u>discharge</u> (see p.116) is <u>low</u>. The <u>velocity</u> (speed) is <u>low</u> due to <u>friction</u> from the <u>rough channel sides</u> and <u>bed</u>.
- The river carries <u>large, angular stones</u>.

River Eden at Appleby

MIDDLE COURSE

- The <u>middle parts</u> of the <u>Eden basin</u> are made from <u>sandstone</u>, a <u>soft</u>, <u>less-resistant rock</u> which is <u>easily eroded</u> by the river. This means that the <u>river valley</u> becomes <u>wider</u> because of <u>lateral</u> (sideways) <u>erosion</u>.

A meander at Salkeld

- The valley sides become <u>gentle slopes</u> and the <u>gradient</u> of the channel is <u>less steep</u>.
- The river channel also becomes <u>wider</u> and <u>deeper</u>. Discharge <u>increases</u> as more <u>streams</u> join the main river.
- The river's <u>sediment load</u> is made up of <u>smaller</u> and <u>more rounded</u> rocks than it was in the <u>upper course</u> as erosion continues (see 108).

LOWER COURSE

- In the lower course, the <u>valley</u> is <u>very wide</u> and <u>flat</u>.

- By the time the Eden reaches <u>Carlisle</u>, it's only <u>a few metres</u> above sea level.

- The river has a <u>high velocity</u> (it's <u>flowing fast</u>) because there's <u>very little friction</u> from the channel's <u>smooth sides</u>. It also has a <u>very large discharge</u> because two other rivers (the Caldew and the Petteril) join the Eden in Carlisle.

- The <u>river channel</u> is <u>very wide</u> and <u>deep</u> — in the centre of Carlisle, the Eden is more than <u>50 m</u> wide. <u>Material</u> carried by the river is <u>fine</u> and <u>well-rounded</u> — most of it is carried by <u>suspension</u> or <u>solution</u> (see p.108).

River Eden at Carlisle

The River Eden is affected by geological changes along its course

Most of the features along the River Eden are caused by changing geology along the basin of the river. Make sure you understand how different rock types are affected by erosion and deposition along a river's course.

CASE STUDY

UK River Basin

Climate and Weather Influence Geomorphic Processes in the Eden Basin...

1) Cumbria is on the <u>west coast</u> of the UK, facing the prevailing <u>south-westerly</u> winds. As a result, Cumbria's <u>climate</u> is <u>mild</u> and <u>wet</u>. The area generally has <u>cool summers</u> and <u>mild winters</u>.

2) Cumbria is one of the <u>wettest</u> parts of the UK, often experiencing periods of <u>intense rainfall</u>. Many of the UK's <u>highest rainfall records</u> were recorded in Cumbria.

Temperature

1) Despite the generally <u>mild winters</u>, temperatures can be <u>much colder</u> on <u>higher ground</u>, such as the land around the <u>source</u> of the River Eden. In winter, this higher ground can <u>regularly freeze</u>.

2) During these cold periods, <u>freeze-thaw weathering</u> can slowly break up the <u>exposed rock</u> of the <u>valley sides</u> in the upper course of the river. If the valley sides are <u>weakened</u>, sudden <u>mass movements</u>, such as <u>landslides</u>, become more likely.

3) <u>Material</u> from landslides is added to the river's <u>load</u> (the rocks, stones and sediment transported by the river), <u>increasing</u> the <u>erosive power</u> of the river through <u>abrasion</u>.

Rainfall

1) During periods of <u>intense rainfall</u>, the ground becomes <u>saturated</u>. This makes it <u>heavier</u> and <u>less stable</u>. This can cause the <u>river banks</u> to slide or <u>slump</u> into the river channel.

2) Heavy rain can <u>flow quickly</u> over the surface and into the river Eden and its tributaries. This can cause the <u>volume</u> of water in the river to <u>rapidly increase</u>.

3) The high volume of water can <u>increase transportation</u> of material by the river, which can cause <u>more erosion</u> by <u>abrasion</u> — particularly in the <u>upper course</u> of the river.

A landslide near Appleby

...and so does the Geology of the Area

1) The <u>harder rocks</u> around the edge of the Eden basin have remained as <u>high ground</u> as they are more <u>resistant</u> to <u>erosion</u>. However, exposed <u>limestone</u> is vulnerable to slow <u>carbonation weathering</u> (p.92).

2) <u>Igneous</u> rocks, such as those found in the west of the Eden basin, tend to be <u>impermeable</u> (i.e. water <u>won't soak</u> into the rock). Because water can't soak into the ground, high rainfall causes lots of <u>surface streams</u> to form, which have a lot of power to erode <u>vertically</u>, creating <u>steep-sided</u> V-shaped valleys.

3) Through the <u>middle</u> and <u>lower courses</u> of the Eden, the river <u>valley</u> is made up of sandstone (a <u>softer</u> rock). The river's increasing volume and <u>energy</u> in its lower course mean that there's lots of <u>lateral</u> (sideways) <u>erosion</u> of the sandstone. This <u>widens</u> the river channel and forms <u>meanders</u> and steep <u>river cliffs</u>.

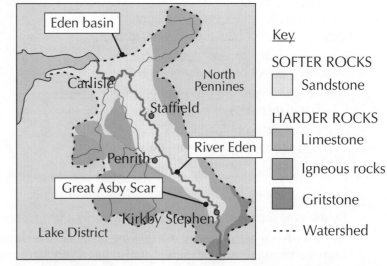

Eden basin

North Pennines

Carlisle

Staffield

River Eden

Penrith

Great Asby Scar

Kirkby Stephen

Lake District

Key

SOFTER ROCKS
☐ Sandstone

HARDER ROCKS
Limestone

Igneous rocks

Gritstone

---- Watershed

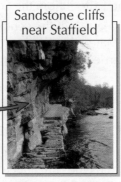
Sandstone cliffs near Staffield

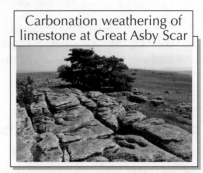
Carbonation weathering of limestone at Great Asby Scar

UK River Basin

The **River Landscape** has been **Altered** by **Management Schemes**

The rivers in the Eden basin have been <u>managed</u> to meet the <u>needs</u> of people in the area. <u>Management strategies</u> have affected the geomorphic processes in the <u>river basin</u>.

Flood Walls & Embankments

1) 10 km of <u>raised flood defences</u> (flood walls and embankments) have been built along the Rivers Eden and Caldew in Carlisle.

2) These are designed to <u>contain</u> the water <u>within</u> the river channel, so that the <u>flood plain</u> can be <u>built on</u>.

3) They <u>interrupt</u> the <u>natural processes</u> of the river and can <u>prevent</u> the <u>natural formation</u> of meanders and the <u>deposition</u> of <u>sediment</u> on the <u>flood plain</u>.

Reservoirs

1) <u>Castle Carrock beck</u> (to the south-east of Carlisle) has been <u>dammed</u> to create a <u>reservoir</u>.

2) Reservoirs limit the <u>natural flow</u> of water downstream. Material carried by the river is <u>deposited</u> in the reservoir and not along the river's <u>natural course</u>. This can increase erosion <u>downstream</u>, and <u>reduce</u> the <u>natural buildup</u> of the flood plain in the lower course of the river.

Planting Trees

1) Near Dalston (south of Carlisle), the landscape has been changed by the planting of <u>1000 trees</u> to <u>reduce flooding</u> and also to <u>reduce erosion</u> by stabilising the soil.

2) Trees <u>intercept rainfall</u> and reduce <u>surface runoff</u>. This <u>prevents</u> rapid <u>increases</u> in the <u>volume</u> of water in the river because it takes longer for water to reach the river channel.

3) As a result, the river will have <u>less energy</u>, reducing <u>lateral</u> and <u>vertical erosion</u>, meaning that <u>meanders</u> may take longer to form.

Channel Management

1) In the past, the river landscape in the Eden basin was changed by <u>channel straightening</u>. Many sections of river were <u>diverted</u> into <u>artificial channels</u> to try to <u>reduce</u> flooding.

2) Channel straightening makes the water flow more <u>quickly</u> than it naturally would, which can <u>increase erosion</u> and <u>decrease deposition</u>. In the <u>artificial channel</u>, conditions <u>aren't right</u> for <u>meanders</u> to form as they normally would — so the <u>natural</u> river landscape is changed.

3) More <u>recently</u>, some areas of the Eden basin have been <u>restored</u> to their original state by having <u>artificial meanders</u> put <u>in</u>, e.g. on the River Lyvennet to the south-west of Appleby.

4) The meanders <u>slow</u> the river's flow, <u>increasing deposition</u>. This <u>encourages</u> the river to begin to <u>meander</u> more naturally, and allows the natural build-up of the <u>flood plain</u>.

Human Activity on the Land also affects **Geomorphic Processes**

1) <u>Deforestation</u> — <u>Natural woodland</u> and <u>heathland</u> have been <u>cleared</u> from many upland areas in the Eden basin. This <u>increases</u> surface <u>runoff</u> when it rains, and means that <u>more water</u> ends up in river channels <u>more quickly</u>. This increase in volume gives rivers more <u>energy</u> for <u>erosion</u>, and can cause <u>sliding</u> and <u>slumping</u> of the river banks.

2) <u>Farming</u> — Some upland areas have been <u>drained</u> of moisture to make them more suitable for farming. This reduces the <u>stability</u> of the soil, meaning that <u>more soil</u> is washed into the river channel by rain. The <u>increased load</u> of the river increases <u>deposition downstream</u>, changing the <u>flood plain landscape</u> from its natural state.

River basins are influenced by both physical and human processes

Whether you choose this river basin or a different one you've studied, make sure you know the landforms in the basin, and understand how geology, climate and human activity influence the processes that impact the landscape.

River Discharge and Flooding

We've not really talked much about the actual water in a river. Well, all that's about to change — hooray.

River Discharge is the Volume of Water Flowing in a River

River discharge is just the volume of water that flows in a river per second. It's measured in cumecs — cubic metres per second (m^3/s). Hydrographs show how the discharge at a certain point in a river changes over time in relation to rainfall:

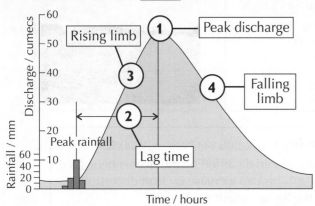

1. Peak discharge: The highest discharge in the period of time you're looking at.
2. Lag time: The delay between peak rainfall and peak discharge.
3. Rising limb: The increase in river discharge as rainwater flows into the river.
4. Falling limb: The decrease in river discharge as the river returns to its normal level.

Lag time happens because most rainwater doesn't land directly in the river channel — there's a delay as rainwater gets to the channel. It gets there by flowing quickly overland (called surface runoff, or just runoff), or by soaking into the ground (called infiltration) and flowing slowly underground.

Rivers Flood due to Physical and Human Factors

Flooding happens when the level of a river gets so high that it spills over its banks. The river level increases when the discharge increases because a high discharge means there's more water in the channel. This means the factors that increase discharge can cause flooding:

Prolonged Rainfall

After a long period of rain, the soil becomes saturated. Any further rainfall can't infiltrate, which increases runoff into rivers. This increases discharge quickly, so flooding is more likely.

Heavy Rainfall

Heavy rainfall means the water arrives too rapidly for infiltration, so there's a lot of runoff. This increases discharge quickly, increasing the risk of a flood.

Geology (rock type)

Clay soils and some rocks, e.g. granite and shale, are impermeable (i.e. they don't allow infiltration) so runoff is increased. When it rains, discharge increases quickly, which can cause a flood.

Relief (change in the height of the land)

If a river is in a steep-sided valley, water will reach the river channel much faster because water flows more quickly on steeper slopes. Discharge increases rapidly, increasing the flood risk.

Changing the land use, e.g. by building on it or removing trees, can also increase the flood risk.

Land use

1) Buildings are often made from impermeable materials, e.g. concrete, and they're surrounded by roads made from tarmac (also impermeable). Impermeable surfaces increase runoff and drains quickly take runoff to rivers — discharge increases quickly, so there's a greater risk of flooding.

2) Trees intercept rainwater on their leaves, which then evaporates. Trees also take up water from the ground and store it. This means cutting down trees increases the volume of water that reaches the river channel, which increases discharge and makes flooding more likely.

You get lag time because rainwater doesn't fall directly into the river channel

Hydrographs are a good way of showing the changes in river discharge when there is a storm or lots of rainfall. There are lots of factors that affect peak discharge and lag time, which can increase the risk of flooding.

UK River Flooding

Here's a <u>case study</u> about a <u>flood</u> that occurred in the <u>north west</u> of <u>England</u> back in <u>December 2015</u>. <u>Extremely wet weather</u> brought way <u>too much water</u> for the river channels to cope with.

The Flood was **Caused** by **Prolonged** and **Heavy** Rainfall

On <u>5th</u> and <u>6th December 2015</u>, Storm Desmond caused widespread <u>flooding</u> across <u>Cumbria</u>, including severe flooding in Carlisle, Keswick, Appleby and Glenridding. Flooding occurred because of a <u>combination</u> of <u>factors</u>:

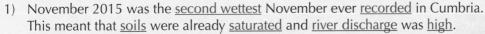

1) November 2015 was the <u>second wettest</u> November ever <u>recorded</u> in Cumbria. This meant that <u>soils</u> were already <u>saturated</u> and <u>river discharge</u> was <u>high</u>.

2) Storm <u>Desmond</u> was a <u>very low pressure system</u> that arrived in Cumbria on 5th December. It caused <u>extremely heavy rainfall</u> — more than <u>300 mm</u> fell across the Cumbrian hills in <u>24 hours</u>. This was the <u>highest rainfall</u> ever recorded in UK and <u>more</u> than many places in the UK <u>normally</u> receive in a whole <u>month</u>.

3) Carlisle, Keswick and Appleby are <u>built-up areas</u> and there has been lots of <u>development</u> on the <u>flood plain</u>. This has affected the flood plain's ability to <u>absorb</u> and <u>store flood water</u>. The lack of <u>soil</u> or <u>vegetation</u> meant there was <u>little infiltration</u> of rainfall, which led to <u>high surface runoff</u>.

4) <u>Natural woodland</u> and <u>heathland</u> have been <u>cleared</u> from many upland areas in the region. This <u>increased</u> surface <u>runoff</u> when it rained, and meant that <u>water</u> ended up in the river channel <u>more quickly</u>.

The **Flooding** Affected **Both People** and the **Environment**

Effects on People

1) 1 person <u>died</u> in Kendal.
2) Several thousand <u>homes</u> and <u>businesses</u> were <u>flooded</u>. Thousands of <u>jobs</u> were put at <u>risk</u> in businesses affected by the floods.
3) More than <u>30 schools</u> and a number of <u>hospitals closed</u>.
4) <u>Roads</u> and <u>railways</u> were <u>damaged</u>, including the <u>West Coast Main Line</u>, the main rail link between London and Glasgow. The <u>road</u> between <u>Grasmere</u> and <u>Keswick</u> was closed for <u>5 months</u>.
5) <u>3 bridges</u> were swept away and others were <u>damaged</u>, cutting off access to some areas.
6) <u>Electrical sub-stations</u> were flooded — thousands of homes were without <u>power</u> for <u>several days</u>.

Effects on the Environment

1) Rivers were <u>polluted</u> with <u>rubbish</u> and <u>sewage</u>.
2) <u>Mudslides</u> and <u>landslides</u> were <u>triggered</u> — a big landslide occurred near <u>Glenridding</u>.
3) <u>1000 sheep</u> and <u>cattle</u> were <u>washed downstream</u>.
4) Large <u>boulders</u> were washed downstream into <u>Glenridding</u>.
5) <u>Trees</u> were <u>torn</u> from <u>river banks</u> by the flood water.
6) <u>Debris</u> was strewn across the <u>flood plain</u> and caught in the <u>trees</u>.
7) Lots of <u>silt</u> and <u>sediment</u> was <u>deposited</u> as the water <u>receded</u>, ruining farmland.

The Cumbrian floods were made worse by development on flood plains

Remember, it's normally a combination of natural and human processes that leads to river flooding. And don't forget the threats to the environment from flooding — it's not just people who suffer the effects. Next up, management...

UK River Flooding

The impacts of the floods were pretty devastating, but fortunately local and national management schemes helped to reduce the impacts of flooding on local communities and the environment.

The Flood was **Managed** in a **Variety** of **Ways**

1) People responded to the Cumbrian floods on a variety of scales — locally, regionally and at a national level.

2) The management of the flood event also occurred at a range of time-scales, from the immediate responses to longer-term rebuilding. There is also ongoing work to try and prevent future flooding.

Local-Scale Management

1) Local community guest houses and cafés offered places to stay and provided free food to rescue workers and those that had to leave their homes.

2) The British Red Cross set up rest centres in Keswick, Appleby and Kendal for people evacuated from their homes.

3) Members of Carlisle United football club helped people to clean up after the flood water went down.

4) Local farmers helped the council to clear away the debris with their tractors and trailers.

5) A community group was founded in Glenridding to oversee the clear-up and repairs from the flood damage. They are also trying to plan for future extreme weather events and prevent future flooding.

Wider-Scale Management

1) Storm Desmond was tracked as it approached the UK across the Atlantic. Flood warnings and alerts were issued by the Met Office giving people in Cumbria some time to prepare.

2) Once the flooding began, the Prime Minister called an emergency meeting to decide how to manage the response to the flood.

3) The government organised a full national emergency response — 200 people from the military were brought in, along with military helicopters. Fire and rescue workers came to help from surrounding areas of the country.

4) The Environment Agency brought in people and resources from other parts of the country to help deal with the flooding.

5) Engineers worked to restore power, using generators to provide temporary power while the main sub-stations were still underwater.

6) The Princes' Countryside Fund gave £40 000 to help rural people recover from the damage caused by the flooding.

7) The public donated £400 000 within 48 hours in response to a relief appeal.

8) The government provided a £50 million 'Repair and Renew' scheme offering up to £5000 to homeowners and businesses to protect their homes against future flood damage.

9) In summer 2016 the Environment Agency published a 'Cumbria Action Plan'. This plan contains strategies to improve protection from future flooding in Cumbria and to reduce surface runoff in upland areas of the region. A lot of this work is still being done, so nobody knows yet how well it will work.

REVISION TIP

Providing help and relief after a flood is part of flood management

These aren't the only examples of flood management schemes (see pages 115 and 121-122 for more). This page show how the Cumbrian floods were managed in the short term. Try drawing yourself a map of the area, then adding notes and pictures to show how people responded to help you remember it all.

Hard vs Soft Engineering

Floods can be <u>devastating</u>, but there are a number of different <u>strategies</u> to stop them or lessen the blow.

Strategies can be classed as Hard Engineering or Soft Engineering

There's <u>debate</u> about <u>which strategies are best</u>, so you'll need to know the <u>benefits</u> and <u>costs</u> of a few of them.

Hard Engineering Strategies can Reduce the Risk of Flooding Occurring

Hard Engineering

<u>Man-made structures</u> built to <u>control the flow</u> of rivers and <u>reduce flooding</u>.

Method	What it is	Benefits	Disadvantages
Dams and reservoirs	<u>Dams</u> (huge walls) are built <u>across</u> the rivers, usually in the <u>upper course</u>. A <u>reservoir</u> (artificial lake) is formed <u>behind</u> the dam.	Reservoirs <u>store water</u>, especially during periods of prolonged or heavy rain, <u>reducing</u> the <u>risk of flooding</u>. The water in the reservoir can be used as <u>drinking water</u> and to <u>generate hydroelectric power</u> (HEP).	Dams are <u>very expensive</u> to build. Creating a reservoir can <u>flood existing settlements</u>. Eroded material is <u>deposited</u> in the <u>reservoir</u> and <u>not</u> along the river's <u>natural course</u> so <u>farmland</u> downstream can become <u>less fertile</u>.
Channel straightening	The river's <u>course</u> is <u>straightened</u> — <u>meanders</u> are <u>cut out</u> by building <u>artificial straight channels</u>.	Water moves out of the area <u>more quickly</u> because it doesn't travel as far — <u>reducing</u> the <u>risk</u> of flooding.	<u>Flooding</u> may happen <u>downstream</u> instead, as water is <u>carried there faster</u>. There's <u>more erosion downstream</u> because the water's <u>flowing faster</u>.
Embankments/ Flood walls	<u>Raised walls</u> are built <u>along</u> the river banks.	The river can hold <u>more water</u> so it will flood <u>less frequently</u>, protecting buildings on the flood plain.	They're quite <u>expensive</u> and there's a risk of <u>severe flooding</u> if the water rises <u>above</u> the level of the embankments or if they <u>break</u>.
Flood relief channels	<u>Channels</u> are built that <u>divert</u> the water around important areas or take it elsewhere if the water level in the river gets <u>too high</u>.	Flooding is prevented because <u>river discharge</u> is <u>reduced</u>. <u>Gates</u> on the flood relief channels mean that the <u>release</u> of water can be <u>controlled</u>.	There will be <u>increased discharge</u> where the relief channel rejoins the river (or joins another river) which could cause <u>flooding</u> in that area. If the water level gets <u>too high</u> for the <u>relief channels</u> they could also <u>flood</u>.

Make sure you know the disadvantages as well as the benefits of each strategy

Flooding can be a nightmare. But, as luck would have it, there are plenty of strategies to reduce the impacts. Hard engineering usually provides a long-term solution to flooding, but can be very expensive.

Hard vs Soft Engineering

The table on the previous page gives some of the <u>disadvantages</u> of <u>hard engineering</u> strategies. Because of these drawbacks, <u>soft engineering</u> strategies can sometimes be a <u>better solution</u>.

Soft Engineering Strategies can Reduce the Effects of Flooding

Soft Engineering

Schemes set up using <u>knowledge</u> of a <u>river</u> and its <u>processes</u> to <u>reduce the effects of flooding</u>.

Method	What it is	Benefits	Disadvantages
Flood warnings	The <u>Environment Agency</u> warns people about possible flooding through <u>TV</u>, <u>radio</u>, <u>newspapers</u> and the <u>internet</u>.	The <u>impact</u> of flooding is <u>reduced</u> — warnings give people time to <u>move possessions upstairs</u>, put <u>sandbags</u> in position and to <u>evacuate</u>.	Warnings <u>don't stop</u> a <u>flood</u> from happening. People may <u>not</u> hear or have <u>access</u> to the <u>warnings</u>.
Preparation	Buildings are <u>modified</u> to <u>reduce</u> the amount of <u>damage</u> a flood could cause. People make <u>plans</u> for what to do in a flood — they keep items like <u>torches</u> and <u>blankets</u> in a <u>handy place</u>.	The <u>impact</u> of flooding is <u>reduced</u> — <u>buildings</u> are <u>less damaged</u> and people <u>know what to do</u> when a flood happens. People are also <u>less likely to worry</u> about the threat of floods.	Preparation <u>doesn't guarantee safety</u> from a flood and it could give people a <u>false sense of security</u>. It's <u>expensive</u> to modify homes and businesses.
Flood plain zoning	Restrictions <u>prevent building</u> on parts of a flood plain that are <u>likely to be affected</u> by a flood.	The <u>risk of flooding</u> is <u>reduced</u> — <u>impermeable surfaces aren't created</u>, e.g. buildings and roads. The <u>impact</u> of flooding is also <u>reduced</u> — there aren't any buildings to damage.	The <u>expansion</u> of an <u>urban area</u> is <u>limited</u> if there aren't any other suitable building sites. It's no help in areas that have <u>already been built on</u>.
Planting trees	Planting trees in the river valley <u>increases interception</u> of rainwater and also increases the <u>lag time</u>.	<u>Discharge</u> and <u>flood risk</u> are <u>reduced</u>. Vegetation <u>reduces soil erosion</u> in the valley and provides <u>habitats</u> for <u>wildlife</u>.	<u>Less land</u> is available for <u>farming</u>.
River restoration	River restoration involves making the river <u>more natural</u>, e.g. by removing man made levees, so that the <u>flood plain</u> can <u>flood naturally</u>.	There is <u>less risk</u> of <u>flooding downstream</u> because <u>discharge</u> is <u>reduced</u>. <u>Little maintenance</u> is needed as the river is left in its natural state and there are <u>better habitats</u> for <u>wildlife</u>.	<u>Local flood risk</u> can <u>increase</u>, especially if nothing's done to prevent major flooding.

Another big table of costs and benefits to learn

Soft engineering strategies work with the river's natural processes, so they tend to be more environmentally friendly than hard engineering strategies. They do have drawbacks though — a big one is that they may not prevent flooding.

Flood Management

Time for a real-world <u>example</u> of <u>flood management</u>, and it's off to Cornwall...

Severe Flash Floods showed the need for Flood Defences in Boscastle

1) The village of <u>Boscastle</u> on the north coast of <u>Cornwall</u> was devastated by a <u>flash flood</u> on 16th August 2004, which caused <u>millions of pounds</u> worth of <u>damage</u>. Despite being <u>vulnerable to flash flooding</u>, it had <u>no modern</u> flood defences.

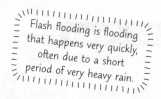

Flash flooding is flooding that happens very quickly, often due to a short period of very heavy rain.

2) The village is surrounded by <u>steep valley sides</u>, and land <u>upstream</u> of the village has been <u>cleared</u> of <u>trees and vegetation</u>. This <u>increases</u> surface <u>runoff</u> and means that during periods of heavy rain, river <u>discharge increases quickly</u>.

Steep sides

Narrow channel

3) The <u>old bridge</u> in the village had a <u>low arch</u> over a very <u>narrow river channel</u>. The flooding in 2004 was <u>made worse</u> because trees and vehicles in the floodwater became <u>trapped</u> under the bridge, forming a <u>dam</u>.

4) The village is a popular <u>tourist destination</u> and <u>90%</u> of the local economy <u>relied on tourism</u>. After 2004, the number of tourists <u>dropped</u> significantly, increasing the <u>demand for protection</u> against future floods.

A Flood Management Scheme is Now in Place

A <u>flood management scheme</u> for Boscastle was completed in <u>2008</u>. It includes both <u>hard</u> and <u>soft</u> engineering strategies...

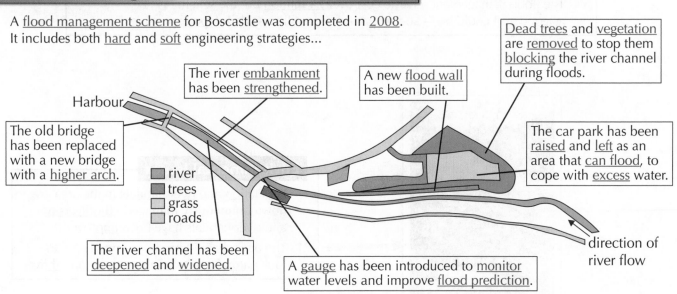

The river <u>embankment</u> has been <u>strengthened</u>.

A new <u>flood wall</u> has been built.

<u>Dead trees</u> and <u>vegetation</u> are <u>removed</u> to stop them <u>blocking</u> the river channel during floods.

Harbour

The old bridge has been replaced with a new bridge with a <u>higher arch</u>.

The car park has been <u>raised</u> and <u>left</u> as an area that <u>can flood</u>, to cope with <u>excess</u> water.

river
trees
grass
roads

The river channel has been <u>deepened</u> and <u>widened</u>.

A <u>gauge</u> has been introduced to <u>monitor</u> water levels and improve <u>flood prediction</u>.

direction of river flow

The devastating floods in 2004 showed the need for management in Boscastle

Whether you've studied Boscastle or a different flood management scheme in the UK, make sure you know details of why the scheme was needed and what the management strategy was. Then move on to the next page...

Flood Management

On the whole, the <u>flood management scheme</u> in Boscastle has been a <u>success</u>, but there are still some <u>issues</u> with it...

The Scheme has **Social, Economic** and **Environmental** Issues

Social Issues

1) Residents' lives were <u>disrupted</u> for years by <u>rebuilding projects</u> and the construction of flood <u>defences</u>.

2) The new defences have made Boscastle a <u>safer place</u> to live.

3) However, they'll only protect against a <u>1 in 75 year flood</u> — they <u>won't prevent</u> flooding of the same size as the 2004 flood. The defences needed for this would <u>spoil</u> the <u>character</u> of the village.

4) Many residents do not <u>like</u> the <u>new bridge</u>, and think that it's <u>not in keeping</u> with the character of the village.

Economic Issues

1) <u>Homes</u> and <u>businesses</u> are now <u>less at risk</u> of <u>flooding</u>. So there is less risk of expensive <u>damage</u> to property, loss of <u>stock</u> and <u>business</u>, and rising <u>insurance costs</u>.

2) The flood management scheme cost over <u>£4 million</u> but the scheme isn't as good as it could be — some options were still considered <u>too expensive</u>.

Environmental Issues

1) <u>Vegetation</u> and <u>river habitats</u> in the area are now continuously managed. <u>Biodiversity</u> and river habitats have been <u>improved</u>.

2) The new channel has been engineered to look <u>natural</u> and to function as a <u>normal river</u>.

There are both pros and cons to every flood management scheme

EXAM TIP Examiners love asking long questions about management schemes. If you've got a lot of lines to fill, planning your answer before you start will help you to remember to include everything you want to say.

Worked Exam Questions

Time to put your knowledge to the test... I've made life easier for you by giving you the answers to the first page of practice exam questions. Read over them to get an idea of what your exam answers should be like.

1   Study **Figure 1**, which shows the long profile of a river.

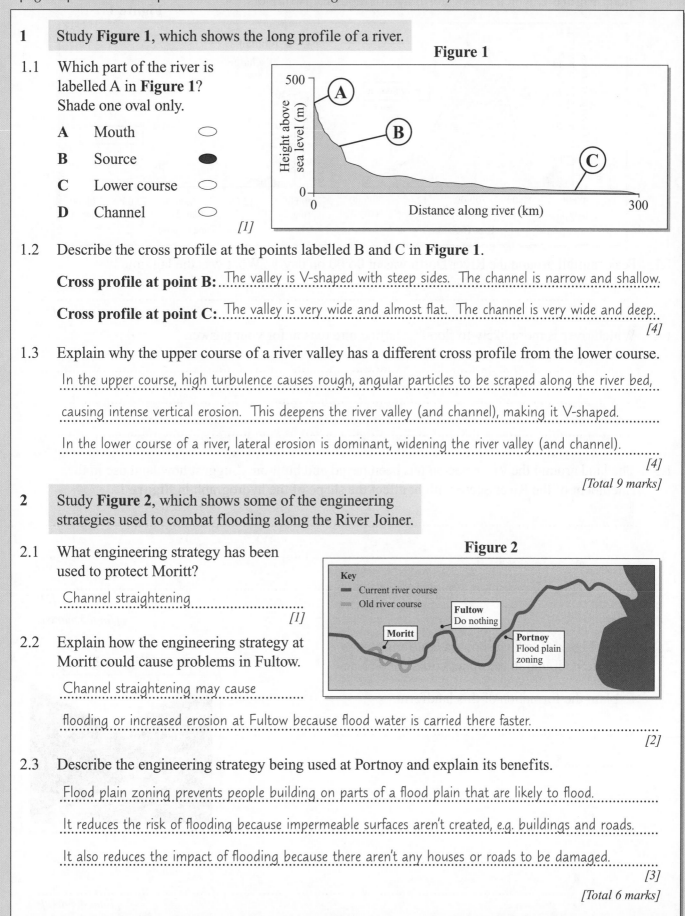

Figure 1

1.1   Which part of the river is labelled A in **Figure 1**? Shade one oval only.

     A   Mouth   ◯

     B   Source   ⬤

     C   Lower course   ◯

     D   Channel   ◯

       [1]

1.2   Describe the cross profile at the points labelled B and C in **Figure 1**.

     Cross profile at point B: The valley is V-shaped with steep sides. The channel is narrow and shallow.

     Cross profile at point C: The valley is very wide and almost flat. The channel is very wide and deep.

       [4]

1.3   Explain why the upper course of a river valley has a different cross profile from the lower course.

     In the upper course, high turbulence causes rough, angular particles to be scraped along the river bed,

     causing intense vertical erosion. This deepens the river valley (and channel), making it V-shaped.

     In the lower course of a river, lateral erosion is dominant, widening the river valley (and channel).

       [4]

       [Total 9 marks]

2   Study **Figure 2**, which shows some of the engineering strategies used to combat flooding along the River Joiner.

2.1   What engineering strategy has been used to protect Moritt?

     Channel straightening

       [1]

Figure 2

2.2   Explain how the engineering strategy at Moritt could cause problems in Fultow.

     Channel straightening may cause

     flooding or increased erosion at Fultow because flood water is carried there faster.

       [2]

2.3   Describe the engineering strategy being used at Portnoy and explain its benefits.

     Flood plain zoning prevents people building on parts of a flood plain that are likely to flood.

     It reduces the risk of flooding because impermeable surfaces aren't created, e.g. buildings and roads.

     It also reduces the impact of flooding because there aren't any houses or roads to be damaged.

       [3]

       [Total 6 marks]

Exam Questions

1 Study **Figure 1**, which shows storm hydrographs for two rivers.

Figure 1

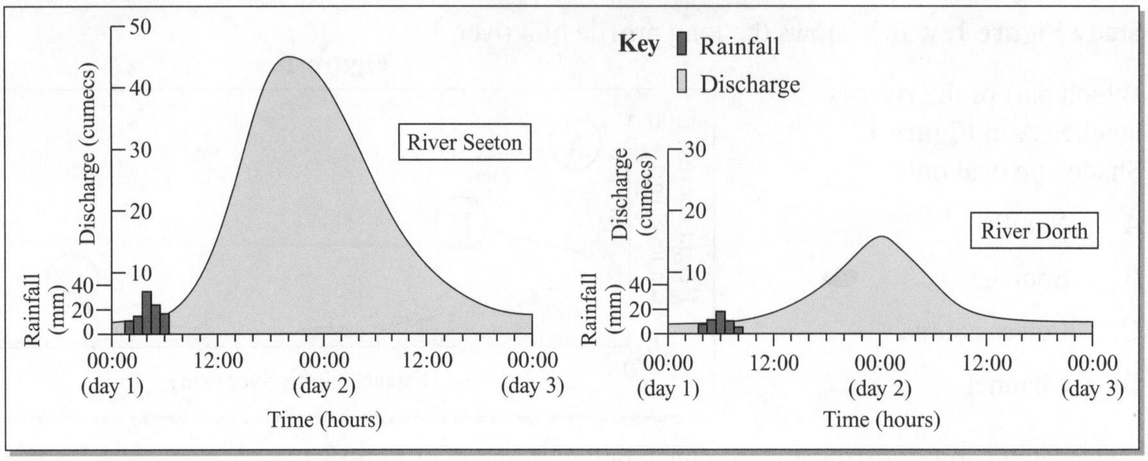

Key ■ Rainfall
     ▯ Discharge

River Seeton

River Dorth

1.1 Peak rainfall around the River Dorth was at 06:00 on day 1. What was the lag time?

....
.... *[1]*

1.2 Which river is more likely to flood? Outline **one** reason for your answer.

....
....
.... *[2]*

1.3 The land around the River Seeton has been paved and built on. Suggest how land use in the catchment of the River Seeton might affect the shape of the hydrograph in **Figure 1**.

....
....
.... *[2]*
[Total 5 marks]

2 Study **Figure 2**, which shows a landform that is likely to be found in the upper course of a river.

Figure 2

2.1 Explain the formation of this landform.

....
....
....
....
....
.... *[Total 4 marks]*

Revision Summary

That's it for <u>UK River Landscapes</u>. Now it's time to see how much information your brain has <u>soaked up</u>.
- Try these questions and <u>tick off each one</u> when you <u>get it right</u>.
- When you've done <u>all the questions</u> for a topic and are <u>completely happy</u> with it, tick off the topic.

River Valley Profiles and Processes (p.107-108) ☑
1) What does a river's long profile show?
2) Describe the cross profile of a river's lower course.
3) Name the part of the river course where vertical erosion is dominant.
4) What's the difference between abrasion and attrition?
5) Name two processes of transportation.
6) When does deposition occur?

Features of Erosion and Deposition (p.109-112) ☑
7) Where do waterfalls form?
8) How is a gorge formed?
9) What are interlocking spurs?
10) a) Where is the current fastest on a meander?
    b) What feature of a meander is formed where the flow is fastest?
11) Name the landform created when a meander is cut off by deposition.
12) What is a flood plain?
13) Outline the main features of a river estuary.
14) What do the contour lines on a map show?
15) Give two pieces of map evidence for a river's lower course.

UK River Basin — Case Study (p.113-115) ☑
16) Describe how the cross profile of a named river changes from the upper to lower courses.
17) a) For a named river basin, describe how climate has influenced the landscape.
    b) Describe how the geology has influenced the landscape.
18) How has human activity changed the landscape of a river basin you have studied?

River Flooding (p.116-118) ☑
19) What is river discharge?
20) What is lag time?
21) Explain how cutting down trees can increase flooding.
22) Give two human effects of a UK river flood you have studied.
23) Describe two local-scale responses to a UK flood event you have studied.

Flood Defences and Management (p.119-122) ☑
24) Define hard engineering.
25) Define soft engineering.
26) Describe how flood walls reduce the risk of flooding.
27) Describe the disadvantages of flood warnings.
28) a) Using a named example of a flood management scheme, explain why the scheme was needed.
    b) Give two features of the scheme and explain how they reduce the flood risk.
    c) Describe the social issues caused by the scheme.

Glacial Erosion

Glaciers are masses of ice that fill valleys and hollows and slowly move downhill. The UK might not have any glaciers any more but it did in the past, and they can seriously carve up the landscape through erosion.

Much of the UK Used to be Covered in Ice

1) There have been lots of glacial (cold) periods during the last 2.6 million years.

2) During some glacial periods, parts of the UK were covered in a massive ice sheet.

3) The map shows the maximum extent of ice cover during the last ice age, about 20 000 years ago.

4) Ice covered most of Scotland, Ireland and Wales and came as far south as the Bristol channel in England.

5) The erosion, transport and deposition of material by ice has been very important in shaping the landscape of the UK.

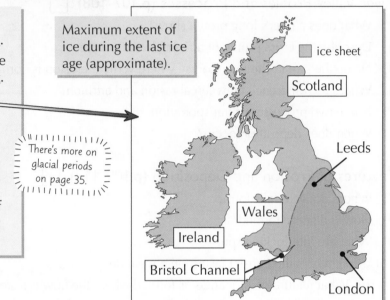

Maximum extent of ice during the last ice age (approximate).

There's more on glacial periods on page 35.

ice sheet

Scotland

Leeds

Wales

Ireland

Bristol Channel

London

Glaciers Erode the Landscape as They Move

1) The weight of the ice in a glacier makes it move downhill (advance), eroding the landscape as it goes.

2) The moving ice erodes the landscape in two ways:

- Plucking occurs when meltwater at the base, back or sides of a glacier freezes onto the rock. As the glacier moves forward it pulls pieces of rock out.

- Abrasion is where bits of rock stuck in the ice grind against the rock below the glacier, wearing it away (it's a bit like the glacier's got sandpaper on the bottom of it).

3) At the top end of the glacier the ice doesn't move in a straight line — it moves in a circular motion called rotational slip. This can erode hollows in the landscape and deepen them into bowl shapes.

4) The rock above glaciers is also weathered (broken down where it is) by the conditions around glaciers.

5) Freeze-thaw weathering is where water gets into cracks in rocks. The water freezes and expands, putting pressure on the rock. The ice then thaws, releasing the pressure. If this process is repeated it can make bits of the rock fall off.

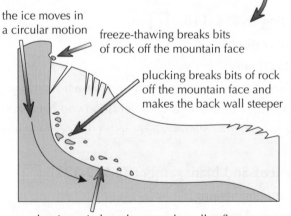

the ice moves in a circular motion

freeze-thawing breaks bits of rock off the mountain face

plucking breaks bits of rock off the mountain face and makes the back wall steeper

abrasion grinds and gouges the valley floor

Glaciers erode valleys in two ways — by plucking and abrasion

You don't have know every detail on the map above, but you should know roughly how far south the ice got. Make sure you also know the difference between plucking, abrasion (types of erosion) and freeze-thaw weathering.

Glacial Landforms

The landscapes of most upland areas in the UK have been massively affected by ice. Here are some of the landforms that are created by glacial erosion that you can see in the UK...

Glacial Erosion Produces Seven Different Landforms

An arête is a narrow, steep-sided ridge formed when two glaciers flow in parallel valleys. The glaciers erode the sides of the valleys, which sharpens the ridge between them giving it a jagged profile. (E.g. Striding Edge, Lake District)

A pyramidal peak is a pointed mountain peak with at least three sides. It's formed when three or more back-to-back glaciers erode a mountain. (E.g. Snowdon, Wales)

Corries begin as hollows containing a small glacier. As the ice moves by rotational slip, it erodes the hollow into a steep-sided, armchair shape with a lip at the bottom end. When the ice melts it can leave a small circular lake called a tarn. (E.g. Red Tarn, Lake District)

Truncated spurs are cliff-like edges on the valley side formed when ridges of land (spurs) that stick out into the main valley are cut off as the glacier moves past.

Hanging valleys are valleys formed by smaller glaciers (called tributary glaciers) that flow into the main glacier. The glacial trough is eroded much more deeply by the larger glacier, so when the glaciers melt the valleys are left at a higher level.

Ribbon lakes are long, thin lakes that form after a glacier retreats. They form in hollows where softer rock was eroded more than the surrounding hard rock. (E.g. Windermere, Lake District)

Glacial troughs are steep-sided valleys with flat bottoms. They start off as a V-shaped river valley but change to a U-shape as the glacier erodes the sides and bottom, making it deeper and wider. (E.g. Nant Ffrancon, Snowdonia)

Glaciers Transport and Deposit Material called Till

1) Glaciers can move material (such as sand, clay and rocks) over very large distances — this is called transportation. This unsorted mixture of material is called till.

2) The material is frozen in the glacier, carried on its surface, or pushed in front of it. It's called bulldozing when the ice pushes loose material in front of it.

3) When the ice carrying the material melts, the material is deposited (dropped) on the valley floor, forming landforms such as moraines and drumlins (see next page).

4) Most glacial deposits aren't sorted by size and weight like river deposits — rocks of all shapes and sizes are mixed up together.

5) However, very fine material such as sand and gravel can get washed away from the front of the glacier by small meltwater streams. The streams sort the material by size and deposit it in layers (called outwash) in front of the glacier.

Learn how ice produces these seven landforms

Make sure you know what each of these landforms looks like — and also make sure you know why they look the way they do. You might be asked to spot them on a map in the exam, or from a photo — see pages 129-130.

Glacial Deposition

Glaciers <u>transport</u> a lot of material — and that material has to <u>end up somewhere</u>.

Glaciers **Deposit Material** as **Different Types** of **Moraine**

<u>Moraines</u> are <u>landforms</u> made out of <u>till</u> dropped by a <u>glacier</u> as it melts.
There are four <u>different types</u>, depending on their <u>position</u>:

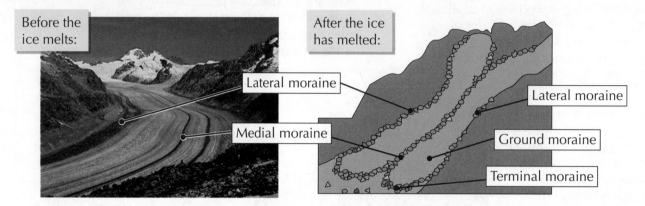

Before the ice melts:

After the ice has melted:

Lateral moraine

Medial moraine

Lateral moraine

Ground moraine

Terminal moraine

1) <u>Lateral</u> moraine is a <u>long mound</u> of material deposited where the <u>side</u> of the glacier was. It's formed by material eroded from the <u>valley walls</u> and carried along on the <u>ice surface</u> at the <u>sides</u> of the glacier.

2) <u>Medial</u> moraine is a <u>long ridge</u> of material deposited along the <u>centre</u> of a valley floor. When <u>two glaciers meet</u>, the <u>lateral moraines</u> from the two edges <u>join</u> and form a line of material running along the <u>centre</u> of the <u>new glacier</u>.

3) <u>Terminal</u> moraine builds up at the <u>snout</u> of the glacier — marking the <u>furthest point</u> reached by the ice. Material that's <u>abraded</u> and <u>plucked</u> from the valley floor is transported at the front of the glacier, and then deposited as <u>semicircular mounds</u> as the ice retreats.

4) <u>Ground moraine</u> is eroded material that was dragged along the <u>base</u> of the glacier and is deposited over a <u>wide area</u> on the <u>valley floor</u> as the ice melts.

Material can also be **Deposited** as **Drumlins and Erratics**

Drumlins

1) <u>Drumlins</u> are <u>elongated hills</u> of <u>glacial deposits</u> — the largest ones can be <u>over 1000 m</u> long, <u>500 m</u> wide and <u>50 m</u> high.

2) They're <u>round</u>, <u>blunt</u> and <u>steep</u> at the <u>upstream</u> end, and <u>tapered</u>, <u>pointed</u> and <u>gently sloping</u> at the <u>downstream</u> end.

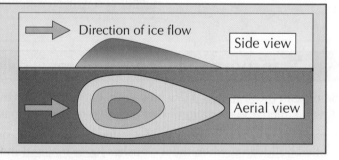

Direction of ice flow

Side view

Aerial view

Erratics

1) <u>Erratics</u> are <u>rocks</u> that have been <u>picked up</u> by a glacier, <u>carried along</u> and <u>dropped</u> in an area that has a completely <u>different rock type</u>.

2) Erratics often look <u>out of place</u>, e.g. a large boulder on its <u>own</u>.

Glaciers deposit material when the ice melts

All those different types of moraine can get a bit confusing when you're just reading about them. To get them memorised, try sketching the diagram from the top of the page and labelling the four different types.

Identifying Glacial Landforms

In the exam you might be asked to spot glacial landforms on an OS® map. It's no problem when you know how, so here are a few tips for you...

Use **Contour Lines** to Spot **Pyramidal Peaks**, **Corries** and **Arêtes** on a Map

Contour lines are the orange lines drawn all over maps. They tell you about the height of the land by the numbers marked on them, and the steepness of the land by how close together the lines are (the closer they are, the steeper the slope). Here are a few tips on how to spot pyramidal peaks, arêtes and corries on a map:

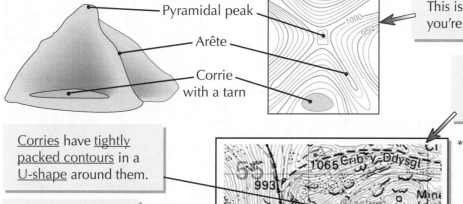

Pyramidal peak
Arête
Corrie with a tarn

This is the sort of thing you're looking for on a map.

But on a real map, like this one of Snowdon in Wales, it's not as blindingly obvious.

Corries have tightly packed contours in a U-shape around them.

Some corries have a tarn in them.

A pyramidal peak has tightly packed contour lines that curve away from a central high point. If you find this you'll find the arêtes and corries around it.

Arêtes are quite hard to see. Look for a really thin hill with tightly packed, parallel contours on either side.

Arêtes often have corries or tarns on either side, and footpaths on them with names like 'Something Edge', e.g. 'Striding Edge'.

You can also use **Maps** to Spot **Glacial Troughs** and **Ribbon Lakes**

You might be asked to spot a glacial trough or a ribbon lake on a map extract. This map of Nant Ffrancon (a glacial trough) and Llyn Ogwen (a ribbon lake) in Wales shows the classic things to look out for:

Glacial troughs are flat valleys with very steep sides. There are no contour lines on the bottom of the valley but they're tightly packed on the sides.

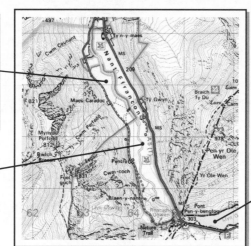

Many glacial troughs have ribbon lakes in them. Look for a flat valley with steep sides surrounding a long straight lake.

Look for a wide, straight valley in a mountainous area with a river that looks too small to have formed the valley.

EXAM TIP

Contour lines are the key to spotting glacial landforms on maps

Don't panic if you're given map extracts in the exam — just study them carefully and try to picture the landforms. Make sure you refer to the map in your answer, and give details about what's shown.

UK Glacial Landscape

Snowdonia is a great place to look for glacial landforms. It may not be covered in ice now, but it has seen a lot of ice in the past. Here's an example of some of the landforms that are found there.

Snowdonia is a Glacial Landscape in North Wales

1) Snowdonia is an area in north Wales. It has been repeatedly covered by ice during glacial periods (see page 35).

2) The upland areas of Snowdonia (e.g. the Glyders — mountains to the north-east of Snowdon) show many of the landforms from pages 127-128.

3) Here are some of the glacial features that are found on the Glyders and the surrounding area:

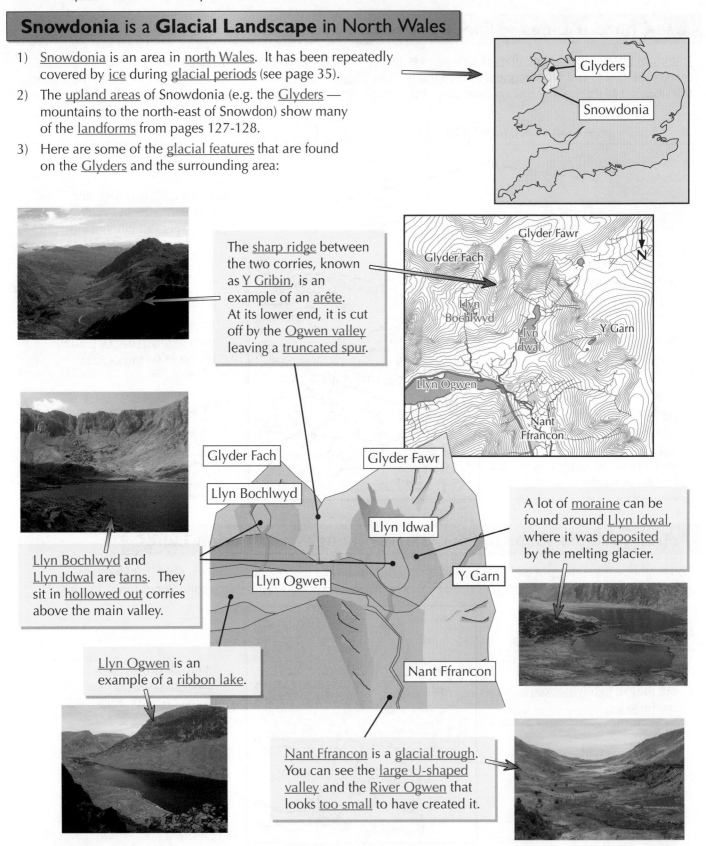

The sharp ridge between the two corries, known as Y Gribin, is an example of an arête. At its lower end, it is cut off by the Ogwen valley leaving a truncated spur.

Llyn Bochlwyd and Llyn Idwal are tarns. They sit in hollowed out corries above the main valley.

A lot of moraine can be found around Llyn Idwal, where it was deposited by the melting glacier.

Llyn Ogwen is an example of a ribbon lake.

Nant Ffrancon is a glacial trough. You can see the large U-shaped valley and the River Ogwen that looks too small to have created it.

There are lots of different glacial landforms in Snowdonia

This is just an example of some of the glacial landforms that can be seen in Snowdonia. You may have studied a different example — that's fine, as long as you can spot and describe the landforms there from maps and photos.

Land Use in Glacial Landscapes

People <u>use</u> glaciated areas in loads of different ways. Unfortunately, these different activities create <u>conflicts</u>.

Glaciated Areas have Many Economic Uses

Farming

1) <u>Sheep farming</u> is common in <u>upland</u> glaciated areas because the <u>steep slopes</u> and <u>poor soils</u> make it <u>unsuitable</u> for most other types of farming.
2) <u>Cattle</u> are sometimes kept on the flatter <u>valley floors</u>.
3) It's usually too cold to grow <u>crops</u>, but <u>grass</u> is grown to make <u>hay</u> to <u>feed</u> the <u>animals</u>.

Forestry

1) <u>Coniferous (evergreen) forests</u> are often planted in upland areas because they can <u>cope</u> with the <u>cold</u> weather and high <u>rainfall</u>.
2) The trees are used for <u>timber</u>, e.g. for <u>building materials</u>.

Quarrying

1) The <u>erosion</u> by glaciers left lots of <u>rock exposed</u>, making it easy to get to.
2) Glacial landscapes are often quarried for <u>slate</u>, <u>granite</u>, and <u>limestone</u>.

Tourism

1) Glaciated areas have <u>dramatic</u> landscapes, making them <u>attractive</u> places to visit.
2) People take part in a <u>variety of activities</u> including hiking, climbing, boating, mountain biking and skiing.

Economic Activity Causes Conflict in Glacial Landscapes

Most <u>upland glacial landscapes</u> in the <u>UK</u> are very <u>attractive</u> areas. Conservationists want to <u>preserve</u> the <u>environmental value</u> of the landscapes, but <u>development</u> is needed to provide <u>employment</u> (e.g. in farming, quarrying, forestry or tourism) and to provide <u>roads</u> and <u>facilities</u> for the many <u>visitors</u> to glacial areas. This creates <u>conflict</u> between <u>conservation</u> and <u>development</u>. For example:

Conflicts caused by Farming

1) Grazing sheep remove <u>vegetation</u> from the landscape. Some conservationists would like the landscape to be more <u>natural</u> — e.g. at Cwm Idwal the area is fenced off to prevent sheep from entering, so more <u>trees</u> and <u>shrubs</u> are now growing.
2) Some farmers don't want lots of tourists <u>walking</u> through their land, and may try to <u>block footpaths</u> or <u>deter walkers</u>.

See pages 132-133 for more on the impacts of tourism.

Conflicts caused by Tourism

1) <u>Conservationists</u> may object to the <u>development</u> of <u>infrastructure</u> to support the tourism industry, e.g. the visitor centre on the top of Snowdon.
2) Tourists can <u>damage stone walls</u>, <u>scare sheep</u>, leave <u>gates</u> open and <u>trample</u> on crops, causing conflict with <u>farmers</u>.

Conflicts caused by Forestry

1) <u>Harvesting</u> trees means <u>chopping</u> forests down, which affects conservation efforts because it can <u>scare off wildlife</u> and <u>damage habitats</u>.
2) Coniferous forests don't support as many different types of <u>species</u> as mixed woodland. This may make the area <u>less attractive</u> to tourists and there may be <u>limited access</u> when the trees are being chopped down.

Conflicts caused by Quarrying

1) Conservationists object to the <u>destruction</u> of <u>habitats</u> and the <u>damage</u> to <u>local wildlife</u>.
2) Quarrying makes the environment <u>less attractive</u> to tourists so they may be discouraged from visiting. This could have <u>economic impacts</u> on <u>local businesses</u> who depend on the tourists.
3) Local residents may object to the <u>large trucks</u> that transport the quarried stone <u>passing</u> close to their homes, and the <u>noise</u> from the quarry itself.

Different land uses in glacial landscapes can cause conflict

If you get a question about conflict between different groups of people in the exam, make sure you write about both points of view. If you're stuck, try putting yourself in the shoes of the groups involved.

Tourism in Glacial Landscapes

Glacial landscapes in the UK are visited by millions of people every year — but popularity comes at a price...

Tourism has Social, Economic and Environmental Impacts

Glacial landscapes are very popular with tourists. This has a number of impacts:

Economic Impacts

1) Tourism can have a positive economic impact on glacial landscapes as it is often the main industry.

2) Tourism offers employment to local people (e.g. in hotels, shops, cafés and the outdoor industry). However, jobs are often seasonal and low paid.

3) Less positive impacts include extremely high house prices due to demand for holiday and second homes. This can often mean that local people are unable to buy houses and so are forced out of the area.

4) The price of goods and services is often higher because tourists are willing to pay more.

Social Impacts

1) Increased traffic causes problems because often the roads are narrow and winding. Congestion is common and there isn't enough car parking available.

2) Shops that used to sell goods for local people (e.g. food, clothes) often sell gifts and outdoor clothing for tourists instead.

3) Holiday homes are usually not occupied all year round. This can lead to some services for local residents being limited, e.g. reduced bus services in off-peak seasons.

Environmental Impacts

1) Footpath erosion is often a problem due to the large numbers of walkers. Vegetation is destroyed and exposed soil is washed away — this damages the landscape and leaves large erosion scars.

2) Litter increases during the tourist season and some tourists light bonfires or BBQs, which can damage the ground.

3) Water sports (e.g. jet skiing and power boating) create noise pollution. The waves created by the boats can erode the shoreline and fuel spills can pollute the water, harming fish, birds and plants.

4) Tourists may park on grass verges, causing damage to vegetation.

5) Wildlife and livestock can be disturbed by walkers and their dogs.

Strategies are Needed to Cope with the Impact of Tourists

The impacts of tourism can be managed in different ways. Here are some examples:

1) Managing footpath erosion:
   - Resurface paths with hard-wearing materials, e.g. rocks, plastic mesh, slabs, etc.
   - Reseed vegetation to reduce the visual impact of the erosion.
   - Encourage visitors to use alternative routes by providing signposting or fencing.

2) Managing traffic congestion:
   - Increase public transport in the tourist season.
   - Improve the road network, e.g. by providing designated passing places on single-track roads.
   - Encourage people to use bikes, buses, boats and trains, e.g. by providing discounts.

3) Protecting wildlife and farmland:
   - Use signs to remind people to take their litter home and provide covered bins at the most popular sites.
   - Encourage visitors to enjoy the countryside responsibly — by closing gates and keeping dogs on leads.

Tourism can bring wealth to an area but it also causes lots of problems

Not everyone is happy with the growth of tourism — local residents can object to high prices, damage to the environment and being stuck in traffic all summer. Don't forget that tourism provides jobs and income though.

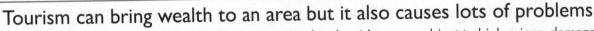

Tourism in Glacial Landscapes

The Lake District is a classic example of a glacial landscape where tourism has had impacts.

The Lake District Attracts Millions of Tourists

The Lake District is a National Park in Cumbria, which gets 16.4 million visitors every year. The attractions for visitors include:

1) Beautiful scenery — large lakes (e.g. Windermere) and mountains (e.g. Scafell Pike).
2) Cultural attractions — e.g. Beatrix Potter's house and the Wordsworth Museum.
3) Activities — e.g. rock-climbing, mountain biking, water sports, bird watching and fishing.

Lake District

Tourism is Having Big Impacts on the Area

Environmental Impacts

1) Catbells is a popular mountain for walkers, but the large number of people using the main footpath from Keswick has led to severe erosion.
2) Tourists often park on the grass verges in the popular Langdale valley, which damages the vegetation.
3) Noise, erosion and pollution of water with fuel is caused by boats and water sports on Lake Windermere.

Economic Impacts

1) Tourism employed over 16 000 people in 2014 and visitors spent over £1 billion.
2) The average price of a house in the village of Grasmere is over £350 000 (due to holiday homes etc.) but the average local household income is only £27 000, so many local people may not be able to afford to stay living in the area.

Social Impacts

1) It's estimated that 89% of visitors to the park arrive by car. Traffic is heavy on the roads linking the National Park with the motorway, especially at the end of the day when day trippers are going home.
2) Businesses in the village of Ambleside mostly cater for tourists — roughly 40% are cafés, restaurants, hotels etc. and around 10% sell outdoor clothing. Prices of everyday goods are high and local residents often travel to Windermere or Kendal to buy most of their food and clothes.
3) More than 16% of properties in the National Park are second homes or holiday homes. This means there are fewer people living in the National Park all year round, so bus services are limited, some primary schools in the Langdale valley have closed and Gosforth no longer has a doctor.

Management Strategies are Reducing the Impact of Tourism

Here are a few strategies being carried out to reduce the problems caused by tourism in the Lake District:

1) Coping with the extra traffic and lack of car parking:
   The Go Lakes Travel scheme aims to reduce car use, e.g. by introducing pay-as-you-go bikes, and Ambleside has Controlled Parking Zones within the town centre where people can park for 1 hour. This encourages a high turnover of parking spaces.
2) Helping local people cope with high property prices:
   In 2012, planning permission was granted for 134 affordable homes and 141 houses that only local people can buy (to prevent them being bought as second homes).
3) Coping with the erosion of footpaths:
   At Tarn Hows, severely eroded paths have been covered with soil and reseeded, and the main route has been gravelled to protect it.
4) Coping with the noise, erosion and pollution from water sports:
   Zoning schemes mean that some water sports are only allowed in certain areas of some lakes, e.g. Windermere has a 10 knot speed limit for all boats, which falls to 6 knots in some zones.

The Lake District is a glacial landscape that is very popular with tourists

If you've read the previous page, this one shouldn't be too tricky — just learn some facts and figures about the Lake District (or whichever example you have studied), and a few management strategies that are being used there.

Worked Exam Questions

With the answers written in, it's very easy to skim these worked examples and think you've understood. But that's not going to help you, so take the time to make sure you've really understood everything here.

1 Study **Figure 1**, a photograph showing land use in Scotland in a glacial landscape.

1.1 Name one of the land uses shown in **Figure 1** and explain why it is commonly found in glacial landscapes in the UK.

Figure 1

Land use: Forestry

[1]

Reason: Coniferous forests are often planted in upland areas because they can cope with the cold weather and high rainfall. The trees are used for timber, e.g. for building materials.

[2]

1.2 To what extent are the benefits from the development of UK glacial landscapes more significant than the problems?

Development of glacial landscapes can bring benefits to an area. It provides employment (e.g. in quarrying or tourism), as well as facilities for visitors and local communities. It brings money into the area, so services will improve (e.g. more frequent buses), improving the quality of life of the people who live there. However, development can also cause problems. For example, conservationists want to preserve the environmental value of the landscapes, but development can damage the environment and destroy habitats. This can make the area less attractive to tourists, reducing income to local businesses who depend on them. On balance, I think the problems caused by development outweigh the benefits.

[6]

[Total 9 marks]

2 Study **Figure 2**, a photograph showing tourists near the summit of Snowdon, in a glacial landscape in north Wales.

Figure 2

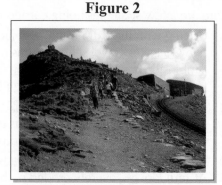

2.1 Use **Figure 2** and your own knowledge to describe the possible negative impacts of tourists visiting glacial landscapes.

Figure 2 shows that footpath erosion can be a problem due to the large numbers of walkers. Vegetation is destroyed and exposed soil is washed away. This damages the landscape and leaves large erosion scars. Also, house prices are often high in glaciated areas due to demand for holiday homes and second homes. This can mean that local people cannot afford to buy houses and are forced to move out of the area. Holiday homes are not occupied all year round. This can lead to some services for local residents being limited, for example, reduced bus services in off-peak seasons.

[Total 4 marks]

Exam Questions

1 Study **Figure 1**, an Ordnance Survey® map of part of the Lake District.

Figure 1

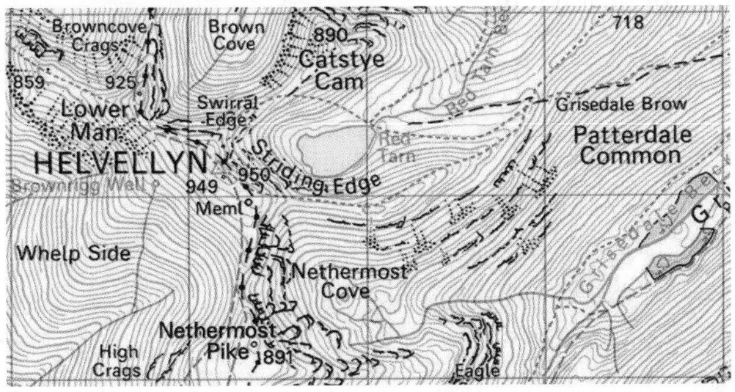

Scale 1:50 000
2 centimetres to 1 kilometre (one grid square)

Kilometres

1.1 Give the four figure grid reference of a grid square that contains a glacial trough and explain how they are formed.

Grid reference:.....................................

Formation:...

....

....

....

....
[2]

1.2 Using **Figure 1**, how far is it between the summits of Catstye Cam and Nethermost Pike?

.... km
[1]

[Total 3 marks]

2 Study **Figure 2**, a diagram showing features of glacial deposition.

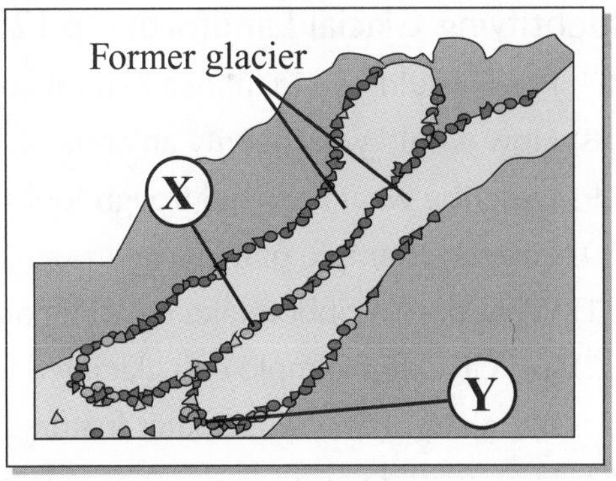

2.1 Identify the depositional feature labelled X on **Figure 2**. Shade **one** oval only.

A Medial moraine ⬭

B Erratic ⬭

C Ground moraine ⬭

D Snout ⬭ [1]

Figure 2

2.2 Outline **one** way in which glaciers transport material.

....

....
[1]

2.3 Explain the formation of the feature labelled Y on **Figure 2**.

....

....

....

....
[3]

[Total 5 marks]

Revision Summary

Right, you've reached the end of <u>UK Glacial Landscapes</u> — time to see how much of it you can <u>remember</u>.
- Try these questions and <u>tick off each one</u> when you <u>get it right</u>.
- When you've done <u>all the questions</u> for a topic and are <u>completely happy</u> with it, tick off the topic.

Glacial Erosion and Glacial Landforms (p.126-127) ☑

1) Describe the maximum extent of ice in the UK during the last ice age. ☑
2) Describe two ways that ice erodes the landscape. ☑
3) What is rotational slip? ☑
4) Explain what freeze-thaw weathering is. ☑
5) What is a corrie? ☑
6) How does a pyramidal peak form? ☑
7) Give an example of a pyramidal peak. ☑
8) Explain how a hanging valley forms. ☑
9) What is a glacial trough? ☑
10) What is bulldozing? ☑
11) Describe the formation of outwash. ☑

Glacial Deposition (p.128) ☑

12) Give one difference between lateral and ground moraine. ☑
13) Where is medial moraine deposited? ☑
14) Describe the formation of terminal moraine. ☑
15) Describe what a drumlin looks like. ☑
16) What is an erratic? ☑

Identifying Glacial Landforms (p.129-130) ☑

17) How would you identify a pyramidal peak on a map? ☑
18) How would you identify an arête on a map? ☑
19) Describe what a glacial trough looks like on a map. ☑
20) Give an example of a glacial trough. ☑
21) What does a ribbon lake look like on a map? ☑
22) a) Give an example of a glaciated upland area in the UK. ☑
    b) Name some of its major features of erosion. ☑
23) How would you identify a corrie in a photograph? ☑
24) Describe what an arête looks like. ☑

Land Use in Glacial Landscapes (p.131-133) ☑

25) Describe the types of farming that commonly take place in glacial landscapes. ☑
26) Name three economic activities, other than farming, that take place in glacial landscapes. ☑
27) Give two examples of conflicts that might be caused by quarrying in glacial landscapes. ☑
28) Describe the conflicts caused by a type of land use other than quarrying in glacial landscapes. ☑
29) Describe the economic impacts of tourism on glaciated upland areas. ☑
30) Give two strategies that might be used to manage the social impacts of tourism. ☑
31) Explain why tourists are attracted to one glacial area you have studied. ☑
32) Using a named example, describe the social impacts of tourism on a glaciated area. ☑
33) For a named upland area, describe one way that environmental impacts
    of tourism have been managed. ☑

Urban Growth

Urban areas (towns and cities) are <u>growing</u> at <u>different rates</u> in <u>different parts</u> of the world.

Urbanisation is Happening **Fastest** in **Poorer Countries**

1) <u>Urbanisation</u> is the <u>growth</u> in the <u>proportion</u> of a country's population living in <u>urban areas</u>.

2) It's happening in countries <u>all over the world</u> — more than <u>50%</u> of the world's population currently live in <u>urban areas</u> (<u>3.9 billion</u> people) and this is <u>increasing</u> every day.

3) Urbanisation happened <u>earlier</u> in developed countries (see p.178), e.g. during the <u>Industrial Revolution</u> (in the 18th and 19th centuries), and <u>most</u> (79%) of the population now <u>already live</u> in <u>urban areas</u>. Developed countries have very <u>slow rates</u> of urban growth.

4) A <u>smaller proportion</u> (35%) of the population in developing countries <u>currently live</u> in urban areas. In general, the <u>fastest rates</u> of urbanisation in the world are in developing countries.

5) The percentage of the population living in urban areas <u>varies</u> in <u>emerging countries</u>. Some, such as <u>Thailand</u> and <u>China</u>, are experiencing <u>rapid urban growth</u>.

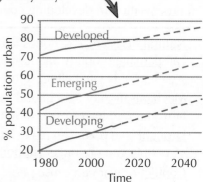

6) Urbanisation is predicted to continue at a <u>fast rate</u> in regions that still have <u>large rural populations</u>. By 2050, the <u>majority</u> of people in <u>every global region</u> are predicted to live in <u>urban areas</u>.

The World's **Biggest Cities** are Now Found in **Poorer Countries**

1) There are different types of cities:

- <u>Megacity</u> — an urban area with <u>over 10 million people</u> living there. A megacity can be a <u>single</u> city, or a <u>conurbation</u> — where neighbouring towns and cities have spread and <u>merged</u> together.

- <u>World city</u> — a city that has an <u>influence</u> over the <u>whole world</u>. World cities are centres for <u>trade</u> and <u>business</u>. Lots of <u>people</u> and <u>goods</u> from <u>international</u> destinations pass through them. They also tend to be hubs of <u>culture</u> and <u>science</u>, with <u>international media</u> centres.

- <u>Primate city</u> — a city that <u>dominates</u> the country it is in. These cities have a <u>much larger population</u> than other cities in the country — usually more than <u>twice</u> as many people as the <u>next biggest city</u>.

2) In 1950 most of the <u>biggest</u> and most <u>influential</u> cities were in <u>developed</u> countries. There were only <u>2</u> megacities — Tokyo and New York.

3) By 2014 there were <u>28</u> megacities and this number is still growing — it's predicted to rise to <u>43</u> by 2030. More than <u>two-thirds</u> of current megacities are in <u>poorer</u> countries (<u>emerging</u> and <u>developing</u> countries), mostly in <u>Asia</u>, e.g. <u>Jakarta</u> in Indonesia and <u>Mumbai</u> in India.

4) In 1950, the only <u>world cities</u> were London, Paris, Tokyo and New York.

5) The number of world cities has also <u>increased</u>, but it's difficult to put an <u>exact number</u> on how many there are. Most are still in <u>developed</u> countries but some, e.g. <u>Beijing</u>, <u>Moscow</u> and <u>Rio de Janeiro</u>, are in <u>emerging</u> countries.

Population growth is higher in developing countries than developed countries

Most countries are urbanising, but rates of urbanisation are usually fastest in developing and emerging countries. As a result, most megacities are found in poorer countries. They can be found in developed countries too though.

Urban Growth

Urban areas are popular places to be and getting even more so. You need to know why...

Urbanisation is Caused by Rural-Urban Migration and Natural Increase

1) Rural-urban migration is the movement of people from the countryside to the cities. The rate of rural-urban migration in developing countries is affected by push factors (things that encourage people to leave an area) and pull factors (things that encourage people to move to an area). Rapid urbanisation in developing countries is being caused by a combination of push and pull factors:

Push factors

1) Natural disasters, e.g. floods and earthquakes, can damage property and farmland, which people can't afford to repair.
2) Mechanisation of agricultural equipment — farms require fewer workers so there are fewer jobs.
3) Drought (see p.26) can make land unproductive, so people can no longer support themselves.
4) Conflict or war can cause people to flee their homes.

Pull factors

1) There are more jobs in urban areas that are often better paid.
2) Access to better health care and education.
3) To join other family members who have already moved.
4) People think they will have a better quality of life.

Natural increase is also known as internal growth.

2) Urbanisation is also caused by natural increase (when the birth rate is higher than the death rate).

3) The birth rate tends to be higher in cities because it's normally young people that move to urban areas (to find work). These people then have children in the cities — increasing the urban population.

4) In developing countries, better healthcare can be found in cities than in rural areas. This means people living in urban areas live longer, reducing death rates and increasing the proportion of people in urban areas.

Economic Change Leads to Migration

Economic change is causing cities in countries of different levels of development to grow or to decline.

Developing

Cities in developing countries are growing. This is because:

1) Rural areas are very poor — loss of jobs in farming (see above) leads to national migration to cities as people seek work. There are lots of opportunities in the informal sector (see p.140) for low-skilled migrants from rural areas.
2) Some cities have good transport links so trade is focused there — providing lots of jobs.
3) Some cities are attracting foreign companies and manufacturing industry is expanding.

Emerging

Some cities in emerging countries are growing and some have stabilising populations.

1) Some cities have become industrial centres — there are lots of manufacturing jobs. Other cities have a rapidly expanding service sector, e.g. the IT industry in India. People move to the cities to work in the new industries and in services supporting them.
2) As countries get wealthier they are investing in flagship projects, e.g. sports stadiums for international events, to attract foreign investment. This creates more jobs, attracting workers.

Developed

Some cities in developed countries have stable populations and others are declining.

1) De-industrialisation has led to the decline of industrial areas (see p.151) — people moved away to find work elsewhere. Some cities are still declining, e.g. Sunderland, however many cities have been regenerated and are attracting people again, e.g. Bristol.
2) A lot of low-skilled workers, e.g. cleaners and factory-line workers, are attracted to more successful cities in the region. This leads to the decline of the cities they are leaving.

People usually move to cities to look for better jobs and services

Nothing too difficult on this page — rural-urban migration and internal growth leads to urbanisation and economic change, which in turn encourages even more migration. Try scribbling down the reasons for population growth.

Urban Growth — Opportunities and Challenges

The lure of the <u>city lights</u> can be strong, but there are plenty of <u>problems</u> caused by <u>urbanisation</u>. Don't worry too much though, there are also a lot of <u>opportunities</u> for these new urban dwellers.

Rapid Urbanisation can cause Lots of Problems in Developing Countries

Cities offer <u>lots</u> of <u>opportunities</u> for the people migrating there — e.g. better access to education, healthcare and employment. The <u>growing population</u> can also help increase the <u>wealth</u> and <u>economic development</u> of the city, as well as the <u>country</u> it's in. However, <u>very rapid growth</u> puts <u>pressure</u> on cities, causing <u>problems</u>:

Economic Consequences

1) There may not be <u>enough jobs</u> for everyone, leading to high levels of <u>unemployment</u>.
2) Lots of people work in the <u>informal sector</u>, where the jobs aren't <u>taxed</u> or <u>regulated</u> by the government. People often work <u>long hours</u> in <u>dangerous conditions</u> for <u>little pay</u>.
3) People may <u>not</u> have access to <u>education</u> so they are unable to develop the skills needed to get better <u>jobs</u>.

Social Consequences

1) There <u>aren't enough houses</u> for everyone — many people end up in <u>squatter settlements</u> that are <u>badly built</u> and <u>overcrowded</u>.
2) <u>Infrastructure</u> can't be built fast enough — people often <u>don't</u> have access to <u>basic services</u>, e.g. clean water, proper sewers or electricity. This can cause <u>poor health</u>.
3) There can be high levels of <u>crime</u>.

Environmental Consequences

If cities grow <u>rapidly</u>, waste disposal services, sewage systems and environmental regulations for factories <u>can't keep pace</u> with the growth.

1) Rubbish often isn't <u>collected</u> or it may end up in big <u>rubbish heaps</u>. This can damage the <u>environment</u>, especially if it's <u>toxic</u>.
2) <u>Sewage</u> and <u>toxic chemicals</u> can get into rivers, <u>harming wildlife</u>.
3) The <u>road system</u> may not be able to <u>cope</u> with all the <u>vehicles</u>. <u>Congestion</u> causes increased <u>greenhouse gas</u> emissions and <u>air pollution</u>.

The Favela-Bairro Project Helped Poor People in Rio de Janeiro's Favelas

Often the <u>poorest people</u> in urban areas are the <u>worst affected</u> by the problems of urban growth. <u>Urban planning schemes</u> can help <u>reduce</u> the <u>impact</u> of these problems and improve the <u>quality of life</u> for the urban poor. An example of an urban planning scheme is the <u>Favela-Bairro Project</u> in Rio de Janeiro:

1) <u>Rio de Janeiro</u> is in south east <u>Brazil</u>. It has more than <u>600</u> squatter settlements (called favelas), housing <u>one-fifth</u> of the city's population (more than <u>one million people</u>).
2) The <u>Favela-Bairro project</u> ran from <u>1995-2008</u> and involved <u>253 000 people</u> in <u>73 favelas</u>. It has led to:
   - <u>Social improvements</u> — e.g. there are now day care centres for children, adult education classes and services to help people with drug or alcohol addictions.
   - <u>Economic improvements</u> — e.g. the project is helping people get legal ownership of their properties and running training schemes to help people find better jobs.
   - <u>Environmental improvements</u> — e.g. wooden buildings are being replaced with brick buildings, streets have been widened and paved, and there are now rubbish collection services.

REVISION TIP

Draw a table of urban opportunities and challenges

Make sure you're familiar with the opportunities and challenges caused by rapid urbanisation. Try making a table or mind map to help you remember them. It would be a good idea to include extra detail about the opportunities and challenges facing people in a named city, e.g. Lagos (see p.143).

Urban Economies

Cities in <u>richer</u> and <u>poorer</u> countries are quite <u>different</u>. This is partly because they have different <u>economic structures</u> — people work in <u>different</u> kinds of <u>jobs</u>. First up, you're going to need some <u>definitions</u>...

There are **Different** Kinds of **Work**

1) There are <u>two</u> different types of <u>employment</u> — <u>formal</u> and <u>informal</u>.

- <u>Formal</u> employment is <u>officially</u> recognised — workers are <u>protected</u> by the <u>laws</u> of the country. There are rules about how many <u>hours</u> people can work, the <u>age</u> of workers, and <u>health</u> and <u>safety</u>. Workers pay <u>tax</u> to the <u>government</u> out of the <u>wages</u> they earn.
- <u>Informal</u> employment is <u>unofficial</u> — jobs <u>aren't taxed</u> or <u>regulated</u> by the government. People often work <u>long hours</u> in <u>dangerous</u> conditions for <u>little pay</u>.

2) There are also <u>four</u> different <u>economic sectors</u> — <u>primary</u>, <u>secondary</u>, <u>tertiary</u> and <u>quaternary</u>.

- The <u>primary</u> sector involves collecting <u>raw materials</u>, e.g. <u>farming</u>, <u>fishing</u>, <u>mining</u> and <u>forestry</u>.
- The <u>secondary</u> sector involves turning a <u>product</u> into <u>another product</u> (<u>manufacturing</u>), e.g. making <u>textiles</u>, <u>furniture</u>, <u>chemicals</u>, <u>steel</u> and <u>cars</u>.
- The <u>tertiary</u> sector involves providing a <u>service</u> — anything from <u>financial</u> services, <u>nursing</u> and <u>retail</u> to the <u>police force</u> and <u>transport</u>.
- The <u>quaternary</u> sector is the <u>information economy</u> — e.g. <u>research and development</u>, where scientists and researchers investigate and develop new products (e.g. in the <u>electronics</u> and <u>IT industry</u>), and <u>consultancy</u> (e.g. advising businesses).

Urban Economies **Vary** By **Level of Development**

	Developing countries	Emerging countries	Developed countries
Formal and informal employment	<u>Many</u> workers are employed in the informal sector.	Number of workers in the informal sector <u>decreases</u> as the country develops.	<u>Few</u> workers in the informal sector.
Economic sectors	Lots of people work in <u>low-skilled tertiary sector</u> jobs, e.g. on market stalls. <u>Few people</u> work in the <u>secondary</u> sector because there's <u>not enough money</u> to <u>invest</u> in the <u>technology needed</u> for this type of industry, e.g. to build large factories. A <u>small percentage</u> of people work in high-skilled <u>tertiary</u> jobs, e.g. in government offices or IT.	<u>Employment</u> in the <u>secondary sector</u> is <u>high</u>. There are established <u>industrial zones</u> and <u>good infrastructure</u>. There are also lots of <u>low-skilled tertiary</u> jobs, e.g. in retail or tourism. As the <u>industrial economy grows</u>, people have <u>more money</u> to spend on services — <u>higher-skilled jobs</u> are created in the <u>tertiary sector</u>, e.g. in medicine or law. Some cities <u>specialise</u> in certain <u>services</u>, e.g. Hyderabad, India specialises in <u>IT development</u>.	<u>Fewer people</u> work in the <u>secondary sector</u> than in <u>emerging</u> countries. <u>Most people</u> work in the <u>tertiary sector</u> because there's a <u>skilled</u> and <u>educated</u> workforce, and there's a <u>high demand</u> for services like banks and shops. There's some employment in the <u>quaternary sector</u> because the country has lots of <u>highly skilled labour</u> and has <u>money</u> to <u>invest</u> in the <u>technology needed</u>.
Working conditions	Conditions are <u>poor</u>. Pay is <u>low</u>, hours are <u>long</u> and conditions can <u>be dangerous</u>.	Conditions <u>improve</u> and workers' rights <u>increase</u>.	Conditions are <u>good</u>. Pay is <u>high</u>, workers have many <u>rights</u> protected by <u>law</u>.

Urban economies differ in different parts of the world

A country's level of development affects urban economies — developing countries have large informal and primary sectors, but the number of people employed in these sectors decreases as the countries develop.

Urban Growth in Lagos

CASE STUDY

Lagos is a great example of the <u>attraction</u> of cities and the <u>problems</u> caused by <u>rapid urban growth</u>.

Lagos is the **Biggest** City in **Africa**

Lagos is a megacity in <u>Nigeria</u> — a <u>developing</u> country, but the <u>richest</u> country in <u>Africa</u>.
The city's population is over <u>21 million</u>, and it's one of the <u>fastest-growing</u> urban areas in the world.

1) Lagos is located at the outlet of the massive <u>Lagos Lagoon</u> (see map below) on the <u>Atlantic western coast</u> of <u>Nigeria</u>.

2) This location is ideal for its <u>port</u>, which is one of the <u>biggest</u> in <u>Africa</u>. The city has spread <u>outwards</u> from its origin on Lagos Island around the <u>lagoon</u> and <u>along the coast</u>.

3) Lagos is well <u>connected</u> by <u>road</u> to the other <u>major towns</u> in <u>Nigeria</u>, e.g. <u>Abuja</u> (the national capital). It has an <u>international port</u> and <u>airport</u>, making it an important centre for <u>regional</u> and <u>global trade</u>.

4) Lagos is Nigeria's <u>biggest city</u> for <u>population</u> and <u>business</u>. It was the <u>national capital</u> until 1991 and remains the <u>main financial centre</u> for the whole of <u>West Africa</u>. The city contains <u>80%</u> of Nigeria's <u>industry</u> and lots of <u>global companies</u> are located there.

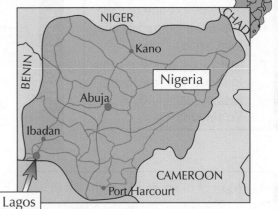

Different **Areas** of Lagos have Different **Functions**

1) The development of Lagos means that land use and <u>building age varies</u> across the city.

2) The <u>oldest parts</u> of the city are on <u>Lagos Island</u>, which is now the CBD. Many of the old buildings have been <u>redeveloped</u> as <u>high rise office blocks</u> and <u>luxury shops</u>. Land is very <u>expensive</u>.

3) By <u>1960</u> the <u>city</u> had <u>spread north</u> and <u>east</u> along the <u>main road</u> and <u>rail links</u>, e.g. creating <u>Mushin</u>. <u>Industries</u> developed <u>near major transport links</u>, e.g. <u>Ikeja industrial estate</u> near the airport.

4) Rapid expansion meant that <u>by 1990</u> Lagos had <u>merged</u> with the <u>smaller surrounding towns</u> to form a <u>continuous urban area</u>. The city has continued to <u>sprawl</u> into the <u>surrounding countryside</u>.

5) It has mainly spread <u>north</u> as it is hemmed in by the <u>lagoon</u> to the <u>east</u> and <u>major rivers</u> to the <u>west</u>. It has also <u>expanded west</u> along the <u>Lagos-Badagry express-way</u>, e.g. in <u>Ojo</u>.

6) <u>Slums</u> have developed on less desirable land on the <u>outskirts</u> of Lagos throughout its history. However, over time, the city has <u>sprawled</u> outwards, <u>beyond</u> many of the slums and they now form part of the <u>main urban area</u> of Lagos.

Key: slum ✈ airport 🚢 port
—— major road —— railway
First developed: 1920 1960 1990

	Area	Age and function
CBD	<u>Lagos Island</u>	<u>Modern high-rise office buildings</u>, local government <u>headquarters</u> and <u>banks</u>.
Inner city	<u>Mushin</u>	<u>Older</u>, <u>high-density</u>, <u>low-quality</u> houses.
	<u>Ikeja</u>	Large <u>industrial estate</u> built in the <u>1960s</u>, with <u>factories</u> making e.g. plastics and textiles.
Suburbs	<u>Victoria Island</u>	<u>Modern</u>, <u>high-class residential</u> and <u>commercial</u> — lots of businesses and shops.
Rural-urban fringe	<u>Ojo</u>	<u>Sprawling</u>, <u>low-density new housing</u> on the <u>outskirts</u> of the city.
	<u>Lekki</u>	<u>New industrial zone</u> and <u>port</u> being built.

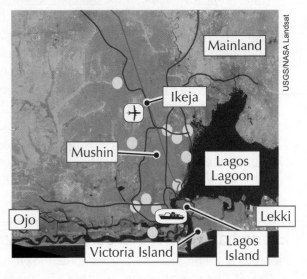

USGS/NASA Landsat

Urban Growth in Lagos

Lagos's Population is **Growing Rapidly**

Lagos's population has <u>grown</u> for <u>different reasons</u> at different <u>times</u>:

Historic

1) The city was under <u>British rule</u> during <u>colonial</u> times and was a centre of <u>trade</u>. This attracted <u>traders</u> and <u>merchants</u> to the city.

2) Many <u>ex-slaves</u> also came to Lagos, e.g. from <u>Sierra Leone</u>, <u>Brazil</u> and the <u>West Indies</u>.

1960s-1990s

1) After Lagos gained <u>independence</u> there was <u>rapid economic development</u> — the <u>export</u> of <u>oil</u> made some people very <u>wealthy</u>.

2) The government financed lots of <u>construction projects</u>, e.g. building <u>sea ports</u>, <u>oil refineries</u> and <u>factories</u>. The <u>jobs</u> created led to <u>rapid urbanisation</u> — lots of people moved <u>to Lagos</u> from <u>rural Nigeria</u>.

3) <u>Birth rates</u> were <u>high</u> and <u>death rates</u> were <u>lower</u> leading to <u>high rates</u> of <u>natural increase</u> — a rapidly <u>growing</u> population.

Recent

1) <u>Most</u> of the population growth in Lagos is due to <u>rural-urban migration</u>.

2) The countries <u>bordering</u> Nigeria, e.g. Chad and Niger, are <u>poor</u> and <u>involved</u> in conflict — many people leave these countries for a <u>better life</u> in Lagos.

3) There are also lots of <u>national migrants</u> from the <u>northern states</u> of Nigeria where there is lots of <u>ethnic</u> and <u>religious conflict</u> and high levels of <u>poverty</u>.

4) There is some international migration from the <u>USA</u>, the <u>UK</u> and <u>China</u>. This is mainly people who are employed by <u>foreign businesses</u> operating in <u>Lagos</u>.

5) The rate of <u>natural increase</u> is still <u>high</u> — <u>birth</u> rates are still higher than <u>death</u> rates though <u>both</u> are slowly falling.

There are **Distinctive Ways** of **Life** in Lagos

1) Lagos has a big <u>film</u> industry, which produces popular 'Nollywood' films. There is also a thriving <u>music</u> scene, which has introduced music styles such as <u>Afrobeat</u> and <u>Afro hip-hop</u> — this gives it <u>cultural importance</u> in Nigeria.

2) <u>Western-style fashion</u> is becoming common among the <u>richer</u> inhabitants, but many people still retain their <u>traditional dress</u> and <u>ways of life</u>, e.g. <u>fishing</u> in the lagoon, or making <u>crafts</u> to sell.

3) There are around <u>250</u> different <u>ethnic groups</u> living in Lagos and there can be ethnic <u>tension</u>, particularly between those with different <u>religions</u>, e.g. Christians and Muslims.

4) About <u>two-thirds</u> of the population live in <u>slums</u>. For those who can afford <u>proper housing</u>, it's a mix of <u>old</u> and <u>new</u> — some of the <u>old colonial buildings</u> remain, alongside new <u>high-rise flats</u> and <u>skyscrapers</u> in the <u>central business district</u>. The very rich live in <u>gated communities</u>, e.g. on <u>Banana Island</u>.

5) <u>Street parties</u>, <u>pool parties</u> and <u>nightclubbing</u> are all popular <u>leisure</u> activities in Lagos, and there are many <u>festivals</u> held throughout the year (e.g. Lagos International Jazz Festival, Badagry Festival, Eyo Festival) celebrating <u>music</u>, <u>food</u> and <u>local culture</u>.

6) <u>Shopping</u> is also popular in Lagos — there are loads of <u>street vendors</u>, lots of <u>markets</u> specialising in different products and rows and rows of <u>small shops</u>. The central business district on <u>Lagos Island</u> has been <u>modernised</u> and has more <u>western-style shops</u> and <u>supermarkets</u>, selling <u>international foods</u>.

7) <u>Consumption</u> of all resources is <u>rising</u> in Lagos — as people get <u>wealthier</u>, they can <u>afford</u> to buy more <u>consumer goods</u> and use more resources. <u>Consumption</u> of energy is rapidly increasing in <u>Nigeria</u>, and Lagos is responsible for more than <u>half</u> of this increase.

Lagos has grown incredibly quickly

Plenty to learn on these two pages about the growth of Lagos. Make sure you've got it sorted before you move on — there's a lot more to come on Lagos. Turn over to see some more of the issues facing its citizens and authorities.

Urban Growth in Lagos

People in Lagos have **More Opportunities...**

There is <u>better access</u> to <u>employment</u> in Lagos than in rural Nigeria and the surrounding countries:

1) Incomes are about <u>4 times higher</u> in Lagos than those in rural areas and <u>informal sector jobs</u> mean most people can find a way of making money — the <u>huge population</u> means there is a <u>large market</u> for <u>services</u>.

2) Lagos is home to many of the country's <u>banks</u>, <u>government departments</u> and <u>manufacturing industries</u> (e.g. making food and drink). There are two major <u>ports</u> and a <u>fishing industry</u>, all of which provide employment. <u>Rapid growth</u> of the city means there are lots of <u>construction</u> jobs.

3) There are more <u>health care centres</u> and <u>hospitals</u> and a better range of <u>medicines</u> in Lagos and there is better access to <u>higher education</u> — Lagos has six <u>universities</u>.

4) It is possible to access <u>electricity</u> and <u>water networks</u> as well as <u>TV</u> and the <u>internet</u>.

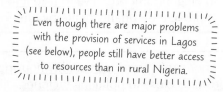

Even though there are major problems with the provision of services in Lagos (see below), people still have better access to resources than in rural Nigeria.

... but **Lagos** faces **Challenges** in **Housing, Traffic, Waste, Jobs** and **Services**

1 Squatter Settlements

Over <u>60%</u> of the city's population live in <u>slums</u>.

1) Houses are often <u>flimsy</u>, <u>wooden huts</u>. These are <u>illegally</u> built — people face <u>eviction</u> if slums are <u>demolished</u> to <u>clean up</u> the city.

2) The only <u>electricity</u> comes from <u>illegal connections</u> that often <u>cut out</u>.

3) There are high levels of <u>crime</u> — many slums are <u>patrolled</u> by gangs called '<u>area boys</u>' who both <u>commit crimes</u> and act as <u>informal</u> '<u>police</u>' in the slum.

2 Traffic Congestion

Lagos has some of the <u>worst traffic congestion</u> in the <u>world</u> because:

1) There has been very little <u>investment</u> in transport <u>infrastructure</u>, despite the city growing enormously.

2) <u>Public transport</u> is <u>limited</u>, although there are plans to improve it, e.g. a light rail train.

3) The <u>CBD</u> is on an <u>island</u>, with only <u>three bridges</u> linking it to the rest of the city.

3 Limited Service Provision

1) There aren't enough schools for the population (e.g. there is only <u>one primary school</u> in Makoko) and many families <u>can't afford</u> to send their children to school.

2) There aren't enough <u>health care facilities</u> and many people can't <u>afford</u> to pay for treatment.

4 Poor Employment Conditions

1) There aren't enough <u>formal jobs</u> for the <u>growing population</u> — people have to make money <u>any way they can</u>, e.g. by <u>scavenging</u> in the Olusosun rubbish dump for items to sell.

2) About <u>60%</u> of the population work in <u>informal</u> jobs (see p.140), e.g. street sellers, barbers.

3) There's <u>no protection</u> for informal workers. <u>Street-sellers'</u> stalls are <u>bulldozed</u> to make way for <u>new developments</u> and <u>road widening</u>.

4) Lots of people live on less than <u>$1.25 per day</u>.

5 Waste Disposal

1) Most of the city doesn't have access to proper <u>sewers</u>, e.g. in Makoko <u>communal toilets</u> are shared by <u>15 households</u> and most of the waste goes <u>straight</u> into the <u>lagoon</u> below — it's always full of <u>rubbish</u> and <u>raw sewage</u>. This <u>causes health problems</u>, e.g. cholera.

2) The <u>huge</u> population produces <u>lots</u> of waste — approximately <u>9000 tonnes per day</u>.

3) Only about <u>40% of rubbish</u> is officially collected and there are <u>large rubbish dumps</u>, e.g. Olusosun, which contain <u>toxic waste</u>. <u>Waste disposal</u> and <u>emissions</u> from factories are <u>not controlled</u>, leading to <u>air</u> and <u>water pollution</u>.

6 Water Supply

1) Only about <u>40%</u> of the city is <u>connected</u> to the <u>state water supply</u>. The pipes are <u>old</u> and <u>rusty</u> — the water often gets <u>contaminated</u> with <u>sewage</u>.

2) The state water company <u>supplies less than half</u> of what is <u>needed</u>. Water is in such short supply that people pay <u>hugely inflated prices</u> to get water from <u>informal sellers</u>.

Urban Growth in Lagos

CASE STUDY

There are **Big Inequalities** in Lagos

There are <u>big differences</u> between the <u>rich</u> and the <u>poor</u> in Lagos, which leads to differences in <u>quality of life</u>.

Rich

1) Wealthy people can afford <u>better housing</u> — the very rich live in luxurious and very expensive <u>gated communities</u>, e.g. on <u>Banana Island</u>.

2) They can also <u>afford</u> to <u>live closer</u> to <u>work</u>, so don't have to <u>face</u> traffic jams every day.

3) Lagos does not have enough electricity-generating <u>capacity</u> to satisfy the <u>whole</u> city, so neighbourhoods have to <u>take it in turns</u> to have electricity. The very wealthy improve their quality of life by running their own <u>powerful generators</u>.

Poor

The poor can't afford <u>high quality housing</u> — they end up living in <u>slums</u> on land that regularly <u>floods</u> or is close to <u>polluting factories</u>. Electricity is not available to the <u>poorest</u> people in slums, meaning they are reliant on <u>polluting cooking stoves</u> or small petrol <u>generators</u>, which cause <u>pollution</u> and <u>reduce quality of life</u>. Lack of <u>waste disposal</u> leads to <u>high health risks</u>.

The <u>inequalities</u> above make <u>political</u> and <u>economic management</u> of Lagos <u>challenging</u>:

1) There are <u>different development priorities</u>, e.g. the <u>wealthy</u> want <u>investment</u> in more high-class, modern <u>office space</u> (e.g. <u>Eko Atlantic</u>) to relieve pressure on the existing CBD, but the poor who live in slums need investment in <u>housing improvement</u> and in <u>more services</u>.

2) <u>Corruption</u> is very common in Nigeria. The government can introduce laws, e.g. to regulate traffic, but the wealthy know they can <u>ignore them</u> and <u>bribe</u> the police if they get caught.

3) The wealthy elite are <u>very powerful</u> — e.g. proposals to improve railways in and around Lagos for people and freight have been <u>stopped</u> by people who have a business interest in the lorries that currently supply the city.

The **Government** is Trying to make Lagos **More Sustainable**

1) <u>Sustainability</u> means <u>improving</u> things for people <u>today</u> without <u>negatively affecting</u> future generations. Basically, it means behaving in a way that doesn't <u>irreversibly damage the environment</u> or <u>use up resources</u> faster than they can be <u>replaced</u>.

2) Some strategies to improve sustainability are <u>top-down</u> (<u>large-scale</u>, <u>expensive</u> infrastructure projects run by <u>governments</u> and IGOs — see p.188). In Lagos, <u>top-down</u> strategies include:

> Sustainability should consider the economy and people as well as the environment.

Improving Water Supply

The government has begun work on a <u>US $2.5 billion plan</u> which includes <u>new water treatment plants</u> and <u>distribution networks</u>. In the meantime <u>water kiosks</u> are being introduced, where people can <u>buy water</u> at a <u>lower price</u> than from informal water sellers, until they are connected.

Improving Waste Disposal

The <u>Lagos Waste Management Authority</u> (LAWMA) is working to improve <u>rubbish collection</u> by making sure collection <u>vans</u> can get to each area of the city, e.g. by doing collections at <u>night</u> when there's <u>less traffic</u>. <u>Recycling banks</u> are being put in <u>every estate</u> and people are <u>encouraged</u> to <u>sort</u> and <u>recycle</u> their <u>waste</u>.

Reducing Traffic Congestion

Two <u>light rail lines</u> are under construction to relieve <u>road congestion</u>. The lines will connect the <u>CBD</u> on <u>Lagos Island</u> with the <u>north</u> and <u>west</u> of the city (including the <u>airport</u>) along major <u>commuter routes</u>. The trains will be <u>emission free</u> to <u>limit air pollution</u> and the route will take <u>35 minutes</u> instead of up to <u>4 hours</u> by car.

Improving Air Quality

<u>Small electricity generators</u> (used by households when the power goes out) are a big source of <u>air pollution</u>. To <u>improve air quality</u> the government <u>banned</u> the <u>import</u> of small generators — instead communities are encouraged to get <u>together</u> to run <u>one larger generator</u>, which will produce <u>less emissions</u> overall.

Urban Growth in Lagos

Communities and NGOs are Also Trying to Improve Lagos's Sustainability

Other strategies to improve sustainability in Lagos are bottom-up (smaller-scale projects run by communities and non-governmental organisations — see p.188). In Lagos, bottom-up strategies include:

Improving Health

CHIEF is an NGO that aims to develop sustainable health care in deprived areas of Lagos by opening community health centres, particularly for disadvantaged women and children. They also run education projects in local communities, to make people more aware of health issues.

Improving City Housing

SEAP is a Nigerian NGO that promotes sustainable livelihoods for the poorest people in society. For example, it offers small loans (microfinance) to poor communities at affordable rates, so that people can afford to get a mortgage on a house. This means that people can move out of slum housing into small affordable apartments with better access to services.

Improving Education

The Oando Foundation is a charity that is aiming to create a sustainable education system in Nigeria by improving school attendance and the quality of education on offer. The foundation involves local communities in each project so they support the school. It has 'adopted' and renovated schools in Lagos — this is reducing the number of primary children out of school. It is also working to improve teachers' skills through training programmes.

There are Pros and Cons to Top-Down and Bottom-Up Strategies

	Advantages	Disadvantages
Top-down	• Can achieve large improvements that affect the whole city, e.g. the improved water supply aimed to provide enough water for everyone at a low cost by 2020. • Can carry out higher-cost projects that communities or NGOs would struggle to fund. • Can address economic, social and environmental sustainability.	• Often very expensive, e.g. Nigeria had to borrow almost US $1 billion from the World Bank to fund construction of its light rail line. • Top-down approaches don't always have the support of communities, who may decide to ignore or undermine the strategy. For example the bus rapid transit is often delayed due to cars and stalls blocking the bus lane. • May not help those most in need, e.g. the ban on small generators affects the poor more than the rich as they are less able to afford cleaner alternatives.
Bottom-up	• Planned with the local community, so it has their support and can target issues that most concern local people. • Often funded by donations from more developed countries or wealthy people, so there's low cost to the people they help or the Nigerian government.	• Smaller scale so projects reach fewer people. • Funds may be limited — especially during economic recessions (periods of economic decline) when the need may be greatest. Schemes often rely on donations from people in more developed countries but people can't afford to give as much during a recession. • Can lack coordination — there may be several NGOs with the same aims working separately.

Include lots of specific facts when you write about a case study

If you've studied a different example of urban growth in class and you'd rather write about that instead, then no problem — just make sure you have enough information to cover the key points on this page.

Worked Exam Questions

Here's some worked exam questions for this section — for an extra bit of practice, try covering the answers and thinking about how you would answer each question before you read the suggested answer.

1   There are a number of challenges that affect life in cities in developing and developed countries.

1.1   Which of the following is **not** likely to be a challenge faced by a worker in the informal sector? Shade **one** oval only.

     A   Working in dangerous conditions.   ⬭

     B   Working long hours.   ⬭

     C   Earning very little.   ⬭

     D   Having to pay high taxes.   ⬬   *[1]*

1.2   Describe the evidence shown in **Figure 1** for challenges faced by many cities in developing and developed countries.

Figure 1

© iStock.com/BluesandViews

     Housing in squatter settlements like the one shown in

     Figure 1 is often badly built and overcrowded. Electricity

     may not be supplied to all houses, causing people to make

     their own dangerous connections.

[2]

1.3   Describe how migration has affected the growth of a city in a developed or developing country.

     A large numbers of migrants move to Lagos every year, and the population is increasing very rapidly.

     The urban area is growing outwards into the surrounding countryside. The housing supply has not

     been able to keep up, with over 60% of the population of Lagos living in slums.

[3]

1.4   Explain how an urban planning scheme in a developing country or emerging country has had a positive effect on people living in the area.

     Around one-fifth of the population of Rio de Janeiro live in squatter settlements (favelas).

     The Favela-Bairro project was a scheme designed the improve quality of life for people in 73 favelas.

     It set up day care centres for children and adult education classes, improving people's social situation.

     It also improved people's economic situation, for example by helping them to get legal ownership

     of their homes and by running training schemes so they could find better jobs and earn more.

     Environmental changes, such as setting up rubbish collection services, made the area more pleasant

     for people to live in.

[4]

[Total 10 marks]

Exam Questions

1   Study **Figure 1**, a graph showing the change in the urban population of developing countries and developed countries between 1950 and 2000.

1.1   Complete the graph to show that the urban population of developing countries in 2000 was 2 billion. *[1]*

Figure 1

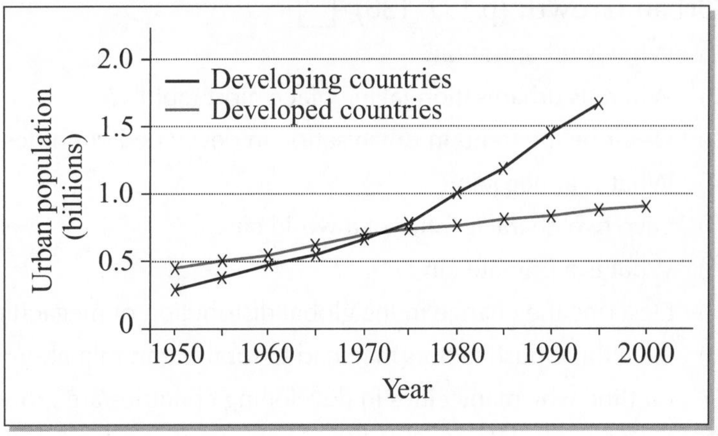

1.2   Describe the trends shown in **Figure 1**.

....

....

....

....

....

....

....
[3]

1.3   Suggest **two** pull factors that encourage people to move to cities.

1:...

....

2:...

....
[2]

1.4   Suggest reasons for the difference in the rate of urbanisation in developing countries and developed countries shown in **Figure 1**.

....

....

....

....

....

....

....
[6]

[Total 12 marks]

Revision Summary

So now you've finished <u>Urban Issues and Challenges</u>, go ahead and see what you can remember.
- Try these questions and <u>tick off each one</u> when you <u>get it right</u>.
- When you've done <u>all the questions</u> for a topic and are <u>completely happy</u> with it, tick off the topic.

Urban Growth (p.137-138) ☑

1) What is urbanisation?
2) Where is urbanisation taking place most rapidly?
3) Describe the trend in urbanisation in developed countries.
4) What is a megacity?
5) Give two characteristics of a world city.
6) What is a primate city?
7) Describe the change in the global distribution of megacities since 1950.
8) Give three push factors that lead to rural-urban migration in developing countries.
9) Outline why many cities in developing countries are growing.
10) Give an example of an economic change that is leading to migration in developed countries.

Urban Characteristics and Trends (p.139-140) ☑

11) Describe the social challenges that have been caused by rapid urban growth in developing countries.
12) List two environmental challenges caused by urban growth in developing countries.
13) a) Give a named example of an urban planning scheme.
    b) Explain how it has improved the quality of life for the urban poor.
14) What is formal employment?
15) What types of work are classified as part of the quaternary sector?
16) In which type of country does most informal employment take place?
17) What are the working conditions like in cities in developing countries?

Urban Growth — Case Study (p.141-145) ☑

For a megacity in a developing or emerging country that you have studied:
18) Where are the oldest buildings found?
19) Describe where most new growth is taking place in the city.
20) Give one reason why the population has grown rapidly in recent years.
21) Give two distinctive characteristics of the ways of life in the city.
22) Give three opportunities that the megacity offers to the people who live there.
23) Outline three challenges that the people in the city face.
24) Give two reasons for the differences in the quality of life within the megacity.
25) Outline one top-down initiative that is trying to make the city more sustainable.
26) Outline one bottom-up initiative that is trying to make the city more sustainable.
27) Give two advantages of top-down sustainability strategies.
28) Give two disadvantages of community-led sustainability strategies.

Urban Land Use

In general, most cities in the UK have a <u>similar layout</u> — there are <u>four distinct zones</u> with <u>different land uses</u>.

Cities Have Different Zones

Most UK cities have <u>distinct areas</u> called <u>zones</u>. You might be asked to spot one of them on a map, so here are the four main zones and what to look out for:

The <u>Central Business District</u> (CBD) is usually in the middle of a town or city. It has <u>commercial</u> and <u>public buildings</u>, e.g. libraries, museums, hotels, <u>shops</u>, offices, restaurants and <u>entertainment facilities</u>. Look for <u>high density</u> buildings and the <u>meeting</u> of <u>major roads</u>.

The <u>suburbs</u> are found towards the edge of the city. They are mainly <u>residential</u> areas, often with <u>semi-detached houses</u>. Look for lots of <u>short</u>, <u>curved</u> streets and <u>cul-de-sacs</u> on the map.

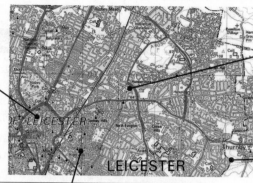

The <u>rural-urban fringe</u> is on the edge of the city. It has farmland and open spaces as well as a mix of <u>commercial</u> business parks and <u>residential</u> (high-class housing). Look for <u>white spaces</u> showing fields <u>mixed</u> with more <u>built-up areas</u>.

The <u>inner city</u> area often has a mix of land uses — mainly <u>industrial</u> and <u>residential</u> (<u>old terraced houses</u>, <u>high-rise tower blocks</u> and <u>modern housing</u> built in redevelopment programmes). There are also some <u>businesses</u> and <u>recreational parks</u>. Lots of <u>short</u>, <u>parallel</u> roads often show areas of <u>terraced housing</u> in the inner city.

Land Use is Influenced by Accessibility, Availability, Cost and Regulations

Accessibility

1) City centres are usually <u>very accessible</u> — they are the location of the main <u>train</u> and <u>bus stations</u> and the <u>centre</u> of the <u>road network</u>.

2) <u>Shops</u> and <u>offices</u> locate in city centres because they need to be <u>accessible</u> to lots of people.

3) Some <u>businesses</u> now locate on the <u>edges</u> of cities — these are near <u>major motorway junctions</u> and <u>out-of-town airports</u>, so <u>avoid traffic congestion</u> in the <u>city centre</u>.

Planning Regulations

1) <u>City planners</u> try to <u>control</u> how cities develop by deciding what <u>types</u> of buildings can be built in <u>different parts</u> of the city.

2) There are often <u>strict</u> planning regulations in city centres — <u>polluting</u> industries may be <u>banned</u>.

3) Some cities have <u>strict limits</u> on development in the <u>rural-urban fringe</u>, e.g. designated greenbelt land that can't be built on. This stops the city <u>sprawling</u> into the <u>countryside</u>.

Availability

1) In the city centre almost all land is <u>in use</u> and <u>demand</u> is <u>high</u>. Businesses may <u>extend upwards</u> as ground space is limited — the <u>tallest</u> buildings are often in the <u>centre</u>.

2) <u>Brownfield</u> land in city centres, such as <u>old industrial sites</u>, may be <u>redeveloped</u> as <u>shops</u> or <u>offices</u>. Some of the <u>old terraced housing</u> and <u>apartment blocks</u> in inner cities are <u>redeveloped</u> as <u>luxury homes</u> for young professionals.

3) There is <u>lots of space</u> on the <u>edges</u> of cities where <u>larger buildings</u>, e.g. shopping centres, science parks, industrial estates and houses, can be built (if allowed).

Cost

1) The <u>city centre</u> has the <u>highest land prices</u> — the cost of land <u>falls</u> towards the <u>edge</u> of the city.

2) Some <u>businesses</u> and <u>shops</u> can <u>afford</u> to locate offices and shops in the <u>city centre</u> but there are <u>few houses</u>.

3) <u>Houses</u> tend to <u>increase</u> in <u>size</u> from the <u>inner city</u> to the <u>suburbs</u> as the <u>price</u> of land <u>decreases</u>.

Land use changes in the different zones of a city

It's a good idea to learn the four main parts of a city and the land use in each bit. Remember that how the land is used is affected by many things. Make sure you've given all the information on this page a good look over.

Urban Change

Urban areas go through a lot of changes as they develop. Changes in the economy mean people move in, then they move out, and then they move in again — this has lots of consequences for cities and surrounding areas.

Suburbanisation is When People Move to the Edge of the City

Suburbanisation is the movement of people from the middle of the city to the edges — urban areas expand rapidly (sprawl) as housing is built on the outskirts. It began occurring in the early 20th century in many developed countries including the UK.

Causes

1) Urbanisation causes urban areas to become overcrowded and polluted, with little 'natural' space. Suburban areas offer more open green spaces and can seem more family-friendly.

2) Improvements in transport networks mean that people can live in the suburbs and commute in to the city to work.

3) As countries develop, governments often clear low quality city centre housing and provide new houses outside the city for residents.

4) Planning laws may be more relaxed outside city centres, so it's easier to build houses. In the UK, developers build new housing estates on the edges of urban areas.

Consequences

1) As urban areas spread, more ground is concreted over. This can increase surface run-off (when water flows quickly overland) and the risk of flooding.

2) There are fewer people living in inner city areas, which may cause businesses (e.g. shops) to close. This increases unemployment, which leads to lower living standards and poverty.

3) Wealthier middle-class people may move to the suburbs, leaving poorer people in inner city areas.

4) As people and businesses move out to the suburbs, buildings in the city centre are abandoned and may become derelict. This can lead to the city centre becoming run down.

Counter-urbanisation is Movement to Rural Areas

Counter-urbanisation is the movement of people away from large urban areas to smaller settlements and rural areas. In the UK and many other developed countries this process began in the 1970s and 80s.

Causes

1) Suburbs and city centres often have problems with traffic congestion and parking. Increased car ownership and improved public transport mean that people can live further from the city and commute to work.

2) Housing in central urban areas and the suburbs is often very expensive. People feel they are not getting value for money and move further from the city, where prices are often lower.

3) Houses in smaller settlements and rural areas are often bigger and have more outside space than those in city centres and the suburbs. People think they'll have a higher quality of life in rural areas.

4) Improved communication services (e.g. high-speed internet connections) make it easier for people to live in rural areas and work from home.

Consequences

1) Some services in rural areas see an increase in business (e.g. pubs that have restaurants). This is because the newer residents are often professionals or retired people who have higher disposable incomes.

2) But it can lead to the creation of commuter settlements — where people live in rural areas but continue to work in the city. This may force some shops and services in rural areas to close because of reduced demand — people spend most of their time away from the area at work.

3) New housing estates are often built on open countryside, which affects wildlife habitats.

4) Rural roads and infrastructure may struggle to cope with the additional traffic.

Urban Change

De-Industrialisation — Manufacturing Moves Out of an Area

1) As countries develop, they experience de-industrialisation (manufacturing moving out of an area). Urban areas are affected by industry moving:
   - out of city centres into rural areas where rents are cheaper.
   - overseas to countries where costs are lower — this is known as global shift.

2) De-industrialisation can lead to de-population as people leave the old industrial areas.

3) The city centre and industrial zones on the edges of cities decline — unemployment increases leading to lower living standards and poverty. Shops, restaurants and other amenities close.

Some City Centres have Undergone Regeneration

Since the 1990s some city centres in developed countries have undergone regeneration to reverse the decline of urban areas because of suburbanisation, counter-urbanisation and de-industrialisation.

Causes

1) To attract people and businesses back to the city centre, governments and private companies invest in new developments, e.g. high quality flats and office blocks, and upgrade infrastructure.

2) Once re-urbanisation has started it tends to continue — as soon as a few businesses invest and people start to return, it encourages other businesses to invest.

3) Young, single people often want to live close to their work in areas with good entertainment services (e.g. bars and nightclubs).

The movement of people back into urban areas is known as re-urbanisation.

Consequences

1) As people move back into the city centre, new shops and services open, which boosts the economy in the city. But jobs created in new businesses may not be accessible to the original residents, many of whom are unskilled or semi-skilled.

2) Original residents in the area being re-urbanised are often on low incomes and may not be able to afford housing as prices increase. They may have to move to cheaper areas of the city.

3) Re-developing derelict brownfield sites in cities instead of greenfield sites in the open countryside protects countryside wildlife habitats.

New Islington has Been Regenerated

Here's how an inner city area in Manchester was regenerated:

The old estate needed regenerating...

1) The Cardroom Estate was built in Manchester in the 1960s, just east of the city centre. It replaced the old, cramped terraces that had housed factory workers.

2) By the mid 1990s the estate had become run-down and had a bad reputation. 50% of the houses were empty or being used as squats.

3) The area had many economic and social problems including high unemployment, joyriding, burglary, drug problems, graffiti and vandalism.

... so people took action

1) The government's regeneration agency worked with private companies and local residents to improve the area — renamed New Islington.

2) 1700 new homes were built in consultation with local residents, and a new tram stop improved public transport links.

3) New community facilities include a health centre, village hall, and restaurants and cafés.

4) The project provided an orchard, an eco-park and a community football pitch — these have made the area a more attractive place to live.

Many UK cities have experienced deindustrialisation and regeneration

If you've studied a different example of urban regeneration, you can use that instead. But make sure you can explain the problems caused by deindustrialisation, and the social and economic impacts of regeneration.

Dynamic UK Cities

CASE STUDY

Right, now that you know the basics of <u>urban change</u>, it's time to get into the specifics with a case study. <u>London</u> is a classic example of how changes in a city provide both <u>opportunities</u> and <u>challenges</u>.

London is a **Global City** in **South East England**

1) London is sited on the <u>flat floodplain</u> of the <u>River Thames</u> where it meets the sea.

2) It is the UK's <u>capital city</u> and is an essential part of the UK's economy. <u>Over 20%</u> of the UK's <u>income</u> comes from London.

3) It is the centre of the UK's <u>transport</u> system. It was a major <u>port</u> until 1981 and still has <u>shipping links</u>. There are <u>two major international airports</u> (Heathrow and Gatwick) plus three <u>smaller</u> ones, e.g. London City Airport. There is <u>easy access</u> to <u>mainland Europe</u> via the Channel Tunnel.

4) It has a major <u>influence</u> on its <u>surrounding area</u>. Companies are attracted to the region by the <u>proximity</u> to London, which <u>increases jobs</u> and <u>wealth</u>. The <u>South East</u> and <u>East of England</u> are the two biggest <u>regional economies</u> in the UK outside London.

5) London's important <u>globally</u> too — it's a <u>world city</u> and, along with New York, one of the two most important <u>financial centres</u> in the world. There are more <u>foreign banks</u> in London than <u>anywhere else</u>.

Learn the **City's Structure**

Land use and building age varies across the city (see p.149).

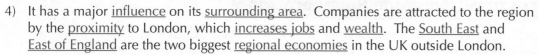
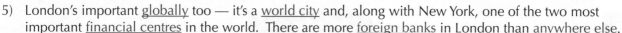

Area (example)	Main Land Use	Description
CBD (Central Business District)	<u>City of London</u>	Commercial	Mix of <u>new high-rise office blocks</u> and <u>historical</u> buildings. Land is <u>expensive</u> so building <u>density</u> is <u>high</u>. There are a <u>few small parks</u>.
Inner city	<u>Newham</u>	Low-class residential	<u>High-density</u>, <u>old</u> terraced housing, <u>1960s-70s high-rise flats</u> and <u>modern apartment</u> buildings. <u>Poor</u> environmental quality, some <u>green space</u>.
	<u>Chelsea</u>	High-class residential	<u>80%</u> houses built <u>before 1919</u>. Land is <u>expensive</u> so building <u>density</u> is <u>high</u>. Lots of <u>large terraced houses</u>, some converted into <u>flats</u>. High quality <u>green space</u> — most houses have <u>gardens</u>.
Suburbs	<u>Surbiton, Kingston upon Thames</u>	Middle-class residential	Good quality <u>20th century semi-detached</u> housing, along with <u>shops</u> and <u>restaurants</u>. Most houses have <u>gardens</u> and there are <u>large</u> areas of good quality <u>green space</u>.
Rural-urban fringe	<u>Crockenhill, Sevenoaks</u>	High-class residential	<u>Large</u>, <u>detached</u> and <u>semi-detached</u> houses with <u>gardens</u> — the area is surrounded by <u>countryside</u>.
	<u>Thurrock</u>	Industrial, commercial	Industry includes <u>oil refineries</u>, <u>manufacturing</u> and a <u>container port</u>. Lakeside <u>retail</u> park opened in <u>1990</u>.

Migration is Causing Parts of London to **Grow**

1) The <u>population</u> of London is now over <u>8.5 million people</u> and it's <u>growing</u> due to:
   - <u>International migration</u> — <u>net</u> migration to London in 2014 was <u>100 thousand people</u>.
   - <u>National migration</u> — within the UK, <u>young</u> adults move <u>to</u> the city for <u>work</u> or to <u>study</u>.
   - <u>Internal population growth</u> — the <u>young population</u> means there are <u>more births</u> than <u>deaths</u> in the city.

2) <u>Inner city</u> London has the <u>highest rate</u> of people moving <u>in</u> and <u>out</u> including both the <u>wealthiest</u> and <u>poorest</u> people. <u>Highly skilled</u> people move to the <u>inner city</u> to work in <u>high-paid jobs</u> (e.g. in banking) along with <u>low-paid migrants</u> looking for jobs in the <u>service sector</u> (e.g. cleaning and catering).

3) Migrants who have been in London for <u>longer</u> tend to move out to the <u>suburbs</u> as they become more <u>settled</u>. About 50% of the population of the <u>outer London boroughs</u> of <u>Harrow</u> and <u>Hounslow</u> are <u>foreign-born</u>.

Dynamic UK Cities

Migration Influences the Character of Different Parts of the City

Age Structure — there is now a high percentage of people aged 25-34 in inner city London and a lower proportion of people over 65. Most immigrants are of working age.

Ethnicity — ethnic diversity is higher in inner city areas, e.g. 52% of people are foreign born in Newham compared to 29% in Kingston upon Thames, but it's increasing rapidly in some suburbs, e.g. Bexley.

Population — population growth rates are increasing in inner city areas because of high immigration rates and because many migrants are of child-bearing age (so birth rates are higher).

Housing — the high rate of immigration is leading to overcrowding. Poorer immigrants often live in older terraces and 1960s-70s council tower blocks in the inner city, which are more affordable.

Services — in inner city areas where immigration rates are high, there is an increasing demand for services such as education and health care (e.g. for school places and maternity care). However, these areas are often amongst the poorest parts of the city, so it's difficult to provide what's needed.

There are Distinctive Ways of Life in London

Chinatown

1) London's West End is home to many theatres where the world's top musicals and plays are regularly performed. Some of the UK's most popular museums and art galleries are in London e.g. the British Museum and the National Gallery. The city is also a centre for fashion — London Fashion Week is one of the four biggest fashion events in the world.

2) London has very high ethnic diversity, and some areas, e.g. Chinatown, have a high proportion of people from one ethnic background. Lots of food, music and goods from that culture can be found in the area and many people are attracted to these areas to shop and eat.

3) There are also many big festivals celebrating different cultures and ethnic backgrounds, for example, the annual Afro-Caribbean Notting Hill Carnival, Chinese New Year parade, Proms and Eid in the Square.

4) Housing in richer areas (mainly west London and the suburbs, e.g. Sutton) tends to be modern apartments or large houses with gardens. In poorer areas (mainly the inner city and east London, e.g. Newham) the housing density is higher and many buildings have been split to house multiple families.

5) Many leisure facilities are available for people in London — cinemas, concert venues, clubs and pubs are all popular and the city is also home to some of the best restaurants and shopping areas in the UK. There are also many popular visitor attractions, such as the London Eye and the Tower of London.

6) London has many world-class sports facilities, e.g. Wembley and Twickenham stadiums. Each year there are lots of popular mass participation sporting events around London, e.g. the London Marathon.

7) London's wealth means that it consumes a huge amount of resources — food, water and energy etc. E.g. Londoners consume nearly 7 million tonnes of food every year, most of which is imported.

London has Environmental Opportunities and Problems

1) Urban greening is important in London — green spaces have environmental benefits and make sure cities remain places where people want to live and work. London is already 40% public green space with lots of parks in the city centre, e.g. Hyde Park, and larger open areas on the outskirts, e.g. Hampstead Heath.

2) However, the growth of the city and movement of people to the suburbs means there is pressure to build on greenfield sites. This has destroyed natural habitats. Building on brownfield sites is better for the environment but the land needs clearing and decontaminating first.

3) Waste disposal is becoming an increasing issue as the city's population grows. Only 33% of rubbish in London is recycled (the lowest level in the whole of England) — the rest goes to landfill.

London is constantly growing and diversifying

This may seem like loads of information, but it's all pretty straightforward really — think about how migration might impact the city's structure and character. The changes in the city will have effects on the environment too.

Dynamic UK Cities

CASE STUDY

UK cities are <u>changing</u> and London's no different. Changes lead to <u>opportunities</u> and <u>challenges</u>.

Urban Change has Created Opportunities in London

Financial and business services and TNC investment

- The <u>growth</u> of <u>finance</u> and <u>business</u> services is <u>revitalising</u> the <u>CBD</u>. The City of London has emerged as a global centre for <u>banking</u>, <u>insurance</u> and <u>law</u> companies, which benefit from being <u>close</u> to each other.

- Many <u>TNCs</u> locate their <u>sales</u> and <u>marketing</u> departments and <u>headquarters</u> in London because of its <u>importance</u> as a <u>financial centre</u>. TNCs based in London include HSBC, Shell, GlaxoSmithKline and Virgin Atlantic Airways. These in turn attract <u>further investment</u> as they help to cement London's <u>identity</u> as a <u>global</u> city.

London also has an integrated transport system, making travel easier (see p.157).

Gentrification and studentification

- Some areas, e.g. Islington, have been <u>gentrified</u> — <u>wealthier</u> people move in to <u>run down areas</u> and <u>regenerate</u> them by <u>improving</u> their houses. New <u>businesses</u> are springing up in gentrified areas to cater for the wealthier newcomers.

- Other areas, e.g. Camden, have been <u>studentified</u> — a high student population has led to <u>thriving services</u> and <u>entertainment venues</u>, generating <u>new jobs</u> and <u>wealth</u> for the area.

Leisure and culture

- London hosted the <u>Olympic games</u> in 2012, with most <u>investment</u> taking place in London's <u>East End</u>. This was one of London's <u>most deprived</u> areas but the area now has <u>new transport links</u> and the <u>athletes' village</u> has been developed into a modern <u>housing estate</u>. The sports stadiums are <u>open</u> for <u>community use</u> as well as <u>world sporting events</u>. New <u>jobs</u> have been <u>created</u> and lots of people are <u>moving to</u> the area.

Modern London faces lots of Challenges

1 Housing Availability

London's <u>population</u> has been <u>growing rapidly</u>, but <u>homes</u> have <u>not</u> been built at the same pace. The <u>supply of homes</u> is <u>not enough</u> to meet the <u>demand</u>, so <u>house prices</u> and <u>rents</u> are <u>rising</u>. Workers on <u>lower incomes</u> often can't afford to live <u>near</u> to where they work, many people can't afford to <u>buy</u> homes, and adults <u>house-sharing</u> is becoming <u>more common</u>.

2 Transport Provision

London has a very good transport system but the <u>rising population</u> and <u>increasing</u> number of <u>commuters</u> is stressing the transport network. Roads are frequently <u>congested</u>, trains are overcrowded and the <u>London Underground</u> is increasingly filled <u>beyond its capacity</u>.

3 Access to Services

London provides some of the <u>best healthcare</u> and <u>education</u> in the UK. However, its <u>large population</u> means that <u>access</u> to these services can be <u>difficult</u>, especially for <u>poorer</u> people.

The <u>best</u> state schools, e.g. Holland Park, are very <u>over-subscribed</u> and difficult to get into. <u>Wealthy parents</u> are able to send their children to <u>fee-paying</u> schools, but many children from <u>poorer families</u> end up in under-performing schools.

4 Inequality

London is home to the <u>richest</u> and the <u>poorest</u> people in the UK and the <u>gap</u> is <u>widening</u>. Many children in deprived areas of London leave school <u>without basic qualifications</u>, leading to <u>low incomes</u> and <u>high unemployment</u> — more than <u>25%</u> of the population are living in <u>poverty</u>, due to <u>unemployment</u> and <u>low wages</u>. <u>Unhealthy lifestyles</u>, e.g. drinking, smoking and poor diets, are <u>more common</u> in <u>deprived areas</u>. <u>Life expectancy</u> is about <u>5 years lower</u> in <u>poorer</u> areas of the city than in wealthier areas.

REVISION TIP

Draw yourself a table of urban opportunities and challenges

Make sure you're familiar with the opportunities and challenges caused by change in urban areas of the UK. Try making a table or drawing a colourful mindmap to help you remember them all.

Dynamic UK Cities

The growth of London has had a massive impact on surrounding rural areas.

London and its Surrounding Rural Areas are Interdependent

London is connected to the rural areas around it — they rely on each other for goods and services.

1) Many people commute into London from the surrounding rural areas to work. This means some villages, e.g. Ivy Hatch, may become commuter settlements — where people live in rural areas but work in London.

2) Students and young professionals move into London to live close to their work in areas with good entertainment facilities, e.g. Camden has lots of pubs, clubs and restaurants.

3) London has excellent hospitals and private schools as well as specialist services, e.g. Great Ormond Street children's hospital — people travel from the surrounding rural areas to use them.

4) London relies on the surrounding rural areas for food — many farmers sell their produce to supermarkets and wholesalers who transport it into the city.

Urban Sprawl is Changing the Rural-Urban Fringe...

1) Most growth has taken place in the rural-urban fringe. Large shopping centres, e.g. Bluewater, have been built on the edge of the city where land is cheaper and there is less congestion and more parking space.

2) Industrial areas, e.g. Crossways Business Park by the QEII bridge, have also been developed on the outskirts of London.

3) The availability of jobs has attracted many people to live there. Large housing estates, e.g. St Clements, have been built on rural greenfield land — open spaces are lost and ecosystems damaged or destroyed.

...Which has Created New Challenges for the Rural Areas Around London

1) Lots of people are moving from London to the surrounding rural areas for a better quality of life (counter-urbanisation — see page 150). This puts pressure on housing, pushing up prices.

2) The population of some areas, e.g. Sevenoaks District (north west Kent), is becoming older. Lots of people retire there because it is a peaceful, pleasant environment. At the same time, younger people are leaving, and many move into London for work. Ageing populations require more healthcare and special facilities, e.g. nursing homes.

3) As the number of young people in rural areas has decreased, schools in some villages have had to close due to declining numbers of pupils, e.g. there is now no secondary school in Edenbridge.

4) Increased use of technology in agriculture and increasing farm sizes has decreased the number of workers needed in rural areas. Finding alternative employment can be a challenge.

Rural Diversification Creates Economic Opportunities

1) Many farmers struggle to earn enough to live on — prices for their goods are forced down by supermarkets and cheaper imports.

2) Some farmers are finding alternative ways of making money, either by farm-based activities or by starting a new business (e.g. farm shops, accommodation and leisure activities). This is known as rural diversification.

3) Tourism can also create new economic opportunities in rural areas. For example, Leeds Castle (in Kent) is a historic building that has developed various attractions (e.g. a maze and golf course) and events to encourage more people to visit. However, this can mean that new tourist facilities are built on greenfield land and lead to an increase in traffic congestion.

Cities have big impacts on the rural areas surrounding them

And there you have it, the last page of this enormous case study. You don't have to learn about London if you've studied a different example in class, just make sure you have enough information to cover all the key points.

Sustainable Urban Living

It's the 's' word again — it wouldn't be a geography topic without it. This time it's sustainable cities.

Urban Areas Need to Become More Sustainable

1) Sustainable living means doing things in a way that lets the people living now have the things they need, but without reducing the ability of people in the future to meet their needs (see p.144).

2) Big cities need so many resources that it's unlikely they'd ever be truly sustainable. But things can be done to make a city (and the way people live there) more sustainable:

Water Conservation Schemes

Only as much water should be taken from the environment as can be naturally replaced. Water conservation schemes reduce the amount of water used. For example:

- collecting rainwater for use on gardens or for flushing toilets.
- installing toilets that use less water to flush.
- installing water meters so that people have to pay for the water that they use.
- encouraging people to use less water, e.g. by turning off taps whilst brushing teeth.

Creating Green Space

Cities can be noisy, dirty, busy and hot — they are unsustainable because people find them unpleasant and stressful. Creating green space within urban areas helps to make sure that they remain places where people want to live and work. This is because:

- they provide naturally cooler areas where people can relax in very hot weather.
- they encourage people to exercise more and to use alternative transport, e.g. bikes. This makes people healthier and less stressed.
- they make people feel happier by providing a break from the noise and bustle of the city.

Green spaces also have environmental benefits. For example:

- they reduce the risk of flooding by reducing surface runoff from rainfall.
- they reduce air pollution by creating pockets of clean air.

Energy Conservation Schemes

Burning fossil fuels to generate power isn't sustainable because they'll run out. Burning them also increases the rate of climate change because it produces greenhouse gases. Energy conservation schemes reduce the use of fossil fuels. For example by:

- promoting renewable energy sources (wind, solar, tidal etc.) over traditional coal or gas fired power stations.
- government incentives to make homes more energy efficient, e.g. allowing homeowners who generate electricity from renewable sources (such as solar panels) to sell any excess energy to the national grid.
- making sure that new homes that are built meet minimum energy efficiency requirements.
- encouraging people to use less energy at home, e.g. by turning off lights when they're not needed.

Waste Recycling

More recycling means fewer resources are used, e.g. metal cans can be melted down and used to make more cans. Less waste is produced, which reduces the amount that goes to landfill. Landfill is unsustainable as it wastes resources that could be recycled and eventually there'll be nowhere left to bury the waste. Decomposing landfill also releases greenhouse gases. Waste recycling schemes include:

- collection of household recycling boxes.
- recycling facilities for larger items, e.g. fridges.
- websites, e.g. Freecycle™ and Freegle™, where items are offered for free so they can be used by others instead of being thrown away.

EXAM TIP

A lot of these strategies are common sense

If you're asked about how cities can be made more sustainable in the exam and you can't remember, don't panic — start off by thinking about all the ways you could avoid throwing stuff away. Then think about how you could save other resources such as water and energy. That'll give you a good start.

Traffic Management

Everyone wants a car but everyone hates being stuck in a traffic jam. Cities have so many people and so many cars that traffic congestion is a massive problem. Fortunately, there are some schemes in place to manage it.

Traffic Congestion is a Big Problem for Urban Areas

Many people have to travel to work in urban areas, often by car. Businesses also use lorries and vans for deliveries. Having so many vehicles on the road leads to lots of traffic congestion, which causes problems:

- Environmental problems — lots of traffic increases air pollution, and the release of greenhouse gases contributes to climate change.
- Economic problems — congestion can make people late for work or meetings and delay deliveries by lorries, which causes companies to lose money.
- Social problems — there is a higher chance of accidents (with other cars, cyclists, or pedestrians). Congestion also causes frustration for drivers, health issues for pedestrians and cyclists (from breathing in polluted air) and can delay emergency vehicles.

Using Public Transport Reduces Traffic Congestion

Many urban transport strategies encourage people to use public transport instead of travelling by car. London is a good example of the strategies used but similar schemes are also used in many other cities.

1) The Docklands Light Railway is an automatic train system that connects east London with the city centre. It operates mostly on tracks raised above street level, though parts are underground. It is used by 110 million people each year.
2) London's Underground system takes 3 million passengers off the roads every day. A new underground line, Crossrail, is being built east to west across the city to increase rail capacity in central London by 10%.
3) Self service bicycles are available to hire for as little as 30 minutes at a time, and are cheaper than other forms of public transport. Bike lanes and special bike signals at junctions can improve safety.
4) Integrated transport systems make public transport easier to use. For example, in London electronic 'Oyster Cards' allow people to travel on buses, trains, the Underground and some boats without buying separate tickets. They can be automatically topped up and are simply swiped on entry and exit from stations and buses, making them quick and easy to use.
5) Many cities (although not London) also have park-and-ride facilities on the outskirts of the city, which allow people to drive to a large car park, then get the bus into the city centre.

Traffic Flow Can Also be Managed

Traffic congestion can also be reduced by managing the flow of traffic through the city. For example:

1) Ring roads and pedestrianised shopping streets keep traffic away from the city centre, making it safer and less polluted, and preventing congestion on narrow city centre roads.
2) Bus priority lanes stop buses being held up in traffic, making them more attractive than driving.
3) Parking restrictions make sure parked cars don't block traffic flow on narrow roads. 'Urban clearways' are major roads along which stopping or parking is very limited.
4) Congestion charging discourages drivers from entering the city centre at peak times. A scheme in Durham cut the number of cars entering the historic city centre by 85%.
5) Car sharing schemes connect people with similar commutes so that fewer cars are needed. Carpool lanes encourage more people to use car shares. These are traffic lanes where only cars with 2 or more occupants can go — reducing journey times.
6) Promoting flexible working hours means workers aren't all working the standard hours of 9am to 5pm. This helps to spread traffic out through the day, avoiding congestion at rush hour.

Getting people to use public transport is a major traffic management scheme in cities

Basically, the aim is to get as many people as possible out of their cars and onto public transport, then cleverly manage the flow of the traffic that's left. Something for you to think over next time you're waiting in a queue of traffic.

Worked Exam Questions

And here's the worked exam questions for this section. Remember, these answers are just suggestions — there are other correct answers — but they should give you an idea of the kinds of things to write.

Figure 1

1 Study **Figure 1**, an area of Newcastle quayside that has been regenerated. The area declined when industry relocated.

1.1 Using **Figure 1**, give **two** features of the regeneration project.

Feature 1: A walkway has been developed along the river.

Feature 2: The environment has been made more attractive.

[2]

1.2 For a UK urban regeneration project that you have studied, explain how the area has been improved.

In the mid 1990s, the Cardroom Estate in Manchester had many economic and social problems,

e.g. high unemployment, joyriding and burglary. The government's regeneration agency worked with

private companies and local residents to improve the area — renamed New Islington. Regeneration

programmes included the construction of 1700 houses, community facilities (e.g. a health centre) and

new green areas. A new tram stop on the estate also helped to improve public transport links.

[4]

[Total 6 marks]

2 Study **Figure 2**, which shows an area of Byrnshire in 1950 and 2016.

Figure 2

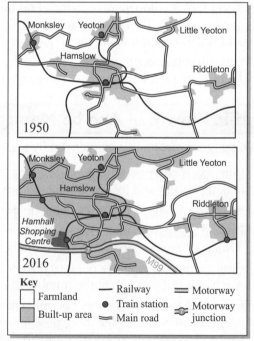

2.1 State **two** ways that cities and the rural areas around them depend on each other.

1: People living in rural areas use city services such as hospitals.

2: Cities rely on farms in the surrounding rural areas for food.

[2]

2.2 Using **Figure 2**, describe **one** environmental cost of the changes to the rural area around Hamslow between 1950 and 2016.

A motorway has been built, which will have increased noise and air pollution.

[2]

2.3 Suggest **one** social challenge that Riddleton might face due to its links with the city of Hamslow.

Schools might be closing down because of declining numbers of pupils, as younger people with

families might not be able to afford rising house prices in Riddleton.

[2]

[Total 6 marks]

Exam Questions

1   Study **Figure 1**, a photograph of
a street in Northern Ireland.

Figure 1

1.1   Using **Figure 1** and your own knowledge,
outline **two** challenges caused by industrial
decline in UK cities.

Challenge 1:..

....

Challenge 2:..

....

[2]

1.2   "Urban change presents more challenges than opportunities."
Using a case study of a UK city, discuss the extent to which you agree with this statement.

[9 + 3 SPaG]

[Total 14 marks]

2   Study **Figure 2**, a graph showing the migration of males into
and out of London in 2013 across a range of age groups.

2.1   Using **Figure 2**, which age group
experienced a net increase in population
due to migration? Shade **one** oval only.

Figure 2

A	0-10 years	⬭
B	11-20 years	⬭
C	21-30 years	⬭
D	31-40 years	⬭

[1]

2.2   What is meant by national migration?

....

....

[1]

2.3   Describe how international migration is changing the growth and character
of a named city in a developed country.

....

....

....

....

[4]

[Total 6 marks]

Revision Summary

Have a go at these questions to see if you've got to grips with UK cities.
* Try these questions and tick off each one when you get it right.
* When you've done all the questions for a topic and are completely happy with it, tick off the topic.

Urban Land Use and Change (p.149-151) ☑

1) Describe how you could identify the rural-urban fringe on a map.
2) Describe where you might find commercial land use in a city.
3) How does accessibility affect urban land use?
4) How do planning regulations affect urban land use?
5) Define suburbanisation.
6) Give two causes of counter-urbanisation.
7) What is de-industrialisation?
8) Give one cause of regeneration.
9) Name one area in the UK where regeneration

Dynamic UK Cities (p.152-155) ☑

For a major city in the UK that you have studied:

10) How is the city connected to the country it is located in?
11) Describe the land use in the inner city.
12) Describe the variations in environmental quality in the city.
13) How has migration affected housing in different parts of a city?
14) Describe the ways of life in the city.
15) Give two environmental problems that the city faces.
16) How has urban change created opportunities for financial and business services?
17) What is gentrification?
18) Describe two challenges that urban change has created in the city.
19) Describe two ways that development is putting pressure on the rural-urban fringe.
20) What are the challenges for rural areas surrounding the city?
21) Give an example of rural diversification.
22) Give two environmental impacts from tourism projects in rural areas.

Urban Sustainability (p.156-157) ☑

23) What does sustainable urban living mean?
24) Describe how water conservation schemes can help make a city more sustainable.
25) Give two examples of energy conservation schemes.
26) Explain the importance of green space for sustainable living in an urban environment.
27) Describe how waste recycling can help make cities more sustainable.
28) Give two economic problems caused by traffic congestion in urban areas.
29) Describe two ways that public transport can be used to reduce traffic congestion in urban areas.
30) Give three strategies for managing traffic flow in urban areas, and explain how they work.

Characteristics of the UK

Time to learn some stuff about the UK. I don't know if you've been, but I hear it's lovely at this time of year.

The **Characteristics** of the UK **Change** Across the Country

<u>UK population density</u>

Population density (the <u>number</u> of people living in a given <u>area</u>) <u>varies</u>:

- Population density is <u>highest</u> in <u>urban cores</u> (the central parts of urban areas, e.g. <u>major cities</u> like London, Glasgow, Birmingham) — in London it's about <u>5500</u> people per km².
- It's also high in areas <u>around</u> major cities, or where there are <u>clusters</u> of cities, e.g. the <u>south-east</u>, <u>Midlands</u> and <u>central Scotland</u>.
- <u>Mountainous</u> regions such as northern Scotland and central Wales have <u>low</u> population densities.
- Other areas of <u>low</u> population density are <u>north England</u> and <u>west Wales</u>. Eden in Cumbria has a population density of about <u>24</u> people per km².

Population density

High
Medium
Low

Glasgow
Eden
Newcastle
Leeds
Manchester
Sheffield
Birmingham
Cardiff
London

High population density can cause <u>problems</u>:

- There may be a <u>shortage</u> of available <u>housing</u> — e.g. in London, up to <u>60 000</u> new homes are needed <u>every year</u> to keep up with <u>population growth</u>. A shortage can drive up the <u>price</u> of houses, so some people <u>can't afford</u> to live there.
- There may be <u>pressure</u> on services such as <u>health care</u> and <u>schools</u> — there can be long <u>waiting lists</u> to see doctors, and children may have to attend a school a <u>long way</u> from home.

<u>UK average annual rainfall</u>   The UK gets <u>quite a lot</u> of <u>rain</u>, but the amount <u>varies</u> hugely around the country:

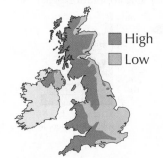

High
Low

- The <u>north</u> and <u>west</u> of the UK generally have <u>high rainfall</u>. E.g. Aultbea in <u>northwest Scotland</u> has an average annual rainfall of <u>1470 mm</u>.
- The <u>south</u> and <u>east</u> of the UK generally have <u>lower rainfall</u>. E.g. London has an annual average rainfall of <u>560 mm</u>.
- Rainfall tends to be <u>higher</u> in <u>coastal areas</u> than inland.
- Rainfall is also <u>higher</u> in areas of <u>higher elevation</u> — <u>mountainous</u> areas get <u>more</u> rainfall than <u>low-lying</u> areas.

The UK's relief (see p.86) helps to determine patterns of population density, rainfall and land use.

Areas with <u>high</u> population density use a lot of <u>resources</u>, e.g. <u>water</u>. If the area also has <u>low rainfall</u>, this can cause <u>water stress</u> — there isn't <u>enough</u> water to meet people's needs. <u>London</u> experiences <u>severe</u> water stress.

<u>Land use</u> is how land is used, e.g. housing or farming. It <u>varies</u> across the UK:

- Most of the UK (about <u>70%</u>) is <u>agricultural</u> land. <u>Arable farming</u> (growing crops) is more common in the <u>south</u> and <u>east</u> of the country, and <u>grazing animals</u> is more common in the <u>north</u> and <u>west</u>.
- Less than <u>10%</u> of the UK is <u>built on</u> — buildings are <u>concentrated</u> in <u>large urban areas</u>, especially in <u>south-east</u> England, the <u>Midlands</u> and <u>central Scotland</u>. These urban areas are <u>expanding</u>. <u>Economic</u> activity is concentrated in <u>urban cores</u> — most <u>jobs</u> are found there.
- <u>Forest</u> covers about <u>13%</u> of the land — some of this is <u>natural</u> and some has been <u>planted</u> and is <u>managed</u> by people.
- Some areas are <u>not used</u> as much by humans and have been left in a fairly <u>natural</u> state, e.g. <u>mountainous</u> or <u>boggy</u> areas in north Scotland.

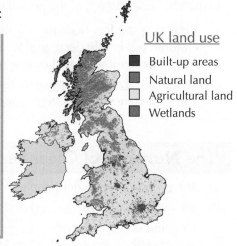

<u>UK land use</u>

Built-up areas
Natural land
Agricultural land
Wetlands

Population density, weather and land use vary across the UK

Don't worry too much about learning specific details on this page — the main thing to learn is the rough patterns of population density, rainfall, land use and relief (see p.86), and some of the issues these patterns can cause.

The Changing Population of the UK

Since 1900, the population of the UK has changed a lot — there are lots more of us, and the average age is increasing.

The UK's Population is Increasing Slowly

1) In 2001, the population of the UK was about 59 million. By 2015, it was about 65 million.

2) Population has increased every year since 2001, but growth rate has slowed down since 2011.

3) The changing population structure of the UK is shown using population pyramids:

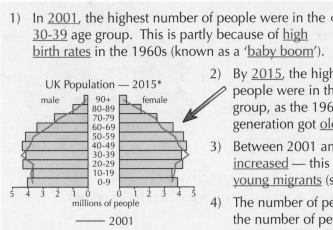

1) In 2001, the highest number of people were in the 30-39 age group. This is partly because of high birth rates in the 1960s (known as a 'baby boom').

2) By 2015, the highest number of people were in the 40-49 age group, as the 1960s 'baby boom' generation got older.

3) Between 2001 and 2015, the number of people aged 20-29 increased — this was partly due to increasing numbers of young migrants (see p.164).

4) The number of people aged 0 to 39 increased by about 6%, and the number of people aged over 39 increased by about 15% — this shows that the UK's population is getting older (see below).

4) The changing population of the UK matches the Demographic Transition Model (see p.179):

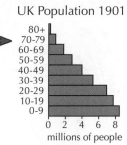

- Between 1900 and 1940 the UK was at stage 3 of the DTM. The population was growing (but not as fast as it had been during the previous 200 years) and there were more younger people than older people.

- Since 1940 birth and death rates have continued to fall (except for baby booms). Birth rate is now 12 births per thousand people and death rate is 9 deaths per thousand people. These are both quite low, but population is still growing slowly — this shows that the UK is at stage 4 of the DTM.

- The UK hasn't yet reached stage 5 — when death rate is higher than birth rate, and population size starts to decrease.

The UK has an Ageing Population

In the UK, around 18% of the population are over 65. The proportion of older people is increasing because:

1) Birth rates are low because couples are having fewer children — in the UK, the average number of children per family decreased from 2.9 in 1964 (the peak of the 1960s 'baby boom') to 1.8 in 2014. Also, more women are choosing not to have children than in the past.

2) People are living longer due to better medical care and a healthier lifestyle (e.g. not smoking). Life expectancy in the UK increased from 72 years in 1964 to 81 years in 2015.

The Number of Older People Varies Around the UK

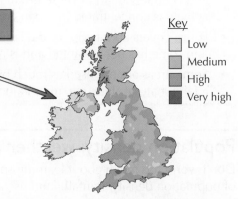

Key
- Low
- Medium
- High
- Very high

1) The proportion of older people isn't the same everywhere in the UK.

2) It's lower in Northern Ireland and Scotland than in England and Wales.

3) It's generally lower in urban cores, such as London, Bristol and Manchester — people often live in cities to be closer to their jobs, so a higher proportion of the population is of working age.

4) The percentage of older people is high in coastal areas, especially in east and south-west England, because lots of people move there when they retire.

The Changing Population of the UK

The Ageing Population Has **Social** and **Economic Effects**

Social

1) <u>Healthcare services</u> are <u>under pressure</u> because <u>demand</u> for medical care has <u>increased</u>.

2) Some people act as <u>unpaid carers</u> for older family members in their free time, so they have <u>less leisure time</u> and are more <u>stressed</u>.

3) People may not be able to <u>afford</u> to have lots of children when they have dependent older relatives. This may lead to a further <u>drop in birth rate</u>.

4) Many retired people do <u>voluntary work</u>, e.g. in hospitals. This <u>benefits</u> the community.

Economic

1) <u>Taxes</u> for working people <u>rise</u> to pay for <u>healthcare</u> and services such as <u>pensions</u> and <u>retirement homes</u>.

2) Older people who <u>aren't working</u> pay <u>less tax</u>, so their economic contribution <u>decreases</u>.

3) However, some older people <u>look after</u> their grandchildren, so their children can <u>work</u>.

4) Many older people have <u>disposable income</u>, which they spend on goods and services that <u>boost</u> the economy.

There are **Different Responses** to the UK's **Ageing Population**

1) As the number of older people <u>increases</u>, the government may need to <u>increase taxes</u> or <u>cut spending</u> in other areas (e.g. education or defence) to fund more <u>support</u> and <u>medical care</u>.

2) The government is <u>raising</u> the <u>age</u> at which people can claim a <u>pension</u> — people <u>stay in work longer</u>, so they contribute to <u>taxes</u> and <u>pensions</u> for <u>longer</u>.

3) The government is encouraging people to <u>save more money</u> to help pay for their <u>retirement</u>. For example, in 2015 the government launched <u>savings accounts</u> for over-65s, known as 'pensioner bonds' — these offer a <u>higher rate of interest</u> than many savings accounts, so older people can <u>save more</u>.

4) The UK government currently offers a <u>winter fuel allowance</u> to <u>all</u> older people. In future, this may <u>only</u> be given to older people who <u>can't afford</u> to heat their homes, meaning <u>less money</u> is spent overall.

London's Population is Different — **Younger** and more **Ethnically Diverse**

1) In <u>2001</u>, the population of London was about <u>7.2 million</u>. By <u>2015</u>, it had increased to more than <u>8.5 million</u>. This is <u>faster</u> growth than <u>anywhere else</u> in the UK.

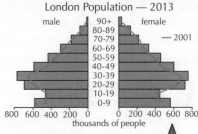

London Population — 2001

male — 90+ 80-89 70-79 60-69 50-59 40-49 30-39 20-29 10-19 0-9 — female

800 600 400 200 0 0 200 400 600 800
thousands of people

London Population — 2013

male — 90+ 80-89 70-79 60-69 50-59 40-49 30-39 20-29 10-19 0-9 — female — 2001

800 600 400 200 0 0 200 400 600 800
thousands of people

2) Growth was <u>higher</u> amongst groups of <u>working age</u> (20-69 years) than for those <u>under 20</u> or <u>over 69</u> — lots of people move to London from elsewhere in the UK or from overseas for <u>work</u>. The <u>highest</u> population growth was in the <u>40-49</u> age bracket, which increased by almost <u>30%</u>.

3) The percentage of <u>men</u> in all age groups <u>increased more</u> than the percentage of <u>women</u> between 2001 and 2013, although the <u>total number</u> of women remained slightly higher.

4) Just like the rest of the UK, population growth in London is driven by <u>natural increase</u> (more births than deaths) and <u>migration</u>. People who migrate there from <u>other countries</u> increase the city's <u>ethnic diversity</u>.

Across the UK as a whole, about <u>13%</u> of the population were <u>born</u> in another country. In <u>London</u>, this value is about <u>37%</u>. Ethnic diversity in London has <u>increased</u> between 2001 and the present — in 2001, <u>60%</u> of the population were <u>white British</u>, but by 2011 this had <u>fallen</u> to <u>45%</u>. The change has been driven by an increase in <u>EU immigrants</u> as well as <u>Black African</u> and <u>Asian</u> people (see next page).

In general, the population of the UK is increasing and getting older

But some areas like London have a much younger and diverse population. Check that you have a good grasp of the ways the population of the UK is changing and the impacts that it's having by jotting down a few points for each.

Migration

The UK's population is changing because people are constantly moving in and out.

Net Migration has been Increasing in the UK

1) Roughly half the UK's population growth is driven by natural increase (more births than deaths), and about half by migration.

2) Between 1970 and 1982 more people left the UK than moved to the UK. There has been a constant flow of British people leaving the UK since 1970 — mostly to Australia, the USA, France and Spain.

3) Overall, since 1983 more people have moved to the UK than have left and net migration has generally been increasing — net migration has more than doubled in the last 10 years.

UK Immigration Policy has Increased Diversity

1) After the second world war, the UK encouraged immigration from Commonwealth countries, e.g. the Caribbean, India and Pakistan, to fill skills shortages in the UK workforce.

2) Later, entry was restricted but work permits for migrants with desirable skills, e.g. IT, were made available — many highly skilled Indians and Pakistanis still come to the UK.

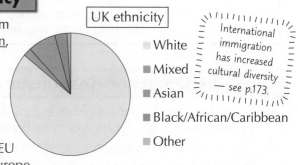

UK ethnicity
- White
- Mixed
- Asian
- Black/African/Caribbean
- Other

International immigration has increased cultural diversity — see p.173.

3) Since 1995 the EU has allowed free movement of people within member countries to find work — while the UK was part of the EU this increased the number of people migrating to the UK from Europe.

4) Between 2001 and 2011, the proportion of non-British white people increased more than any ethnic group — Polish people are now one of the largest non-UK born groups.

Immigration Impacts the UK in Many Ways

1) Immigration affects the population distribution. Most international migrants move to major cities — this is where most jobs are and where universities are located. The most popular destinations for international migrants are London and the West Midlands.

2) Immigration also affects the age structure of the population. The large number of young migrants (20-29) increases the population in this age group. Immigration also increases the birth rate, because many migrants are of child-bearing age. Immigrants make up about 13% of the UK population, but account for about 27% of babies born.

3) Immigration also has social and economic impacts. For example:

Social Impacts

1) Immigrants introduce languages, food, arts etc. giving the UK a rich cultural mix.

2) Sometimes immigrants live in communities with others from the same ethnic group — this can create ethnic segregation and may result in racial tension and violence.

3) Local services like schools can be strained by rapidly increasing local populations. E.g. children may speak English as a second (or third) language, so may need extra help to succeed in schools. Services may need more staff to meet demand.

Economic Impacts

1) Like all workers, immigrants contribute to the local and national economy through taxes.

2) Immigrants claiming state benefits for unemployment and housing and putting increased pressure on public services can cause resentment among other members of the population.

3) In the UK, many immigrants work long hours for low salaries compared to UK-born people. This can reduce average salaries or make working conditions worse.

Immigration has led to increased diversity

Examiners like to ask questions about immigration in the UK, so give this page plenty of attention. Make sure you know the trends and impacts of migration to the UK, both social and economic.

The UK Economy

The UK economy has <u>changed a lot</u> since <u>1960</u>, but is still one of the <u>largest</u> in the world.

The UK's **Economy** is **Changing**

Key <u>causes</u> of economic change include:

1) <u>De-industrialisation</u> and the <u>decline</u> of the UK's <u>industrial base</u> — <u>fewer jobs</u> are available in <u>manufacturing</u> and <u>heavy industries</u> (such as <u>coal mining</u> and <u>steel production</u>). These industries were once a primary source of <u>employment</u> and <u>income</u> for the UK.

2) <u>Globalisation</u> — a lot of manufacturing has moved <u>overseas</u>, where <u>labour costs</u> are <u>lower</u> (global shift), though headquarters of manufacturing companies have often remained in the UK. <u>Trade</u> with other countries is an <u>increasingly important</u> part of UK GDP.

3) <u>Government policies</u> — government <u>decisions</u> on <u>investment</u> in new <u>infrastructure</u> and <u>technology</u> and support for <u>businesses</u> (e.g. tax breaks) affect how well the <u>economy grows</u>. Membership in government groups, e.g. <u>World Trade Organisation</u>, makes it <u>easier</u> for companies in the UK to <u>operate across the world</u>.

Primary and **Secondary** Industries have **Declined**

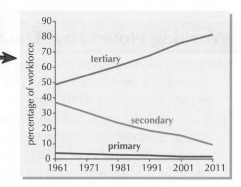

1) Since 1960, jobs in <u>primary</u> industries have <u>decreased</u>. Farming has become more <u>mechanised</u> so fewer people are needed. The <u>mining</u> industry also declined due to <u>competition</u> from abroad and <u>cheaper alternative fuels</u>.

2) Jobs in <u>secondary</u> industries have also <u>decreased</u> — people employed in <u>manufacturing</u> fell from <u>36%</u> of the workforce in 1961 to just <u>9%</u> in 2011. This was partly a result of <u>global shift</u>.

Tertiary and **Quaternary** Industries are **Growing**

1) Tertiary and quaternary industries are becoming <u>more important</u> as the economy becomes <u>post-industrial</u>.

2) In 2011, tertiary and quaternary industries employed over <u>80%</u> of the UK's workforce — and this proportion is <u>increasing</u>. Important industries include:

- <u>Services</u> — e.g. retail, entertainment and personal services (e.g. hairdressers). <u>Retail</u> is the UK's largest sector, employing <u>4.4 million people</u>.

- <u>Information technology</u> — this is now an <u>important</u> part of the UK's economy. Over <u>60 000 people</u> are employed in the <u>IT sector</u> by companies like <u>Microsoft</u>® and <u>IBM</u>®.

- <u>Finance</u> — the UK, and especially the <u>City of London</u>, is home to many <u>global financial institutions</u>. Some, like <u>HSBC</u>, have their <u>global headquarters</u> in the UK.

- <u>Research</u> — <u>research and development</u> (R&D) is <u>increasing</u> in the <u>UK</u>, making use of the UK's <u>skilled university graduates</u>. In 2013, nearly <u>£30 billion</u> was spent on <u>R&D</u> in the UK.

Science and Business Parks

Quaternary industries are increasingly found in <u>science parks</u> or <u>business parks</u>. These are often:

1) On the <u>outskirts</u> of cities near to <u>good transport links</u>, e.g. motorways, A-roads and airports.

2) <u>Close to housing</u> to accommodate the workforce.

3) <u>Near universities</u> so that research businesses in science parks can have <u>access</u> to <u>university research</u>, allowing them to <u>develop cutting edge technology</u>.

The number of them has <u>grown</u> because:

- There is a <u>large</u> and <u>growing demand</u> for <u>high-tech</u> products. Science parks can help develop <u>new technology</u> for these products.

- The UK has a <u>high number</u> of <u>strong research universities</u> for businesses on science parks to form <u>links</u> with.

- <u>Clusters</u> of <u>related businesses</u> in one place can <u>boost</u> each other.

The UK Economy

Changes to the Economy Have Been Driven by Politics

1) Between <u>1997</u> and <u>2007</u>, the UK economy <u>grew strongly</u> and unemployment <u>decreased</u>. This was partly because of the <u>government's priorities</u>:

Investment in technology and education boosted growth of quaternary industries (see p.140).

- Encouraging <u>investment</u> in new <u>technologies</u>, e.g. computing industries.
- Investing in <u>university education</u>, leading to a more <u>skilled workforce</u>.

2) However, in <u>early 2008</u> the UK entered a <u>recession</u>. Businesses <u>failed</u>, <u>GDP decreased</u> and <u>unemployment increased</u>. The government had to <u>change</u> their priorities to <u>end</u> the recession:

- <u>Supporting businesses</u> so they didn't <u>collapse</u> — their collapse would increase <u>unemployment</u>.
- <u>Decreasing taxes</u> on goods to <u>encourage spending</u> and international <u>trade</u>.

Getting people into work means there are fewer people claiming benefits and more paying taxes.

3) The recession ended in <u>late 2009</u>. The government had to focus on <u>paying off</u> money <u>borrowed</u> during the recession and helping people to find <u>jobs</u>:

- Cutting spending on <u>public services</u> such as pensions, education and defence to <u>raise money</u>.
- Providing <u>training</u> for <u>job-seekers</u> and support for <u>new businesses</u> to decrease <u>unemployment</u>.

Working Hours Have Decreased Since 2001

1) Overall, working hours are decreasing — the average number of hours worked in a week was <u>34.7</u> in <u>2001</u> and <u>33.1</u> in <u>2014</u>. The number of hours worked <u>decreased</u> slightly more for <u>men</u> than for <u>women</u> over this time.

Since 1998, the maximum working time per week is 48 hours, and workers are entitled to at least 5.6 weeks of holiday each year.

2) There has been an increase in people doing <u>part-time jobs</u> and <u>zero-hours contracts</u> (where the employee <u>isn't</u> guaranteed <u>any</u> hours of work).

3) However, the number of families with <u>both</u> parents in <u>full-time work</u> has <u>increased</u> since 2003, when the government <u>increased financial support</u> for low-income working parents.

The UK Imports and Exports Lots of Goods

The changes in the UK <u>economy</u> are reflected in the <u>goods</u> it trades in.

1) The UK <u>imports</u> over <u>£500 billion</u> of goods each year — this is <u>more</u> than it <u>exports</u>, which means it has a <u>trade deficit</u>. The UK imports the most from <u>Germany</u>, <u>China</u> and the <u>Netherlands</u>. The UK's main imports include <u>cars</u>, <u>crude oil</u> and <u>petrol</u> — it is wealthy so can afford to import <u>high value goods</u> like cars and <u>fuels</u> to provide energy for industry, homes and transport.

2) The UK <u>exports</u> over <u>£350 billion</u> of goods each year. The UK exports the most to the <u>USA</u>, <u>Germany</u> and the <u>Netherlands</u>. The UK's main exports include <u>cars</u>, <u>machinery</u> and <u>medicines</u>. The development of medicines and high-tech machinery are examples of <u>quaternary</u> industries.

The Effect of Industry on the Physical Environment can be Reduced

1) Industry can have <u>negative effects</u> on the <u>environment</u>, for example by releasing <u>pollutants</u>, <u>greenhouse gases</u> or by damaging the environment through <u>raw material extraction</u>.

2) <u>Modern</u> industrial developments are <u>more environmentally sustainable</u> than older plants as a result of more strict environmental <u>regulations</u>, better environmental <u>awareness</u> and increasing <u>energy</u> and <u>waste disposal costs</u>.

3) For example, <u>Jaguar Land Rover</u> opened a new <u>engine manufacturing centre</u> in <u>Wolverhampton</u> in 2014. The factory is designed to operate more sustainably — it was built to maximise <u>natural cooling</u> and <u>natural light</u> to reduce <u>energy use</u>, and has <u>solar panels</u> in the roof that can generate <u>30%</u> of the plant's <u>electricity</u>. <u>Almost all</u> of the <u>waste</u> from the plant is <u>recycled</u>, with only a <u>small proportion</u> going to <u>landfill</u>.

The UK economy is complex and dynamic

Our economy is constantly changing, driven by de-industrialisation, globalisation and political decisions.

Uneven Development

Economic change has created <u>uneven development</u> — some regional economies are <u>growing</u>, others are <u>declining</u>.

The **Changing** UK **Economy** is Leading to **Uneven Development**

1) Places with a lot of <u>tertiary</u> and <u>quaternary</u> industries are experiencing <u>rapid economic growth</u>:

- <u>Well-connected</u>, <u>desirable</u> locations with <u>good infrastructure</u> find it easier to attract business, so generally have <u>higher</u> levels of development. For example, in <u>Cambridge</u>, links to the <u>university</u> and good access to <u>transport</u> means that industries like <u>technology</u> and <u>biomedicine</u> are growing rapidly.

2) But some areas of the UK are <u>struggling</u> to <u>grow economically</u>. These include:

- <u>Former industrial areas</u>, e.g. north east England and parts of the Midlands, where the loss of <u>manufacturing industry</u> has caused <u>high unemployment</u> and new jobs haven't been created.

- <u>Isolated</u> rural areas on the <u>periphery</u> (edge) of the UK (e.g. north Wales, north west Scotland), which are relatively <u>inaccessible</u>. There are <u>few employment opportunities</u> because they are difficult to farm and have few natural resources (see p.180).

Burnley is a **Former Industrial Area** with **High Unemployment**

1) <u>Burnley</u> is a town in Lancashire, about 20 miles north of <u>Manchester</u>.

2) In the <u>early 20th Century</u> Burnley had a <u>thriving economy</u> based on <u>textiles</u> — it was one of the world's leading <u>cotton weaving</u> towns. From <u>1914</u>, the textiles industry in the UK began to <u>collapse</u> — partly due to cheap <u>imports</u>. The last cotton mill <u>closed</u> in the <u>1980s</u>.

3) Other <u>primary</u> and <u>secondary</u> industries also <u>struggled</u>. Several major factories <u>closed</u> in the <u>1990s</u> and <u>early 2000s</u> with the <u>loss</u> of <u>hundreds of jobs</u>.

4) Burnley has <u>struggled to recover</u> economically. The <u>employment</u> rate is only about 65% and <u>wages</u> are <u>well below</u> the UK average — low-skilled service sector jobs <u>don't pay well</u>. There is <u>very little</u> population <u>growth</u> — with few jobs on offer, people are more likely to <u>leave</u> than to move there.

5) The <u>manufacturing skills</u> existing in the area and the <u>low costs</u> of operating there have begun to attract <u>aerospace</u> engineering firms — meaning the area is still largely <u>dependent</u> on <u>manufacturing</u> industries for employment.

Derelict street

Rural Areas are Changing

Uneven development is also causing <u>changes</u> in <u>rural</u> landscapes:

1) In <u>Cumbria</u> (a rural area in <u>north west England</u>, which includes the <u>Lake District National Park</u>) the <u>population</u> of some villages has <u>decreased</u> recently, especially in <u>western Cumbria</u>. This is mainly due to there being <u>fewer jobs</u> — <u>agriculture</u> and <u>manufacturing</u> are big industries in Cumbria but they're both in <u>decline</u>.

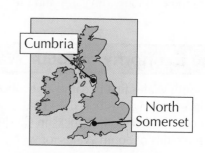

Cumbria

North Somerset

2) In <u>North Somerset</u> (a mainly rural area in the <u>west of England</u>, close to <u>Bristol</u>), the <u>population</u> of some North Somerset towns and villages have <u>increased</u> a lot in recent years, particularly close to <u>Bristol</u>. People are moving to <u>quieter towns</u> and <u>villages</u> with <u>easy access</u> to the centre of <u>Bristol</u>.

3) These changes have <u>social</u> and <u>economic</u> effects:

- As the population has <u>dropped</u> it's caused a <u>decrease in services in Cumbria</u>. Schools, shops and other businesses in some areas are <u>closing</u>. <u>Unemployment</u> is <u>above</u> the national <u>average</u> in <u>two</u> of the <u>districts</u> in Cumbria.

- In <u>North Somerset</u>, house prices are <u>rising</u> which risks <u>pricing out locals</u>. Roads are <u>congested</u> with people <u>commuting</u> to Bristol, and services like schools are <u>oversubscribed</u>.

There are regional differences in development in the UK

Make sure you know why lots of people are moving to some rural areas and the reasons why they are leaving other areas. Then swot up on uneven development and its impacts on former industrial areas like Burnley.

UK Economic Hubs

Uneven development (see previous page) has led to the creation of economic hubs.

An **Economic Hub** is an **Economically Important Place**

1) Economic hubs are places where economic activity is concentrated — e.g. they often have lots of businesses. They have economic influence beyond the hub itself, for example companies located in the hub may trade with companies in other countries.

2) Economic hubs occur at a range of scales. E.g. a region, a city or just part of a city:

- Region — South Wales (see below).
- City — London is an economic hub for the UK, and has a global economic influence, e.g. through trade and financial markets. The headquarters of many banks and other businesses (both UK-based and global) are located there, and the city creates 22% of the UK's GDP.
- Part of city — Electric Works, a large office building in central Sheffield, is home to many digital, creative and media companies.

South Wales is an Economic Hub

1) South Wales is much richer than other parts of Wales — e.g. GDP per capita in Cardiff is £22 000 compared to £15 500 in Wales as a whole. The difference in wealth is caused by the large number of companies that have located in the south, and the high number of visitors the area attracts.

2) Some of the biggest employers in South Wales are digital and media companies — digital companies in South Wales grew by 87% between 2010 and 2013, which is much faster than in the UK as a whole.

3) South Wales also has major manufacturing and service industries, e.g. Ford have a car manufacturing plant in Bridgend and insurance providers Admiral have their headquarters in Cardiff.

4) Most companies are based in the cities, creating inequalities in wealth between the cities and surrounding areas. However, growth has a positive effect on the whole region by creating jobs, attracting visitors and prompting further development, e.g. out-of-town shopping centres.

5) Through business investment, employment and exports, South Wales contributes significantly to the economy of Wales and the UK as a whole.

The **Economy** of South Wales Has **Changed Over Time**

1) South Wales first became an economic hub in the 18th century. For much of the 18th and 19th centuries, its economy was based on coal mining and ironmaking. Canals and rail networks were built to transport coal and iron to the docks in Cardiff, Swansea and Newport, to be exported. Lots of people moved to the cities of South Wales for work, and the area became quite wealthy.

2) In the 20th century, coal mining and ironworking in South Wales declined due to overseas competition. Unemployment levels were high, and many people lived in poverty.

3) In 1992, the different parts of the region started to work together more to achieve economic growth. They aimed to improve transport networks, attract businesses, increase skills and draw visitors to the area. The European Union (EU) gave millions of pounds of funding to help South Wales develop, e.g. nearly £4 million to construct the National Waterfront Museum in Swansea and nearly £80 million to improve the A465 between Hereford and Swansea and improve the accessibility of South Wales.

4) This has helped to attract private investors, including lots of high-tech companies, to the region, making it the economic hub it is now. These industries are likely to expand in future, driving further economic growth in South Wales.

Economic hubs are centres for business, finance and manufacturing

Economic hubs are great for economic growth and job opportunities, and they often lead to further development. Make sure you understand how economic hubs affect the national and regional economies before you move on.

UK Regional Differences

There are <u>social</u> and <u>economic divisions</u> between different parts of the country caused by <u>uneven growth</u>.

Employment, Health, Education and more Vary Across the UK

In general, <u>economic</u> and <u>social</u> indicators tend to be <u>better</u> in the <u>south</u> than the north. This is the north-south divide. There are <u>exceptions</u> — some cities <u>don't fit</u> the trends, and <u>it's not all worse</u> in the north.

Employment — De-industrialisation (see p.151) has had a <u>greater negative impact</u> on the <u>north</u> of the UK, but the <u>growth</u> of the <u>post-industrial service industry</u> has mostly benefited the <u>south</u>. This means there are <u>regional variations</u> in <u>unemployment</u>. Unemployment is <u>highest</u> in the <u>north east</u> of England, and lowest in the <u>south east</u>.

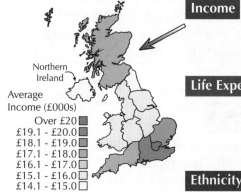

Northern Ireland

Average Income (£000s)
Over £20
£19.1 - £20.0
£18.1 - £19.0
£17.1 - £18.0
£16.1 - £17.0
£15.1 - £16.0
£14.1 - £15.0

Income — The <u>average disposable household income</u> in the UK is about <u>£17 500</u>. But it <u>varies</u> hugely over the UK. <u>Wages</u> are generally <u>lower</u> in the <u>north</u> than the south, e.g. the 2014 <u>average weekly wage</u> was <u>40% lower</u> in <u>Huddersfield</u> than <u>London</u>.

Life Expectancy — Generally, people living in the <u>South</u> of England are <u>healthier</u> than people living in the <u>North</u> of England and in <u>Scotland</u>. The <u>highest life expectancy</u> at birth for <u>males</u> (2011-2013) was in south-east England (<u>80.4 years</u>) and the <u>lowest</u> was in Scotland (<u>76.8 years</u>).

Ethnicity — In 2011, the <u>largest</u> ethnic groups in England and Wales were <u>White</u> (86%), <u>Indian</u> (2.5%) and <u>Pakistani</u> (2.0%). <u>London</u> had the <u>greatest ethnic diversity</u> in 2011. <u>Wales</u> was the <u>least diverse</u>.

Education — <u>GCSE results</u> are generally <u>better</u> in the <u>south</u> of England than the <u>Midlands</u> or the <u>north</u>. There is also a strong <u>link</u> between <u>educational attainment</u> and <u>household income</u> — students from <u>wealthier families</u> tend to get <u>better grades</u>.

Access to Broadband — <u>Most</u> households in the UK <u>have internet access</u> — only around 10% don't. Almost <u>every household</u> with internet has a <u>broadband</u> connection. However, some areas have <u>faster broadband</u> than others — people living in '<u>notspots</u>' in <u>rural areas</u> (and some <u>towns</u>) can have <u>very slow broadband</u>.

The Government and EU have Tried to Resolve Regional Differences

There are <u>schemes</u> at a <u>range of scales</u> designed to <u>reduce differences</u> in wealth:

1 Creating Enterprise Zones

1) The UK government has created <u>55 Enterprise Zones</u> across England, Scotland and Wales.

2) These offer companies a range of benefits for locating in enterprise zones, including <u>reduced taxes</u>, <u>simpler planning rules</u>, and <u>improved infrastructure</u> (e.g. superfast broadband).

3) These measures can be used to <u>encourage</u> companies to <u>locate</u> in areas of <u>high unemployment</u>, bringing <u>jobs</u> and <u>income</u> which could help <u>poorer rural</u> areas to develop.

4) For example, the new <u>Dorset Green</u> Enterprise Zone has already created <u>2000 new jobs</u> in the region.

2 Regional Development

1) The EU used the <u>European Regional Development Fund</u> (<u>ERDF</u>) to promote <u>growth</u> in poorer rural areas by investing in <u>small high-tech businesses</u>, providing <u>training</u> to improve local people's <u>skills</u> and funding infrastructure, e.g. high speed broadband to attract businesses. For example, the EU funded <u>superfast broadband</u> in Cornwall, which attracted <u>digital businesses</u>, such as Gravitas.

2) The <u>Common Agricultural Policy</u> (<u>CAP</u>) is an EU initiative to make sure <u>EU farmers</u> can earn a <u>living</u> from farming. It includes <u>training</u> for farmers and <u>assistance</u> for young farmers starting up, as well as <u>subsidies</u> for <u>rural diversification</u> projects (see p.155). Since leaving the EU in 2020, the UK has introduced its own <u>Agriculture Bill</u> and is starting to <u>transition away</u> from the CAP.

UK Regional Differences

3 Devolving More Powers

1) <u>Scotland</u>, <u>Wales</u> and <u>Northern Ireland</u> have their <u>own devolved governments</u>, and <u>some powers</u> are being devolved to <u>local councils</u> in <u>England</u> too.

2) This allows them to use money on schemes they feel will best benefit the <u>local community</u>, e.g. <u>better public transport</u> or <u>regeneration projects</u> to turn disused buildings into modern office spaces to <u>attract business</u> to the area.

4 Transport Infrastructure

1) The <u>UK government</u> plans to link London, Birmingham, Leeds and Manchester with a new <u>high speed rail line</u>, HS2. This will increase <u>capacity</u> and allow <u>faster journeys</u> into major cities — promoting <u>industry</u> and <u>jobs</u> in poorer areas in the north of England.

2) On a local scale, Lancashire county council has built a <u>new road</u> to link the <u>port</u> of Heysham in Lancashire to the <u>M6</u>. This will encourage <u>businesses</u> to <u>invest</u> by <u>reducing travel times</u> and <u>easing congestion</u>, creating more <u>job opportunities</u> for people in the <u>surrounding rural areas</u>.

The UK has a Good but Improving Transport Network

As well as using transport infrastructure to <u>reduce regional differences</u>, the government is upgrading <u>transport networks</u> to increase capacity. <u>Congested</u> transport networks can <u>slow</u> economic development, so it is important to <u>improve</u> them to ensure continued <u>economic growth</u> across the whole of the UK. For example:

<u>Roads</u> — <u>capacity</u> on <u>motorways</u> is being increased by <u>upgrading</u> to "<u>smart motorways</u>" with <u>extra lanes</u>, e.g. the M4.

<u>Railways</u> — <u>Crossrail</u> (opened in 2022) has <u>increased</u> central London's <u>rail capacity</u> by <u>10%</u>.

<u>Airports</u> — the UK Government has agreed that a <u>new runway</u> is <u>needed</u> in the <u>south east</u> as existing airports are <u>full</u> or <u>filling up</u>.

<u>Ports</u> — a <u>new port</u>, <u>London Gateway</u>, is operating at the <u>mouth</u> of the <u>River Thames</u>. It is able to handle the world's <u>largest container ships</u> and hopes to become a <u>hub</u> for <u>global trade</u>.

The UK has Strong Links to Other Countries

The UK has formed <u>strong links</u> with <u>other countries</u> as it has <u>developed</u> — these links help <u>promote economic development</u> throughout the UK.

1) <u>Trade</u> — the UK trades globally, with links to the <u>USA</u>, <u>Europe</u> and <u>Asia</u> being <u>particularly significant</u>. The UK's <u>overseas exports</u> are worth over <u>£250 billion</u> per year.

2) <u>Transport</u> — the <u>Channel Tunnel</u> links the <u>UK</u> to <u>France</u> by <u>rail</u>, providing a route for <u>goods</u> and <u>people</u> to access <u>mainland Europe</u>. Large <u>airports</u> like <u>Heathrow</u> act as a <u>hub</u> and provide <u>links</u> to <u>hundreds of countries</u> around the world.

3) <u>Electronic Communications</u> — as well as being home to <u>offices</u> for many <u>global IT firms</u>, most of the <u>trans-Atlantic cables</u> (carrying <u>phone lines</u> and <u>internet connections</u>) linking <u>Europe</u> with the <u>USA</u> are routed <u>via the UK</u>.

4) <u>European Union (EU)</u> — the <u>EU</u> is an <u>economic</u> and <u>political partnership</u> of <u>27 countries</u>. <u>Goods</u> and <u>people</u> can <u>move freely</u> between EU countries, <u>strengthening links</u> between members. The <u>UK left</u> the EU in <u>2020</u>, but the two still have <u>economic</u> and <u>political ties</u>.

5) <u>The Commonwealth</u> — the <u>Commonwealth</u> is an <u>association</u> of <u>54 independent states</u>, including the <u>UK</u>. It exists to <u>improve the well-being</u> of <u>everyone</u> in Commonwealth countries.

Make sure you know how the UK is connected to the rest of the world

It's easy to assume you know everything in this section because it's about the UK and you probably know the UK quite well. But you might need to know specific details for the exam, so don't be tempted to just skim read.

UK Links to the Wider World

The UK's links with other countries mean that <u>more</u> and <u>more businesses</u> are arriving in the <u>UK</u>.

FDI is **Increasing** in the UK...

1) A <u>company</u> based in one country can <u>invest money</u> in a <u>different country</u> — this is <u>foreign direct investment</u> (<u>FDI</u>). FDI can take two forms:
   - companies can <u>buy land</u> or <u>buildings</u> and locate their <u>factory</u> or <u>office</u> there.
   - companies can <u>buy</u> all or part of an already <u>existing business</u>.
2) FDI has been <u>increasing</u> in the <u>UK</u> — it <u>rose</u> from <u>£726 billion</u> in 2010 to <u>£1 065 billion</u> in 2014.
3) Most of this <u>investment</u> comes from <u>transnational corporations</u> (<u>TNCs</u> — see p.186).

... Due to **Globalisation, Free Trade Policies** and **Privatisation**

Globalisation

<u>Globalisation</u> is the process of countries become more <u>integrated</u> (see p.186). It is increasing FDI because:

1) <u>Transport</u> and <u>communications</u> links have <u>improved</u> making it <u>easier</u> for companies to <u>operate</u> in the UK.
2) London has <u>developed</u> as a <u>global financial centre</u> — many <u>foreign banks</u>, e.g. the German Deutsche Bank, have located here because of the <u>business culture</u> and <u>networking opportunities</u>.

Privatisation

1) Services that were <u>previously</u> run by the <u>UK government</u> have been offered to <u>private</u> firms. This has increased FDI because <u>foreign firms</u> can buy them or <u>merge</u> them with their existing businesses.
2) For example, many UK <u>electricity boards</u> are now owned by <u>foreign companies</u> — Scottish Power is owned by the <u>Spanish</u> energy company, Iberdrola.

Free Trade Policies

1) Free trade policies <u>reduce import</u> and <u>export restrictions</u>, making it <u>easier</u> for countries to <u>trade</u>.
2) The EU allows <u>free trade</u> between members. The UK <u>left</u> the EU in <u>2020</u>, but the two agreed a <u>trade deal</u>, so companies can still move <u>goods</u> and <u>services</u> easily between the <u>UK</u> and <u>EU</u> countries.
3) Free trade agreements with <u>other countries</u> can attract <u>investors</u> to the UK who want access to <u>other markets</u>. They often include <u>special agreements</u> for <u>investment</u> as part of the deal.

The UK **Economy** is **Increasingly Affected** by **TNCs**

On the plus side...

1) <u>Jobs</u> are <u>created</u>, e.g. the US firm Grand Heritage Hotel Group is investing in a new resort in Derbyshire creating <u>1000 jobs</u>.
2) <u>Large scale projects</u> can be built that the UK government <u>can't afford</u> to pay for, e.g. <u>£15 billion</u> has been invested in <u>UK infrastructure</u>, such as offshore wind turbines, sub-sea power cables etc.
3) TNCs often lead the way in developing <u>new products</u>, <u>technology</u> and <u>business practices</u> which can be used by other firms to <u>increase productivity</u>.

But there are also downsides...

1) It can lead to <u>over-reliance</u> on TNCs — if there's a problem elsewhere in the world, the <u>UK's economy</u> is <u>affected</u>, e.g. the world <u>economic recession</u> led to <u>redundancies</u> at the Nissan factory in Sunderland in 2009.
2) There are <u>big effects</u> if TNCs choose to <u>relocate</u> or <u>change suppliers</u>, e.g. many UK farmers are dependent on just <u>one</u> or <u>two</u> large TNCs who <u>buy</u> their <u>produce</u>.
3) Local businesses <u>struggle to compete</u> against TNCs, e.g. in some towns the <u>arrival</u> of the coffee chain <u>Starbucks</u> has forced <u>independent</u> coffee shops to <u>close down</u>.

Learn the ways in which the UK's economy is linked to the wider world

This is important stuff — economic growth in the UK has been influenced by FDI and transnational corporations. Make sure you understand the benefits of TNCs, and also the problems that they cause to the UK economy.

The UK's Role in the World

The UK may be a relatively <u>small</u> state, but it has an important role in <u>global politics</u> and <u>conflicts</u>.

The UK is a **Member** of Several **International Organisations**

1) Lots of <u>international organisations</u> have been set up to try to <u>avoid conflict</u>, and to ensure that member countries <u>work together</u> to help <u>resolve</u> conflict elsewhere.

2) The <u>UK</u> is a member of several international <u>groups</u>, such as:

- The <u>North Atlantic Treaty Organisation</u> (<u>NATO</u>) is a group of <u>30</u> countries, including the USA and many European countries, who work together to ensure their own <u>security</u>. They aim to <u>prevent conflict</u> by <u>promoting cooperation</u> and to <u>resolve conflicts</u> by <u>political means</u> (e.g. overseeing negotiations) and <u>military</u> means (as a last resort).

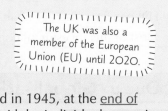
The UK was also a member of the European Union (EU) until 2020.

- The <u>United Nations</u> (<u>UN</u>) is made up of <u>193</u> member states. It was founded in 1945, at the <u>end of WWII</u>, to <u>maintain peace</u>. The UN tries to solve issues that can't be dealt with by individual countries, e.g. helping countries <u>develop sustainably</u> and delivering <u>aid</u> during crises.

- The <u>Group of Seven</u> (<u>G7</u>) has <u>seven</u> members — the US, Canada, France, the UK, Japan, Germany and Italy. Members meet once a year to discuss relevant <u>issues</u>, including <u>economic policies</u>, <u>conflict</u>, <u>energy supply</u> and <u>security</u>, and come to <u>agreements</u> about how best to approach them.

The UK has been Involved in **Resolving Conflict** in **Ukraine**

1) <u>Ukraine</u> is a country in eastern Europe — it is bordered by <u>Russia</u> to the north and east. Ukraine was <u>governed</u> by Russia until 1991.

2) In <u>2013</u>, backed by <u>Russia</u>, the Ukraine government decided not to form closer <u>trade links</u> with the <u>EU</u>, but to strengthen their ties with Russia <u>instead</u>. This was <u>unpopular</u> with many Ukrainians, who wanted to build a closer <u>relationship</u> with <u>western Europe</u>, and there were <u>protests</u> and <u>violence</u>.

3) In <u>2014</u>, the <u>Russian President</u>, Vladimir Putin, <u>took control of Crimea</u> (part of Ukraine) and moved large numbers of Russian <u>troops</u> to the <u>Russia-Ukraine border</u>. There has been <u>fighting</u> between the <u>Ukrainian army</u> and <u>pro-Russian Ukrainians</u> ever since.

4) <u>International organisations</u> in which the <u>UK</u> plays a part have reacted in <u>various ways</u> to the crisis:

NATO — <u>NATO</u> is trying to <u>settle</u> the conflict by encouraging <u>negotiations</u> between the two sides. In 2015, they created a <u>rapid-response force</u> of around <u>5000 soldiers</u> stationed in surrounding countries to <u>deter</u> future attempts by Russia to gain territory. The rapid-response force will be led by different countries in rotation — the <u>UK</u> led it in <u>2017</u>, as well as <u>supplying troops</u> and <u>RAF jets</u>.

UN — The <u>UN</u> is also trying to <u>end</u> the fighting in Ukraine and <u>preserve</u> Ukraine's borders. They are supporting <u>peace talks</u> between Russian and Ukrainian leaders, and <u>providing aid</u> (e.g. food, medicine and blankets) to people forced to <u>leave their home</u> because of fighting. In 2015, the UK gave <u>£15 million</u> in aid to Ukraine, as well as <u>military support</u> and <u>training</u> for the Ukrainian <u>army</u>.

G7 — <u>G7</u> used to be <u>G8</u> — the other countries <u>forced Russia out</u> in 2014, after its seizure of Crimea. The UK, along with the other G7 countries, has imposed <u>sanctions</u> on Russia — e.g. <u>restricting</u> the <u>money</u> that Russian banks can borrow and <u>limiting trade</u> with Russia. By threatening the Russian <u>economy</u>, they hope to make Russia agree to a <u>ceasefire</u> and the <u>withdrawal</u> of Russia's troops.

EXAM TIP

The UK is involved in many different global peacekeeping efforts
If you've studied a different example of the UK's role in an international conflict, feel free to discuss it in the exam. Just make sure you have enough information about the UK's part in that conflict.

UK Media and Culture

The UK's media and culture is one of its most important exports — British books and films can be found all over the world and have helped shape what people in different parts of the world imagine Britain to be like.

The UK Exports Lots of Media Products

1) Media products are things like films, TV and radio shows, music and books.

2) The UK produces lots of media and exports it all over the world. This makes a big contribution to the UK's economy — in 2012, media industries employed nearly 1.7 million people and exported over £17 billion of products worldwide.

> **Examples**
>
> - TV drama series — e.g. 'Downton Abbey' is watched by around 120 million people in more than 100 countries, including the USA and China.
> - TV reality shows — e.g. 'The X Factor UK' is watched by more than 360 million people in 147 territories, and 51 countries have produced their own national version.
> - Films — UK films are distributed all over the world, but are most popular in New Zealand, Australia and Europe. For example, 'The King's Speech' took over US $400 million at the box office, of which two-thirds was outside the UK.

3) Media produced in the UK and reflecting life here are distributed all over the world, and some successful British artists have become internationally famous. This means that media exports have a big influence:

- Most exported UK media are in English, so people in other countries develop a better understanding of the English language. The different lifestyles, values and beliefs of UK residents also become more widely known and understood.

- Media exports affect the way the UK is perceived in other countries — e.g. in some films and TV shows it is portrayed as an ugly, industrial country, while in others it is shown as scenic and rural.

- Seeing the UK portrayed positively in different media makes people want to come here — either to work, to study or just to visit. For example, tourism in the UK increased after the 2012 Olympic Games in London, which was broadcast on TV around the world.

See page 164 for more on immigration to the UK.

Ethnic Groups Influence Life and Culture in the UK

1) The UK is a multicultural country — for centuries, people have moved here from all over the world.

2) People moving to the UK bring their own culture, which they share — e.g. by setting up businesses such as shops and restaurants or building religious centres.

3) People from the same ethnic background often settle in the same area of a city, creating a distinctive character in that area (because of e.g. the architecture and types of businesses that people create there).

4) Ethnic groups have influenced food, media and fashion in the UK:

Food — food that originates in other countries has become a staple for many Brits, e.g. curry and pizza. Different national dishes need different ingredients, so shops specialising in those ingredients often open in areas with a high number of people from a particular ethnic background.

Media — people from ethnic minorities have written, acted in and produced a number of successful TV shows, such as 'The Kumars' and 'Youngers'. Music styles including soul, reggae and dubstep all have roots in Black African and Caribbean music. They have been extremely influential in shaping music in the UK.

Fashion — as traditional cultural clothes become more common, people from other cultures start to wear them. Asian and middle-eastern fashion has become popular in the UK, e.g. harem trousers and kaftans. Fashion houses and high-street shops start to sell their own versions of these clothes, often combining traditional and UK styles — e.g. Indonesian-style batik prints on strapless tops.

Incoming migrants bring their culture and customs to the UK with them

UK culture has been shaped by historical and modern migration — food, media and fashion have all been affected by immigration. Cover the page and see if you can explain some ways migration has influenced life in the UK.

Worked Exam Questions

Another set of worked exam questions to look at here. It's tempting to skip over them without thinking, but it's worth taking time to look carefully — similar questions might just come up in your own exams...

1   Study **Figure 1**, photographs of Chadderton, a northern town, and Bath, a southern city.

Figure 1

Chadderton

Bath

1.1   Using **Figure 1**, outline **one** piece of evidence for a north-south divide.

The quality of housing in the photograph of Bath is higher than that in the photograph of Chadderton.

[1]

1.2   Give **one** reason for the development of the north-south divide.

The growth of post-industrial service industries has mostly benefited the south.

[1]

1.3   Explain how the north-south divide can be reduced.

Devolving more powers to Scotland, Wales, Northern Ireland and some local councils in the north of

England can help to reduce the development gap by providing money that can be used on schemes

they feel will best help the development of the local area. Creating Enterprise Zones could help to

reduce the north-south divide by encouraging companies to locate in areas of high unemployment,

bringing jobs and income to areas that need them. Transport links between the north and the south of

the country could be improved, e.g. the development of the HS2 line, which will allow faster journeys.

[4]

[Total 6 marks]

2   Study **Figure 2**, a photograph showing vehicles boarding a shuttle at the Channel Tunnel terminal in the UK.

Figure 2

2.1   Using **Figure 2**, describe how the UK's transport links help it to connect to the wider world.

Links such as the Channel Tunnel make it quick and easy for people

to get to and from other countries in Europe. Goods can also be

transported easily, increasing the UK's potential for trade with other countries.

[Total 2 marks]

Exam Questions

1   Study **Figure 1**, a map of central Newcastle in 2016.

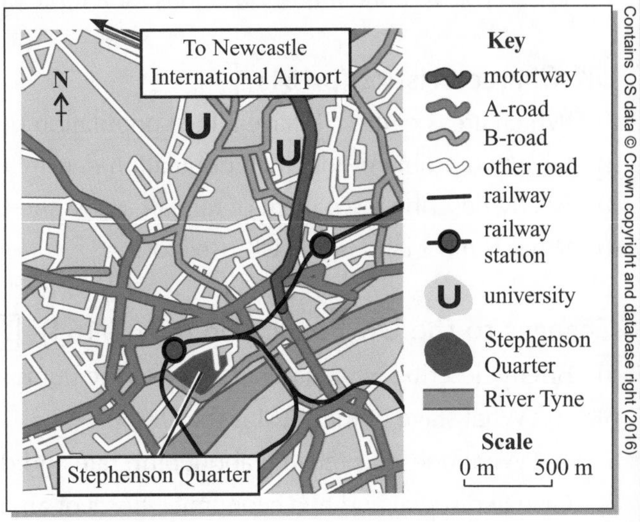

1.1   Suggest **two** reasons why the Stephenson Quarter may be a desirable location for a computing business.

Figure 1

Reason 1: ....

....

....

Reason 2: ....

....

....

[Total 2 marks]

---

2   Study **Figure 2**, a table showing net international migration into the UK between 2001 and 2015.

2.1   Using **Figure 2**, calculate the range of the net international migration values.

....

[1]

2.2   Explain how international migration has altered the age structure of the UK.

....

....

....

....

....

....

[4]

Figure 2

	Net international migration
2001	153 200
2002	190 900
2003	194 200
2004	209 900
2005	336 000
2006	254 800
2007	304 900
2008	284 100
2009	220 100
2010	255 600
2011	270 500
2012	165 500
2013	188 500
2014	264 900
2015	341 400

2.3   State **two** trends in national migration in the UK.

1: ....

2: ....

[2]

[Total 7 marks]

Revision Summary

Well done for making it to the end of Section 12. Time for some revision questions to check what you know.
- Try these questions and <u>tick off each one</u> when you <u>get it right</u>.
- When you've done <u>all the questions</u> for a topic and are <u>completely happy</u> with it, tick off the topic.

UK Characteristics (p.161) ☑
1) Which areas of the UK have a high population density?
2) Give two problems that high population density might cause.
3) Briefly describe the pattern of rainfall across the UK.
4) What is most land in the UK used for?

Changes to the UK Population (p.162-164) ☑
5) Briefly describe what has happened to the number of people in the UK since 2001.
6) a) What stage of the DTM is the UK at?
   b) What does this tell you about birth rate and death rate in the UK?
7) Give two social and two economic effects of an ageing population on the UK.
8) 'The UK has positive net migration.' What does this mean?

The UK Economy (p.165-166) ☑
9) What are the main causes of economic change in the UK?
10) What has happened to the number of people employed in secondary industries since 2001?
11) What sort of industry has become more important as the UK becomes post-industrial?
12) Describe how average working hours have changed since 2001.
13) Give three major exports of the UK.

Uneven Development and Economic Hubs (p.167-168) ☐
14) Give two reasons why some areas of the UK struggle to grow economically.
15) Give two contrasting ways that changes in the UK's economy are affecting rural areas.
16) What is an economic hub?
17) Give three examples of economic hubs in the UK.
18) Give two examples of major industries in South Wales.
19) How is industry in South Wales different now compared to the 19th century?

If you've studied an economic hub other than South Wales, you can answer about that instead.

UK Regional Differences (p.169-170) ☑
20) What is the north-south divide?
21) Describe how employment varies across the UK.
22) Give two ways that transport infrastructure can reduce regional differences in wealth.
23) Give examples of the UK's strong links with other countries.

The UK's Global Significance (p.171-173) ☐
24) Give two examples of international organisations that the UK is a member of.
25) a) Give an example of an international conflict that the UK has been involved in trying to resolve.
   b) Describe how an international organisation involving the UK has reacted to this conflict.
26) Give two ways in which media exports may have influenced people in other countries.
27) a) Give one example each of ethnic food, media and fashion.
   b) For each example, give one way in which it has influenced UK life or culture.

Measuring Development

This topic is a little <u>tricky</u> — but this <u>page</u> will set you up well, so make sure you take a <u>good look</u> at it.

Development is when a **Country is Improving**

When a country <u>develops</u> it basically gets <u>better</u> for the people living there.
There are <u>different aspects</u> to development:

- <u>Economic</u> — progress in <u>economic growth</u>, e.g. how <u>wealthy</u> a country is, its level of <u>industrialisation</u> and use of <u>technology</u>.
- <u>Social</u> — improvement in people's <u>standard of living</u>, e.g. <u>better health care</u> and access to <u>clean water</u>.
- <u>Political</u> — having a <u>stable</u> political system with <u>institutions</u> that can <u>meet the needs</u> of society.

There Are Loads of **Measures of Development**

1) Development is <u>pretty hard to measure</u> because it <u>includes so many things</u>. But you can <u>compare</u> the development of different countries using 'measures of development'.

Name	What it is	A measure of...	As a country develops, it gets...
<u>Gross Domestic Product (GDP)</u>	The <u>total value</u> of <u>goods</u> and <u>services</u> a <u>country produces</u> in a <u>year</u>. It's often given in US$.	Wealth	Higher
<u>GDP per head</u>	The GDP <u>divided</u> by the <u>population</u> of a <u>country</u>. It's often given in <u>US$</u> and is sometimes called <u>GDP per capita</u>.	Wealth	Higher
<u>Gross National Income (GNI)</u> and <u>GNI per head</u>	The <u>total value</u> of <u>goods</u> and <u>services</u> produced by a <u>country</u> in a <u>year</u>, including income from <u>overseas</u>. It's often given in <u>US$</u>. <u>GNI per head</u> is the GNI <u>divided</u> by the <u>population</u> of a <u>country</u>.	Wealth	Higher
<u>Birth rate</u>	The number of <u>live babies born per thousand</u> of the population <u>per year</u>.	Women's rights	Lower
<u>Death rate</u>	The number of <u>deaths per thousand</u> of the population <u>per year</u>.	Health	Lower
<u>Infant mortality rate</u>	The number of <u>babies</u> who <u>die under 1 year old</u>, <u>per thousand babies born</u>.	Healthcare	Lower
<u>Doctors per 1000 of population</u>	The number of <u>working doctors per thousand</u> of the population.	Access to healthcare	Higher
<u>Internet users (ITU)</u>	The <u>number</u> of <u>people</u> who have used the <u>internet</u> in the <u>last year</u> per 100 people.	Wealth	Higher
<u>Literacy rate</u>	The <u>percentage</u> of <u>adults</u> who <u>can read and write</u>.	Education	Higher
<u>Access to safe water</u>	The <u>percentage</u> of people who can <u>get clean drinking water</u>.	Health	Higher
<u>Life expectancy</u>	The <u>average age</u> a person can <u>expect to live to</u>.	Health	Higher
<u>Human Development Index (HDI)</u>	This is a number that's calculated using <u>life expectancy</u>, <u>education level</u> (e.g. average number of years of schooling) and <u>income per head</u>. Every country has an HDI value between <u>0</u> (least developed) and <u>1</u> (most developed).	Lots of things	Higher
<u>Corruption Perceptions Index (CPI)</u>	A measure of the level of <u>corruption</u> that is believed to exist in the public sector on a scale of <u>1-100</u>. The <u>lower</u> the score, the <u>more corruption</u>.	Corruption	Higher

2) <u>Single</u> indicators can be <u>misleading</u> if they are used <u>on their own</u> because, as a country develops, some aspects <u>develop before others</u>. So it might seem that a country's <u>more developed</u> than it <u>actually is</u>.

3) Using a composite indicator of development, where <u>more than one measure</u> is used (i.e. wealth and something else) avoids these problems. The <u>Human Development Index</u> is a composite indicator.

Measuring Development

Development isn't just about money. But when it comes to classifying HICs and LICs, well, it pretty much is.

Countries can be **Classified** based on **How Wealthy** they Are...

A simple way to find a country's level of development is to look at its wealth.

Higher Income Countries (HICs)

HICs are the wealthiest countries in the world, where the GNI per head is high and most citizens have a high quality of life.
For example: UK, USA, Canada, France.

Lower Income Countries (LICs)

LICs are the poorest countries in the world, where the GNI per head is very low and most citizens have a low quality of life.
For example: Afghanistan, Somalia, Uganda and Nepal.

Newly Emerging Economies (NEEs)

NEEs are rapidly getting richer as their economy is moving from being based on primary industry (e.g. agriculture) to secondary industry (manufacturing). Quality of life for many citizens is improving.
For example: China, Brazil, Russia, India.

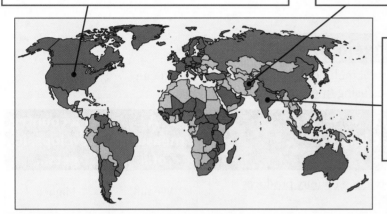

...But Using Wealth **On Its Own** Can Cause **Problems**

GNI per head can be misleading when used on its own because it is an average — variations within the country don't show up.

1) It can hide variation between regions in the country, and between classes — the rich in big cities may have much higher measures of development than the poor in rural areas.

2) For example, if you looked at the GNI per head of Russia it might seem quite developed (because it is high enough to be an HIC), but in reality there are a small number of extremely wealthy people and a lot of very poor people.

You Can Also **Classify Countries** Based on their **Human Development**

1) The human development of a country is based on measures like birth rates and death rates, as well as its HDI score.

2) Developed countries, e.g. the UK, have very high human development.

3) Emerging countries, e.g. India, have medium to high human development.

4) Developing countries, e.g. Chad, have low human development.

	Chad	India	UK
Human Development Index (2014)	0.392	0.609	0.907
Fertility rate (average number of births per woman)	4.45	2.5	1.9
Birth rate (per 1000)	36.1	19.3	12.1
Death rate (per 1000)	14	7.3	9.4
Maternal mortality rate (number of women who die due to pregnancy-related problems per 100 000)	856	174	9
Infant mortality rate (per 1000 babies born)	87	40.5	4.3

There are lots of ways of measuring development

You might come across different names for the three main classifications of countries. Countries with the highest level of development are sometimes called ACs ('advanced countries') or just 'developed countries'. These names are defined slightly differently — some countries will be categorised differently depending on the system used.

Development and the DTM

The Demographic Transition Model can be used to show how countries develop over time.

Development is Linked to the Demographic Transition Model

1) The Demographic Transition Model (DTM) shows how changing birth rates and death rates affect population growth.

2) When the birth rate is higher than the death rate, more people are being born than are dying, so the population grows — this is called natural increase. It's called natural decrease when the death rate's higher than the birth rate.

3) Birth rates and death rates differ from country to country. This means that population growth is faster in some countries than others, especially in less developed countries.

4) Population growth also changes within a country over time as it develops.

5) Changing birth and death rates are linked to a country's economic development (see p.177).

6) So the five stages of the DTM are linked to a country's level of development.

Stage 1 is the least developed — the birth rate is high because there's no use of contraception. People also have lots of children because poor healthcare means that many infants die.

The death rate is also high due to poor healthcare or famine, and life expectancy is low (few people reach old age).

Income is very low.

	Stage 1	Stage 2	Stage 3	Stage 4	Stage 5
Birth rate	High and fluctuating	High and steady	Rapidly falling	Low and fluctuating	Slowly falling
Death rate	High and fluctuating	Rapidly falling	Slowly falling	Low and fluctuating	Low and steady
Population growth rate	Zero	Very high	High	Zero	Negative
Population size	Low and steady	Rapidly increasing	Increasing	High and steady	Slowly falling
Example countries	No countries, some tribes in Brazil	Gambia (HDI = 0.4)	India (HDI = 0.6)	UK (HDI = 0.9)	Japan (HDI = 0.9)

DEVELOPMENT

Stage 2 is not very developed — many developing countries are in stage 2.

The economy is based on agriculture so people have lots of children to work on farms, which means that birth rates are high.

Death rates fall due to improved healthcare and diet so life expectancy increases.

Stage 3 is more developed — most emerging countries are at stage 3. The birth rate falls rapidly as women have a more equal place in society and better education.

The use of contraception increases and more women work instead of having children.

The economy also changes to manufacturing, so income increases and fewer children are needed to work on farms. Healthcare improves so life expectancy increases.

Stages 4 and 5 are the most developed — most developed countries are at one of these stages.

Birth rates are low because people want possessions and a high quality of life, and may have dependent elderly relatives, so there is less money available for having children.

Healthcare is good, so the death rate is low and life expectancy is high. Income is also high.

Population often increases rapidly as countries start to develop

Lots of information here, but don't panic — you don't have to memorise all the information on the diagram. Just make sure you understand what's happening at each stage and how population and development are connected.

Factors Affecting Development

You need to know the <u>factors</u> that <u>affect development</u> — i.e. why <u>countries differ</u> in how <u>developed</u> they are. There are a fair few, but take it steady and you'll be OK...

Physical Factors can Affect How Developed a Country is

1 Climate

1) If a country has a poor climate (<u>really hot</u> or <u>really cold</u> or <u>really dry</u>) not much will grow. This <u>reduces</u> the amount of <u>food produced</u>, which can lead to <u>malnutrition</u>. People who are malnourished have a <u>low quality of life</u>.

2) People also have <u>fewer crops to sell</u>, so <u>less money</u> to <u>spend</u> on <u>goods and services</u>. This also <u>reduces</u> their <u>quality of life</u>.

2 Topography & Farming Land

1) Topography is the <u>shape of the land</u>. If the land in a country is <u>steep</u>, then it <u>won't produce a lot of food</u>. This has the same effect as a <u>poor climate</u> (see left).

2) <u>Steep land</u> can also make it difficult to develop <u>infrastructure</u>, e.g. roads, power lines etc. This can <u>limit trade</u> and make it hard to provide <u>basic services</u>.

3 Few Raw Materials

1) Countries <u>without</u> many <u>raw materials</u> like <u>coal</u>, <u>oil</u> or <u>metal ores</u> tend to <u>make less money</u> because they've got <u>fewer products to sell</u>.

2) This means they have <u>less money</u> to <u>spend on development</u>.

3) Some countries <u>do</u> have a lot of raw materials but still <u>aren't very developed</u> because they don't have the <u>money</u> to <u>develop</u> the <u>infrastructure</u> to <u>exploit them</u> (e.g. roads and ports).

4 Location

1) In countries that are <u>landlocked</u> (don't have any coastline) it can be <u>harder</u> and <u>more expensive</u> to <u>transport goods</u> into and out of the country.

2) This means it's harder to <u>make money</u> by <u>exporting goods</u>, so there's <u>less</u> to spend on development.

3) It's also harder to <u>import goods</u> that might <u>help</u> the country to <u>develop</u>, e.g. medicine and farm machinery.

5 Lots of Natural Hazards

1) A natural hazard is a <u>natural process</u> which <u>could</u> cause <u>death</u>, <u>injury</u> or <u>disruption</u> to humans or <u>destroy property</u> and possessions. A <u>natural disaster</u> is a natural hazard that has actually <u>happened</u>.

2) Countries that <u>have a lot of natural disasters</u> (e.g. Bangladesh, which floods regularly) have to <u>spend a lot of money rebuilding</u> after disasters occur.

3) So natural disasters <u>reduce quality of life</u> for the people affected, and they <u>reduce</u> the amount of <u>money</u> the government has to spend on <u>development projects</u>.

There can also be Human Factors for Uneven Development

1 Poor Trade Links

1) Trade is the <u>exchange</u> of <u>goods</u> and <u>services between countries</u>.

2) <u>World trade patterns</u> (who trades with whom) seriously influence a country's <u>economy</u> and so affect their <u>level of development</u>.

3) If a country has <u>poor trade links</u> (it trades a small amount with only a few countries) it <u>won't make a lot of money</u>, so there'll be <u>less to spend on development</u>.

2 Debt

1) Very poor countries <u>borrow money</u> from <u>other countries</u> and <u>international organisations</u>, e.g. to help cope with the aftermath of a natural disaster.

2) This money has to be <u>paid back</u> (sometimes with <u>interest</u>).

3) Any <u>money</u> these countries make is <u>used to pay back</u> the debt, so <u>isn't used to develop</u>.

Factors Affecting Development

3 Colonialism & Neo-colonialism

1) Countries that were <u>colonised</u> (<u>ruled</u> by a <u>foreign country</u>) are often at a <u>lower</u> level of development when they gain <u>independence</u> than they <u>would be</u> if they had <u>not been colonised</u>.

2) <u>European countries</u> colonised much of Africa in the 19th century. They controlled the economies of their colonies, engaged in the <u>slave trade</u> and <u>removed raw materials</u>, and sold back expensive <u>manufactured goods</u>. This was <u>bad</u> for African development as it made parts of Africa <u>dependent</u> on Europe, and led to <u>famine</u> and <u>malnutrition</u>.

3) After colonies gained their <u>independence</u>, <u>richer</u> countries <u>continued</u> to <u>control</u> them <u>indirectly</u>. For example, some transnational corporations (TNCs) <u>exploit</u> the <u>cheap labour</u> and <u>raw materials</u> of <u>poorer</u> countries (see p.186). This is called <u>neo-colonialism</u>.

4 An Economy Based On Raw Materials

1) Countries that mostly export <u>primary products</u> (raw materials like wood, metal and stone) tend to be <u>less developed</u>.

2) This is because you <u>don't make much profit</u> by selling primary products. Their <u>prices</u> also <u>fluctuate</u> — sometimes the <u>price falls below</u> the <u>cost of production</u>.

3) This means people <u>don't make much money</u>, so the government has <u>less to spend on development</u>.

4) Countries that export <u>manufactured goods</u> tend to be <u>more developed</u>.

5) This is because you usually make a <u>decent profit</u> by selling manufactured goods. Wealthy countries can also <u>force down</u> the <u>price of raw materials</u> that they buy from poorer countries.

5 Politics

1) <u>Corrupt</u> governments can <u>hinder development</u>, e.g. by <u>taking money</u> that's intended for building <u>new infrastructure</u> or <u>improving facilities</u> for people. They might also prevent a <u>fair election</u> from happening, so there is <u>no chance</u> for a <u>democratically elected government</u> (chosen by the people) to gain power.

2) If a government is <u>unstable</u> (i.e. likely to lose power at any time), companies and other countries are <u>unlikely to invest</u> or want to <u>trade</u>, meaning that level of development stays <u>low</u>.

3) Governments need to invest in the <u>right things</u> to help a country <u>develop</u>, e.g. <u>transport</u> and <u>schools</u>. If they invest in the <u>wrong areas</u>, the country <u>won't</u> develop as quickly.

6 Conflict

1) <u>War</u>, especially <u>civil wars</u>, can <u>slow</u> or <u>reduce</u> levels of development. E.g. <u>health care</u> becomes much <u>worse</u> and things like <u>infant mortality increase</u> a <u>lot</u>.

2) <u>Money</u> is spent on <u>arms</u> and <u>fighting</u> instead of <u>development</u>, people are <u>killed</u> and <u>damage</u> is done to <u>infrastructure</u> and <u>property</u>.

3) Countries have to spend money <u>repairing</u> this <u>damage</u> when the fighting <u>ends</u>.

7 Disease and Healthcare

1) In some developing countries, <u>lack of clean water</u> and <u>poor health care</u> mean that a large number of people suffer from <u>diseases</u> such as <u>malaria</u> and <u>cholera</u>.

2) People who are ill <u>can't work</u>, so they're not contributing to the <u>economy</u>. They may also need <u>expensive medicine</u> or <u>health care</u>.

3) Increased <u>spending</u> on health care means that there's <u>less money</u> available to spend on <u>development</u>.

Learn these physical and human causes of uneven development

If you get a long answer question about the factors that affect development, scribble down a quick plan with the key points before starting your answer — examiners are looking for a logical structure.

Consequences of Global Inequalities

Countries have a tough time trying to develop. And things don't look great if you can't make it off the bottom of the pile either. Inequalities affect all of us though — just some more than others...

Uneven Development Leads to Inequalities Between Countries

Wealth is not spread evenly across all countries in the world. People in the richest 20% of the world's countries (the 5th quintile) have 70.1% of the world's wealth (GDP per capita), whereas people in the poorest 20% (the 1st quintile) have just 1.0% of the world's wealth.

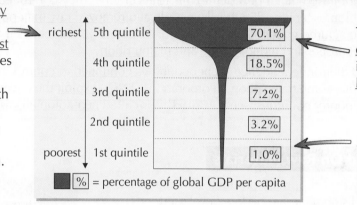

richest 5th quintile — 70.1%
4th quintile — 18.5%
3rd quintile — 7.2%
2nd quintile — 3.2%
poorest 1st quintile — 1.0%

■ % = percentage of global GDP per capita

The UK is in the 5th quintile. Other countries in the 5th quintile include Norway and Japan.

Chad is in the 1st quintile. Other countries in the 1st quintile include Malawi and Cambodia.

Global Inequalities have Social and Political Consequences

Differences in wealth can make things difficult for poorer people and developing countries:

- **EDUCATION** — poorer countries can't afford to invest as much in education as richer countries. Poorer people may not be able to afford school fees or children may have to work to support their families instead of attending school. Lack of education means people can't get better-paid, skilled jobs in the future, so the cycle of poverty continues.

- **HEALTH** — people in developing countries are at higher risk for many diseases than people in developed countries leading to lower life expectancies. Infant mortality is also much higher in developing countries. Poorer people find it harder to get quality health care and healthy food.

- **POLITICS** — inequalities can increase political instability, crime and discontent in poorer countries. This means civil wars are more likely in developing countries. Conflict can increase inequality — poverty increases as money is spent on fighting rather than development. Developing countries are often dependent on richer countries. This means they have less influence over regional and global decisions.

- **INTERNATIONAL MIGRATION** — if neighbouring or nearby countries have a higher level of development, people will seek to enter that country to make use of the opportunities it provides to improve their quality of life.

Global Inequalities also Cause Environmental Problems

1) Economic development leads to more consumption of food, water and energy as people get wealthier. This puts pressure on scarce resources and can threaten ecosystems, e.g. as more land is built on.

2) Industrialisation leads to increased air, water and land pollution. The release of greenhouse gases enhances the greenhouse effect, contributing to climate change. Waste is dumped in landfill sites and untreated sewage, chemical waste and runoff from farmland ends up in rivers and lakes.

3) Many developed countries have factories in developing countries or buy goods that are produced there. This means that local pollution levels are often much higher in developing countries.

4) Poorer people can also be trapped in a cycle of environmental damage, e.g. if they can't afford fuel they have to collect firewood from their local environment which can lead to deforestation.

The development gap has major consequences for people and the environment

There are huge differences between the world's poorest and richest countries. Make sure you can list some examples of social, political and environmental problems that have come about as a result of uneven development.

Worked Exam Questions

Here are some handy worked exam questions to get you in the exam mood. Use them wisely.

1   Study **Figure 1**, which shows measures of development for Canada, Malaysia and Angola.

1.1   "Canada is the most developed of these three countries." Do you agree with this statement? Justify your answer using **Figure 1**.

Figure 1

	Canada	Malaysia	Angola
GNI per head	$51 770	$11 120	$4800
Birth rate	10.28	19.71	38.78
Death rate	8.42	5.03	11.49
Infant mortality rate	4.65	13.27	78.26
Life expectancy	81.76	74.75	55.63
Literacy rate	97.1%	94.6%	71.1%

I agree that Canada is the most developed of the three countries. It has a much greater GNI per head than the other countries, which indicates that its citizens are wealthier and can probably afford a high quality of life. Measures of health, such as infant mortality rate and life expectancy, both indicate that Canada is more developed than Malaysia and Angola. Canada's literacy rate is higher than Malaysia's, and much higher than Angola's, suggesting that there is a formal education system, and that children have the time to go to school. This also suggests that Canada is the most developed of the three countries.

[4]

1.2   Outline **one** limitation of only using GNI per head as a measure of development.

GNI per head is an average, so it can hide variation between regions in the country, and between classes.

[2]

[Total 6 marks]

2   In 2014, Nicaragua had a 0.03% share of the world's total exports while the UK had a 2.66% share. Study **Figure 2**, which shows the types of goods exported by each country.

Figure 2

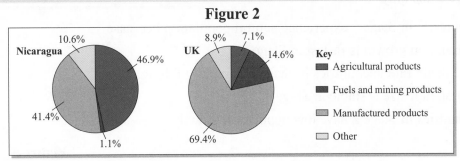

2.1   In 2014, what percentage of UK exports was not agricultural products, fuels or mining products?

69.4 + 8.9 = 78.3%

[1]

2.2   Using **Figure 2**, suggest a reason why Nicaragua is less developed than the UK.

Nicaragua's largest exports are agricultural products (which are primary products), and manufactured goods make up less of its exports than in the UK. Primary products don't generate as much money as manufactured goods, which means there is less money to spend on development in Nicaragua.

[2]

[Total 3 marks]

Exam Questions

1 Study **Figure 1**, which shows damage caused by fighting in Libya's civil war, which has been ongoing since 2011.

Figure 1

1.1 Using **Figure 1** and your own knowledge, suggest how the conflict may have affected Libya's level of development.

....

....

....

....

[3]

1.2 Libya is a former Italian colony. Explain how being a former colony may affect a country's economic development.

....

....

....

[3]

[Total 6 marks]

2 Study **Figure 2**, which shows the Demographic Transition Model (DTM).

Figure 2

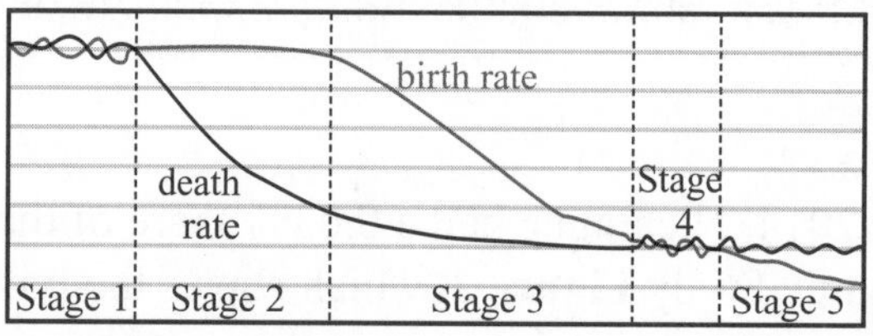

2.1 Using **Figure 2**, which **two** of the statements below are true? Shade **two** ovals only.

A Countries in Stage 5 experience natural population decrease. ◯

B Population growth is fastest in Stage 1. ◯

C The death rate in countries in Stage 3 is rapidly falling. ◯

D Population size is stable in Stage 4. ◯

E Countries in Stage 2 have low population growth. ◯

[2]

Figure 3

2.2 **Figure 3** shows birth and death rates in Morocco.

Using **Figure 2** and **Figure 3**, assess Morocco's level of economic development. Justify your answer.

Birth rate	18.2
Death rate	4.81

....

....

....

[3]

[Total 5 marks]

Theories of Development

Rostow and Frank came up with theories about how countries develop (or don't develop in Frank's case).

Rostow's Theory shows Five Stages of Economic Development

1) Rostow's modernisation theory predicts how a country's level of economic development changes over time — it describes how a country's economy changes from relying mostly on primary industry (e.g. agriculture), through secondary industry (e.g. manufacturing goods) to tertiary and quaternary industry (e.g. services and research).

2) At the same time, people's standard of living improves.

3) Stage 1 is the lowest level of development and Stage 5 is the highest.

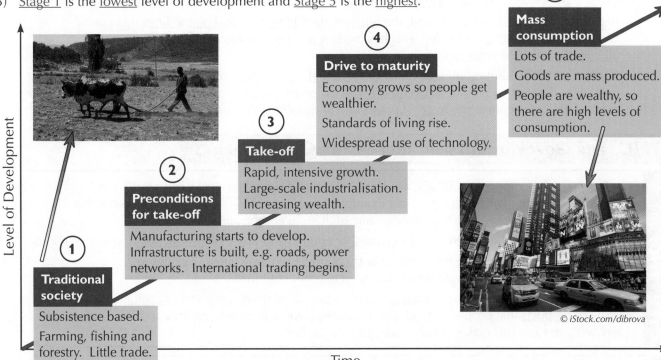

5 Mass consumption
Lots of trade.
Goods are mass produced.
People are wealthy, so there are high levels of consumption.

4 Drive to maturity
Economy grows so people get wealthier.
Standards of living rise.
Widespread use of technology.

3 Take-off
Rapid, intensive growth.
Large-scale industrialisation.
Increasing wealth.

2 Preconditions for take-off
Manufacturing starts to develop.
Infrastructure is built, e.g. roads, power networks. International trading begins.

1 Traditional society
Subsistence based.
Farming, fishing and forestry. Little trade.

Level of Development

Time

© iStock.com/dibrova

Frank's Dependency Theory says Poor Countries Rely On Rich Countries

1) Frank's dependency theory was developed as an alternative to Rostow's model to explain why some countries are more developed than others.

2) The theory suggests that some poorer, weaker countries (the periphery) remain poor because they are dependent on the core countries (those that are richer and more powerful).

3) It argues that the exploitation that started during the colonial period has continued — this is neo-colonialism (see p.181). The richer, former colonial countries continue to dominate the trading system even though the colonised countries have gained independence — richer countries continue to take advantage of the cheap raw materials and labour available in poorer countries.

4) For example, poorer countries have been encouraged to plant crops for export and produce primary products to sell cheaply to richer countries. This means they need to import manufactured goods at higher cost from richer countries to provide for their own population. This traps them in poverty and makes them dependent on the economy of the core countries.

5) Richer countries may also exploit poor countries by interfering in local politics in poorer countries or loaning them money with high rates of interest, leading to large debts.

6) This means that poor countries remain dependent on richer countries. Some people think that as long as they remain part of the capitalist (free trade, profit-seeking) system, these countries can't develop.

REVISION TIP

Neither of these theories is perfect

See if you can come up with a way to summarise Frank's dependency theory in five phrases or sentences. Then make sure you spend plenty of time revising the differences between the two theories on this page.

Globalisation

Reducing global inequalities is a massive task. Let's start at the very beginning with some globalisation...

Globalisation is the Process of Countries Becoming More Integrated

1) Every country has its own political and economic systems as well as its own culture.

2) Globalisation is the process of all the world's systems and cultures becoming more integrated — it's the whole world coming together like a single community.

3) It happens because of the movement of money and people between countries, as well as businesses locating their operations and selling their products in more countries. Here are a few reasons why globalisation is increasing:

- Improvements in ICT include e-mail, the internet, mobile phones and phone lines that can carry more information and faster. This has made it quicker and easier for businesses all over the world to communicate with each other.

- Improvements in transport include more airports, high-speed trains and larger ships. This has made it quicker and easier for people all over the world to communicate with each other face to face. It's also made it easier for companies to get supplies and to distribute their products all over the world.

TNCs and Governments are Increasing Globalisation

TNCs

1) Transnational corporations (TNCs) are companies that produce products, sell products or are located in more than one country. For example, Sony is a TNC — it manufactures electronic products in China and Japan, and sells many of them in Europe and the USA.

2) TNCs increase globalisation by linking together countries through the production and sale of goods.

3) They also bring the culture from their country of origin to many different countries, e.g. McDonald's brings Western-style fast food to other countries.

4) TNCs also promote a culture of consumerism — people in developing and emerging countries see all the products that people in developed countries have, e.g. mobile phones and TVs, and want to have them too. This makes people's lifestyles more similar.

Governments

1) Free trade — governments increase globalisation by promoting free trade, e.g. reducing tariffs on goods. This means it's much easier to move goods, money and services between countries.

2) Investment — governments compete with each other to attract investment by TNCs. They think that TNCs will bring jobs, increase income from taxes and promote economic growth in their country.

3) Privatisation — governments hand over services and industries to private companies, e.g. in the UK, some rail services are now run by companies from the Netherlands, Germany and France.

Globalisation Benefits Some Countries More than Others

1) Some countries have benefited from globalisation, e.g. China, India, Brazil. This is because they have, e.g:

- large, cheap workforces
- governments open to foreign investment
- less strict environmental, labour and planning laws
- lots of cheap raw materials
- reasonable infrastructure
- available land

2) However, some people think that globalisation is increasing global inequality.

- Free trade benefits richer countries — TNC profits normally return to their headquarters, which are often in developed countries, and poor countries can struggle to compete, i.e. produce cheaper goods.

- Richer countries benefit from freer movement of labour — skilled workers are attracted by higher wages and better living conditions in richer countries, leading to a 'brain drain' in poorer countries.

Globalisation is increasing the amount of links between countries

Draw a rough outline of the UK, then take another look at this page and add a labelled arrow to your outline for everything that is increasing links between the UK and other countries across the world.

Approaches to Development

Strategies to help countries to develop can be divided into <u>two categories</u>, depending on who makes the decisions.

Development Strategies can be Top-Down or Bottom-Up

1) Some people are trying to <u>decrease global inequalities</u> by helping <u>poor</u> countries <u>develop</u>.
2) Development projects can include building <u>schools</u> to <u>improve literacy</u> rates, making <u>dams</u> to provide <u>clean water</u> or providing <u>farming education</u> and <u>equipment</u> to <u>improve agriculture</u>.
3) There are <u>two</u> different approaches to development strategies:

	Top-down approaches	Bottom-up approaches
Type of strategy	A <u>government</u> or <u>large organisation</u>, e.g. an inter-governmental organisation (IGO) (see p.188) or transnational corporation (TNC) makes <u>decisions</u> about how to increase development and <u>direct</u> the project.	<u>Local people</u> and <u>communities</u> decide on ways to improve things for their own community. <u>Non-governmental organisations</u> (NGOs) are often involved (see p.188).
Scale and aims	• Often used for <u>large projects</u>, e.g. <u>dams</u> for hydroelectric power (HEP) or <u>irrigation schemes</u>. • These aim to solve <u>large scale</u> problems and improve the lives of <u>lots</u> of people.	• Usually <u>small-scale</u>, e.g. building or maintaining a well in a village. • They often aim to <u>improve</u> the <u>quality of life</u> for the <u>poorest</u> and <u>most vulnerable</u> people in society.
Funding	• The projects are usually very <u>expensive</u>. • Some projects are <u>funded</u> by <u>TNCs</u> or <u>governments</u> from <u>developed</u> countries who will <u>profit</u> from the <u>development</u>, e.g. by selling the HEP produced. • Other projects may be <u>funded</u> by <u>loans</u> from <u>international organisations</u>, e.g. the World Bank or the International Monetary Fund (IMF). The money may have to be <u>paid back later</u> or the <u>organisation</u> may have <u>conditions</u> for lending the money, e.g. removing trade barriers.	• Projects are usually much <u>cheaper</u>. • Most <u>money</u> comes from <u>charities</u>, which often rely on <u>donations</u> from people in richer countries.
Technology	• The projects are often <u>high-tech</u> and <u>energy intensive</u>. The construction usually involves <u>machinery</u> and <u>technology</u>, which is often operated by <u>skilled workers</u> from <u>developed</u> countries rather than local people. • The <u>recipient</u> country becomes <u>dependent</u> on <u>technology</u> and <u>workers</u> from the <u>donor</u> country for <u>operation</u> and <u>maintenance</u>.	• Projects involve <u>intermediate</u> technology. • <u>Local materials</u> are used and <u>local people</u> are employed. This means people have the <u>materials</u> and <u>skills</u> to <u>maintain</u> the project.

Top-down schemes are often large-scale and expensive

Bottom-up approaches tend to be cheaper, but they might not make as big a difference as top-down strategies. Development is a complicated matter with no easy solutions. There's more on the pros and cons of different approaches on the next page but, for now, concentrate on learning the differences between them.

Approaches to Development

There are <u>lots</u> of different ways to help a country to <u>develop</u>, but none of them are <u>trouble-free</u>...

Approaches to **Development** Include **NGO-Led Intermediate Technology...**

1) <u>Non-governmental organisations</u> (NGOs) are not-for-profit groups which are <u>independent</u> from governments. They're often charities, e.g. the <u>British Red Cross</u> or <u>Oxfam</u>.

2) <u>NGO-led development projects</u> often involve the use of <u>intermediate technology</u>. This includes tools, machines and systems that are <u>simple to use</u>, <u>affordable</u> to buy or build and cheap to <u>maintain</u>.

Advantages

1) Projects are designed to <u>address</u> the <u>needs</u> of people <u>local</u> to where the projects are carried out.

2) <u>Locally available</u>, <u>cheap</u> materials are used so the community <u>isn't</u> dependent on <u>expensive imports</u>.

3) Projects are <u>labour intensive</u> — they create <u>jobs</u> for <u>local people</u>.

Disadvantages

1) Projects are often <u>small-scale</u>, so they may <u>not</u> benefit <u>everyone</u>.

2) Different organisations may <u>not work together</u>, so projects may be <u>inefficient</u>.

...**IGO-Funded** Large **Infrastructure...**

<u>Inter-governmental organisations</u> (IGOs), e.g. the World Bank, the International Monetary Fund (IMF) and the United Nations (UN), are made up of the <u>governments</u> of <u>several countries</u>.

Advantages

1) <u>IGOs</u> can afford to fund <u>large infrastructure</u> projects in <u>developing</u> and <u>emerging</u> countries.

2) Projects can improve the country's <u>economy</u>, helping with <u>long-term development</u>, e.g. HEP stations may <u>promote industry</u>, which <u>provides jobs</u> and <u>boosts</u> the <u>economy</u>.

3) Projects can also <u>improve</u> people's <u>quality of life</u>, as people have better access to <u>reliable power</u>, <u>clean water</u> etc.

Disadvantages

1) Large projects are often <u>expensive</u> and the country may have to <u>pay back the money</u> (if it's a loan). This can lead to lots of <u>debt</u>.

2) They <u>may not benefit everyone</u> — e.g. HEP may not supply power to remote areas.

3) If governments are <u>corrupt</u>, they may use the <u>money</u> for their <u>own purposes</u>.

4) Projects tend to be <u>energy intensive</u> — they use <u>scarce resources</u>, <u>release greenhouse gases</u> and lead to <u>loss</u> of <u>ecosystems</u>.

...and **Investment** by **TNCs**

<u>TNCs</u> (see p.186) are also involved in <u>development</u> through <u>investment</u> in the <u>countries</u> they operate in.

Advantages

1) TNCs provide <u>employment</u> for <u>local</u> people.

2) More <u>companies</u> mean a <u>greater income</u> from <u>taxes</u> for the <u>host</u> country.

3) Some TNCs run programmes to <u>help development</u>.

4) TNCs may also <u>invest</u> in <u>infrastructure</u>, <u>improving</u> <u>roads</u>, <u>basic services</u> and <u>communication links</u> in the area. This may improve the <u>quality of life</u> of local people.

Disadvantages

1) Some <u>profits leave</u> the <u>host</u> country.

2) TNCs can cause <u>environmental problems</u> — <u>developing</u> countries may have <u>less strict environmental regulations</u>, leading to e.g. the dumping of <u>toxic waste</u>.

3) TNCs may <u>move around</u> the country to take advantage of <u>local tax breaks</u>, leaving people <u>jobless</u> as the company moves on.

All approaches to development have both advantages and disadvantages

Different projects might benefit different people, and some might cause financial problems. Try covering each section of this page and drawing a table of the pros and cons for each type of approach.

Reducing the Development Gap

Some people think that the <u>best way</u> to <u>reduce</u> the global development gap is for everyone to <u>work together</u>...

The **Millennium Development Goals** Aimed to **Increase Development**

1) The <u>Millennium Development Goals</u> (<u>MDGs</u>) aimed to <u>improve life</u> in <u>developing countries</u>. They were targets set by the United Nations (UN) in <u>2000</u> — all UN member states agreed to try to achieve the goals by <u>2015</u>.

2) There were <u>eight MDGs</u>, which aimed to:

1) <u>Halve</u> the number of people living in <u>extreme poverty</u> or suffering from <u>hunger</u>.

2) Make sure that <u>all children</u> had a <u>primary education</u>.

3) <u>Increase</u> the number of <u>girls</u> and <u>women</u> in <u>education</u> and in <u>paid employment</u>.

4) <u>Reduce death rates</u> in <u>children</u> under five years old by <u>two-thirds</u>.

5) <u>Reduce death rates</u> amongst <u>women</u> caused by pregnancy or childbirth by <u>three-quarters</u>.

6) Stop the <u>spread</u> of major <u>diseases</u>, including HIV/AIDS and malaria.

7) <u>Protect</u> the <u>environment</u> and make sure development was <u>sustainable</u>, while <u>improving quality of life</u>.

8) Make sure that countries <u>around the world</u> worked <u>together</u> to help <u>poorer</u> countries develop.

© iStock.com/africa924

3) By <u>2015</u>, the UN had gone some way to achieving these goals, but success was <u>variable</u> in different parts of the world. The UN has set a new series of <u>Sustainable Development Goals</u> (<u>SDGs</u>) to achieve by <u>2030</u>.

Tourism is Helping Kenya to **Increase** its **Development**

EXAMPLE

1) <u>Kenya</u> is a low-income country in <u>East Africa</u>. It attracts <u>tourists</u> because of its <u>tribal culture</u>, <u>safari wildlife</u>, <u>warm climate</u> and <u>beautiful unspoilt scenery</u>. Kenya's <u>government</u> is trying to <u>boost tourism</u> as a way of <u>increasing</u> its <u>development</u>.

2) <u>Visa fees</u> for <u>adults</u> were <u>cut by 50%</u> in <u>2009</u> to make it <u>cheaper to visit</u> the country. They were also <u>scrapped</u> for <u>children under 16</u> to encourage <u>more families</u> to visit.

3) <u>Landing fees</u> at airports on the Kenyan <u>coast</u> have been <u>dropped</u> for charter airlines.

4) Tourism has increased from <u>0.9 million</u> visitors per year in <u>1995</u> to <u>1.8 million</u> in <u>2011</u>.

Effectiveness — Benefits

1) Tourism now contributes <u>over 12%</u> of Kenya's <u>GDP</u> — money that can be spent on <u>development</u> and <u>improving quality of life</u>.

2) Nearly <u>600 000 people</u> are <u>directly</u> or <u>indirectly</u> <u>employed</u> by the <u>tourism industry</u> — that's 10% of <u>all employment</u> in Kenya.

3) The <u>24 national parks</u> charge <u>entry fees</u> to tourists. This money is used to <u>maintain</u> the national parks, which helps to protect the <u>environment</u> and <u>wildlife</u>.

4) Since 2000, Kenya's score on the <u>Human Development Index</u> has <u>increased</u> from <u>0.45</u> to <u>0.55</u>.

Effectiveness — Negatives

1) Only a <u>small proportion</u> of the money earned goes to <u>locals</u>. The rest goes to <u>big companies</u>, often based in <u>developed countries overseas</u>, so <u>doesn't</u> help to <u>close</u> the development gap.

2) Some Maasai tribespeople were <u>forced off their land</u> to create national parks for tourists.

3) Tourist vehicles <u>damage</u> the <u>environment</u>, e.g. <u>safari vehicles</u> destroying vegetation and disturbing animals.

Tourism has brought wealth and jobs to Kenya

International schemes, like the MDGs, can help development, but so can schemes in individual countries. Things have generally improved in Kenya — many people have a better quality of life, but it's not been good for everyone.

Reducing the Development Gap

Here are a load more ways of reducing the development gap, each with their own pros and cons.

There are Lots of Other Strategies that can Reduce the Development Gap

Aid

1) Aid is given by one country to another as money or resources (e.g. food, doctors).

2) It is spent on development projects, for example constructing schools to improve literacy rates, building dams and wells to improve clean water supplies and providing farming knowledge and equipment to improve agriculture.

3) Aid can definitely help, but sometimes it is wasted by corrupt governments. Or once the money runs out, projects can stop working if there isn't enough local knowledge and support to keep the projects going.

Debt Relief

1) Debt relief is when some or all of a country's debt is cancelled, or interest rates are lowered. This means they have more money to develop rather than to pay back the debt.

2) For example, Zambia (in southern Africa) had $4 billion of debt cancelled in 2005. In 2006, the country had enough money to start a free healthcare scheme for millions of people living in rural areas, which improved their quality of life.

3) An advantage of debt relief is that donor countries can specify how the saved money should be spent, so it can be directed to e.g. health care or education. However, some countries may be reluctant to cancel debts for countries with corrupt governments.

Fair Trade

1) The fair trade movement is all about farmers getting a fair price for goods produced in developing countries, e.g. coffee and bananas, allowing them to provide for their families.

2) Companies who want to sell products labelled as 'fair trade' have to pay producers a fair price.

3) Buyers also pay extra on top of that to help develop the area where the goods come from, e.g. to build schools or health centres.

4) But there are problems — only a tiny proportion of the extra money reaches the original producers. Much goes to retailers' profits.

Investment

1) Foreign-direct investment (FDI) is when people or companies in one country buy property or infrastructure in another.

2) FDI leads to better access to finance, technology and expertise, and improved infrastructure, improved industry and an increase in services.

Industrial Development

In countries with a very low level of development, agriculture makes up a large portion of the economy. Developing industry increases GNI and helps improve levels of development as productivity, levels of skill and infrastructure are improved.

Increasing Trade

1) Trade between a developing country and other countries can help to increase development.

2) Trade increases the amount of money a country has to spend on things like health care and education, and on development projects, such as improving transport infrastructure.

3) But trade can have a negative effect on people. E.g. to keep prices low, wages and working conditions may be very poor. So increased trade won't necessarily improve quality of life for everyone.

Microfinance Loans

1) Microfinance is when small loans are given to people in developing countries who may not be able to get loans from traditional banks. The loans enable them to start their own businesses and become financially independent.

2) Although microfinance works for some people, it's not clear that microfinance can reduce poverty on a large scale.

Aid, trade and investment help poor countries develop

Poorer countries can improve their own level of development through industry and trade. Other countries can also help by providing aid or trading more fairly. Small scale schemes, e.g. microfinance, can be effective too.

Development in India

CASE STUDY

India's level of development is fairly low, but increasing, and its rapid growth is causing lots of change.

India is an Emerging Country in Southern Asia

1) India is a rapidly developing emerging country. It has the second largest population in the world (approx. 1.3 billion) and is still growing.

2) India was a British colony until 1947, but now has its own democratically elected government.

3) India has a rich and diverse cultural background. It's renowned for its production of 'Bollywood' films, which are exported worldwide.

4) India has a beautiful and varied landscape, including areas of mountains, desert, great plains and a large coastline, making it an attractive tourist destination.

5) The large coastline also allows the development of ports, such as Mumbai, increasing trade.

India's Economy has Changed a lot Since 1990

	1990	2015
GDP ($ trillion)	0.3	2.1
GNI per capita ($)	390	1600

1) India is getting rapidly wealthier.

2) India has a medium level of development (HDI = 0.61). There are large inequalities — some people are very wealthy, but the majority are poor.

3) Primary industry (e.g. agriculture) is becoming a smaller part of India's economy. It makes up only 17% of its GDP.

4) Secondary industry (manufacturing) has grown to employ 22% of the workforce. Secondary industries are stimulating economic development. They provide people with reliable jobs (compared to seasonal agricultural work), and selling manufactured goods overseas brings more income into India than selling raw materials.

5) India's tertiary service and high-tech quaternary industries have grown hugely in recent years, now accounting for 45% of GDP.

6) These changes have affected what India imports and exports.

	1990	2015
Exports	Low-value manufactured goods, e.g. clothing, and primary products, e.g. tea	High-value manufactured goods, e.g. machinery
Imports	Manufactured goods, e.g. machinery, chemicals	Crude oil (for transport and industry)

Globalisation and Government Policies have Increased Development

Globalisation

1) More than 50% of all Indians now own a mobile phone. This has enabled lots of people to start their own small businesses, giving them a larger income.

2) India has 12 major ports and more than 20 international airports. It also has an extensive rail network, carrying 8 billion passengers a year and almost 3 million tonnes of freight per day. This makes it easier to transport goods, so trade can increase, and TNCs are more likely to invest.

3) Some large TNCs, e.g. Microsoft®, Nokia, Unilever and Coca-Cola®, outsource some manufacturing and IT to India. These bring jobs, greater income from taxes and the latest technology and business practices.

Government Policy

1) In 2009 India made primary education free and compulsory — 96% of children now enrol for school. Having a more educated workforce helps to fuel development.

2) The rail network is being upgraded and new roads and airports are being built. These reduce travel time — e.g. the Delhi metro enables thousands of commuters to get to work.

3) India is one of the top locations in the world for FDI (foreign direct investment — foreign companies buy land, buildings or parts of companies in a country). Most investment comes from Singapore, Mauritius, Japan and the USA. India is trying to attract more FDI by relaxing the rules on how much land, property etc. foreign companies can own.

Development in India

Lots of Trans-National Corporations Operate in India

Unilver is one of the world's biggest food and consumer goods manufacturers.

There are <u>advantages</u> and <u>disadvantages</u> to TNCs operating in India.

Advantages

1) TNCs provide <u>employment</u> — e.g. Coca-Cola® directly employs <u>25 000 people</u> and indirectly employs <u>150 000</u> people in India.

2) More companies mean a <u>greater income</u> from tax for <u>India</u>.

3) Some TNCs run programs to <u>help development</u> in India. E.g. Coca-Cola® has established <u>retail training</u> programmes to help businesses become more <u>profitable</u> and <u>efficient</u> — the <u>Parivartan</u> programme has trained over <u>260 000 retailers</u>.

Disadvantages

1) TNCs can cause <u>environmental problems</u> — e.g. the concern of local communities about the amount of <u>water</u> being <u>extracted</u> by Coca-Cola® bottling plants led to plants in Kerala and Varanasi being <u>closed</u>.

2) Large global <u>retail chains</u> can offer <u>cheap</u> prices on goods — Indian <u>street traders</u> are concerned that this will <u>destroy</u> their <u>livelihoods</u> as people choose to shop in supermarkets instead.

3) TNCs could <u>withdraw</u> their <u>business</u> from India at <u>any time</u>, e.g if the <u>economic climate</u> changes.

India Receives Different Types of Aid

Short-term Aid

1) Intended to help recipient countries cope with <u>emergencies</u>. Can come from <u>foreign governments</u> or <u>non-governmental organisations</u> (NGOs).

2) The <u>UK</u> sent <u>£10m</u>, a <u>rescue team</u> and <u>1200 tents</u> to India after an <u>earthquake</u> in 2001. <u>NGOs</u> like Oxfam provided <u>supplies</u> and <u>temporary buildings</u>.

3) Helps with <u>immediate disaster relief</u>, but often <u>not able</u> to help <u>longer-term</u> recovery efforts.

'Top-down' Aid

1) When an <u>organisation</u> or <u>government receives</u> the aid and <u>decides</u> where it should be <u>spent</u>.

2) Often <u>large infrastructure projects</u> like <u>dams</u> for hydroelectric power or <u>irrigation schemes</u>.

3) Can improve a country's <u>economy</u>, but may not improve the <u>quality of life</u> of the <u>poorest people</u>.

Long-term Aid

1) Intended to help the recipient countries to become <u>more developed</u>.

2) E.g. until 2015, India received over <u>£200m</u> each year from the <u>UK</u> to <u>tackle poverty</u>.

3) Impact can <u>vary</u> — India has had problems with <u>corruption</u> and aid does not always reach the <u>poorest people</u>.

'Bottom-up' Aid

1) Money is given <u>directly to local people</u>, e.g. to build or maintain a well.

2) E.g. WaterAid trains local people to <u>maintain</u> village <u>handpumps</u> in rural India.

3) Can have a large impact — schemes are generally <u>supported</u> by local people and can improve <u>health</u>, <u>skills</u> and <u>income</u>.

Development is Causing Population Change in India

1) <u>Birth rates</u> in India are <u>high</u>. <u>Death rates</u> and <u>infant mortality</u> have <u>fallen</u>, partly due to <u>better health care</u> and <u>health education</u>, e.g. encouraging people to wash their hands. This means that:

- India's population is <u>rapidly increasing</u> — it grew from about <u>870 million</u> in 1990, to <u>1.3 billion</u> in 2015.
- The majority of the population are <u>young</u> — about 28% are <u>under 14</u>.
- <u>Life expectancy</u> has <u>increased</u> from <u>58</u> in 1990 to <u>68</u> in 2014.

2) The <u>fertility rate</u> is starting to <u>fall</u> — it <u>decreased</u> from <u>4.0</u> in 1990 to <u>2.4</u> in 2014, partly due to growing <u>wealth</u> and better <u>education</u>. So <u>population growth rates</u> are gradually <u>slowing down</u>.

3) As the country gets <u>wealthier</u>, <u>urban</u> areas are growing because of <u>migration</u> and <u>natural increase</u>:

- In 1990, only <u>26%</u> of the population lived in <u>urban</u> areas. By 2015 this had risen to <u>33%</u>.
- India already has <u>5 megacities</u> (see p.137) — New Delhi, Mumbai, Kolkata, Bengaluru and Chennai, and is expected to have <u>2 more</u> by <u>2030</u>.

Development in India

CASE STUDY

Some **Regions** of **India** are **Developing Faster** than **Others**

1) Rapid economic growth has increased inequality within India — the gap between the richest and poorest states has been widening.

2) The growth of manufacturing and services has benefited urban areas more than rural areas. GDP per capita is highest in the south and west states, e.g. Maharashtra, which have the highest urban population.

3) More money gets spent on these areas in order to attract more FDI and TNCs. The wealth generated can then be spent on development projects improving literacy rates and quality of life.

4) More rural states, e.g. Bihar, have higher rates of poverty. This has led to undernourishment and health problems because people can't afford to buy enough food. Many children have to work rather than attend school leading to low literacy rates. Poor health and education leads to a low HDI score. Older people are less likely to migrate to urban areas, instead remaining in rural areas.

	Maharashtra	Bihar
Urban Population (%)	45	11
GDP per capita ($)	2561	682
HDI	0.572	0.367
Literacy rate (%)	83	64

Economic Development has **Pros** and **Cons** for **Different Groups** of **People**

Economic development is good news for some people, but can cause problems for others:

Positive Impacts

1) All age groups have better health:
   - Elderly people are living longer.
   - There is a lower infant mortality rate.
   - There is a lower maternal mortality rate.

2) Some age groups have better education:
   - Higher education has given young graduates access to better jobs, e.g. in technical firms and ICT.
   - Many adults have better literacy.

3) There can be better gender equality:
   - Women have better access to education — literacy rates for Indian women have increased from 34% in 1991 to 59% in 2011.
   - Women have better access to contraception and family planning advice.

Negative Impacts

1) Rapid industrialisation means young workers may have to do dangerous jobs. Working conditions may also be poor due to a lack of regulations put in place by Indian authorities.

2) As young people move to urban areas to find work, there are fewer workers in rural villages. This means:
   - Children in rural areas may get a poor education due to a lack of skilled teachers — nearly 50% of teachers have only completed secondary education.
   - Children may have to work as agricultural labourers to support their families.

3) There is still a lot of gender inequality:
   - It is unsafe for women in many urban areas. E.g. in Delhi, crimes against women increased by 20% from 2014-15.
   - If men leave to find work in cities, women may be left to care for and provide for the entire household — balancing a job with housework.

Economic Development has **Impacts** on **Quality of Life...**

Quality of Life

1) There are more jobs and India's daily wages have increased by about 42 Rupees since 2010. This means that people have more money to improve their life, for example by securing access to clean water, a higher quality home and medical care when they need it.

2) But some jobs in industry, e.g. coal mining, can be dangerous or include poor conditions (see above), which can reduce workers' quality of life.

Development in India

...and on the **Environment**

Environment

1) <u>Industrialisation</u> leads to higher <u>energy consumption</u>. Increased <u>demand</u> for <u>fossil fuels</u> in industry, homes and vehicles means <u>more greenhouse gases</u> are released, contributing to <u>climate change</u>. India releases almost <u>7%</u> of all global greenhouse gas emissions.

2) More <u>factories</u> and <u>cars</u> mean more <u>air pollution</u>. The pollution is so <u>bad</u> in some cities, e.g. New Delhi, that a thick, toxic <u>smog</u> often forms. <u>Gases</u> such as sulfur dioxide and <u>smoke particles</u> damage people's health and cause <u>breathing problems</u> and <u>lung diseases</u>. More than <u>0.5 million</u> people in India <u>die</u> from diseases related to air pollution each year.

3) <u>Urban sprawl</u> leads to <u>land</u> and <u>water pollution</u> — lack of <u>infrastructure</u> means that about <u>70%</u> of India's sewage flows <u>untreated</u> into <u>rivers</u>. Waste may not be <u>correctly sorted</u> and <u>disposed of</u>, e.g. <u>dangerous contaminated waste</u> from a factory in Kodaikanal was initially <u>dumped</u> instead of being <u>disposed</u> of <u>safely</u>.

4) However, <u>increased income</u> from economic development means people can <u>afford</u> to <u>protect</u> the <u>environment</u>. For example, since 1990 India's <u>forest cover</u> has <u>stopped decreasing</u> and <u>started to grow</u>.

India's **Global Influence** is **Increasing**

1) India is playing a <u>larger role</u> in <u>regional</u> and <u>global politics</u> as it develops. In recent years the Indian government has <u>improved relations</u> with its immediate <u>neighbours</u> (e.g. joining <u>ASEAN</u>, a <u>political</u> and <u>economic</u> organisation made up of countries in <u>southeast Asia</u>).

2) India is a member of several <u>international organisations</u> — India was one of the founding members of the <u>United Nations</u> (UN), which works towards <u>sustainable development</u>. It is also part of the <u>World Trade Organisation</u> (WTO) and a member of <u>G20</u>, a group of 20 of the world's <u>largest economies</u>.

3) Economic <u>growth</u> has also <u>changed</u> India's <u>relationship</u> with the <u>USA</u> and <u>EU</u>:

India and the USA

1) India used to have a <u>poor</u> relationship with the <u>USA</u> but this has been <u>improving</u>.

2) The USA expects the economic development of India to <u>increase trade</u>, <u>employment</u> and <u>economic growth</u> in <u>both</u> countries.

3) The <u>USA</u> also sees <u>India</u> as a <u>huge market</u> for <u>renewable</u> and <u>nuclear energy</u> because of the number of <u>increasingly wealthy</u> people and the <u>growth</u> of <u>industry</u>.

India and the EU

1) India has had a <u>good</u> relationship with the EU and they became <u>strategic partners</u> in 2004, agreeing to <u>cooperate</u> on certain issues.

2) Negotiations for a <u>free trade</u> agreement began in 2007. The EU is one of India's <u>biggest markets</u> and <u>trading partners</u>.

3) The EU supports <u>health</u> and <u>education</u> programmes in India to promote <u>continued development</u>.

4) Changing <u>international relations</u> have <u>costs</u> and <u>benefits</u>:
   - <u>Costs</u> — there is increasing <u>tension</u> between <u>India</u> and <u>China</u> — both have <u>rapidly growing economies</u>. <u>Developed</u> nations are also concerned about <u>losing economic power</u> as India grows.
   - <u>Benefits</u> — improved relations mean India can <u>cooperate</u> with <u>other countries</u> on <u>global issues</u>, e.g. climate change. FDI brings <u>economic benefits</u> to <u>both</u> India and the country of origin, and global trade agreements mean that <u>political actions</u>, e.g. sanctions, are more <u>effective</u>.

India is experiencing rapid change

You might have studied a different country in class — it's fine to learn that one instead. Just make sure you know about the economic changes caused by globalisation, the impacts on people and its changing role in the world.

Worked Exam Questions

These worked questions will show you the kinds of answers you should be writing in the exam.

---

1 Study **Figure 1**, which shows the yearly level of foreign direct investment (FDI) in a region of an emerging country between 2008 and 2016.

1.1 Using **Figure 1**, describe how FDI in the region changed between 2008 and 2016.

The level of FDI stayed around the same level (about US$ 4 million) between 2008 and 2011 before increasing rapidly between 2011 and 2016 to US$ 34 million.

[2]

Figure 1

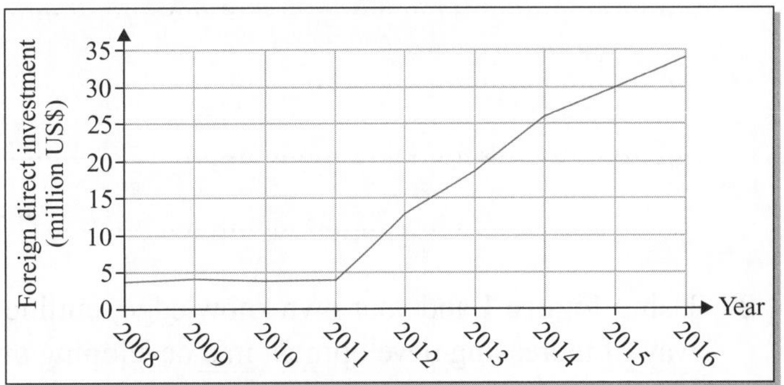

1.2 Explain one negative impact of FDI for an emerging country.

Large global retail chains can offer cheap prices on goods, which can destroy the livelihoods of local street traders as people choose to shop where the prices are cheaper.

[2]

[Total 4 marks]

---

2 Large-scale infrastructure projects may be funded by inter-governmental organisations (IGOs) or transnational corporations (TNCs).

2.1 Which statement best describes a benefit of TNC investment for developing countries?

A TNCs bring in workers from other countries to do skilled jobs. ◯

B New technology is developed in developed countries. ◯

C TNCs send money back to their country of origin. ◯

D Employees get a more reliable income. ⬤

[1]

2.2 Compare the benefits for the recipient country of infrastructure projects funded by IGOs or TNCs.

Large infrastructure projects funded by both TNCs and IGOs can improve the country's economy by promoting industry. However, IGO projects may be funded through loans to the country, leaving that country in debt, whereas TNCs don't usually offer loans. Governments may be corrupt and use the money provided by IGOs for their own benefit, but TNCs only invest in infrastructure where they'll benefit, so the projects may be more likely to be completed.

[3]

2.3 State one advantage of development strategies being led by NGOs.

Projects are designed to address the needs of people local to where they're being carried out.

[1]

[Total 5 marks]

Exam Questions

1   Study **Figure 1**, which shows some tourists on safari in Africa.

Figure 1

1.1   Outline **one** way in which tourism can help deal with the problems of uneven development.

....

....

....

....

[2]

1.2   Using **Figure 1** and your own knowledge, outline two negative impacts of promoting tourism as a way of increasing development in a developing or emerging country.

Impact 1:...

....

Impact 2:...

....

[4]

[Total 6 marks]

2   Study **Figure 2**, an article about an aid project in Ghana.

Figure 2

UK Government Support for Ghana

The UK is the second largest aid donor to Ghana. The UK Government's Department for International Development (DFID) gave over £205 million between 2005 and 2007 towards Ghana's poverty reduction plans. This level of aid continues, with donations of around £85 million per year. The aid is used in several ways, including to improve healthcare, education and sanitation.

About 15% of the UK's funding in 2008 was used to support the healthcare system in Ghana —

£42.5 million was pledged to support the Ghanaian Government's 2008-2012 health plan. On top of that, in 2008 the UK gave nearly £7 million to buy emergency equipment to reduce maternal deaths.

Thanks to a £105 million grant from the UK in 2006, Ghana has been able to set up a ten year education strategic plan. It was the first African country to do this. The UK pledged additional money to help 12 000 children in North Ghana to get a formal basic education.

2.1   Outline one potential advantage and one potential disadvantage for the recipient country of long-term aid projects.

Advantage:...

....

Disadvantage: ....

....

[2]

2.2   To what extent do trans-national corporations (TNCs) improve economic development and quality of life in developing and emerging countries? Reference at least one country you have studied.

[9 + 3 SPaG]

[Total 14 marks]

Revision Summary

Hurrah, you've finally reached the end of <u>Section 13</u> — time to see how good your <u>understanding</u> of this topic is.
- Try these questions and <u>tick off each one</u> when you <u>get it right</u>.
- When you've done <u>all the questions</u> for a topic and are <u>completely happy</u> with it, tick off the topic.

Development (p.177-179) ☑

1) List five measures of development. ☑
2) What is HDI? ☑
3) Give two ways that countries can be classified based on their development. ☑
4) Describe the five stages of the demographic transition model. ☑

Causes and Consequences of Global Inequalities (p.180-182) ☑

5) Give four physical factors that can affect how developed a country is. ☑
6) Give four human factors that can affect how developed a country is. ☑
7) Give two possible social consequences of global inequality. ☑
8) Give one possible political consequence of global inequality. ☑

Theories of Development and Globalisation (p.185-186) ☑

9) List the five stages of economic development according to Rostow's theory. ☑
10) Briefly summarise Frank's dependency theory. ☑
11) What is globalisation? ☑
12) Give one reason why globalisation is increasing. ☑
13) What does TNC stand for? ☑
14) Give two ways in which governments are increasing globalisation. ☑
15) Give one reason why some people think that globalisation increases global inequality. ☑

Reducing the Development Gap (p.187-190) ☑

16) Explain what is meant by a top-down approach to development. ☑
17) Give one advantage and one disadvantage of the top-down approach. ☑
18) Explain what is meant by a bottom-up approach to development. ☑
19) What is intermediate technology? How can it help development? ☑
20) What was the aim of the Millennium Development Goals? ☑
21) Name one country that is promoting tourism as a way to increase its development. ☑
22) What is debt relief? How can it help increase development? ☑
23) How can microfinance loans help reduce the development gap? ☑

Development in India (p.191-194) ☑

24) Give one example of India's cultural importance. ☑
25) How has the economy of India changed since 1990? ☑
26) How is India's industrial structure changing? ☑
27) How has globalisation helped increase development in India? ☑
28) What is the difference between short-term and long-term aid? ☑
29) Explain how development has changed India's population structure. ☑
30) How have some age and gender groups in India been negatively impacted by development? ☑
31) How has development had impacts on the environment in India? ☑
32) How is India's global influence changing? Is this causing any problems? ☑

If you have studied a different country, you can answer these questions for that country instead.

Demand for Resources

There are an awful lot of <u>people</u> on our planet, and they all want <u>resources</u> — it can all get a bit <u>complicated</u>...

Everyone Needs **Food, Energy** and **Water**

<u>Resources</u>, such as <u>food</u>, <u>energy</u> and <u>water</u>, are needed for <u>basic human development</u>:

1) <u>Food</u> — without <u>enough nutritious food</u>, people can become <u>malnourished</u>. This makes them more likely to get <u>ill</u>, and may stop them from <u>working</u> or doing well at <u>school</u>.

2) <u>Energy</u> — a good supply of energy is needed for a <u>basic standard of living</u>, e.g. to provide <u>lighting</u> and <u>heat</u> for cooking. It's also essential for <u>industry</u> and <u>transport</u>.

3) <u>Water</u> — people need a constant supply of <u>clean</u>, <u>safe water</u> for <u>drinking</u>, <u>cooking</u> and <u>washing</u>. Water is also needed to <u>produce food</u>, <u>clothes</u> and lots of other products.

<u>Access</u> to food, water and energy affects the <u>economic</u> and <u>social well-being</u> of <u>people</u> and <u>countries</u>.

Population Growth is **Increasing Demand** for Resources

The world's population is <u>increasing</u>. <u>More people</u> require <u>more resources</u>, so demand <u>increases</u>.

Population Projections

- Population projections are <u>predictions</u> of <u>how many people</u> there will be in the world in the <u>future</u>.

- We know <u>past</u> and <u>present</u> values of population pretty <u>accurately</u>, but it's <u>more difficult</u> to predict <u>future</u> global population — it gets <u>harder</u> the <u>further forward</u> in time you go.

- The <u>UN</u> has made three <u>predictions</u> about <u>population growth</u> up to the <u>end of this century</u>. The <u>highest</u> prediction shows the <u>world's total population</u> reaching <u>14 billion people</u>.

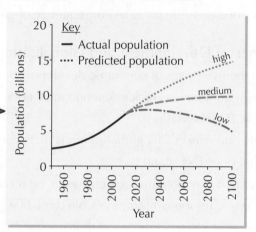

Other Factors Also **Increase Demand** for Resources

Increasing <u>wealth</u>, <u>urbanisation</u> and <u>industrialisation</u> are increasing the demand for resources.

In <u>emerging</u> countries, e.g. China and Brazil, there has been <u>rapid industrialisation</u> and <u>urbanisation</u> and people are getting <u>wealthier</u> (see page 137).

Over the next few decades most <u>economic</u> growth is expected to take place in <u>Africa</u>.

These factors are affecting the regional demand for resources.

① Increasing Wealth

1) <u>Economic development</u> means that people are getting <u>wealthier</u> (more <u>affluent</u>).

2) Wealthier people have <u>more disposable income</u>, which affects their <u>resource consumption</u>:

- They can afford to buy <u>more food</u> (see p.200).

- They can afford <u>cars</u>, <u>fridges</u>, <u>televisions</u> etc., all of which use <u>energy</u>. Manufacturing these goods and producing energy to run them also uses a lot of <u>water</u>.

- More people can <u>afford</u> flushing toilets, showers, dishwashers etc. This <u>increases water use</u>.

② Urbanisation

1) <u>Urbanisation</u> is the <u>growth</u> in the <u>proportion</u> of a country's population living in urban areas.

2) Urbanisation tends to <u>increase resource consumption</u> because:

- Cities tend to be more <u>resource-intensive</u> than rural areas — street lights and neon signs use <u>energy</u>, and fountains and urban parks require <u>water</u>.

- Food and water have to be <u>transported</u> long distances to meet the increased demand in cities, and <u>waste</u> needs to be <u>removed</u> — this increases <u>energy use</u>.

Demand for Resources

③ Industrialisation

1) Industrialisation is the <u>shift</u> in a country's main economic activity from <u>primary production</u> (e.g. farming) to <u>secondary production</u> (e.g. manufacturing goods).

2) <u>Manufacturing goods</u> such as cars, chemicals and electrical appliances uses a lot of <u>energy</u> — e.g. to run machines or heat components so they can be shaped. Manufacturing also uses a lot of <u>water</u> — e.g. for cooling and washing components. As countries become more <u>industrialised</u>, their demand for energy and water <u>increases</u>.

3) Industrialisation is <u>increasing</u> the <u>production</u> of <u>processed</u> goods, e.g. foods such as margarine. This <u>increases</u> the <u>demand</u> for ingredients such as <u>palm oil</u>, which are often grown on huge <u>plantations</u>.

Malthus and Boserup Had Different Theories About Resource Supply

Malthus and Boserup both came up with theories about how <u>population growth</u> and <u>resource availability</u> are <u>related</u>:

Malthus's Theory

- <u>Thomas Malthus</u> was an 18th-century economist. He thought that <u>population</u> was increasing <u>faster</u> than <u>supply of resources</u>, so eventually there would be <u>too many people</u> for the <u>resources</u> available.

- He believed that when this happened, people would be killed by catastrophes such as <u>famine</u>, <u>illness</u> and <u>war</u>, and the population would <u>return</u> to a level that could be <u>supported</u> by the resources available.

- The point where the <u>lines cross</u> on the graph is the point of <u>catastrophe</u> — population starts to <u>decrease</u> after this, until it is <u>low enough</u> that there are enough resources to <u>support</u> it again.

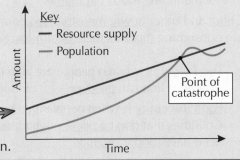

Boserup's Theory

- <u>Ester Boserup</u> was a 20th-century economist. Her theory was that <u>however big</u> the world's population grew, people would always produce <u>sufficient resources</u> to meet their needs.

- She thought that, if <u>resource supplies</u> became <u>limited</u>, people would come up with <u>new ways</u> to <u>increase production</u> (e.g. by making technological advances) in order to <u>avoid hardship</u>.

- The graph shows that, as population <u>increases</u> to be <u>equal</u> with resource supply, resource supply <u>increases</u> so there are always <u>enough resources</u> available for the population.

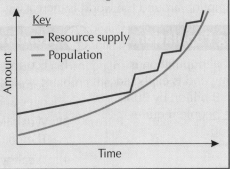

Neither theory has been proved completely <u>right</u> or completely <u>wrong</u>. There have been <u>famines</u> in some areas, but on a <u>global scale</u>, food production has <u>so far kept up</u> with population growth.

People in richer countries consume more food, water and energy

That was a quick dash through some pretty big ideas. Don't worry, there's more coming up on managing resources — but if you can get your head round this lot, it'll really help with the rest of the topic, so go back and read it again.

Global Demand for Food

The world needs <u>more</u> and <u>more food</u>, but in some areas there just isn't <u>enough</u>.

Global **Food Supply** is **Uneven**

The <u>amount</u> of food that countries <u>produce varies</u>. The map on the right shows the production of <u>cereals</u> by country from 2012 to 2014. The production of other food follows a <u>similar pattern</u>.

1) <u>East Asia</u> and <u>North America</u> produce <u>a lot</u> of food.

2) <u>Central America</u> and <u>Africa</u> only produce <u>small</u> amounts of food.

The <u>factors</u> that affect <u>how much food</u> can be <u>produced</u> are explained on the next page.

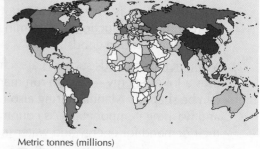

Metric tonnes (millions)
- ■ >410
- ■ 90-410
- ■ 50-90
- ■ 16-50
- □ 2.8-16
- □ <2.8
- □ No data available

The <u>amount</u> of food people <u>eat</u> also <u>varies</u> across the world. This can be shown by comparing the <u>average daily calorie intake</u> of people in different countries, or by the <u>Global Hunger Index</u>.

1) <u>More developed</u> areas like <u>North America</u> and <u>Europe</u> eat <u>a lot</u>. They can <u>afford</u> to <u>import</u> a large variety of foods and many people have a <u>high income</u> so can buy more food.

2) <u>Less developed</u> areas like <u>Africa</u>, <u>Central America</u> and parts of <u>Asia</u> consume <u>less</u> food per person as they <u>can't afford</u> as much and less food is <u>available</u>.

3) <u>China</u> and other <u>newly industrialised</u> countries are consuming <u>more</u> as their <u>wealth increases</u>.

The <u>Global Hunger Index</u> shows how many people are suffering from <u>hunger</u> or <u>illness</u> caused by lack of food. It gives a value for each country from 0 (<u>no hunger</u>) to 100 (<u>extreme hunger</u>). Countries are divided into <u>categories</u> depending on the <u>severity</u> of the problem.

Categories (2014)[*]
- ■ Low
- ■ Moderate
- □ Serious
- ■ Alarming
- ■ Extremely alarming
- □ No data/not calculated

- <u>Food security</u> is when people are able to eat enough <u>nutritious food</u> to stay <u>healthy</u> and <u>active</u>. Countries that can <u>produce a lot</u> of food or are <u>rich</u> enough to <u>import</u> the food they need have <u>food security</u>.

- <u>Food insecurity</u> is when people <u>aren't</u> able to get enough food to stay healthy or lead an active life. Countries that <u>don't grow enough</u> to feed their population and <u>can't afford to import</u> the food they need have <u>food insecurity</u>.

Global **Food Consumption** is **Increasing**

Food <u>consumption</u> around the world is <u>increasing</u>. This is down to <u>two</u> main reasons:

(1) Rising Population

The global population is <u>increasing</u> and is expected to reach 9 billion by 2040 — <u>more people</u> require <u>more food</u>.

(2) Economic Development

1) <u>Economic development</u> means that countries are getting <u>wealthier</u>.

2) Some <u>emerging countries</u> are experiencing <u>high</u> population growth rates and <u>lots</u> of people are getting a lot <u>richer</u>, very <u>quickly</u>.

3) Wealthier people have <u>more disposable income</u> to spend on <u>food</u>. They often buy a greater <u>variety</u> of food and <u>more</u> than they <u>need</u>.

4) Wealthy <u>countries</u> can afford to <u>import</u> food <u>all year round</u> so people no longer eat just what is <u>seasonally available</u>.

5) <u>Industrialisation</u> of <u>agriculture</u> means some countries are able to <u>produce more</u> food at <u>lower cost</u>. Food becomes <u>cheaper</u>, so people can <u>afford</u> to <u>eat more</u>.

More people and more money = more food required

If you can get this lot under your belt it'll really help with understanding the rest of the topic. Make sure you're clear on the meaning of food security and insecurity — it's all about whether people have a reliable source of food.

    * Source: von Grebmer et al. (2015). Reproduced with permission from the International Food Policy Research Institute.

Food Insecurity

Food insecurity is a pretty complex issue — there are loads of factors that affect how much food is available.

Food Supply is Affected by Physical Factors...

Food insecurity occurs for two reasons — not enough food is being produced or people are unable to access food supplies. Food production and accessibility are affected by physical factors:

Climate

Countries that have climates that are unsuitable for farming (e.g. too hot, too cold, or too little rainfall) can't grow much food of their own. Extreme weather events, such as floods and droughts, can also affect food supply.

Water stress

Crops and livestock need water to survive. Areas that have low rainfall or where water for irrigation is scarce struggle to grow enough food.

Pests and diseases

Pests reduce yields by consuming crops, e.g. rats cause big problems by eating stored grain, and huge locust swarms eat all the vegetation in their path. Diseases affect most crops and livestock and can cause a lot of damage if they spread through crops and herds, e.g. 37% of the world's wheat crops are under threat from a disease called wheat rust.

...and Human Factors

Food production and accessibility are also affected by human factors:

Poverty

People living in poverty often don't have their own land where they can grow food. Poverty can also affect people's ability to farm the land effectively, e.g. they may not be able to buy the fertilisers or pesticides they need. At a global scale, poverty means that countries which can't grow enough can't afford to import food from countries with a surplus.

Technology

The mechanisation of farm equipment (e.g. use of tractors) increases the amount of food that can be grown by making the process more efficient. New technologies (e.g. genetic engineering — see p. 203) can help protect plants from disease, increase their yields and help them grow better in harsh climates.

Conflict

Conflict — fighting may damage agricultural land or make it unsafe, making it difficult to grow enough food. Access to food becomes difficult for people who are forced to flee their homes. Conflicts also make it difficult to import food because trade routes are disrupted and political relationships with supply countries may break down.

Learn these six factors that can lead to food insecurity

Food insecurity is a complex issue, and is usually caused by a combination of these factors. Knowing the factors listed on this page won't help solve world hunger I'm afraid, but it will help you to write great exam answers.

Food Insecurity

Time to delve into what happens when there isn't enough food to go round... There's a lot more to it than you might think, but don't worry — as long as you can remember these impacts of food insecurity you'll be fine.

Food Insecurity has Negative Impacts

Food insecurity doesn't just mean that people go hungry — it can lead to a whole load of other problems too:

Famine

A serious lack of food across a large area is known as a famine. During a famine people are unable to get enough food of any sort, which leads to starvation and death if the situation continues.

Undernutrition

To stay healthy, people need to eat a balanced diet. Undernutrition is when you don't get enough nutrients of a particular sort to keep your body healthy.

Soil erosion

If people are struggling to get enough food, they may not use the best agricultural practices, e.g. they may over-cultivate the land (grow crops repeatedly, without allowing time for the soil to recover its nutrients). Pressure to get enough to eat may also lead to overgrazing, when there are more animals than the land can support. Over-cultivation and overgrazing lead to soil erosion.

Rising prices

When there isn't enough food available, food prices usually increase. This is because shops don't have to lower their prices to compete for customers — people will pay any price to get the food they need. Rising prices mean that the poorest people can't afford to feed themselves properly.

Refugees from a civil war receiving food aid

*

Social unrest

People expect governments to help them get enough food during times of food insecurity, e.g. during a drought. If governments don't appear to be doing enough, make the situation worse or distribute aid unfairly, it can cause rioting and even turn into a bigger conflict, e.g. a civil war.

EXAM TIP

Food insecurity can cause a variety of problems

Some of the impacts of food insecurity are not particularly obvious. If you're asked about them in the exam, bear in mind things like soil erosion, rising food prices and social unrest, and don't try to answer an essay question by only writing about people being hungry. You'll need more than that to get top marks.

Increasing Food Production

If you've read the previous page you'll know why food insecurity can make things difficult. We need to produce more food — and there are some pretty interesting ways people are doing just that.

New Technologies can Increase Food Supply

With the global demand for food increasing, new ways of increasing food supplies are urgently needed. Trying to increase yields (how much food is produced in a given area) is important. Solutions exist at a range of scales from a complete change in agricultural methods, to smaller, local techniques to improve crop growth using existing technology. Here are some examples:

Irrigation

Irrigation is artificially watering the land so crops can grow. It can be used to make dry areas more productive, or to increase the number of harvests and the yield of crops.

There are three main types of irrigation:

1) Gravity flow — digging ditches and channels to transport ground or surface water to fields.

2) Sprinklers — spraying water across fields.

3) Drip systems — dripping water from small holes in pipes directly onto the soil around the roots of crop plants.

Hydroponics and Aeroponics

Hydroponics and aeroponics are methods of growing plants without soil:

1) In hydroponics plants are grown in a nutrient solution, supported by a material such as rockwool, gravel, or clay balls.

2) In aeroponics plants are suspended in air and a fine mist of water containing nutrients is sprayed onto the roots. The water drips off the roots and is used again.

3) Plants are monitored closely and nutrients adjusted to maximise the yield of crops.

4) Less water is required than plants grown in soil and reduced risk of disease and pests means less need for pesticides.

5) Hydroponics and aeroponics are very expensive, so these methods are currently only used for high value crops.

Biotechnology

Biotechnology involves genetically engineering crops to improve production. Genetically modified (GM) crops allow more food to be grown in smaller areas with fewer resources.

For example, GM crops can be designed to have:

1) Higher yields, e.g. C4 rice is a breed of rice that is being developed to produce high yields.

2) Resistance to drought, disease or pests (which reduces the need for pesticides).

3) Higher nutritional values, e.g. potatoes with more protein, rice with more vitamin A.

However, there are ethical and environmental concerns:

- They may reduce biodiversity because fewer varieties of crops are planted.

- GM plants may interbreed with wild plants and pass on their genes or disrupt ecosystems.

The New Green Revolution

The Green Revolution (1960s-70s) involved using mechanisation, chemicals and new strains of plants to increase the yield of crops. However, it caused lots of environmental problems and mainly benefited large-scale producers and richer farmers. The new green revolution aims to improve yields in a more sustainable way (see page 205). This will involve using a combination of:

1) GM varieties, including varieties with pest and disease resistance.

2) Traditional and organic farming methods, including soil nutrient recycling, crop rotation and natural predators to control pests.

Increasing Food Production

Appropriate Technology

1) The <u>high-tech</u> methods discussed on the previous page all have <u>disadvantages</u>. They also all tend to be <u>extremely expensive</u>, so aren't a <u>practical choice</u> to use in <u>less-wealthy countries</u>. For these countries, <u>appropriate technologies</u> are a much <u>better option</u>.

2) Using <u>appropriate technologies</u> involves choosing ways of increasing food production that are <u>suited</u> to <u>local environments</u> and the <u>needs</u>, <u>skills</u>, <u>knowledge</u> and <u>wealth</u> of the <u>people</u> in those areas.

3) For example, in <u>poorer countries</u>:

- <u>Individual</u> wells with <u>easy to maintain</u>, mechanical pumps are more suitable than <u>larger</u>, diesel powered pumps.

- A <u>drip irrigation system</u> constructed from <u>local materials</u> is more appropriate than an imported, high-tech sprinkler system.

- Planting a <u>variety</u> of <u>local species</u> that can cope with <u>local environmental conditions</u> and have seeds that can be <u>collected</u> and <u>re-planted</u> may be more appropriate than planting a single GM variety that may have to be <u>repurchased</u> each year.

Mechanised Food Production is Harmful to the Environment

1) Since the <u>1960s</u>, there has been a <u>growth</u> in <u>large-scale</u>, <u>industrial</u> farming where <u>processes</u> are increasingly done by <u>machines</u>, e.g. tractors and combine harvesters, rather than <u>people</u>.

2) <u>Industrial farming</u> can increase the <u>amount</u> of food that can be produced, because <u>processes</u> such as milking, ploughing and harvesting can be done more <u>quickly</u>.

3) However, changes to farms have had <u>impacts</u> on <u>ecosystems</u> and the <u>environment</u>:

- <u>Field sizes</u> have <u>increased</u> so that food can be produced more cheaply. <u>Removal</u> of <u>hedgerows</u> has led to a <u>decline</u> in <u>biodiversity</u>.

- The amount of <u>chemicals</u> used in food production has been <u>increasing</u> — large quantities of <u>artificial fertilisers</u> and <u>pesticides</u> are applied to crops, and animals are given <u>special feed</u> to encourage growth. If they enter <u>water courses</u> (e.g. rivers), these chemicals can <u>harm</u> or <u>kill organisms</u>.

- Increased use of <u>heavy machinery</u>, e.g. in planting and harvesting, can cause <u>soil erosion</u>.

4) Global <u>demand</u> for <u>fish</u> is <u>increasing</u>. Most <u>fish</u> and <u>seafood</u> is provided by <u>commercial fishing</u> methods — these include <u>trawling</u> (towing <u>huge nets</u> behind boats) and <u>dredging</u> (dragging a <u>metal frame</u> along the <u>seabed</u> to harvest shellfish such as oysters and scallops).

5) Since the <u>1950s</u>, fishing has become increasingly <u>mechanised</u> — this mean that boats can now carry <u>bigger nets</u> and haul in <u>bigger catches</u> than used to be possible, helping to <u>meet demand</u> for fish.

6) <u>Fish farms</u> (aquaculture) are also being used to <u>breed fish</u> and <u>shellfish</u> in <u>contained spaces</u>.

7) Commercial fishing is having a number of <u>impacts</u> on <u>ecosystems</u> and the <u>environment</u>:

- <u>Over-fishing</u> of some fish (e.g. cod) means that some species are now <u>endangered</u>. Decreasing the number of one species in an ecosystem can have <u>knock-on impacts</u> on other species (see p.46).

- <u>Dredging</u> can damage seafloor <u>habitats</u> and disturb <u>organisms</u> such as sea urchins and starfish.

- <u>Fish farms</u> are often overcrowded, and the large number of fish produce a lot of <u>waste</u>. If this waste is <u>released</u> into the natural environment, it can cause large blooms of <u>algae</u>. The algae absorb a lot of <u>oxygen</u> from the water, causing other plants and animals to <u>die</u>.

New technologies are having an environmental impact

Although new technologies help to create a more sustainable source of food, they can be harmful to the environment. To help you remember the impacts of each new technology, draw a table which explains the positive and negative impacts of each. Then try comparing and contrasting these impacts.

Sustainable Food Supply

Developing more sustainable food production systems is a big challenge in the modern world. New methods of farming are being adopted to reduce the environmental impacts of new technologies and mechanisation.

Low Impact Farming Makes Food Supplies More Sustainable

To make food supplies sustainable, alternatives to industrial agriculture are needed, which don't damage the environment. These can be environmentally, economically and socially sustainable:

- Environmental sustainability means keeping the environment in a healthy state in the long-term.
- Economic sustainability means making sure the wealth of individuals and countries continues to grow.
- Social sustainability means maintaining a high quality of life for everyone indefinitely.

Organic Farming

1) Organic farming uses natural processes to return nutrients to the soil, so that crops can continue to be grown. E.g. crops, animals and empty (fallow) areas are rotated and natural fertilisers, such as cow manure, are used, which can be less damaging to the environment.

2) Artificial herbicides and pesticides are restricted and animals aren't given extra supplements or vaccinations. This reduces the reliance on unsustainable resources and can protect biodiversity.

3) Organic farmers are encouraged to sell their produce as close to where it is produced as possible, reducing the amount of road and air transport required.

Permaculture

1) Permaculture is a way of living sustainably. It includes trying to produce food in a way that recreates natural ecosystems in an effort to protect the soil, insects and other wildlife.

2) People are encouraged to grow their own food and change their eating habits — eating fewer animal products and more fruit and vegetables, and buying local, organic or fair trade food wherever possible.

3) The production of food is designed to be low maintenance and to keep soils healthy so that crops can continue to be grown. For example, mixed cropping is used, which involves having plants of different heights and lots of different types in one area. This means the available space and light are used better, there are fewer pests and diseases and less watering is required.

Urban Farming Initiatives

1) Urban farming initiatives use empty land, roof tops and balconies to grow food and raise animals in towns and cities.

2) Urban farming makes food locally available, reducing the need to transport food long distances. This means it is often fresher and more nutritious and can also be cheaper — improving the food security of poorer residents.

3) It adds greenery to cities, making them healthier and more attractive places to live and makes urban areas less dependent on industrial agriculture.

Agroforestry Schemes in Mali are Producing a Sustainable Food Supply

1) In the Koutiala region of Mali (a developing country), many local farmers have begun to use agroforestry techniques to make sure that their food supply is sustainable.

2) Mali is a very dry country. Intensive use of land for farming is causing desertification of the land (see p.70), making it less fertile.

3) Farmers were shown how to plant staple crops like maize in amongst trees and nitrogen-fixing plants.

4) The plants add nitrogen to the soil so artificial fertilisers aren't needed. The trees provide shade and prevent soil erosion. They also increase the nutrient and water content of the soil — leaf fall increases the organic content of the soil so that it holds water better. The trees can also be used for building materials.

5) This system increases the yield of maize at the same time as protecting the soil. The system is sustainable because farmers can provide the food they need without damaging the local environment, so they can continue to produce food using these methods in the future.

Sustainable Food Supply

Ethical Consumerism Can Help to Increase Sustainability

1) Ethical consumerism means choosing to buy goods that have been produced with minimal harm to people and the environment. It's also about how we use goods — e.g. whether we throw lots of food away.

2) Ethical consumerism can help to increase food security and sustainability by, for example:

- reducing the amount of food thrown away.
- making food production profitable, so farmers can afford to carry on producing it.
- paying more money to poorer countries for goods, so poverty decreases.

There are Lots of Ways of Making Food Consumption More Ethical

Buy Fair Trade Products

1) Companies who want to sell products labelled as 'fair trade' have to pay farmers a fair price. This helps farmers in poorer countries make enough to improve their quality of life.

2) Food produced under fair trade schemes is ethical and sustainable because:
- Buyers pay extra on top of the fair price to help develop the area where the goods come from, e.g. to build schools or health centres. This makes buying fair trade products more socially sustainable.
- Only producers that treat their employees well can take part in the scheme, e.g. all employees must have a safe working environment. This improves the workers' quality of life.
- There are rules about how fair trade food is grown — farmers must use environmentally friendly methods that e.g. protect biodiversity, limit greenhouse gas emissions and preserve soil health.

Buy Fish and Meat from Sustainable Sources

1) Many fish species are at risk from over-fishing, due to increased consumption. Sustainable fishing includes catch quotas that limit the amount of fish taken and fishing methods that are less harmful to the environment. Labelling allows consumers to choose to eat fish that have been fished sustainably.

2) The raising of cattle is bad for the environment — forests are often cleared to make space for them and they produce a lot of methane (a greenhouse gas). However, eating grass-fed meat is much more sustainable. These animals are raised on natural grassland — they don't need feeding on grain (which requires lots of space and artificial fertilisers to grow) and they provide natural manure for the soil.

Buy Local and Seasonal Food

1) In many wealthy countries, people expect to buy the foods they like all year round. This means that foods have to be imported for all or part of the year.

2) Consumers can choose to eat more food that has been produced locally (e.g. choosing potatoes that have been grown on a nearby farm). They can also eat seasonally — this means eating foods that grow locally at that time of year (e.g. only eating strawberries in summer, when they are grown in the UK).

3) Importing lots of food is not sustainable because transport pollutes the environment.

Reduce Waste and Losses

1) Globally one third of food that is produced is lost or wasted — reducing this will make more food available, so less needs to be grown to feed the world's population.

2) Schemes such as 'Think.Eat.Save' and 'Love Food Hate Waste' encourage individuals, businesses and governments to be less wasteful with food, e.g. by helping people plan their meals better and sharing recipe ideas for using up leftovers. They also encourage people to compost waste rather than putting it in the bin (food in landfill sites produces methane, which is a greenhouse gas).

Consumers' food choices can affect how sustainable food supplies are

It's not just farmers and agricultural companies that affect how sustainable food supplies are — what people choose to buy and eat is important too. Learn a few examples of each way of making food consumption more ethical.

Food in the UK

The way we grow food, and the amount and variety we consume has changed dramatically in the UK since 1940.

Food Consumption Has Decreased Since 1940...

1) Average daily calorie intake in the UK increased from about 2350 in 1940 to about 2600 in 1960, then decreased to about 2150 by 2000.

2) In the past, people were more active so they needed more calories. Nowadays, there's more awareness of and concern about obesity and good nutrition.

... but Food Availability Has Increased

In the UK, food availability is high — most people have enough to eat. Food availability has changed over time:

- The Common Agricultural Policy (CAP) was introduced in the 1950s — it increased production of crops such as wheat by intensifying agriculture (see p.203). Since the 1990s, food production has been more sustainable, and yields have been fairly stable.

- There has been a growth in agribusiness in the UK since the 1960s (see p.204). Agribusiness is large-scale, industrial farming where processes from the production of seeds and fertilisers, to the processing and packaging of the food are controlled by large firms.

- There's also been a growing demand for seasonal products (e.g. strawberries) all year round and high-value foods, such as exotic fruits, coffee and spices. These are often grown in developing countries and exported to the UK. Imports of these foods into the UK have increased, so they are constantly available.

- Organic produce is becoming increasingly popular because people are becoming more concerned about the environmental impacts of food production and the effect of chemicals on their health. Some organic food is produced in the UK, but lots of it is imported too.

Food Banks Have Helped Increase Food Security in Newcastle

1) Although food availability in the UK is high, there are about 5 million people who don't have enough to eat.

2) One way of tackling this is with food banks — people and companies donate food, which is handed out to those in need. Recipients get a package containing enough nutritious food to last them for three days.

3) One city where food banks are needed is Newcastle — around 8% of people in the city have used one of the food banks there. Food banks in Newcastle have helped increase food security:

- They help reduce hunger and improve people's diets — this also improves their health.
- Some shops and bakeries donate unsold fresh food at the end of the day, reducing waste.
- Some food banks give lessons in cooking and budgeting, to help people with limited money eat healthily.

4) However, food banks don't solve underlying problems, such as low wages and benefit cuts.

There's lots of food in the UK, but not everyone has enough to eat

Although the amount of food available has increased, many people today still rely on food banks. Make sure you understand the reasons behind this, and the ways in which food banks are increasing food security in the UK.

Food in the UK

Because we only have a <u>limited amount of land</u>, food production has been <u>intensified</u> in order to <u>increase yields</u>. However, intensification can be <u>harmful</u> to the <u>environment</u> and increases our <u>carbon footprint</u>.

<u>Intensification</u> Increased Food Supplies in the UK

<u>Intensification</u> of <u>farming</u> from the 1940s to the 1980s was an attempt to <u>increase food security</u> by <u>increasing production</u>. The methods used included:

- <u>Higher yielding</u> crops and animals (developed by breeding individuals that gave higher yields initially).
- <u>Monoculture</u> — growing <u>just one crop</u> over a large area.
- <u>Irrigation</u> technologies, e.g. groundwater pumping, electric sprinklers.
- <u>Chemicals</u>, e.g. fertilisers, pesticides and herbicides.
- <u>Mechanisation</u>, e.g. use of machines for sowing, harvesting, weeding and spraying.

This was effective in <u>increasing food security</u> in the UK — in 1940, the UK <u>imported 70%</u> of its cereal crops, but by 1980 this had decreased to <u>20%</u>. However, intensification also had <u>negative impacts</u>, such as:

1) <u>Monoculture crops</u> could be wiped out by a <u>single pest</u>, <u>drought</u> or <u>disease</u>, e.g. cereal crop yields <u>decreased</u> by about 500 000 tonnes because of <u>drought</u> in 1976.
2) Intensive methods caused <u>environmental damage</u>, for example:
   - Monoculture reduced <u>biodiversity</u>, especially of <u>flowering plants</u> and <u>insects</u>.
   - The chemicals used caused <u>pollution</u> of land and water, disrupting <u>ecosystems</u>.
   - Over-exploiting the land led to <u>reduced soil fertility</u> and <u>increased soil erosion</u> in some areas.

The **Carbon Footprint** of Our Food is **Growing**

1) The <u>growing</u>, <u>processing</u> and <u>packaging of food</u> produces CO_2 and other <u>greenhouse gases</u>.

2) <u>Transporting</u> food from where it is grown to where it is sold also produces CO_2. The <u>distance food is transported to the market</u> is called its <u>food miles</u>. The <u>higher the food miles</u>, the <u>more CO_2</u> is produced.

3) The <u>amount of greenhouse gas produced</u> during <u>growing</u>, <u>packing</u> and <u>transporting</u> a food is called its <u>carbon footprint</u>. A <u>larger</u> carbon footprint means <u>more greenhouse gases</u> and <u>more global warming</u>.

4) <u>Imported foods</u> have to be <u>transported a long way</u> so have <u>high food miles</u> and a <u>large carbon footprint</u>.

5) People are becoming aware of the <u>environmental issues</u> caused by transporting food over <u>long distances</u>. Environmentalists are encouraging people to buy food grown <u>locally</u>. <u>Farmers' markets</u>, <u>farm shops</u> and <u>locally-produced</u> vegetable boxes are becoming more and more <u>popular</u>.

Intensifying food production produces more greenhouse gases

Farming has always contributed to greenhouse gas emissions, but intensification has increased agriculture's carbon footprint. Learn how the carbon footprint of our food is growing, and ways to reduce these impacts.

Food in the UK

In <u>Kent</u>, people have been developing a <u>new system</u> of agriculture which <u>reduces</u> the <u>impacts</u> of <u>intensification</u>, but still produces <u>large amounts</u> of food for the UK. It has got disadvantages as well as advantages though. Read on...

Thanet Earth Grows Crops in Huge Greenhouses

1) <u>Thanet Earth</u> is a <u>large-scale</u> agricultural development in <u>Kent</u>, in south-east England.

2) <u>4 greenhouses</u>, each the size of 10 football pitches, are used to grow <u>salad vegetables</u> — tomatoes, cucumbers and peppers — using <u>hydroponics</u>, nearly <u>all year round</u>.

3) The development aims to be <u>sustainable</u>. Each greenhouse has its own <u>power station</u> to provide <u>heat</u> and <u>lighting</u> and <u>rainwater</u> collected from the roofs is used to provide the <u>water supply</u>. <u>Hot air</u> and <u>carbon dioxide</u> from the power stations is <u>pumped</u> back into the <u>greenhouses</u>.

4) The scheme has many <u>advantages</u>, but <u>not everyone</u> is <u>happy</u> with it:

Advantages

- More than <u>500 jobs</u> have been created in an area with relatively <u>high unemployment</u>.
- British salad vegetables can be grown nearly <u>all year round</u>, reducing reliance on foreign imports. This gives the UK better <u>food security</u> and reduces food miles (see p.208).
- <u>Bees</u> are used for <u>pollination</u> and <u>natural predators</u> are used to <u>reduce pest</u> numbers, <u>reducing</u> the need for <u>artificial pesticides</u>.
- The <u>hydroponic</u> system is completely <u>automated</u> so each plant gets the <u>right amount</u> of nutrients, <u>limiting</u> the amount of <u>fertiliser</u> needed.

Disadvantages

- A large area of <u>farmland</u> has been <u>built on</u>.
- <u>Natural habitats</u> have been <u>lost</u> and <u>ecosystems disrupted</u>.
- The <u>money generated</u> goes mostly to the <u>large companies</u> that have invested in it, rather than to <u>local communities</u>.
- The greenhouses are built on high land and are artificially lit, causing <u>visual</u> and <u>light pollution</u>.
- A <u>large amount</u> of <u>energy</u> is required to <u>power</u> the greenhouses, as well as to <u>package</u> and <u>deliver</u> the produce to the supermarkets.

EXAM TIP

There are pros and cons to large-scale agricultural developments

You might be asked to write about a named example of a large-scale agricultural development — Thanet Earth is a good example, but if you've learnt a different one in class then go ahead and use that instead. If you're asked about how successful it is, make sure you cover both its advantages and disadvantages.

Worked Exam Questions

You know the routine by now — work carefully through these examples and make sure you understand them. Then it's on to the real test of doing some exam questions yourself.

1   There are differing theories about the relationship between population growth and resource availability.

1.1   Which one of the following is not a feature Malthus's theory about population and resources?

A   Population will increase faster than the supply of resources.   ◯

B   Population will fall after a 'point of catastrophe'.   ◯

C   Technological advances mean that access to resources will increase.   ●

D   Resource supply dictates population numbers.   ◯

[Total 1 mark]

2   Study **Figure 1**, which shows corn production in Canada (a developed country) and Zimbabwe (a developing country) between 1961 and 2013.

2.1   Compare corn production in Canada and Zimbabwe over the time period shown in **Figure 1**.

Canada increased its corn production from roughly 1 million tonnes per year in 1961 to about 14 million tonnes per year in 2013. However, there was no overall increase in corn production in Zimbabwe, with production varying between about 0.5 and 3 million tonnes.

[2]

Figure 1

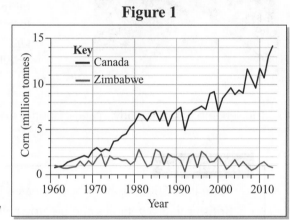

2.2   Outline **one** way in which appropriate technologies could be used to increase corn production in Zimbabwe.

Water supply could be improved by using individual wells with easy-to-maintain, mechanical pumps.

[1]

2.3   Evaluate the success of a large-scale agricultural development you have studied.

Thanet Earth uses hydroponics to grow salad vegetables in large greenhouses nearly all year round. This has created more than 500 jobs in an area with relatively high unemployment. The hydroponic system is automated so each plant gets the right amount of nutrients. This limits the amount of fertiliser needed, making food production more sustainable. However, a large area of farmland has been built on, so natural habitats have been lost and ecosystems disrupted. Also, a large amount of energy is required to power the greenhouses, as well as to deliver the produce to shops, which releases greenhouse gases. In conclusion, the benefits of the scheme outweigh the downsides, so it has been generally successful.

[4]

[Total 7 marks]

Exam Questions

1   Study **Figure 1**, a graph showing real and projected changes in global population from 1950 to 2050.

1.1   Using **Figure 1** and your own knowledge, describe how changes in global population are affecting demand for resources.

....

....

....

....

....

....
[3]

Figure 1

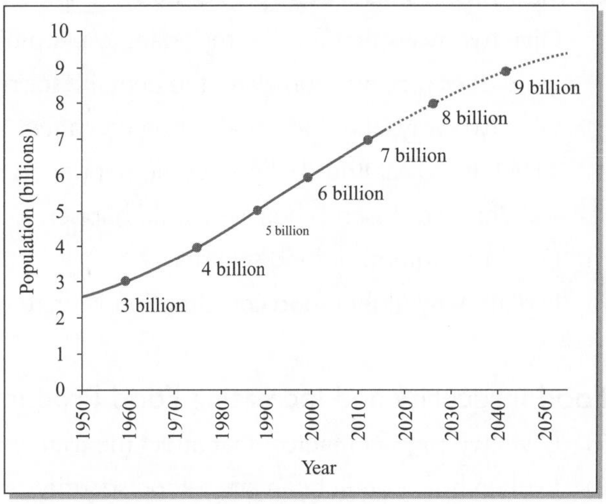

1.2   State two ways that increasing affluence affects people's resource consumption.

1:...

2:...
[2]

[Total 5 marks]

2   Farming practices have changed over time.

2.1   Which of the following is a way of intensifying farming? Shade **one** oval only.

A   Reducing the amount of resources used.   ◯

B   Increasing the size of the area in which food is produced.   ◯

C   Increasing the amount of chemicals used on crops.   ◯

D   Ensuring animals have access to outside space.   ◯   *[1]*

2.2   Outline **one** way in which organic farming is environmentally sustainable.

....

....

....
[2]

2.3   For a country you have studied, compare the effectiveness of one past and one present attempt to increase food security at a national scale.

[8 + 3 SPaG]

[Total 14 marks]

Revision Summary

Well, that's it for <u>Food</u>. Make sure you've remembered all the information by having a go at these questions.
- Try these questions and <u>tick off each one</u> when you <u>get it right</u>.
- When you've done <u>all the questions</u> for a topic and are <u>completely happy</u> with it, tick off the topic.

Demand for Resources (p.198-200) ☑

1) Give two ways that food is important to people's well-being.
2) How does urbanisation affect the demand for resources?
3) Give two ways that industrialisation can affect the demand for resources.
4) a) What did Malthus believe would happen to resource supply as population increased?
    b) What did Boserup believe would happen to resource supply as population increased?
5) Give a definition of food security.
6) Explain why global food consumption is increasing.

Food Insecurity and Increasing Food Production (p.201-204) ☑

7) Give two physical factors that affect the availability of food.
8) Explain how conflict can affect food security.
9) List five impacts of food insecurity.
10) Explain how irrigation can increase food production.
11) Give two ways that biotechnology can increase food production.
12) What is the new green revolution?
13) What is appropriate technology?
14) Give two environmental impacts of commercial fishing.

Sustainable Food Supply (p.205-206) ☑

15) Briefly describe the three types of sustainability.
16) Describe how permaculture can sustainably increase food supply.
17) a) Give an example of a local scheme in a developing country to increase
        sustainable supplies of food.
     b) Explain how the scheme works.
18) What is ethical consumerism?
19) Explain how fair trade can increase food security.
20) Give three other ways that changing consumption can help make food supplies more sustainable.

Food in the UK (p.207-209) ☑

21) True or false: daily calorie consumption in the UK is higher now than in 1940.
22) How has food availability in the UK changed since 1940?
23) How did the Common Agricultural Policy affect food availability?
24) Describe how demand for seasonal food has changed in the UK.
25) Why has demand for organic food increased in the UK?
26) What are food miles?
27) a) Give one example of a <u>local</u> attempt to increase food security.
     b) How has it helped to increase food security?
28) a) Give one example of a <u>national</u> attempt to increase food security.
     b) Give one advantage of this attempt.
     c) Give one disadvantage of this attempt.

Global Demand for Water

The <u>availability</u> of water <u>varies</u> from place to place and the world keeps requiring <u>more</u> and <u>more</u>...

Water Insecurity is **Not** Having Enough **Clean Water**

1) <u>Water security</u> means having a <u>reliable</u> and <u>sustainable</u> source of enough <u>good quality water</u> to meet <u>everyone's needs</u> — for industry, agriculture and personal health.

2) <u>Water security</u> depends on the <u>amount</u> of water available (e.g. from rainfall, rivers, groundwater etc.) and the <u>number of people</u> who need to use the water. It also depends on being able to <u>access the water</u> — which can be hard if you're <u>poor</u>.

3) Having <u>more water</u> than is needed is known as a <u>water surplus</u>. When there's not <u>enough water</u> to meet people's needs it's called a <u>water deficit</u>.

4) A water deficit can lead to <u>water insecurity</u> — when there's <u>not enough clean water</u> to keep everyone <u>healthy</u>, or enable them to make a <u>living</u> (e.g. to water their crops, provide energy etc.).

5) When <u>demand</u> for water <u>exceeds supply</u> during a certain period, or when water is not of high enough <u>quality</u> to use, places are said to experience <u>water stress</u>.

Global Patterns of Water **Security** and **Insecurity Vary**

This map shows the <u>global patterns</u> of water <u>insecurity</u>. A <u>high percentage</u> means that there are <u>more people</u> competing for <u>less water</u> — causing <u>water stress</u>.

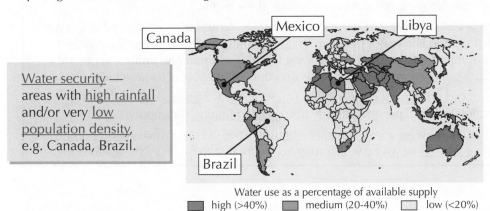

Water security — areas with <u>high rainfall</u> and/or very <u>low population density</u>, e.g. Canada, Brazil.

Water insecurity — areas with <u>low rainfall</u> and/or <u>high population density</u>, e.g. Libya, Mexico.

Water use as a percentage of available supply
■ high (>40%)   ■ medium (20-40%)   □ low (<20%)

Water Demand is **Rising** because there are **More People** with **More Money**

The <u>global demand</u> for water is <u>rising</u> for two main reasons:

① Rising population

1) Global <u>population</u> is <u>increasing</u> — each person needs water for <u>drinking</u>, <u>washing</u>, <u>preparing food</u> etc.

2) <u>More people</u> also means that <u>more food</u> needs to be grown — <u>irrigation</u> for agriculture uses <u>70%</u> of the world's freshwater resources.

② Economic development

The world is becoming <u>increasingly developed</u>.

1) <u>Industrialisation</u> — as countries become more developed, they <u>produce</u> more goods. <u>Manufacturing</u> uses <u>a lot of water</u>.

2) <u>Energy production</u> — <u>15%</u> of all water withdrawn globally is used to produce energy, e.g. in cooling thermal power plants.

3) <u>Rising living standards</u> — as countries develop, people's <u>wealth increases</u> and they can afford a <u>higher standard of living</u>. This <u>increases water use</u>, as more people can afford flushing toilets, showers, dishwashers, etc.

Make sure you understand all these terms

Test yourself on these definitions before you move on — knowing them will help you with the rest of the topic. You might need to know the global patterns of water security too, so take a good look at the map.

Water Insecurity

Loads of <u>factors</u> come together to <u>cause</u> water insecurity. Here are the ones you need to <u>know</u> about...

Water Availability is Affected by Many Factors

<u>Water availability</u> isn't just about how much <u>rainfall</u> you get — there are a load of <u>other factors</u> that affect it too.

Physical Factors

1) <u>Climate</u> — most places rely on <u>rainfall</u>, which feeds <u>lakes</u> and <u>rivers</u>, for their <u>water supply</u>.
If climates are <u>hot</u>, lots of water is also lost from lakes and rivers due to <u>evaporation</u>.
<u>Climate change</u> is altering the <u>total amount</u> of rainfall in places, as well as <u>how often</u> it rains
and <u>how heavy</u> it is. Many <u>dry areas</u> are getting <u>drier</u>, increasing the <u>risk</u> of <u>droughts</u>.

2) <u>Geology</u> — when rain falls on <u>impermeable rock</u>, e.g. clay, it can't soak in, so <u>flows off</u>
into <u>rivers</u> and <u>lakes</u>. These are <u>easy</u> to get water from. When rain falls on <u>permeable rock</u>,
e.g. sandstone, it <u>flows down</u> through them and can form <u>underground water stores</u> (aquifers),
which are <u>harder</u> to get to. However, <u>groundwater</u> can make <u>water available</u> in very <u>dry</u> places,
e.g. the Sahara desert.

Economic and Social Factors

1) <u>Over-abstraction</u> is when <u>more water</u> is being used than is being <u>replaced</u>. It is caused by:
   - <u>Population growth</u> and <u>economic development</u> (see previous page).
   - <u>Improvements</u> in <u>sanitation</u> and <u>personal hygiene</u> — e.g. people take more frequent showers.
   - <u>High demand</u> from <u>businesses</u> — tourism and recreation can put <u>water stress</u> on places during
   peak holiday seasons, e.g. keeping golf courses in arid regions green.

2) The <u>pollution</u> of water sources, e.g. rivers, lakes and groundwater, reduces the amount of <u>clean water</u>
that is <u>available</u>. Water pollution is a major problem in <u>rapidly industrialising countries</u>, where a
lot of <u>industrial waste</u> is dumped into rivers without being <u>treated</u>. Human and animal <u>waste</u> are a
<u>hazard</u> where people <u>share water sources</u> with animals and don't have access to sanitation.

3) <u>Limited infrastructure</u> — <u>rapid urbanisation</u> means that <u>water pipes</u> and <u>sewers</u> can't be built <u>quickly</u>
<u>enough</u> to supply the population and prevent sewage from <u>contaminating</u> the supply.

4) <u>Poverty</u> — water providers charge a <u>fee</u> for <u>supplying water</u> to homes. People who are <u>too poor</u> to
pay for it have to find <u>other sources</u> of water, which may not be treated to make them <u>safe</u> to drink.

Water Insecurity Can Have a Wide Range of Impacts

<u>Water insecurity</u> leads to lots of <u>problems</u>. For example:

1) <u>Pollution and disease</u> — where water is scarce, supplies of <u>drinking water</u> can become polluted by <u>sewage</u>,
<u>industrial chemicals</u> or <u>nitrogen</u> from <u>fertilisers</u>. Some diseases, e.g. <u>cholera</u> and <u>typhoid</u>, are caused
by <u>microorganisms</u> that are <u>passed on</u> through water <u>containing</u> untreated <u>sewage</u>. Without access to
<u>alternative</u> water supplies, people may be <u>forced</u> to drink <u>polluted water</u>, which can cause <u>death</u> or <u>disease</u>.

2) <u>Food production</u> — <u>irrigation</u> for <u>agriculture</u> uses a lot of water. A shortage of water means that <u>less food</u>
can be grown, which could lead to <u>starvation</u>.

3) <u>Industrial output</u> — <u>manufacturing</u> industries are hugely water-intensive so they can't <u>produce as much</u>
during <u>water shortages</u>, reducing people's <u>wages</u> and affecting the <u>economy</u> of the country.

4) <u>Conflict</u> — when areas of water insecurity <u>share</u> the <u>same water supplies</u>, e.g. a <u>river</u> or an <u>aquifer</u>,
water shortages can trigger <u>conflicts</u>. For example, if one country tries to <u>improve</u> its water security
by taking <u>more water</u> from a <u>river</u>, it can <u>reduce</u> the water security of countries <u>downstream</u>.

Learn the causes and impacts of water insecurity

In the exam, you might be asked to identify the causes or impacts of water insecurity from a photo or a
diagram — it'll be much easier to spot them if you know what you're looking for, so learn them...

Increasing Water Supply

There are some pretty <u>large-scale technological solutions</u> that can <u>improve water supply</u>...

Reservoirs Can Provide a Reliable Water Supply

1) <u>Seasonal variations</u> in rainfall or <u>unpredictable</u> rainfall can cause a <u>water shortage</u> at certain times of year. One way of coping with this problem is by <u>increasing storage</u>.

2) Building a <u>dam</u> across a river <u>traps</u> a large amount of water behind the dam, creating a <u>reservoir</u> — this provides a <u>reliable</u> source of water <u>all year</u>. However, dams and reservoirs have <u>environmental impacts</u>:

- Reservoirs <u>flood</u> large amounts of land, <u>destroying habitats</u> and <u>agricultural land</u>.
- Reservoirs impact local <u>ecosystems</u>. Water is often <u>released</u> through the dam at <u>regular intervals</u> making the river flow much more <u>uniform</u> — this often <u>reduces species diversity</u>. Dams also act as a <u>barrier</u> to species' <u>movements</u>, e.g. <u>salmon</u> that migrate upstream to lay their eggs.
- The <u>natural flow</u> of <u>sediment downstream</u> is disrupted, <u>reducing</u> the <u>fertility</u> of areas downstream.
- Reservoirs create <u>new</u> aquatic environments, which can become home to <u>non-native species</u>.

Water Transfer Moves Water to Places Where It's Needed

1) Water is often not <u>where</u> it is most <u>needed</u>. E.g. the <u>south</u> and <u>east</u> of the UK is much <u>drier</u> than the <u>north</u> and <u>west</u>, and has a <u>higher population density</u>, so there isn't always <u>enough water</u> to go round.

2) <u>Water transfers</u> use <u>canals</u> and <u>pipes</u> to move water from a river that has <u>surplus</u> water to a river that has a water <u>shortage</u>. This can cause <u>problems</u> for <u>ecosystems</u> and the <u>environment</u>:

1) <u>Large-scale engineering works</u> are needed to create new <u>channels</u>. These can <u>damage ecosystems</u>.

2) There may be <u>water shortages</u> in areas where the water is coming <u>from</u>, particularly in <u>dry years</u>. This can put <u>pressure</u> on <u>local ecosystems</u>.

3) Lots of <u>energy</u> is needed to <u>pump</u> the water over <u>long distances</u> if there isn't a natural downhill route. This can <u>release greenhouse gases</u>, adding to <u>climate change</u>.

4) Water transfer schemes often involve building <u>dams</u> and <u>reservoirs</u> (see above).

Desalination allows Seawater to be Used as a Water Source

1) <u>Desalination</u> is the removal of <u>salt</u> from <u>seawater</u> so that it can be <u>used</u>. There are two main processes that are used — either the seawater can be <u>heated</u> to <u>evaporate</u> it and then <u>condensed</u> to collect the freshwater or the seawater can be passed through a <u>special membrane</u> to remove the salt.

2) It is <u>expensive</u> because <u>energy</u> is needed to <u>heat</u> the water or to <u>force</u> it through the membrane. Most plants are also powered by <u>fossil fuels</u>, though Saudi Arabia is building the world's first <u>large scale</u>, <u>solar powered</u> desalination plant.

3) In the <u>UK</u>, desalination is mainly used during <u>droughts</u>, rather than being the <u>main source of water</u>.

4) However, <u>wealthy desert countries</u> often use desalination as their main source of clean, drinking water. <u>Dubai</u> supplies <u>98.8%</u> of its water through desalination — up to 140 million gallons a day.

5) Desalination plants in countries that are more dependent on them have developed more <u>efficient technology</u>, e.g. Dubai's new plant is <u>82% efficient</u> compared to about 45% for plants in Europe.

Strategies for increasing water supply have social and environmental costs

These solutions all require large-scale construction projects — they can be very effective in drastically improving water supply, but they're are often expensive to develop and may involve major disruption to ecosystems.

Sustainable Water Supply

Massive engineering works aren't always the answer to water insecurity. We can all do our bit to make sure that we use water resources sustainably, to help make sure that there's enough for everyone.

Sustainable Water Supplies — Use Less and Re-Use More

Water needs to be used more sustainably to make sure there is enough to meet everyone's current needs without preventing future generations from meeting their needs.

Water Conservation

Water conservation is about trying to use less water. For example by:

1) Fixing leaking reservoirs, pipes and dripping taps to stop water being wasted.

2) Fitting dual-flush toilets, as they use less water, or using devices in the cistern (the toilet water tank) that can save up to 3.5 litres of water for every flush.

3) Buying efficient washing machines and dishwashers and only running them with full loads.

4) Irrigating farmland using drip pipes and sprays that direct the water exactly where it is needed, so use less water than traditional irrigation channels and ditches.

5) Fitting homes and businesses with water meters. Charging for metered water makes people more aware of how much they use are using, so are more likely to reduce their usage.

6) Educating people to take shorter showers and turn off taps when not in use.

Groundwater Management

Groundwater is water found underground in soil and in cracks in rock.

1) The amount of groundwater being extracted can be monitored to ensure it is not extracted faster than it is naturally replaced. Laws can be passed to prevent too much groundwater being extracted.

2) To prevent pollution of groundwater making it unusable, farmers can be encouraged to apply less artificial fertiliser and pesticides to farmland and companies that leak toxic industrial waste can be fined.

3) When groundwater supplies are shared between countries, international agreements are needed to make sure one country doesn't take an unsustainable amount of water from the aquifer, leaving other countries unable to meet the needs of their population. Agreeing how much water each country should take from the aquifer can be very difficult.

Recycling and 'Grey' Water

1) Recycling water means taking water that has already been used and using it again rather than returning it to a river or the sea straight away. This makes water use more sustainable because less water needs to be extracted from rivers or from groundwater to meet people's needs.

2) Water from homes and industries can be piped to water treatment plants where it is treated to make it safe enough to reuse.

3) Most recycled water is used for irrigation, industry, power plants and toilet flushing, though it can also be treated enough to make it safe to drink.

4) 'Grey' water is a type of recycled water — it is usually reused immediately rather than being treated first. It is mostly waste water from peoples homes, e.g. from washing machines, showers, or sinks. (It doesn't include water from toilets though, as this water is contaminated.)

5) Because it is relatively clean, it can be safely used for irrigating gardens or farmland, washing cars and flushing toilets. It's not safe for washing hands or drinking though.

6) These methods have the benefit of also conserving energy, as less energy is needed for treating water unnecessarily.

Water needs to be managed sustainably

As you've probably figured out by now, sustainability is a bit of a buzz word. Remember, sustainable solutions are often quite cheap and can be done on a local scale. Study these water examples until you know them inside out.

Increasing Water Supply

Solutions to water insecurity can be <u>large scale</u> and expensive, or <u>local</u> and <u>sustainable</u>.

China is **Transferring Water** from the **Wetter South** to the **Drier North**

To cope with water insecurity, the Chinese government has planned a <u>$62 billion project</u> that will transfer <u>44.8 billion cubic litres</u> of water <u>every year</u> from the <u>south</u> to the <u>north</u> of the country. <u>Two</u> out of <u>three</u> planned routes have been <u>completed</u> — the <u>Central</u> and <u>Eastern Routes</u>.

The water transfer project has <u>advantages</u>:

1) The project provides <u>clean water</u> to over <u>20 cities</u>, including Beijing and Tianjin.
2) The Chinese government estimates that up to <u>100 million people</u> have benefited from the project.
3) Water is important for industry, so an increased water supply means that <u>industrial development</u> can continue in the north. This can increase the country's <u>wealth</u>.
4) The scheme provides water that can be used to <u>irrigate</u> farmland, so crops can be grown.
5) It should prevent <u>over-abstraction</u> in the north, helping to stop land <u>subsidence</u>.

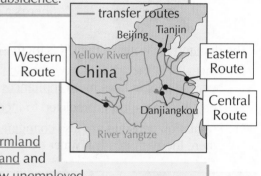

However, the project also has <u>disadvantages</u>:

1) Large areas have been <u>flooded</u>, <u>destroying</u> natural habitats. The huge construction works are <u>damaging</u> fragile <u>ecosystems</u>.
2) Diverting so much water may increase <u>water stress</u> in the <u>south</u>, e.g. a drought in 2010-2011 significantly reduced China's wheat yields.
3) Raising the dam of the Danjiangkou Reservoir <u>flooded</u> productive <u>farmland</u> and forced <u>345 000 people</u> to <u>move</u>. Many of them now have <u>less land</u> and poorly built <u>housing</u>. Many received little <u>compensation</u> and are now <u>unemployed</u>.
4) The water supplied to Beijing is very <u>expensive</u> due to the project's high cost and it's only available in <u>urban areas</u>. The urban poor and many people in rural areas have <u>no access</u> to the diverted water.

Kenya is Using **Sand Dams** to Create a **Sustainable Water Supply**

Kenya is a developing country with a <u>hot</u>, <u>dry</u> climate. Most rain falls in just a <u>few heavy downpours</u> each year. Most <u>rivers</u> only flow during the <u>rainy season</u> — during the <u>dry season</u> the water <u>evaporates</u>. It is difficult for rural communities to <u>store</u> water for <u>future</u> use. People in Kenya's <u>Machakos District</u> have been helped to build <u>sand dams</u>, which now give them access to water <u>all year round</u>:

1) A <u>low dam</u> (about 1 m high) is built across the river.
2) During the <u>rainy season</u>, when water is <u>flowing</u> in the river, <u>coarse</u> material (e.g. sand) is <u>trapped</u> behind the dam.
3) <u>Water</u> gets <u>trapped</u> between the sand particles (about a <u>third</u> of what is trapped behind the dam is actually water).
4) The <u>sand</u> prevents the water from being <u>evaporated</u> by the hot sun during the <u>dry season</u>.
5) When the river <u>stops flowing</u>, water can be <u>extracted</u> from the sand by digging a <u>well</u>, <u>piping</u> the water through the dam to a <u>tap</u> or simply <u>digging holes</u> and scooping out the water.
6) The dams are <u>cheap</u> to build, use <u>local materials</u> and don't require much <u>maintenance</u>.
7) The <u>height</u> of the dam can be <u>raised</u> each year to trap <u>more sand</u>, and <u>more water</u>.

Water supply can be increased through transfer projects or dams

Here's an example of a water transfer scheme and an example of a scheme to increase water supply in a poorer country. Give them a good read over in case you're asked about different water supply schemes in the exam.

Managing the UK's Water

The UK may be famous for being <u>grey</u> and <u>wet</u>, but apparently the <u>rain</u> doesn't fall in the <u>right places</u>...

The **Demand** for **Water Varies** Across the **UK**

In the UK, the places with a <u>good supply</u> of water <u>aren't the same</u> as the places with the <u>highest demand</u>:

<u>UK average annual rainfall</u>

<u>UK population density</u>

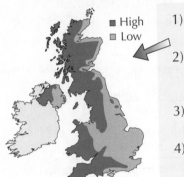

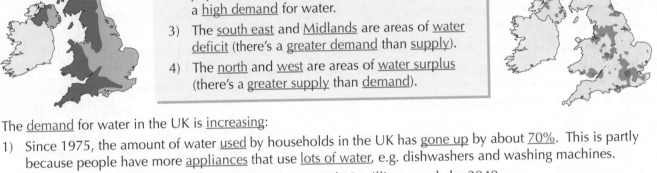

- High
- Low

1) The <u>north</u> and <u>west</u> of the UK have <u>high rainfall</u>, which means there's a <u>good supply</u> of water.
2) The <u>south east</u> and <u>Midlands</u> have <u>high population densities</u>, which means there's a <u>high demand</u> for water.
3) The <u>south east</u> and <u>Midlands</u> are areas of <u>water deficit</u> (there's a <u>greater demand</u> than <u>supply</u>).
4) The <u>north</u> and <u>west</u> are areas of <u>water surplus</u> (there's a <u>greater supply</u> than <u>demand</u>).

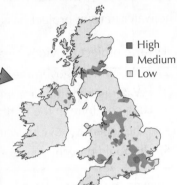

- High
- Medium
- Low

The <u>demand</u> for water in the UK is <u>increasing</u>:

1) Since 1975, the amount of water <u>used</u> by households in the UK has <u>gone up</u> by about <u>70%</u>. This is partly because people have more <u>appliances</u> that use <u>lots of water</u>, e.g. dishwashers and washing machines.
2) The <u>UK population</u> is predicted to <u>increase</u> by around <u>10 million</u> people by <u>2040</u>.
3) Population <u>densities</u> are also <u>changing</u> — lots of <u>new homes</u> are planned to be built in the <u>south east</u> where there is already a water deficit.

Water **Pollution** Needs to be **Managed**

See p.216 for more on groundwater.

1) <u>Polluted</u> or <u>low quality</u> water <u>reduces</u> the amount <u>available</u> for use. This puts more <u>pressure</u> on <u>water resources</u>, especially in areas with a water deficit.
2) Overall, the <u>quality</u> of <u>river water</u> in the UK has been <u>improving</u>. However, there are still some <u>problems</u>:
   - <u>Nitrates</u> and <u>phosphates</u> from <u>fertilisers</u> used on crops are being <u>washed</u> into <u>rivers</u> and <u>groundwater</u>.
   - <u>Pollutants</u> from <u>vehicles</u> are being washed into water sources through <u>runoff</u> when it rains.
   - Accidental <u>chemical</u> and <u>oil spills</u> at factories are <u>polluting local water sources</u> and <u>groundwater supplies</u>.
3) Up to <u>80%</u> of water in some parts of <u>southern England</u> comes from groundwater, but <u>pollution</u> is affecting the water quality of nearly <u>50%</u> of <u>groundwater</u> used for public supply in the UK. Many groundwater sources have been <u>closed</u> or have had to have <u>expensive treatment</u> to make them <u>safe to use</u>.
4) <u>Strategies</u> to manage water quality include <u>improving drainage systems</u> (e.g. by slowing down the movement of rainwater to rivers so that pollutants can be broken down in the soil) and imposing <u>regulations</u> on the amount and types of <u>fertilisers</u> and <u>pesticides</u> used.

Water **Transfers** Can Help **Maintain Supplies**

1) One way to deal with the <u>supply and demand problem</u> is to <u>transfer water</u> from areas of <u>surplus</u> to areas of <u>deficit</u>. For example, <u>Birmingham</u> (an area of <u>deficit</u>) is supplied with water from the <u>middle of Wales</u> (an area of <u>surplus</u>).
2) However, water transfer can cause a variety of <u>issues</u>:
   - The <u>dams</u> and <u>aqueducts</u> (bridges used to <u>transport water</u>) that are needed are <u>expensive</u> to build.
   - It can <u>affect the wildlife</u> that lives in the rivers, e.g. <u>fish migration</u> can be disrupted by dams.
   - There might be <u>political issues</u>, e.g. people <u>may not want</u> their <u>water transferred to another area</u>.

The demand for water is increasing and there's not always enough available

Remember, the availability of water depends on how much there is and how many people want to use it. If there's a deficit, one way to solve the problem is to transfer water from somewhere else. Get this page thoroughly learnt.

Worked Exam Questions

Read through this page carefully — it shows you the sorts of things the examiners are looking for in the exam.

1 Study **Figure 1**, which shows population density in Huffland and average monthly rainfall at two settlements in the region.

Figure 1

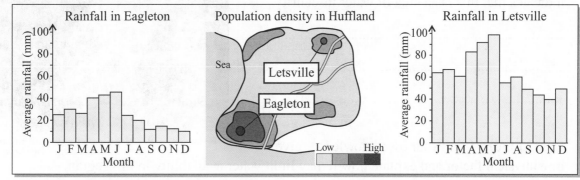

1.1 Using **Figure 1**, describe the amount and pattern of rainfall at Eagleton.

Rainfall is relatively low all year round (less than 50 mm on average per month). Rainfall generally increases between January and June and is at its lowest levels between July and December.

[2]

1.2 Using **Figure 1**, explain why a water transfer scheme might be necessary in Huffland.

In Eagleton the population density is high but rainfall is low, so there is likely to be a water deficit. In Letsville the population density is lower and rainfall is higher, so it's likely to have a water surplus that could be transferred to Eagleton.

[2]

1.3 Other than water transfer, describe **one** large-scale way of increasing water supply and explain how it could help make water supply in Eagleton more reliable.

Desalination could be used to remove salt from seawater so that it can be used. The seawater can either be heated to evaporate it and then condensed to collect the freshwater, or passed through a membrane to remove the salt. This could be used to provide a reliable supply of water all year round.

[3]

1.4 Using an example of a local scheme from a developing or emerging country, explain how water supply has been made more sustainable.

Water supply in Kenya is irregular because most rivers only flow during the rainy season. In the Machakos District, low dams have been built across rivers. During the rainy season, these dams trap coarse material such as sand. Water is trapped between particles, so it doesn't evaporate when the river stops flowing. During times of water shortage, water can be extracted from the sand. The stored water is replenished during each rainy season, and the dams can be raised to trap more sand and water. This means they will continue to provide water in the future, making water supply sustainable.

[6]

[Total 13 marks]

Exam Questions

1   Study **Figure 1**, a photo showing children collecting water in Kenya, Africa.

Figure 1

© iStock.com/ journalturk

1.1   Give **one** piece of evidence from **Figure 1** that indicates that this is an area of water insecurity.

....

....

....
         [1]

1.2   Using **Figure 1** and your own knowledge, give **one** physical factor and explain how it may limit water availability in this region.

....

....

....
         [2]

1.3   Describe **two** human factors that can affect the availability of water.

Factor 1:...

....

Factor 2:...

....
         [2]

1.4   Using **Figure 1**, suggest **one** impact of water insecurity on the people in this community.

....

....
         [1]

1.5   Outline **one** possible effect of water insecurity on industry.

....

....

....
         [2]

1.6   Explain how water insecurity could lead to conflict.

....

....

....
         [2]

[Total 10 marks]

Global Demand for Energy

Energy is a pretty important resource — but some countries have a better energy supply than others...

Energy Security Depends on Energy **Production** and **Consumption**

1) Energy security means having a reliable, uninterrupted and affordable supply of energy available.

2) It depends on the supplies available (either produced or imported), the size of the population, and the amount of energy that a typical person uses.

3) Producing more energy than is required by the population is an energy surplus (this can then be exported to other countries). Having too little energy to meet people's needs is a deficit.

Global **Energy Production** is **Unevenly Distributed**

The map on the right shows the total amount of energy produced, per country, in 2012.

1) Some countries produce lots of energy because they have large energy reserves and the money to exploit them. For example:
   - Iran, Saudi Arabia — large oil reserves.
   - China, Australia — large coal reserves.
   - UK, Russia — large oil and gas reserves.

2) Some countries produce little energy because they have few resources or are unable to exploit their resources due to lack of money or political instability.
   - Sudan — politically unstable and little money.
   - Ireland — few resources that can be exploited.

Energy production (million tonnes oil equivalent)
- 200 and over
- 100-199
- 50-99
- 20-49
- 2-19
- Less than 2

Global **Energy Consumption** is also **Unevenly Distributed**

The map below shows the energy consumption per person across the world in 2014.

Energy consumption per person (tonnes oil equivalent)
- 6.0 and over
- 4.5 – 6.0
- 3.0 – 4.5
- 1.5 – 3.0
- 0 – 1.5

There's a strong relationship between wealth and energy consumption:

1) Wealthy, developed countries tend to consume lots of energy per person because they can afford to. Most people in these countries have access to electricity and heating, and use energy-intensive devices like cars. E.g. Australia, Sweden, USA.

2) Poorer, less developed countries consume less energy per person as they are less able to afford it. Less energy is available and lifestyles are less dependent on high energy consumption than in wealthier countries. E.g. Burkina Faso, Mongolia.

The **Global Demand** for **Energy** is **Increasing**

There are three main reasons why the global demand for energy is increasing:

1) The world's population is increasing — in 2011 the world population was just over 7 billion and it's projected to increase to over 9 billion in 2040 — more people means more energy is needed.

2) Recent economic development has increased the wealth of some poorer countries so people are buying more things. A lot of these things use energy, e.g. cars, fridges and televisions.

3) Technological advances have created loads of new devices that all need energy, e.g. computers, mobile phones and tablets. These are becoming more popular so more energy is needed.

Energy insecurity is not having a reliable source of energy

You don't have to learn every detail of these maps but have a good look in case you have to describe the global patterns of energy production. Having a few example countries up your sleeve won't hurt either.

Energy Supply

There's a lot more to energy supply than just flicking a switch — read on and all will be illuminated...

Energy Supply is Affected by Many Factors

Physical Factors

1) There is unequal distribution of energy resources in the world, so some countries have fewer resources than others and some resources are harder to access, e.g. Antarctic oil reserves.

2) Geology can affect energy supply. Oil and gas are found in sedimentary rocks, where impermeable rocks have trapped the oil and gas in the permeable rocks below. Countries located on plate boundaries (see p.3) may be able to access geothermal energy (using the earth's heat to generate power).

3) Variations in climate and landscape affect the potential for use of solar, wind power, hydroelectric power, wave and tidal power.

Technological Factors

Some countries are not able to exploit their energy resources as the technology required is unavailable or too expensive. For example:

1) Niger has large uranium reserves but does not have the technology to develop nuclear power plants.

2) Some oil reserves in the USA are trapped in rocks and do not flow freely.

Economic Factors

1) The non-renewable energy sources (see p.224) that are left in the world are becoming increasingly difficult to reach, so are more costly to extract.

2) The prices of fossil fuels such as oil and gas are very volatile — they can vary a great deal due to complex economic and political factors. Countries that rely on energy imports might not always be able to afford them.

3) Some developing countries may have potential energy sources but cannot afford to exploit them.

4) The cost of building new energy infrastructure (e.g. new nuclear power stations, wind farms, solar powered technology) can be very high.

Political Factors

1) Wars and political instability in countries with large energy reserves can affect their ability to export their resources, e.g. exports of oil from the Middle East decreased during the Gulf War.

2) Climate change linked to burning fossil fuels has resulted in international agreements to reduce the amount of CO_2 emissions. In some countries, this means that they can't burn fossil fuels as much as they used to.

3) Concerns over the safety of nuclear power and nuclear waste disposal have resulted in stricter regulations. This means it's become harder to build nuclear power stations to generate electricity.

Energy Insecurity has a Range of Impacts

1) As fossil fuels get used up, reserves in more difficult and environmentally sensitive areas are exploited. This increases the cost of producing energy and risks environmental damage.

2) Demand for cleaner and cheaper energy sources increases demand for biofuels. Growing crops for biofuels has negative impacts on the environment and takes up land that could be used for growing food.

3) Energy shortages and higher energy costs reduce industrial output — factories have to produce less (e.g. by only using power at certain times) or relocate to somewhere with better energy security.

4) There is the potential for political instability or conflict between countries with an energy surplus and countries with an energy deficit, e.g. gas supplies from Russia to Ukraine and on to Europe have been disrupted several times due to conflict between Russia and Ukraine.

There are many reasons for variations in energy security

Political instability and conflict can be both a cause and an impact of energy insecurity. Once you're done here, turn over for a page on a source of energy that's been particularly closely linked with politics — oil.

Supply and Demand of Oil

Oil is one of the world's <u>main energy sources</u>. It's <u>constantly</u> in demand, so it's <u>pretty vital</u> that you learn about it.

Oil Reserves and Oil Production are Unevenly Distributed

1) Oil <u>reserves</u> are the amount of <u>recoverable oil</u> — oil that can be <u>extracted</u> using <u>today's technology</u>. Oil <u>production</u> is the process of <u>extracting</u> and <u>refining</u> crude (<u>unrefined</u>) oil.

2) The world's major <u>oil reserves</u> are found in a <u>handful</u> of countries — most of these are in the <u>Middle East</u>.

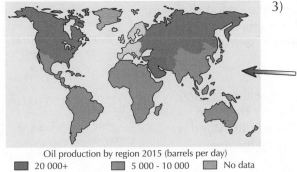

Oil production by region 2015 (barrels per day)
- 20 000+
- 10 000 - 20 000
- 5 000 - 10 000
- 2 500 - 5 000
- No data

3) Oil production doesn't just depend on a country's oil reserves — there are <u>several factors</u> that affect it:

- <u>Infrastructure</u> — in order to produce oil, a country needs the right <u>equipment</u> and <u>technology</u>. Russia, Saudi Arabia and the USA are the world's <u>biggest</u> oil producers.

- <u>Domestic demand</u> — Saudi Arabia relies on oil to meet its <u>own</u> energy needs.

- <u>Shrinking reserves</u> — oil production from <u>North Sea</u> reserves has been <u>declining</u> as reserves are <u>used up</u>.

4) <u>Global oil consumption</u> is <u>increasing</u> as countries develop. Between 2015 and 2016, the amount of oil consumed worldwide rose by <u>1.4 million barrels a day</u>.

- As <u>GDP per capita</u> (see p.177) increases, so does oil <u>consumption</u>. People in <u>wealthier</u> countries have more <u>energy-intensive goods</u>, e.g. cars. Around <u>65%</u> of all oil is used to <u>fuel vehicles</u>.

- <u>Rapid industrialisation</u> in <u>emerging economies</u>, e.g. China and India, also increases oil consumption. The combination of a <u>growing population</u>, a <u>boom</u> in industry and the <u>expansion of cities</u> leads to <u>higher consumption</u> of oil.

Oil Supply and Oil Prices are Affected by Different Factors

1) Oil <u>supply</u> and oil <u>prices</u> are <u>closely linked</u> and can <u>fluctuate</u> for a number of reasons.

2) Generally, periods of <u>oversupply</u> cause oil prices to <u>fall</u> and periods of <u>undersupply</u> cause prices to <u>increase</u>.

- <u>CONFLICTS</u> (e.g. those in the <u>Middle East</u> in the 1970s) can <u>disrupt</u> oil production, which leads to a <u>decrease</u> in oil <u>supply</u>. <u>Shortages</u> of oil cause <u>prices</u> to <u>increase</u>.

- <u>DIPLOMATIC RELATIONS</u> — oil prices may <u>increase</u> because of <u>tensions</u> between <u>oil-producing countries</u>. For example, relations between <u>Saudi Arabia</u> and <u>Iran</u> have led to <u>uncertainty</u> about oil production in the region.

- <u>RECESSIONS</u> (e.g. the <u>global financial crisis</u> in 2008) <u>lower</u> the <u>demand</u> for oil because <u>industrial activities</u> and <u>economic growth</u> slow down. This <u>causes</u> prices to <u>fall</u>.

- <u>ECONOMIC BOOMS</u> — oil prices <u>increase</u> during periods of <u>rapid economic growth</u> because of <u>increased consumption</u> and <u>demand</u>.

The Earth only has a limited supply of oil

We don't know when oil reserves will run out, but if we all keep consuming oil at the rate we are today, it won't be long before we need to look at exploiting new reserves. The next page has some alternative sources of energy.

Increasing Energy Supply

Finding ways to increase energy supply is really important. Luckily there are lots of different options.

Renewable Energy Sources will Never Run Out

Renewable energy can be a good option for increasing energy supply — the sources won't run out, produce little or no waste products, and often need less maintenance than non-renewable power stations. For example:

BIOMASS — wood, plants or animal waste burnt for power or used to produce biofuels. Burning biomass doesn't require much technology, so it's a good choice for developing countries. But it's only renewable if the biomass used is managed sustainably. Growing crops for biofuels reduces the amount of food crops that can be grown and requires lots of water.

Biofuels made from waste products, e.g. used cooking oil, are sometimes referred to as a recyclable energy source.

WIND — turbines use the energy of the wind to generate electricity, either on land or out at sea, often in large windfarms with lots of turbines. There are no greenhouse gas emissions once the turbines have been built. Wind is variable though, so wind farms can't generate electricity all the time.

See p.226 for some more disadvantages of renewable energy sources.

SOLAR — energy from the Sun is used to heat water and solar cookers or to generate electricity using photovoltaic cells. Solar cookers and water heaters can be a cheap source of heat energy for developing countries, but the cells for generating electricity are much more expensive.

HYDROELECTRIC POWER (HEP) — uses the energy of falling water. Water is trapped by a dam and allowed to fall through tunnels, where the pressure of the falling water turns turbines to generate electricity. The flow of water through the turbines can be controlled, so the supply of energy is reliable. However, building dams for hydroelectric power can destroy environments and communities, and they may be too expensive for developing countries.

TIDAL — currents or changes in water level caused by tides are used to turn turbines and generate electricity. It can't generate power all day long, but it can reliably predicted.

WAVE — wind blowing across water makes waves, which drive turbines to generate electricity. The turbines are currently quite expensive and don't produce much energy in calm conditions.

GEOTHERMAL — water is pumped into the ground, where heat deep in the Earth's crust turns it into steam, which drives a turbine to generate electricity. It's a cheap source of energy to set up, but works best in tectonically active areas, which not every country has.

HYDROGEN FUEL — hydrogen gas can be packaged into fuel cells, which generate electricity via a chemical reaction. The only emission is water, but energy is required to obtain pure hydrogen. The energy often comes from burning fossil fuels.

Non-renewable Energy Sources Will Run Out Eventually

However, there are ways that we can increase energy supplies from non-renewable sources:

FOSSIL FUELS — the supply of fossil fuels can be increased by searching for new reserves to exploit, or by exploiting reserves that have been discovered but not yet used (see next page).

NUCLEAR — nuclear power can be used to generate a large amount of energy from a small amount of uranium fuel. However, nuclear power plants are very expensive to build and decommission, nuclear waste must be safely stored for 1000s of years and accidents can be catastrophic. More energy can be extracted by improving the efficiency of reactors by developing new technology. New breeder reactors can also generate more fuel during the reaction — making nuclear energy more like a renewable or recyclable energy source.

Increasing Energy Supply

Conventional Oil and Gas Reserves are being Exploited in Sensitive Areas

1) Despite the development of <u>renewable energy</u>, we still rely heavily on <u>fossil fuels</u>.

2) The <u>pressure</u> of meeting <u>growing</u> energy demands means new, <u>ecologically-sensitive areas</u> are being explored for conventional energy reserves, e.g. the Arctic circle and the Amazon rainforest.

> Conventional energy reserves are easily exploited, e.g. through drilling. Extracting oil or gas from them is quick and cheap.

3) Exploiting new oil and gas reserves brings <u>economic benefits</u>:

- Countries with oil and gas reserves can save money by <u>reducing energy imports</u>.
- These countries can also <u>make money</u> from <u>exporting</u> energy.
- Oil and gas companies bring <u>investment</u> and <u>jobs</u> to an area.

4) However, these economic benefits come at a <u>cost</u> to the <u>environment</u>:

- In order to reach new reserves (e.g. in the Amazon), land may have to be <u>cleared</u> to make way for <u>pipelines</u> and <u>roads</u>. This can disrupt <u>fragile ecosystems</u> and cause a <u>loss of biodiversity</u>.
- Exploring <u>offshore</u> oil and gas reserves, e.g. in the Arctic Ocean, can have a big impact on <u>marine life</u>. <u>Noise</u> and <u>vibrations</u> from drills can <u>confuse whales</u> and other <u>marine mammals</u> that rely on <u>sound</u> to communicate, navigate and find food.
- <u>Opening up</u> isolated areas with <u>roads</u> and <u>industry</u> can increase <u>air, soil and water pollution</u>.

Shale Gas is an Unconventional Gas Reserve

1) <u>Unconventional</u> energy reserves are exploited using more <u>expensive methods</u>, e.g. <u>hydraulic fracking</u>, that need <u>specialist technology</u>. Extraction takes a lot <u>longer</u> than from conventional reserves.

2) <u>Shale gas</u> is a form of <u>natural gas</u> that is trapped in <u>shale rock</u> underground. It's extracted by <u>fracking</u>. This involves <u>liquid</u> being <u>pumped</u> into the shale rock at <u>high pressure</u>. This causes the rock to <u>crack</u> (fracture), releasing the <u>gas</u>, which is collected as it comes out. Fracking has <u>advantages</u> and <u>disadvantages</u>:

Advantages

1) <u>Gas</u> is <u>less polluting</u> than <u>other</u> fossil fuels. It releases <u>half</u> the CO_2 of <u>coal</u>.

2) Fracked gas is a <u>cheaper</u> energy source than <u>some renewables</u> — although it can cost <u>more</u> to extract than gas from some other sources.

3) The technology has already been <u>tested</u> (in the USA) and <u>shown</u> to <u>work</u>, unlike some renewable sources.

Disadvantages

1) The <u>chemicals</u> used in <u>fracking liquid</u> as well as the shale gas itself can <u>pollute water sources</u>.

2) It uses <u>lots</u> of <u>water</u> (a limited resource).

3) It's known to cause <u>small earthquakes</u>.

4) Land has to be <u>cleared</u> to build <u>drilling pads</u>, <u>destroying</u> animal habitats and <u>disrupting ecosystems</u>.

Tar Sands are an Unconventional Oil Reserve

1) <u>Tar sands</u> contain <u>bitumen</u>, which can be refined to produce oil. It's mainly extracted by <u>mining</u>. <u>Surface mines</u> collect tar sand and transport it to <u>processing plants</u>, which use <u>water</u> and <u>chemicals</u> to <u>separate</u> the bitumen from the sands.

2) Surface mining <u>negatively affects</u> the <u>environment</u>:

- Vast amounts of <u>space</u> are needed, which <u>devastates habitats</u> (see p.81). This can cause a <u>reduction</u> in the <u>biodiversity</u> of the area as organisms have <u>less space</u> to <u>live</u> and find <u>food</u>.
- Processing tar sands creates huge amounts of <u>liquid waste</u> full of <u>harmful chemicals</u>. These can <u>pollute</u> water supplies if they aren't <u>managed</u> properly.

Decisions about energy supply cause a lot of debate

This stuff is a hot topic at the moment — turn on the news and there's likely to be something about fracking, wind farms or nuclear power stations. Examiners love relevant geographical topics, so make sure you learn it.

Impacts of Energy Production

Producing energy can cause all sorts of problems — particularly for the environment.

Mining and Drilling have Impacts on the Environment...

1) The extraction of fossil fuels, e.g. by mining and drilling, can damage the environment.

2) Mining has several environmental impacts:

- Surface mining strips away large areas of soil, rock and vegetation so that miners can reach the materials they want. This can permanently scar the landscape.
- Habitats are destroyed to make way for mines, e.g. through clearing forests, leading to loss of biodiversity.
- Clearing forests also affects the water cycle (see p.49) because there are fewer trees to take up water from the ground. This can lead to increased soil erosion.
- Mining processes can release greenhouse gases, e.g. carbon dioxide (CO_2) and methane (CH_4), into the atmosphere. These gases contribute to global warming (see p.37).

3) Extracting oil and gas involves drilling into underground reserves. It can be done inland (onshore) and at sea (offshore).

4) Drilling has negative impacts on the environment:

- Onshore drilling requires land to be stripped of vegetation to make space for the drills and roads to access the sites.
- Oil spills cause major damage to the environment — especially out at sea. The Deepwater Horizon oil spill in 2010 leaked around 4 million barrels of oil into the Gulf of Mexico. Oil coats the feathers and fur of animals, which reduces their ability to move freely or feed.
- Extracting natural gas from underground reserves can cause methane to leak into the atmosphere, making the greenhouse effect stronger and contributing to global warming.

...and so do Some Forms of Renewable Energy

Although it usually has fewer impacts than non-renewable energy, generating renewable energy can still affect the environment:

Wind Energy

1) Large numbers of wind turbines are needed to produce significant amounts of electricity and they need to be set quite far apart. This means they take up lots of space.

2) Wind farms produce a constant humming noise — some people living close to wind farms have complained about this noise pollution.

3) The spinning blades on turbines can kill or injure birds and bats.

Solar Energy

1) Some solar farms use ground and surface water to clean their solar panels. This can lead to water shortages in arid areas, which disrupts ecosystems.

2) The heat reflected from mirrors in solar farms can kill wildlife, e.g. birds.

3) Solar panels built on the ground can disturb and damage habitats.

Hydroelectric Power (HEP)

1) HEP plants use dams to trap water for energy production — this creates a reservoir, which floods a large area of land.

2) The river on which the dam is built can be affected by changes in water flow, e.g. sediment is deposited in the reservoir instead of further downstream.

3) A build-up of sediment can block sunlight, causing plants and algae in the river to die.

Even renewable energy sources can damage the environment

If you get asked about the negative impacts of energy production, fossil fuels might be the first thing to spring to mind — don't forget you could also write about wind farms, solar farms, and HEP plants.

Sustainable Energy Use

There are lots of things that can help us use <u>less energy</u> and use it more <u>efficiently</u>.

Sustainable Energy means Future Generations can Meet their Energy Needs

1) <u>Sustainable energy</u> provides energy <u>today</u> without preventing <u>future generations</u> from <u>meeting their energy needs</u>.

2) It's important because <u>demand</u> for <u>energy</u> is <u>increasing</u> as the world's <u>population</u> is <u>increasing</u>, but <u>non-renewable</u> energy resources (such as coal, oil and gas) are <u>running out</u>.

3) Humans need to find <u>new renewable energy sources</u> and use energy <u>more efficiently</u> so that future generations can meet their energy needs.

A Carbon Footprint is a Measure of Energy Use

Carbon footprints can also be worked out for products, businesses, entire countries, etc.

1) A <u>carbon footprint</u> is a measure of the <u>amount</u> of greenhouse gases (<u>carbon dioxide</u> and <u>methane</u>) an individual's <u>activities</u> produce.

2) It includes <u>direct emissions</u> (those produced from things that <u>use energy</u>) as well as <u>indirect emissions</u> (those produced making things that we <u>buy</u>).

3) <u>Examples</u> of direct emissions include having the <u>heating</u> on, using <u>electrical appliances</u>, <u>commuting</u> and <u>air travel</u>. <u>Examples</u> of an individual's <u>indirect</u> emissions are those produced making their <u>food</u> and <u>clothing</u> etc.

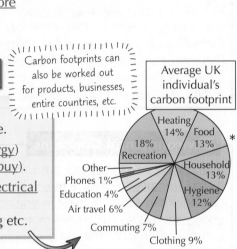

Average UK individual's carbon footprint

Heating 14%
Food 13% *
Household 13%
Hygiene 12%
Clothing 9%
Commuting 7%
Air travel 6%
Education 4%
Phones 1%
Other
Recreation 18%

Energy can be Conserved in Various Ways

1) The demand for energy can be <u>reduced</u> by conserving energy and making energy use more efficient:
   - <u>Energy conservation</u> — <u>changing our behaviour</u> to reduce the amount of energy used. E.g. drying clothes on a <u>washing line</u> instead of in a <u>dryer</u>, insulating our homes.
   - <u>Energy efficiency</u> — doing the <u>same job</u> but using <u>less energy</u>. E.g. a <u>low-energy lightbulb</u>.

2) There are <u>lots of ways</u> that <u>energy</u> use can be <u>reduced</u>:

Sustainable Design

<u>Homes</u>, <u>workplaces</u> and <u>transport</u> can be designed to use energy more sustainably, for example:

1) <u>Insulation</u> — by insulating <u>walls</u>, <u>roofs</u> and <u>floors</u>, less energy is required to <u>heat</u> homes and workplaces.

2) <u>Modern boilers</u> — new boilers are <u>more efficient</u> than older models, so will use <u>less energy</u> in homes and workplaces.

3) <u>Switching</u> to <u>electric</u> — electric cars, vans and trains are <u>more efficient</u> than <u>petrol</u> or <u>diesel</u> versions.

4) <u>Solar panels</u> can be fitted to the <u>roofs</u> of homes and workplaces providing <u>renewable</u>, <u>low-carbon</u> energy.

Increasing Efficiency

Doing the <u>same job</u> but using <u>less fuel conserves</u> energy:

1) <u>Hybrid</u> cars, vans and trains combine <u>diesel</u> or <u>petrol</u> with <u>electric</u> power to increase efficiency. E.g. <u>hybrid trains</u> use <u>electricity when possible</u> and <u>diesel</u> the rest of the time.

2) <u>Regenerative braking</u> — road vehicles and trains can be fitted with devices to <u>store</u> the <u>energy lost under braking</u> to be used <u>later</u> or return it to the national grid.

3) <u>Engine manufacturers</u> are making <u>more efficient engines</u> in response to <u>laws</u> and <u>rising fuel costs</u>.

4) <u>Power stations</u> are becoming more efficient by switching to <u>gas</u> and using <u>Gas Turbine Combined Cycle</u> technology.

Demand Reduction

<u>Demand reduction</u> can reduce the amount of electricity that needs to be <u>generated</u>:

1) <u>Demand</u> can be reduced by, e.g. encouraging people to <u>turn off</u> lights when they're not needed, boiling only the water <u>needed</u> and using <u>more efficient appliances</u>.

2) <u>Improving public transport</u> and <u>encouraging walking</u> or <u>cycling</u> reduces <u>demand</u> for <u>energy</u> used for <u>transport</u>.

*Pie chart based on the data from a study by the government-funded Carbon Trust.

Sustainable Energy Use

Attitudes to Energy Use are Changing

In recent years, many people have become more aware of the need to make energy use sustainable and reduce their carbon footprint (see previous page). This is especially true in developed countries:

Rising Affluence

People with more money can afford to make a choice about energy use, e.g. buying newer cars that are more fuel-efficient or investing in solar panels for their homes. Governments in developed countries have more money to invest in public transport and renewable energy.

Education

People in developed countries have better access to education through school and the media. This means they have a better understanding of the consequences of unsustainable energy use and increasing emissions. People learn how to reduce their carbon footprint, which means there's more interest in using cleaner energy sources and reducing energy consumption.

Environmental Concerns

Increased access to education means people are more worried about permanently damaging the environment — they're more likely to try to reduce their carbon footprint. Developed countries can afford to invest in research into the environmental impacts of different energy sources — this creates more awareness about energy consumption and how to reduce carbon footprints. In developing countries, economic development can overshadow environmental concerns. As a country develops, the environment can become a higher priority.

Rice Husks are used to Generate Sustainable Power in Bihar

Bihar is a rural state in north-east India. Around 85% of people who live in Bihar are not connected to the electricity grid, particularly those in rural areas. Those that are connected often have an unreliable supply. In 2007, a scheme began to use local biomass (a renewable energy source) to supply homes in rural parts of Bihar with electricity. The scheme uses rice husks — a waste product from producing rice for food.

1) Rice husks are collected and used to generate electricity in small, local power plants. Each power plant has a simple design and contains a rice husk gasifier, filters to clean the gas, a gas turbine, a generator and a distribution system that can supply electricity to homes within a 1.5 km range.

2) By 2015, 84 rice husk powered plants were operating in Bihar, supplying electricity to around 200 000 people.

3) Producing electricity locally is very efficient, as the energy sources do not have to be transported long distances and the electricity produced does not need to be transferred over long distances to homes.

4) Providing electricity from biomass has reduced the need for small diesel generators and kerosene lamps in rural homes — and so reduced the use of fossil fuels.

5) As well as supplying electricity, the power plants provide employment for local people. They are trained in management, operation or maintenance. This keeps the scheme sustainable as it reduces reliance on external organisations and expertise.

6) The government now offers financial support to help set up biomass plants.

People are getting more interested in reducing their energy use

Long answer questions are good opportunities to bring in real world evidence. If you're asked about sustainable energy generation, the use of rice husks in Bihar is a great example to support your answer.

Energy Futures

The future of global energy use is uncertain. Some people think we need to make significant changes to make sure we have enough energy in the future, but others are quite happy to carry on as usual...

There are **Contrasting Views** about **Energy Futures**

1) There are two main energy futures:

- **BUSINESS AS USUAL** — Everything carries on as normal. We go on getting most of our energy from fossil fuels and don't increase the use of renewable energy sources.
- **MOVE TO SUSTAINABILITY** — We reduce the amount of fossil fuels we use and increase our use of renewable energy sources.

2) Different groups have different attitudes towards energy futures:

1 Consumers

1) Consumers want secure energy supplies that won't be disrupted in the future.
2) When fossil fuels start to run out, energy security will decrease, increasing the risk of energy shortages.
3) Consumers also want cheap power — sustainable energy requires investment, which can increase the price.
4) Many consumers currently favour business as usual, as it provides a cheap, secure supply of energy. However, as supplies of fossil fuels run out, and environmental awareness increases, some consumers are beginning to favour a move to sustainability (see previous page).

2 TNCs (Transnational Corporations)

1) Many TNCs, e.g. Shell, are involved in extracting and refining fossil fuels and invest a lot of money into the energy sector.
2) Controlling oil reserves gives TNCs lots of power and wealth, which means they may lose money if there is a shift towards using more renewable energy sources.
3) Sustainable energy needs more investment than fossil fuels, so these TNCs would have higher costs and potentially lower gains — this means they may favour the business as usual scenario.
4) TNCs not involved in the fossil fuel industry may also favour business as usual as sustainable energy is more expensive and would be likely to increase their energy costs.

3 Governments

1) Governments want to secure future energy supplies — fossil fuels are a cheap and reliable way of supplying energy in the short-term, but a more sustainable approach will be needed in the long-term.
2) In developed countries, governments are starting to come under pressure from some consumers to protect the environment — this means they want to start using more sustainable energy.
3) Fossil fuels have helped countries to develop and the governments of many emerging countries have concerns about whether sustainable energy sources will continue to help them develop.

4 Climate Scientists

1) Climate scientists study climate and how human activities are affecting it. The IPCC's climate change scenarios (see p.41) predict a temperature increase of up to 4 °C by the year 2100 under the business as usual scenario.
2) They want to reduce reliance on fossil fuels in order to lessen the consequences of climate change, e.g. serious temperature increases and rising sea levels.

5 Environmental Groups

1) Environmental groups, e.g. Greenpeace, want to stop people relying on fossil fuels for energy because their extraction and use damages the environment.
2) They want people to reduce their use of fossil fuels and switch to renewable energy sources in line with the move to sustainability scenario.

Energy in the UK

In the UK, we still get most of our energy from underground as coal, oil and gas, but there is a general trend towards using more renewable energy sources, and reducing reliance on fossil fuels before they run out.

The UK's Energy Mix Has Changed

1) Traditionally, the UK has relied on fossil fuels (coal, oil and gas) to supply its energy. In 1950, 96% of our energy came from coal and oil.

2) The discovery of large gas reserves under the North Sea meant that by 1980, 22% of the UK's energy was supplied by gas.

3) The use of nuclear energy to produce electricity also increased during the 1990s.

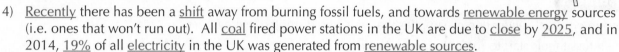

4) Recently there has been a shift away from burning fossil fuels, and towards renewable energy sources (i.e. ones that won't run out). All coal fired power stations in the UK are due to close by 2025, and in 2014, 19% of all electricity in the UK was generated from renewable sources.

5) Wind and bioenergy (energy from the break down or burning of biological sources) are the biggest sources of renewable energy, but the use of solar and hydroelectric power has also increased.

6) Changes to the energy mix of the UK have been influenced by government decisions and international organisations. For example, the UK government has previously offered subsidies to support the building of wind and solar farms. The Kyoto protocol, set up by the United Nations, has set targets to reduce greenhouse gas emissions, leading to a growth in the use of renewables and a reduction in the use of coal.

The UK's Supplies of Coal, Oil and Gas are Running Out

1) North Sea oil and gas reserves are being rapidly used up and production has been declining since 2000.

2) The UK still has coal reserves but coal production has fallen hugely since the mid-20th century. There has been a decline in demand due to an effort to reduce CO_2 emissions, and the cost of mining the remaining reserves is increasing. The last deep coal mine in the UK closed in December 2015.

3) The government must ensure that future energy policy provides enough energy to continue to meet the UK's demand. They need to find ways to reduce energy use and find alternative energy sources as well as decide how best to use the remaining non-renewable energy sources (see below).

Future Energy Sources Need to be Considered Carefully

1) Energy production needs to be sustainable (see p.227).

2) However, energy supply also needs to be reliable and affordable.

3) This means there's some debate about the extent to which non-renewable energy sources should and could be used in the future. Here are some arguments for and against non-renewables in the future:

For	Against
1) The UK still has large coal reserves, which would provide cheap energy for a long time.	1) Non-renewable resources will eventually run out, so we are going to have to switch to renewable energy eventually.
2) There are large amounts of natural gas that could be released by fracking (see p.225).	2) It's more important to protect the environment, than to have cheap energy.
3) We already have the infrastructure to supply non-renewable energy.	3) Non-renewable sources have higher emissions, which contribute to climate change.
4) Using gas would help produce enough energy to meet everyone's needs — this would improve energy security.	4) The UK has legally binding targets to reduce the amount of fossil fuels used.

Energy in the UK

Local and National Schemes aim to Make Energy Use More Sustainable

Local authorities and the government have introduced various schemes on a local and national scale to ensure the UK has enough energy to meet its needs in the future. For example:

Local

The Lewes town council works with OVESCO, a group who are using community investment to fund the installation of solar panels on the roofs of local buildings. The solar power provided lowers energy bills, and any excess energy is sold to the national grid for a profit. The scheme has been very successful so far, however changes to the amount paid by the national grid for the excess energy mean that future projects may not be able to go ahead.

National

The government is supporting the installation of 'smart meters' in every UK home. These are electricity and gas meters that come with a wireless display unit that tells the user exactly how much electricity and gas they are using in real-time and how much it is costing. It's hoped that this will help people make decisions on how to reduce their overall energy usage. The government believes that the scheme will be successful in reducing people's bills as well as reducing the amount of energy used. However, there have been some teething problems with the technology during the roll-out of the scheme, and many people believe that the equipment could quickly become outdated.

Lots of Factors Will Affect UK Energy Supply

It's important to think carefully about the economic, environmental and political factors involved in our energy supply. Here are some of the things that may affect the energy sources we use in the UK in the future:

Environmental Factors

1) The burning of fossil fuels releases greenhouse gases.
2) Fracking may pollute groundwater and cause small earthquakes — it has been halted in the UK unless it can be proven that it's safe.
3) Accidents, such as oil spills or nuclear disasters, can be devastating to surrounding environments.
4) Natural ecosystems can be damaged by renewable energy generators like large dams or the tidal barrage system planned for Swansea in Wales.
5) Power stations and wind farms can be eyesores.

Political Factors

1) Emissions targets — e.g. the UK government has committed to reaching net zero emissions by 2050.
2) Relationships with countries that export energy to the UK.
3) Public pressure over concern for the environment could encourage the development of renewable energy sources.
4) Tax from oil companies is an important source of government funding.

Economic Factors

1) Extracting fossil fuels can be expensive and the cost increases as reserves are used up. North Sea oil is especially expensive. Depending on the market, it may cost more to produce than it can be sold for.
2) The cost of producing electricity from nuclear and renewable energy sources is relatively high.
3) Money is needed for research into alternative energy sources, e.g. shale gas, and for initial investment, e.g. building the new nuclear power station at Hinkley Point.
4) Many renewable sources don't provide a reliable enough supply of energy, so the UK still has to pay to import energy from other countries.

Energy supply in the UK is changing

How the energy mix changes in the future will depend on many factors, such as the decisions made by the government, the technological advances made by scientists, and the changing prices of different energy sources.

Worked Exam Questions

Exams can be pretty scary, but the best preparation you can do is practise answering exam questions.
Read this page to get an idea of how to answer them, then turn over and have a go at the next lot yourself.

1   Study **Figure 1**, a data table showing the amount of oil produced and amount of oil products used in Brazil and Sudan and South Sudan.

1.1   State one possible reason for the decrease in oil production in Sudan and South Sudan in 2012.

Oil production may have been

disrupted by conflict.

   [1]

Figure 1

	Brazil		Sudan & South Sudan	
Year	Oil produced (1000 barrels per day)	Oil products used (1000 barrels per day)	Oil produced (1000 barrels per day)	Oil products used (1000 barrels per day)
2008	1812	2205	478	94
2009	1950	2481	483	125
2010	2055	2699	486	115
2011	2105	2777	453	111
2012	2061	2923	112	107
2013	2024	3033	247	107
2014	2255	3144	259	108

1.2   Calculate the percentage change in oil products used in Brazil between 2008 and 2014.

$$\frac{3\,144\,000 - 2\,205\,000}{2\,205\,000} \times 100 = 42.59\% \text{ (2 d.p.)}$$

   [2]

1.3   In 2008, there was a global financial recession. Explain how this recession may have affected oil prices.

Recessions lower the demand for oil because industrial activities and economic growth slow down.

This is likely to have caused oil prices to fall.

   [3]

   [Total 6 marks]

2   Study **Figure 2**, pie charts showing the proportion of UK energy from different sources in 1970 and 2014.

2.1   State which source of energy the UK most relied on in 1970.

Coal

   [1]

2.2   State which energy source increased its share the most between 1970 and 2014.

Gas

   [1]

Figure 2

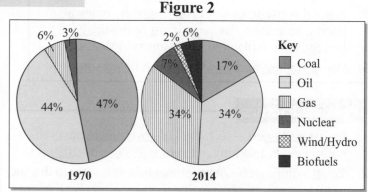

Key
■ Coal
□ Oil
▥ Gas
▨ Nuclear
▧ Wind/Hydro
■ Biofuels

1970   2014

2.3   The changes in energy sources shown in **Figure 2** are similar in many developed countries. State two reasons why rising affluence can lead to more sustainable energy use.

1: *People with more money can afford to buy more energy efficient products for their homes.*

2: *Governments in developed countries have more money to invest in renewable energy.*

   [2]

   [Total 4 marks]

Exam Questions

1 Study **Figure 1**, a map of Barmouth Bay, Wales.

Figure 1

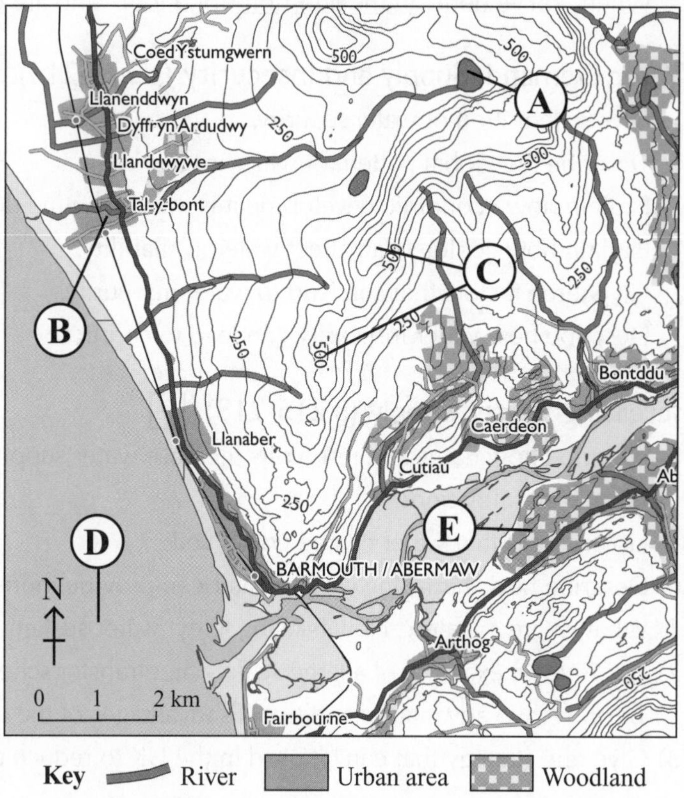

1.1 Which location, A-E, would be the best site for an onshore wind farm? Give one reason for your choice.

Location:..

[1]

Reason: ....

....

....

....

[1]

1.2 Suggest why location E is not suitable for a solar power plant.

....

....

....

....

[2]

1.3 Outline one advantage of using hydropower to increase energy supply.

....

....

[1]

1.4 Discuss the advantages and disadvantages of the extraction of a fossil fuel you have studied.

....

....

....

....

....

....

....

[6]

[Total 11 marks]

Revision Summary

Well, that's Water and Energy out of the way — all that remains is to try these questions.

- Try these questions and <u>tick off each one</u> when you <u>get it right</u>.
- When you've done <u>all the questions</u> for a topic and are <u>completely happy</u> with it, tick off the topic.

Water Demand, Supply and Insecurity (p.213-214) ☐

1) Give a definition of water security. ☑
2) Describe the global pattern of water insecurity. ☑
3) Explain how economic development is increasing the demand for water. ☑
4) Explain how geology can affect water availability. ☑
5) Give three factors that can lead to water insecurity. ☑
6) Describe how water insecurity can lead to conflict. ☑

Increasing Water Supply (p.215-218) ☐

7) Describe how dams and reservoirs increase water supply. ☑
8) What is desalination? ☑
9) List six ways that water can be conserved. ☑
10) Describe how managing groundwater can provide more sustainable water supplies. ☑
11) What is 'grey' water? How is using 'grey' water sustainable? ☑
12) a) Give an example of a large scale water transfer scheme. ☑
    b) Give two advantages and two disadvantages of the scheme. ☑
13) Give one strategy that can be used in the UK to reduce groundwater pollution. ☑

Energy Demand, Supply and Insecurity (p.221-223) ☐

14) Give a definition of energy security. ☑
15) Describe the global distribution of energy production. ☑
16) Why is global energy consumption unevenly distributed? ☑
17) Give three reasons why the global demand for energy is changing. ☑
18) Give two physical, economic, political and technological factors that affect energy security. ☑
19) What are the impacts of energy insecurity? ☑
20) Give two things that can affect the supply of oil. ☑

Increasing Energy Supply and Energy in the UK (p.224-231) ☐

21) Give seven renewable energy sources that could be used to increase energy supply. ☑
22) Describe one way that the energy supply from non-renewable energy sources can be increased. ☑
23) Give an example of an unconventional energy reserve. ☑
24) Give one way that mining can affect the environment. ☑
25) How does wind power have negative environmental effects? ☑
26) What does 'sustainable use of energy' mean? ☑
27) What does a person's carbon footprint measure? ☑
28) How can demand for energy be reduced? ☑
29) Give examples of improvements in efficiency that have helped to conserve energy. ☑
30) Describe a renewable energy scheme in a developing or emerging country which improves sustainability. ☑
31) What is the energy future 'business as usual'? ☑
32) Outline how the energy mix of the UK has changed. ☑
33) Give three environmental factors that could affect the energy supply of the UK in the future. ☑

Geographical Decision Making

Knowing all the <u>facts</u> isn't quite enough to get you through your exams — you'll also have to use what you've learnt to come to a <u>decision</u> about a geographical dilemma.

Decision Making is All About Analysing and Interpreting Information

Your <u>exam</u> will probably have a section where you have to write about some <u>information</u> you're given, which could relate to <u>any part</u> of your course.

1) In the exam, you'll have a <u>resource booklet</u> containing information about a <u>geographical issue</u>.
2) You need to study <u>all</u> the information <u>carefully</u> and work out <u>what it all means</u>.
3) You might have to answer <u>questions</u> drawing on both the information you're <u>given</u> and your <u>knowledge</u> of geography from the <u>rest of the course</u>.
4) You'll also have to write a <u>longer answer</u> where you'll have to <u>make a decision</u> about something related to the issue you've been presented with, and <u>justify</u> that decision (see below).

Ask your teacher about the requirements of the exam board you're with.

There'll be Lots of Different Information Sources in the Resource Booklet

1) Depending on your <u>exam board</u>, you might be given the resource booklet to study in the weeks <u>before</u> the exam, or you might have to <u>wait</u> until you're in the exam.
2) The booklet could include <u>several</u> different types of information, such as:

- Maps
- Graphs
- Photographs
- Diagrams
- Statistics
- Newspaper articles
- Quotes from people involved

Make sure you can read all the common types of maps and graphs.

Use All the Information to Form an Opinion About the Issue

1) You'll be asked to <u>argue</u> your <u>point of view</u> using the <u>information</u>, e.g. <u>suggesting</u> how an area could best be <u>managed</u> to meet the needs of <u>everyone</u> involved.
2) <u>There's no single right or wrong answer</u> — but you need to be able to <u>justify</u> your argument, so make sure you can use the <u>data</u> from the resource booklet to <u>support it</u>.
3) <u>Whatever</u> your view is, you need to give a <u>balanced argument</u>. Try to think of the potential <u>impacts</u> of the decision, both <u>positive</u> and <u>negative</u>, including:

- <u>Economic impacts</u> — e.g. will the decision bring more money to a country?
- <u>Political impacts</u> — e.g. are other countries likely to approve of the decision? If not, what effect might this have?
- <u>Social impacts</u> — e.g. will the decision improve quality of life for people in the area?
- <u>Environmental impacts</u> — e.g. is the decision likely to damage natural habitats?

You could also think about how any <u>negative impacts</u> could be <u>reduced</u>.

4) It's likely to be a <u>complex issue</u> with <u>lots</u> of <u>different parties involved</u>. So think about <u>possible conflicts</u> that your solution might cause <u>between different groups</u> of people, or between <u>people</u> and the <u>environment</u>, and how they could be <u>resolved</u>.

You'll need to justify your decision by giving reasons why you chose it

This might seem a bit daunting, but don't panic — just read the information you're given carefully and then try and relate it to what you've learnt on the rest of your course. Do that and you're well on the way to exam success.

Exam Questions

Figure 1

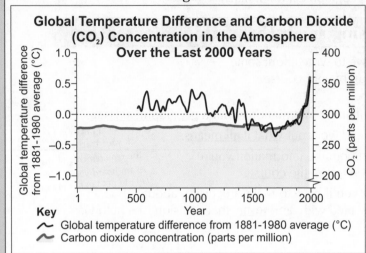

Global Temperature Difference and Carbon Dioxide (CO₂) Concentration in the Atmosphere Over the Last 2000 Years

Key

∿ Global temperature difference from 1881-1980 average (°C)

∿ Carbon dioxide concentration (parts per million)

Figure 3

Carbon footprint (tonnes per person)

	USA (a developed country)	Malawi (a developing country)
2011	17.0	0.1

Figure 4

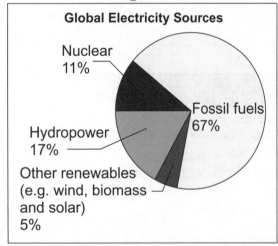

Global Electricity Sources

Nuclear 11%

Fossil fuels 67%

Hydropower 17%

Other renewables (e.g. wind, biomass and solar) 5%

Figure 2

Deforestation and greenhouse gas emissions

- Greenhouse gas emissions from deforestation account for about 12% of the CO₂ emitted by human activities.
- Most deforestation takes place in developing and emerging countries, especially in Brazil and Indonesia. Since 1978, more than 750 000 km² of the Amazon rainforest has been deforested.
- The majority of this deforestation is driven by demand for meat from cattle farmed on deforested land, and for rainforest products such as hardwoods (e.g. teak and mahogany). Much of this demand comes from developed countries.

Figure 5

Renewable Energy Sources in the UK

Biomass

Some power stations in the UK have been converted to run on biomass. Like conventional power stations, biomass plants can generate large amounts of power reliably.

> Currently, half the Drax power station in Yorkshire has been converted from coal to run on sustainably-sourced biomass.
>
> Using biomass emits 86% less carbon dioxide than using coal, even though biomass is often imported from the US and Canada.

Wind

The UK has a number of onshore and offshore wind farms. In total, they generate 6% of the UK's electricity.

Solar

The amount of energy generated by solar power is increasing, but as of 2012 it provided only 0.4% of the UK's electricity.

Figure 6

Scheme 1

An international agreement signed by the vast majority of countries, that requires all new vehicles to meet a minimum level of fuel efficiency. Additionally, the vehicles must emit fewer pollutants and less carbon dioxide than current models.

Scheme 2

A project run by an international charity that aims to educate people in countries with a large carbon footprint about the need to reduce their energy usage. It will offer advice about ways to save energy, such as improving home insulation and driving less.

Scheme 3

Governments and NGOs will work together to ensure those most affected by climate change receive help. A response team will be formed to deliver aid to affected areas, and a fund will be available to support farmers affected by changing weather patterns.

Exam Questions

1   Study **Figures 1-6** on p.236.

1.1   'Human activities are the main cause of climate change over the last 200 years.'
       With the help of **Figures 1-3**, discuss this statement.

       ....

       ....

       ....

       ....

       ....

       ....

       ....

       ....

                                                                                                                              [6]

1.2   'Renewable energy sources are always small-scale and unreliable. They are not a viable
       alternative to fossil fuels.'
       Use **Figures 4-6** and your own knowledge to discuss this statement.

       ....

       ....

       ....

       ....

       ....

       ....

       ....

       ....

       ....

                                                                                                                              [6]

1.3   **Figure 6** describes three schemes that have been proposed to reduce the effects of climate change.

       Which of the three schemes do you think will best reduce the effects of climate change on people
       and the environment?

       Use **Figures 1-6** and your own knowledge to explain your choice.

                                                                                                       [9 + 3 SPaG]

                                                                                                       [Total 24 marks]

Fieldwork

For your Geography GCSE you need to complete some <u>fieldwork</u>, which you'll be asked about in the <u>exam</u>.

You have to Write About **Two Geographical Enquiries** in the Exam

1) There's no assessed <u>coursework</u>, but you need to be able to <u>write about</u> fieldwork that you have done in the exam.

2) You need to have done at least one <u>human</u> and one <u>physical</u> geographical enquiry. You could be asked about <u>both</u> in the exam.

'Geographical enquiry' is just fancy exam-speak for fieldwork.

3) The fieldwork part of the exam will have <u>two</u> types of questions:

- In one part you'll be asked about fieldwork techniques in <u>unfamiliar</u> situations. You might have to answer questions about <u>techniques</u> for <u>collecting data</u>, how to <u>present data</u> you've been given or how <u>useful</u> the <u>different techniques</u> are.

- In the other part you have to answer questions about <u>your investigation</u> — you might be asked about your <u>question</u> or <u>hypothesis</u>, <u>methods</u>, what <u>data</u> you <u>collected</u> and <u>why</u>, how you <u>presented</u> and <u>analysed</u> it, how you could <u>extend your research</u> and so on.

For **Each** of your **Enquiries**, You'll **Need to Know...**

1 Why You Chose Your Question

You'll need to explain <u>why</u> the question or hypothesis you chose is <u>suitable</u> for a <u>geographical enquiry</u>.

You'll also need to know the <u>geographical theory</u> behind your question.

Make sure you know what the <u>risks associated</u> with <u>collecting</u> your data were, how they were <u>reduced</u>, and why the <u>location</u> you chose was <u>suitable</u>.

2 How and Why You Collected Data

You need to <u>describe</u> and <u>justify</u> what data <u>you collected</u>. This includes whether it was <u>primary data</u> (data that you collected <u>yourself</u>) or <u>secondary</u> data (data that <u>someone else</u> collected and you <u>used</u>), <u>why</u> you collected or used it, <u>how</u> you <u>measured</u> it and <u>how</u> you <u>recorded</u> it.

3 How You Processed and Presented Your Data

The way you <u>presented</u> your data, and <u>why</u> you <u>chose</u> that option, could come up.

You'll need to <u>describe what you did</u>, <u>explain</u> why it was <u>appropriate</u>, and <u>how</u> you <u>adapted</u> your presentation method for <u>your data</u>.

You might also be asked for a <u>different way</u> you <u>could</u> have presented your data.

There's more on analysing, concluding and evaluating on the next page.

4 What Your Data Showed

You'll need to know:

- A <u>description</u> of your data.
- How you <u>analysed</u> your data.
- An <u>explanation</u> of your data.

This might include <u>links</u> between your <u>data sets</u>, the <u>statistical techniques</u> you used, and any <u>anomalies</u> (odd results) in the data that you spotted.

5 The Conclusions You Reached

This means you'll need to <u>explain how</u> your data provides <u>evidence</u> to <u>answer</u> the <u>question</u> or <u>support</u> the <u>hypothesis</u> you set at the <u>beginning</u>.

6 What Went Well, What Could Have Gone Better

You might be asked to <u>evaluate</u> your fieldwork:

- Were there <u>problems</u> in your <u>data collection methods</u>?
- Were there <u>limitations</u> in your <u>data</u>?
- What <u>other data</u> would it have been <u>useful</u> to have?
- How <u>reliable</u> are your <u>conclusions</u>?

Plan your fieldwork before you start...

... but don't worry if it doesn't quite go to plan. It's more important that you can write about it and say why things went wrong. It does help if you at least attempt to make it work though — so have another read through the page.

Fieldwork

Analysis, conclusions and evaluations can be pretty tricky, so here's a load of stuff to help you with them.

You need to Describe and Explain what the Data Shows

Analysing and interpreting data is about:

1) Describing what the data shows — you need to describe any patterns and correlations and look for any anomalies. Make sure you use specific points from the data and reference what graph, table etc. you're talking about. You might also need to make comparisons between different sets of data. Statistical techniques help make the data more manageable, so it's easier to spot patterns and make comparisons.

2) Explaining what the data shows — you need to explain why there are patterns and why different data sets are linked together. Use your geographical knowledge to help you explain the results and remember to use geographical terms.

Conclusions are a Summary of the Results

A conclusion is a summary of what you found out in relation to the original question. It should include:

> Be careful when drawing conclusions. Some results show a link or correlation, but that doesn't mean that one thing causes the other.

1) A summary of what your results show.

2) An answer for the question you are investigating, and an explanation for why that is the answer.

3) An explanation of how your conclusion fits into the wider geographical world — think about how your conclusion and results could be used by other people or in further investigations.

Evaluations Identify Problems in the Investigation

Evaluation is all about self assessment — looking back at how good or bad your study (or the data you are given in the exam) was. You need to be able to:

1) Identify any problems with the methods used and suggest how they could be improved. Think about things like the size of the data sets, if any bias (unfairness) slipped in and if other methods would have been more appropriate or more effective.

2) Describe how accurate the results are and link this to the methods used — say whether any errors in the methods affected the results.

3) Comment on the validity of your conclusion. You need to talk about how problems with the methods and the accuracy of the results affect the validity of the conclusion. Problems with methods lead to less reliable and accurate results, which affects the validity of the conclusion.

- Accurate results are as near as possible to the true answer — they have few errors.
- Reliable means that data can be reproduced.
- Valid means that the data answers the original question and is reliable.

For example:

> I concluded that the river flowed faster further downstream. However, one problem with my data collection method was that it was difficult to put the float in at exactly the same point each time. This reduced the accuracy of my measurements. To make my investigation more accurate, I could have placed a tape measure across the river to mark the exact point of entry. Another problem was that I only took two readings at each site and I only used one upstream site and one downstream site. To make my data more reliable I could have taken more readings at each site, and used a larger number of sites both upstream and downstream. These improvements would have produced a more valid conclusion.

You'll have to analyse your own data and data you're given

In the exam, you'll need to write about how you analysed your data and your conclusion, so make sure you have some points ready before you hit the exam. You might also be asked to analyse some data that you're given and draw conclusions from it — the more practice you get now, the easier that'll be.

Exam Questions

When you've finished your fieldwork, have a go at these exam questions. On this page, you'll have to write about someone else's data, and on the next page, you'll be asked about your own fieldwork.

1   A student wanted to investigate how the cross-profile of a beach is affected by different coastal management strategies along the shore. **Figure 1** shows the method she used to find the cross-profile of the beach. She measured the profile at three points along the beach. The results are shown in **Figure 2**.

Figure 1

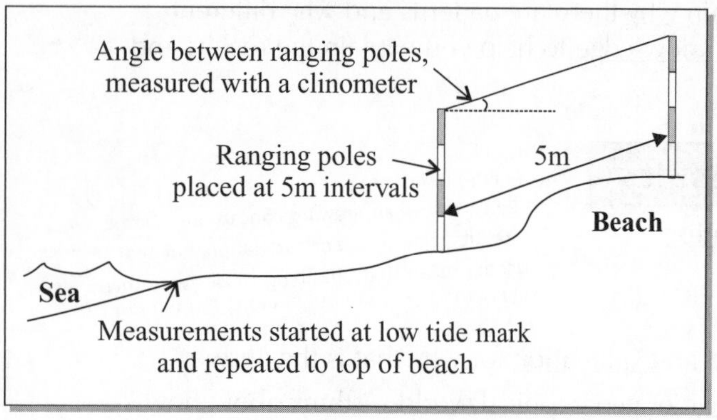

Angle between ranging poles, measured with a clinometer

Ranging poles placed at 5m intervals

5m

Beach

Sea

Measurements started at low tide mark and repeated to top of beach

Figure 2

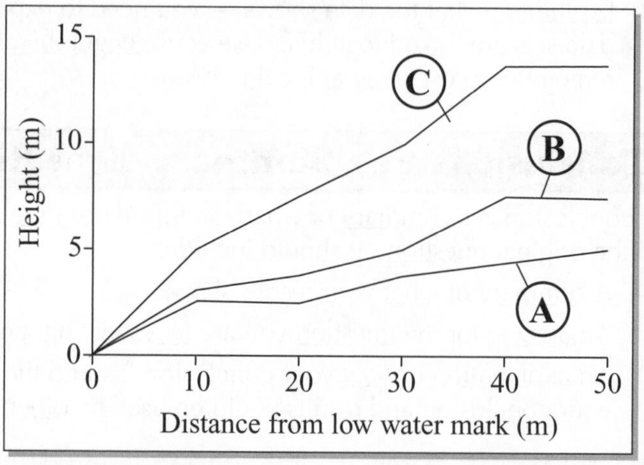

Height (m) vs Distance from low water mark (m)

1.1   Describe two possible sources of inaccuracy in the method used.

    1:..

    ....

    2:..

    ....
                                                                                                        [2]

1.2   Suggest how the student might have chosen the points along the beach at which to measure the cross-profiles.

    ....

    ....
                                                                                                        [2]

1.3   Suggest one way in which the student could add to **Figure 2** so that the data is presented more effectively.

    ....

    ....
                                                                                                        [2]

1.4   Suggest one way in which the reliability of the data could be improved.

    ....

    ....
                                                                                                        [2]

[Total 8 marks]

Exam Questions

2 This question is about your fieldwork enquiry that involved the collection of **physical geography** data.

Give the title of your enquiry that involved the collection of physical geography data.

Title of enquiry: ....

....

2.1 Identify one risk that you needed to manage in your fieldwork location.

....

....

[1]

2.2 Justify the statistical techniques you used to analyse your data.

....

....

....

....

....

[4]

[Total 5 marks]

3 This question is about your fieldwork enquiry that involved the collection of **human geography** data.

Give the title of your enquiry that involved the collection of physical geography data.

Title of enquiry: ....

....

3.1 Assess the effectiveness of your data collection methods in helping you to answer your original question.

....

....

....

....

....

....

....

[Total 6 marks]

Answers

Section 1 — Tectonic Hazards

Page 12

1.1 This question is level marked. How to grade your answer:

Level 0: There is no relevant information. *[0 marks]*

Level 1: There is a basic description of one or two building features. *[1-2 marks]*

Level 2: There is a clear description of specific building features and a detailed explanation of how they might help to reduce the effects of tectonic hazards. *[3-4 marks]*

Here are some points your answer may include:

- Buildings, bridges etc. might have been designed to withstand earthquakes, e.g. by using materials like reinforced concrete or building special foundations that absorb an earthquake's energy.
- Existing buildings and bridges might have been strengthened (e.g. by wrapping pillars in steel frames) so they're less likely to collapse under the weight of falling ash or due to shaking from an earthquake.
- Adaptations like these would make buildings less likely to collapse during a tectonic hazard, so fewer people would be killed, injured or trapped. Also, less rebuilding would be necessary, so the economic effects would also be reduced.
- Automatic shut-off switches that can turn off gas and electricity supplies if an earthquake is detected by a monitoring system might have been installed. This prevents fires and therefore could reduce the death toll and damage to the city.

1.2 E.g. earth movements and volcanoes can be monitored *[1 mark]*, so that people have time to evacuate the area or prepare before an earthquake or eruption occurs *[1 mark]*.

2.1 Volcanic eruptions — any two from: e.g. buildings and roads are destroyed or buried by ash *[1 mark]*. / Buildings may collapse if enough ash falls on them *[1 mark]*. / Vegetation is damaged when ash falls on it *[1 mark]*.

Earthquakes — any two from: e.g. buildings and bridges collapse, and homes are destroyed *[1 mark]*. / Roads are damaged *[1 mark]*. / Electricity cables and communications networks are damaged, cutting off supplies *[1 mark]*.

Section 2 — Weather Hazards

Page 24

1.1 Predicting where and when a tropical storm will hit gives people in Miami time to evacuate, so fewer people will be injured or killed *[1 mark]*. It also gives people time to protect their homes and businesses, e.g. by boarding up windows, so there will be less damage to property *[1 mark]*.

1.2 This question is level marked. How to grade your answer:

Level 0: There is no relevant information. *[0 marks]*

Level 1: There is a basic explanation of how immediate and/ or long-term responses reduced the effects of a named tropical storm. *[1-2 marks]*

Level 2: There is a clear explanation of how immediate and/ or long-term responses reduced the effects of a named tropical storm. *[3-4 marks]*

Level 3: There is a detailed explanation of how immediate and/ or long-term responses reduced the effects of a named tropical storm. *[5-6 marks]*

Your answer must refer to a named example.

Here are some points your answer may include:

- The immediate responses to the event, e.g. evacuation before the hurricane reached land; setting up control centres and emergency shelters; stockpiling supplies; the coastguard, police, fire service and army rescuing people; charities providing aid.
- How the immediate responses helped to reduce the effects of the storm, e.g. rescuing people from affected areas prevented deaths.
- The long-term responses to the event, e.g. government funds to rebuild homes and repair other essential infrastructure; not rebuilding on high risk areas; placing new buildings on stilts in high risk areas; repairing and improving flood defences.
- How the long-term responses helped to reduce the effects of the storm, e.g. aid to rebuild houses meant that people were not left homeless.

- Answers may refer to tropical storm events such as Hurricane Katrina, which struck the Gulf of Mexico in 2005. Although 1800 people were killed and hundreds of thousands made homeless, the majority of residents were evacuated before it arrived. The US government provided $16 billion for rebuilding homes and funded other infrastructure repairs to help speed up the recovery.

2.1 A *[1 mark]*

2.2 In high pressure areas there are few clouds, due to the sinking air *[1 mark]*. This means there is little to block the Sun's energy, which causes high temperatures *[1 mark]*.

Page 33

1.1 6 °C *[1 mark]*

1.2 B *[1 mark]*

1.3 Anticyclones form when air is falling, creating high pressure and light winds *[1 mark]*. The falling air means that clouds aren't formed and skies remain clear *[1 mark]*. In winter, this means that temperatures drop *[1 mark]* because there are no clouds to prevent heat loss from the Earth's surface *[1 mark]*.

2 This question is level marked. There are 3 extra marks available for spelling, punctuation and grammar. How to grade your answer:

Level 0: There is no relevant information. *[0 marks]*

Level 1: There is a basic description of the consequences of and responses to a drought or heat wave event. *[1-2 marks]*

Level 2: There is a clear description of the consequences of and responses to a drought or heat wave event. *[3-5 marks]*

Level 3: There is a detailed description of the consequences of and responses to a drought or heat wave event. *[6-8 marks]*

Make sure your spelling, punctuation and grammar are consistently correct, that your meaning is clear and that you use a range of geographical terms correctly *[0-3 marks]*.

Your answer should refer to one named drought or heat wave event. Here are some points your answer may include:

- The effect of the drought or heat wave on people, including any injuries and deaths.
- Damage to property and infrastructure.
- The cost of the drought or heat wave.
- How people and organisations responded during the drought or heat wave.
- How people and organisations responded immediately after the drought or heat wave.
- How people and organisations responded in the months and years after the drought or heat wave.
- Answers may refer to the Millennium Drought in Australia. As a result of the drought, farmers lost income and livestock, vegetation loss and soil erosion increased, and wildfires affected 30 000 km² of land. In response, water allocations were reduced during the drought, the government gave families and businesses income support to help them survive, and cities like Sydney built new desalination plants to turn sea water into drinking water.

Section 3 — Climate Change

Page 44

1.1 3.2 million km² (accept 3.1-3.3 million km²) *[1 mark]*

1.2 The sea ice extent fluctuated around 7 million km² between 1979 and 1997 *[1 mark]*. It then fell to 3.6 million km² in 2012 *[1 mark]* before recovering to 4.7 million km² by 2016 *[1 mark]*.

2.1 Ice sheets are made up of layers of ice, with one new layer formed each year *[1 mark]*. By analysing the gases trapped in the layers of ice, scientists can tell what the temperature was in each year *[1 mark]*.

2.2 E.g. changes in the Earth's orbit affect the amount of solar radiation/ energy that the Earth receives *[1 mark]*. Periods of warming could have been caused by the Earth receiving more solar energy as it came closer to the Sun *[1 mark]*. / The Sun's output of energy changes in short cycles of about 11 years *[1 mark]*, so periods of cooling could have been caused by periods of reduced solar output *[1 mark]*.

You could also have written about material released from volcanic eruptions or thrown up by asteroid collisions reflecting the Sun's rays back out to space, meaning that less energy reached the Earth.

Section 4 — Ecosystems 1

Page 54

1.1   D *[1 mark]*

A producer is an organism that uses energy from sunlight to produce food, so producers are usually plants rather than animals.

1.2   Any one from: sea urchins *[1 mark]* / sea otter *[1 mark]* / crab *[1 mark]* / octopus *[1 mark]* / periwinkle *[1 mark]* / sea snail *[1 mark]*.

1.3   When dead material decomposes, nutrients are released into the soil *[1 mark]*. The nutrients are then taken up from the soil by plants *[1 mark]*. The plants may be eaten by consumers, so the nutrients they contain are transferred to the consumers *[1 mark]*. When the plants or consumers die, the nutrients are returned to the soil, and the cycle continues *[1 mark]*.

2.1   A: There is lots of light but it is exposed to wind and heavy rainfall *[1 mark]*.
B: It is sheltered and quite dark because of the trees above *[1 mark]*.

2.2   The climate is the same all year round *[1 mark]*. It's hot (the temperature is generally between 20 and 28 °C and only varies by a few degrees over the year) *[1 mark]*. Rainfall is very high (around 2000 mm per year) and it rains every day *[1 mark]*.

Page 64

1.1   C *[1 mark]*

Sustainable forest management is when a forest is used in a way that prevents long-term damage, whilst allowing local people to benefit from the resources it provides in the present and in the future.

1.2   Only some trees are felled — most trees are left standing, so the forest is less damaged *[1 mark]*. The overall forest structure is kept — the canopy's still there and the soil isn't exposed, so the soil remains fertile and is able to support plant growth *[1 mark]*. This means that the forest will be able to regenerate so it can be used in the future *[1 mark]*.

1.3   E.g. the economic benefits of sustainable management are only seen in the long-term *[1 mark]*, so it is difficult for poorer countries who need income immediately *[1 mark]*. Also, even though the trees may be replaced, the newly planted forest may not resemble the natural forest *[1 mark]*, so the entire ecosystem may not be restored *[1 mark]*.

1.4   This question is level marked. There are 3 extra marks available for spelling, punctuation and grammar. How to grade your answer:

Level 0:   There is no relevant information. *[0 marks]*

Level 1:   There is a basic description of some of the benefits of deforestation to the people that live in the rainforest. *[1-3 marks]*

Level 2:   There is a clear description of some of the benefits of deforestation to the people that live in the rainforest and some reference to the problems that it may cause. *[4-6 marks]*

Level 3:   There is a detailed description of some of the benefits of deforestation to the people that live in the rainforest and a clear analysis of the problems that it may cause. The answer comes to a clear conclusion. *[7-9 marks]*

Make sure your spelling, punctuation and grammar is consistently correct, that your meaning is clear and that you use a range of geographical terms correctly *[0-3 marks]*.

Your answer must refer to a named example.

Here are some points your answer may include:

• Deforestation brings some benefits to the people who live in the rainforest, e.g. it clears land for subsistence farming, so people can feed themselves and their families; industries such as logging and mining create jobs.

• Deforestation brings wealth to countries (e.g. through exporting hardwood, minerals etc. from the rainforest). This may have knock-on benefits for the people living in the area, such as investment in providing education or electricity to the area.

• However, deforestation also brings problems for the people living in rainforests. E.g. local rubber tappers who extract natural rubber from rubber trees may lose their livelihoods as trees are cut down.

• Subsistence and commercial farmers may find that their land soon becomes unproductive, and they are forced to move or clear more land. This is because removing tree cover removes the means by which soil nutrients are replenished, and leaves the soil exposed to erosion by heavy rainfall, so it quickly becomes infertile.

• Your answer may refer to deforestation in the Amazon rainforest, including logging and commercial farming in Brazil and mining in Peru.

The question asks you to 'assess the extent'. This means you need to weigh up the pros and cons of the deforestation of tropical rainforests for the people who live there, and come to a clear conclusion about whether the benefits outweigh the problems.

2.1   Coral reefs are found between 30° north and south of the equator because they need warm water to grow *[1 mark]*. They are found close to the coast because they only grow in shallow water *[1 mark]*. The low latitude and shallow water mean that there is plenty of sunlight, which they need to grow *[1 mark]*.

2.2   Your answer will vary depending on the reef you have chosen. Any two from: e.g. runoff from farmland, boats and sewage all cause pollution in the waters surrounding the Great Barrier Reef *[1 mark]*, which can kill wildlife in the area *[1 mark]*. / Coastal developments near the Great Barrier Reef can destroy mangrove forests *[1 mark]*. This increases the amount of nutrients and sediment that are added to the reef ecosystem, which can affect the organisms living there *[1 mark]*. / Human activities in the Great Barrier Reef may interfere with breeding, e.g. tourists disturbing nesting sea birds *[1 mark]*. This may lead to some species dying out in the area *[1 mark]*. / Global warming caused by the release of greenhouse gases into the atmosphere may cause sea temperatures to rise *[1 mark]*. If they increase above 29 °C, coral in the reef can't provide enough nutrients to support the algae that live in it *[1 mark]*.

Section 5 — Ecosystems 2

Page 72

1.1   E.g. low rainfall means that soils are dry *[1 mark]*, while high temperatures mean that evaporation rates are high so soils are dry and salty *[1 mark]*. Dry soils are easily eroded and can form dust clouds, which inhibit rainfall *[1 mark]*.

1.2   Any two from: e.g. extracting groundwater by digging wells means people are able to grow more crops in the short-term, so human populations in the area may increase *[1 mark]*. / In the long-term, extracting water reduces soil moisture, leaving soil drier and more easily eroded *[1 mark]*. / Drier soil means that plants will die, so vegetation cover decreases *[1 mark]*.

2.1   This question is level marked. How to grade your answer:

Level 0:   There is no relevant information. *[0 marks]*

Level 1:   There is a basic description of at least one human cause of desertification. *[1-2 marks]*

Level 2:   There is a clear description of some of the ways that humans contribute to the process of desertification. *[3-4 marks]*

Level 3:   There is a detailed description of a number of ways that humans contribute to the process of desertification. *[5-6 marks]*

Here are some points your answer may include:

• People living in the area may have removed vegetation for firewood. Removal of trees leaves the soil exposed so it is more easily eroded.

• Keeping too many animals in a small area can cause overgrazing of vegetation, whilst trampling can contribute to erosion.

• Over-cultivation of the land can mean that nutrients are used up. This means that plants can no longer be grown in those soils and, without plants, soil erosion increases because their roots no longer hold the soil together.

• Population growth puts pressure on the land, leading to more deforestation (for firewood), more over-grazing and more over-cultivation.

• Human activities are also contributing to climate change.

• Climate change is expected to reduce rainfall in areas that are already quite dry. Less rain means that less water is available for plant growth, so plants begin to die. Plant roots hold the soil together. If the plants die, the soil is easily eroded.

• Climate change is expected to increase global temperature. Higher temperatures would mean that more water would evaporate from the land and from plants. This would make soils drier and mean that plants would die (so their roots would no longer hold the soil together).

Page 84

1.1 Any one from: e.g. it has a light-coloured coat in the winter to camouflage it against the winter snow *[1 mark]*, helping it to hide from predators *[1 mark]*. / It has thick fur *[1 mark]* to reduce the amount of energy needed to keep it warm *[1 mark]*.

1.2 Any two from: e.g. they are evergreen *[1 mark]*, so they can make the best use of available light *[1 mark]*. / They have needles instead of flat leaves *[1 mark]*, which have a smaller surface area, so reduce water loss caused by strong, cold winds *[1 mark]*. / They are cone-shaped *[1 mark]*, which means that heavy winter snowfall can slide straight off the branches without damaging them *[1 mark]*. / Their branches are quite bendy *[1 mark]*, so are less likely to snap under the weight of snow *[1 mark]*.

2.1 Economic opportunities at location A include fishing and tourism *[1 mark]*. The settlement is on the coast with easy access to fishing areas *[1 mark]*. The nearby airport and roads make the settlement accessible to tourists, who may visit to go whale-watching *[1 mark]*.

2.2 E.g. the only access route to location B by land is a long, twisty ice road that may not be usable all year round *[1 mark]*. This could make it difficult for people to access the area, which could limit the development of e.g. tourism *[1 mark]*.

The question tells you to use evidence from the map, so make sure your answer refers to features you can see on the map.

Section 6 — The UK Physical Landscape

Page 91

1.2 E.g. in the past, the UK was much closer to a plate boundary than it is now *[1 mark]*. Active volcanoes forced magma to the surface, forming igneous rocks *[1 mark]*. The heat and pressure caused by plate collisions formed metamorphic rocks *[1 mark]*. This also caused rocks to be folded and uplifted, forming mountain ranges *[1 mark]*.

2.1 Any one from: e.g. carboniferous limestone *[1 mark]* / clay *[1 mark]* / chalk *[1 mark]*.

2.2 A rock formed when magma cools and hardens *[1 mark]*.

2.3 Any one from: e.g. igneous rocks are usually hard *[1 mark]*. / Igneous rocks contain crystals that form as the rock cools *[1 mark]*. / They are often impermeable *[1 mark]*.

2.4 Igneous rocks are generally found in the north and west of the UK *[1 mark]*, mostly in Scotland and Northern Ireland *[1 mark]*.

Section 7 — UK Coastal Landscapes

Page 105

1.1 991802 *[1 mark]*

1.2 2.0 km (accept between 1.9 km and 2.1 km) *[1 mark]*

1.3 Longshore drift transported sand and shingle north east past a sharp bend in the coastline *[1 mark]* and deposited it in the sea, forming a spit *[1 mark]*.

2.1 Any one from: e.g. beach nourishment is when sand and shingle from elsewhere or from lower down the beach is added to the upper part of beaches *[1 mark]*. / Dune regeneration is when sand dunes are created or restored by nourishment, or by planting vegetation to stabilise the sand *[1 mark]*.

2.2 Advantage: Any one from: e.g. beach nourishment creates wider beaches which slow the waves, giving greater protection from flooding and erosion *[1 mark]*. / Dune regeneration restores or creates sand dunes that provide a barrier between the land and the sea. This means wave energy is absorbed, which prevents flooding and erosion *[1 mark]*.
Disadvantage: Any one from: e.g. taking material from the sea bed for beach nourishment can kill organisms like sponges and corals *[1 mark]*. / Beach nourishment is a very expensive defence that has to be repeated *[1 mark]*. / Dune regeneration only protects a small area *[1 mark]*. / Nourishment of existing dunes is very expensive *[1 mark]*.

Section 8 — UK River Landscapes

Page 124

1.1 18 hours *[1 mark]*

1.2 Any one from: the River Seeton is more likely to flood *[1 mark]* because it has a higher peak discharge, meaning that there is more water in the channel *[1 mark]*. / The River Seeton is more likely to flood *[1 mark]* because it has a shorter lag time, meaning that discharge increases more quickly *[1 mark]*.

1.3 Built-up areas contain lots of impermeable surfaces and drains *[1 mark]*. Impermeable surfaces increase runoff and drains quickly take runoff to rivers, so the hydrograph will have a higher peak discharge and a shorter lag time *[1 mark]*.

2.1 This question is level marked. How to grade your answer:
Level 0: There is no relevant information. *[0 marks]*
Level 1: There is a basic explanation of the formation of interlocking spurs. *[1-2 marks]*
Level 2: There is a detailed explanation of the formation of interlocking spurs, which uses geographical terms accurately. *[3-4 marks]*
Here are some points your answer may include:
• In the upper course of a river most of the erosion is vertically downwards, creating steep-sided, V-shaped valleys.
• In the upper course, rivers aren't powerful enough to erode laterally (sideways), so they wind around the high hillsides that stick out into their paths on either side.
• The hillsides interlock with each other as the river winds around them, forming interlocking spurs.

Section 9 — UK Glacial Landscapes

Page 135

1.1 Grid reference: 3614 *[1 mark]*.
Formation: Glacial troughs start off as V-shaped river valleys *[1 mark]*. Glaciers erode the sides and bottom of the valley, forming a U-shaped glacial trough *[1 mark]*.

1.2 1.7 km (allow 1.6-1.8km) *[1 mark]*

2.1 A *[1 mark]*
Medial moraine is a ridge of material deposited along the centre of a valley.

2.2 Any one from: the material can be frozen in the glacier *[1 mark]*. / The material can be carried on the surface of the glacier *[1 mark]*. / The material can be transported by bulldozing, when the ice pushes loose material in front of it *[1 mark]*.

2.3 Terminal moraine forms at the snout of the glacier *[1 mark]*. Material is abraded and plucked from the valley floor and transported at the front of the glacier *[1 mark]*. When the ice retreats, the material is deposited as semicircular mounds *[1 mark]*.

Section 10 — Urban Issues and Challenges

Page 147

1.1

[1 mark]

1.2 The urban population of developed countries increased gradually from about 0.5 billion to 0.9 billion *[1 mark]*. The urban population of developing countries was less than that of developed countries in 1950 but much greater by 2000 *[1 mark]*. It increased rapidly from about 0.3 billion to 2 billion *[1 mark]*.

1.3 Any two from: e.g. there are more jobs in urban areas, and they are often better paid *[1 mark]*. / To get access to better health care and education *[1 mark]*. / To join other family members who have already moved *[1 mark]*. / People think they will have a better quality of life in cities *[1 mark]*.

1.4 This question is level marked. How to grade your answer:

Level 0: There is no relevant information. *[0 marks]*

Level 1: There are a few points about the rate of urbanisation in either developed countries or developing countries. *[1-2 marks]*

Level 2: There is a clear explanation of the rate of urbanisation in developed countries and developing countries. *[3-4 marks]*

Level 3: There is a detailed explanation of the rate of urbanisation in developed countries and developing countries. *[5-6 marks]*

Here are some points your answer may include:

- Urbanisation happened earlier in developed countries than in developing countries, e.g. during the industrial revolution, so most of the population now already live in urban areas. This means that there are fewer people moving into cities in developed countries than in developing countries.

- Good transport and communication networks mean that people in developed countries can live in rural areas and commute to cities, or work from home. This means that many people in developed countries are moving away from cities.

- Decline of heavy industry in cities in developed countries caused mass unemployment. People desiring a better quality of life moved away from overcrowded cities to rural areas, meaning that urban population growth slowed.

- A lower proportion of the population in developing countries currently live in urban areas, so there are more people living in rural areas who might move to cities.

- Many people in developing countries are moving to cities to get a better quality of life, e.g. access to better healthcare, jobs and education. This causes rapid urban growth in developing countries.

Section 11 — Cities in the UK

Page 159

1.1 E.g. derelict buildings became a target for crime and graffiti *[1 mark]*. / Areas in many inner cities became deprived, with poor access to health care, education and a lack of job opportunities *[1 mark]*.

1.2 This question is level marked. There are 3 extra marks available for spelling, punctuation and grammar. How to grade your answer:

Level 0: There is no relevant information. *[0 marks]*

Level 1: There is a basic description of some challenges and/or opportunities caused by urban change. *[1-3 marks]*

Level 2: There is some discussion of the challenges and opportunities caused by urban change and some attempt to come to a conclusion. *[4-6 marks]*

Level 3: There is a detailed discussion of the challenges and opportunities caused by urban change and the answer comes to a clear conclusion. *[7-9 marks]*

Make sure your spelling, punctuation and grammar is consistently correct, that your meaning is clear and that you use a range of geographical terms correctly *[0-3 marks]*.

Your answer must present both challenges and opportunities in a named UK city. You must decide whether the challenges or opportunities are more significant and justify your decision. Here are some points your answer may include:

- A brief description of how the city has changed.

- A discussion of the challenges this change has presented. This may include social and economic challenges, e.g. urban deprivation leading to inequalities in housing, education, health and employment. It may also include environmental challenges, such as buildings and land being left derelict, the loss of greenfield land due to new developments, and the difficulties of waste disposal.

- A discussion of the opportunities the change has presented. This may include social and economic opportunities, e.g. a greater mix of cultures and more possibilities for recreation and entertainment; different employment opportunities; the development of integrated transport systems. It may also include environmental opportunities, such as urban greening, e.g. the creation of parks and community woodlands and the development of cycle ways and footpaths.

- Your answer may also discuss the effects of urban sprawl on the environment and on the character of the settlements in the rural-urban fringe.

- Your answer may refer to London, the capital of the UK which has changed from a former industrial city to a modern tourist destination and centre for finance.

2.1 C *[1 mark]*

For the 21-30 age group, the 'Migration to London' line is higher than the 'Migration out of London' line — more people moved to London than moved away, so the population of this age group must have increased.

2.2 The movement of people within a country *[1 mark]*.

2.3 Your answer will vary depending on the city you have chosen. E.g. in London, international migration has led to an increase in population *[1 mark]*, e.g. about 100 000 more people arrived in London than left in 2014, much of which will have been international migration *[1 mark]*. International migration has also led to London becoming a very ethnically diverse city *[1 mark]*, which has influenced its character, creating distinctive ethnic areas, e.g. the Brick Lane Bangladeshi curry houses *[1 mark]*.

Section 12 — Change in the UK

Page 175

1.1 Any two from: e.g. near to the central business district (CBD) for easy access to banks etc. *[1 mark]* / close to good road and rail links for easy access *[1 mark]* / close to Newcastle International Airport for international travel *[1 mark]* / near to two universities for collaborations with researchers *[1 mark]*.

2.1 188 200 *[1 mark]*

Work out the range by subtracting the lowest value from the highest value, which here is 341 400 − 153 200.

2.2 International migration has increased the number of young adults in the UK *[1 mark]*, because lots of people have moved to the UK for work *[1 mark]*. The number of children in the UK has increased *[1 mark]*, because many immigrants are of child-bearing age *[1 mark]*.

2.3 Any two from: e.g. young adults tend to move into cities *[1 mark]*. / Wealthy people tend to move into rural areas (counter-urbanisation) *[1 mark]*. / Older people tend to move to rural and coastal areas *[1 mark]*.

Section 13 — Development

Page 184

1.1 E.g. conflict is likely to decrease Libya's level of development *[1 mark]*. This is because damage is done to infrastructure and property, such as the building in Figure 1 *[1 mark]*, and money is spent on arms and fighting instead of development *[1 mark]*.

1.2 Countries that were colonised often have a lower level of development when they gain independence than they would if they had not been colonised *[1 mark]*. This is because colonisers control the economies of their colonies, e.g. by exploiting raw materials *[1 mark]*. The money made goes to the colonising country, so it is not used to develop the colonised country, which remains relatively undeveloped *[1 mark]*.

2.1 A *[1 mark]* and D *[1 mark]*.

In Stage 5, birth rate is lower than death rate, so population decreases.
In Stage 4, birth rate and death rate are equal, so population remains stable.

2.2 Morocco has a relatively high birth rate and a low death rate *[1 mark]*, so it is likely to be at Stage 3 of the demographic transition model *[1 mark]*. Countries at Stage 3 are poorer countries, but with increasing levels of economic development *[1 mark]*.

Page 196

1.1 Any one from: e.g. tourism can provide extra employment *[1 mark]*, providing people with an income they might not have had otherwise *[1 mark]*. / Tourism contributes to a country's income *[1 mark]*, allowing it to invest in improving development and quality of life *[1 mark]*. / Entry fees can be charged *[1 mark]*, which fund preservation or protection schemes, e.g. national parks *[1 mark]*.

1.2 Any two from: e.g. most of the income from tourists goes to large, international companies based in developed countries overseas *[1 mark]*, so the effect on development can be small *[1 mark]*. / Local people can be forced to move from land that is wanted for tourism, e.g. national parks *[1 mark]*, so they lose their homes and livelihoods *[1 mark]*. / Tourism vehicles can damage the environment *[1 mark]*, e.g. safari vehicles can destroy vegetation and disturb animals *[1 mark]*.

2.1 Advantage: e.g. helps to improve the level of development of the recipient country (by improving health, education and agriculture) *[1 mark]*.
Disadvantage: e.g. the aid may not reach the poorest people *[1 mark]* / aid may be lost through corruption *[1 mark]*.

2.2 This question is level marked. There are 3 extra marks available for spelling, punctuation and grammar. How to grade your answer:
Level 0: There is no relevant information. *[0 marks]*
Level 1: There is a basic description of how TNCs can affect economic development and quality of life in developing and emerging countries. *[1-3 marks]*
Level 2: There is a clear description of the advantages and disadvantages of TNCs for economic development and quality of life in developing and emerging countries, and a basic judgement of the extent of improvements in a named country. *[4-6 marks]*
Level 3: There is a detailed description of the advantages and disadvantages of TNCs for economic development and quality of life in developing and emerging countries, and a clear judgement of the extent of improvements in a named country. *[7-9 marks]*

Make sure your spelling, punctuation and grammar is consistently correct, that your meaning is clear and that you use a range of geographical terms correctly *[0-3 marks]*.
Your answer must outline ways in which TNCs can improve economic development and quality of life, and ways in which they do not generate improvements, using examples of TNCs in at least one country. You must come to a conclusion about how far they can improve economic development and quality of life, and explain your decision. Here are some points your answer may include:

- TNCs help increase economic development and improve quality of life by employing people, which provides an income for workers and tax income for the state. Some TNCs also run programs to help development, and work with charities to improve quality of life.
- TNCs may not help to improve economic development and quality of life as profits made by the company normally leave the country in which they were made. TNCs may also move around within countries or internationally to take advantage of local government incentives, which can reduce the income from TNCs or prevent long-term development.
- Some TNCs may also cause environmental damage, particularly if environmental regulations are not strict or enforced. This can affect places where people live, which negatively affects quality of life.
- Answers may refer to TNCs in India, for example Unilever, which employs 16 000 people in India and runs development initiatives, but which has been accused of causing environmental damage and threatening the livelihoods of Indian street traders.

Section 14 — Resource Management: Food

Page 211

1.1 The global population has increased from about 2.6 billion in 1950 to about 7.3 billion now and is predicted to continue to rise *[1 mark]*. The increase in population means more resources, e.g. food, water and energy, are required *[1 mark]*. Increasing demand for one resource can also increase the demand for other resources, e.g. more people means more food needs to be grown, which increases the demand for water *[1 mark]*.

1.2 Any two from: e.g. people tend to buy more food than they need *[1 mark]*. / People buy goods that use a lot of energy *[1 mark]*. / Manufacturing these goods uses a lot of water *[1 mark]*. / People use more water because of flushing toilets etc *[1 mark]*.

2.1 C *[1 mark]*
Intensifying farming means producing as much food as possible in as small an area as possible. It usually requires large quantities of chemicals, such as fertilisers and pesticides, to maximise crop yields.

2.2 E.g. organic farming uses natural fertilisers, e.g. manure, instead of chemical fertilisers to return nutrients to the soil *[1 mark]*. Not using chemical fertilisers helps to protect natural ecosystems, making organic farming more environmentally sustainable *[1 mark]*.
You might have written about not using artificial pesticides instead — pesticides can be harmful to organisms, so not using them helps to preserve biodiversity.

2.3 This question is level marked. There are 3 extra marks available for spelling, punctuation and grammar. How to grade your answer:
Level 0: There is no relevant information. *[0 marks]*
Level 1: There is a basic description of one past and/or one present attempt to increase food security at a national scale in a named country. *[1-2 marks]*
Level 2: There is a clear comparison of one past and one present attempt to increase food security at a national scale in a named country. *[3-5 marks]*
Level 3: There is a detailed comparison of one past and one present attempt to increase food security at a national scale in a named country. *[6-8 marks]*

Make sure your spelling, punctuation and grammar are consistently correct, that your meaning is clear and that you use a range of geographical terms correctly *[0-3 marks]*.
Here are some points your answer may include:

- A brief introduction to food security issues in the country you have chosen.
- A description of one past scheme to increase food security, e.g. intensifying farming or the 'Green Revolution'.
- An evaluation of the scheme's effectiveness, e.g. to what extent it increased food security and any issues it caused (e.g. for the environment or people's health).
- A description of one present scheme to increase food security, e.g. GM crops or food production methods.
- An evaluation of the scheme's effectiveness, e.g. to what extent it is increasing food security and any issues it has caused (e.g. for the environment or people's health).
- A conclusion that compares the effectiveness of the two methods and reaches a decision about which was more successful.
- Your answer could refer to intensification of farming in the UK from the 1940s to the 1980s, which used mechanisation, higher yielding plants and large amounts of chemicals to increase food production. It decreased the UK's cereal imports from 70% to 20%, increasing food security. However, the use of monoculture meant that a high proportion of crops were harmed by drought in 1976, while the methods caused environmental problems such as water pollution and loss of biodiversity. Your second example could be the use of new technologies, such as hydroponics, that are currently being used in the UK. Hydroponics allows plants to be grown in a nutrient solution, sometimes in disused spaces such as old tunnels. It is increasing UK production of salad vegetables, and therefore increasing food security. However, the schemes can be expensive to set up and run, so the produce can be expensive. Some sites have been located in rural areas, damaging ecosystems.

Section 15 — Resource Management: Water and Energy

Page 220

1.1 Any one from: e.g. the children are collecting water from an open pool, suggesting that there's no piped water supply *[1 mark]*. / The children are collecting water that looks unclean/unsafe to drink *[1 mark]*.

1.2 E.g. the climate looks dry and hot *[1 mark]* so there may not be much rainfall and lots of water may be lost due to evaporation *[1 mark]*.

1.3 Any two from: e.g. population growth increases the amount of water used, which decreases availability *[1 mark]*. / Industry uses a lot of water, so industrial development can decrease water availability *[1 mark]*. / The pollution of water sources, e.g. rivers, lakes and groundwater, can reduce the amount of clean water that is available *[1 mark]*. / Limited infrastructure, e.g. lack of water pipes and sewers, might mean that sewage contaminates the water supply, decreasing water availability *[1 mark]*. / People may not be able to afford to have water supplied to their home and may not have a water source nearby *[1 mark]*.

1.4 E.g. people may become ill from drinking contaminated water *[1 mark]*. / A shortage of water means that less food can be grown, which could lead to starvation *[1 mark]*.

1.5 Manufacturing industries are very water-intensive, so they can't produce as much during water shortages *[1 mark]*. This may force industries to close *[1 mark]*.

1.6 E.g. when countries in areas of water insecurity share the same water supplies *[1 mark]*, water shortages may trigger one country to take more water from the shared supplies, causing conflict *[1 mark]*.

Page 233

1.1 Location: C *[1 mark]*
Reason: C is exposed on all sides, so turbines will be powered by wind from all directions *[1 mark]*. / It is high up, where winds are stronger *[1 mark]*.
Locations A, B and E are ruled out because they are sheltered by hills, buildings or trees. Location D is ruled out because it is offshore.

1.2 E.g. E would not be suitable for a solar plant because it is in a forest in a valley *[1 mark]*, where trees and the valley sides would block the sunlight *[1 mark]*.

1.3 Any one from: e.g. it's a renewable energy source so it won't run out *[1 mark]*. / It produces no waste products *[1 mark]*.

1.4 This question is level marked. How to grade your answer:
Level 0: There is no relevant information. *[0 marks]*
Level 1: There is a basic discussion of the benefits or costs of extracting a named fossil fuel. *[1-2 marks]*
Level 2: There is a clear discussion of the benefits and costs of extracting a named fossil fuel. *[3-4 marks]*
Level 3: There is a detailed discussion of the benefits and costs of extracting a named fossil fuel. *[5-6 marks]*
Your answer must refer to a specific fossil fuel.
Here are some points your answer may include:
- A brief description of the fossil fuel and how it is extracted.
- A discussion of the benefits of extracting it, e.g. it may be a readily available source of energy, it may cause less pollution than other fossil fuels, it may be cheaper to extract than investing in the technology needed to get energy from other renewable resources.
- A discussion of the costs of extracting it, e.g. there is not an unlimited supply of it so it will run out if it continues to be extracted, using it releases greenhouse gases so extracting it may contribute to global warming, its extraction may cause environmental damage.
- Answers may refer to the extraction of shale gas by fracking. Shale gas is less polluting than coal or oil and is cheaper than some renewables. However, extracting it risks polluting groundwater and air, could cause small earthquakes, and often destroys habitats to clear space for building drilling pads.

Geographical Decision Making

Page 237

1.1 This question is level marked. How to grade your answer:
Level 0: There is no relevant information. *[0 marks]*
Level 1: There is a basic discussion of the statement with limited reference to the figures and some use of knowledge. *[1-2 marks]*
Level 2: There is a clear discussion of the statement with analysis of the figures and use of knowledge. *[3-4 marks]*
Level 3: There is a detailed discussion of the statement with extensive analysis of the figure and appropriate use of knowledge. *[5-6 marks]*
Your answer should come to a conclusion about whether human activities are the main cause of climate change or not. Here are some points your answer may include:
- The climate changes naturally due to variations in the Earth's orbit, changes in the output of the Sun, volcanic activity and asteroid collisions.
- Climate change may also be related to changing concentrations of greenhouse gases in the atmosphere, as they trap heat and create a warming effect.
- CO_2 concentration in the atmosphere was almost constant from year 1 to 1800, and then increased rapidly from 280 parts per million in 1800 to 360 parts per million in 2000. This rapid increase coincided with a rapid increase of about 0.7 °C in global temperature over the same period.
- This increase in CO_2 occurred at the same time as humans began to burn large amounts of fossil fuels, which releases greenhouse gases into the atmosphere.
- Deforestation has also been extensive during this period, for example over 750 000 km² of the Amazon rainforest had been lost since 1978. Deforestation reduces the amount of CO_2 that is removed from the atmosphere by trees, and if the trees are burnt, CO_2 is added to the atmosphere.

- The evidence suggests that humans have caused the increase in atmospheric CO_2 concentration. This increase coincides with increasing temperature, which may suggest that humans are the main cause of climate change.

1.2 This question is level marked. How to grade your answer:
Level 0: There is no relevant information. *[0 marks]*
Level 1: There is a basic discussion of whether renewable energy sources are always small-scale and unreliable. *[1-2 marks]*
Level 2: There is a clear discussion of whether renewable energy sources are always small-scale and unreliable, which uses evidence from Figures 4-6 and other knowledge. *[3-4 marks]*
Level 3: There is a detailed discussion of whether renewable energy sources are always small-scale and unreliable, which uses evidence from Figures 4-6 and other knowledge. *[5-6 marks]*
Your answer must come to a conclusion about whether renewable energy sources are always small-scale and unreliable. Here are some points your answer may include:
- Fossil fuels have traditionally supplied most of our energy and are likely to be able to do so for some years yet.
- Renewable energy sources currently produce 22% of the world's electricity. Most (17%) of this is hydropower.
- Hydropower can be reliable and large-scale. However, it requires a constant supply of flowing water, so it is not a viable alternative to fossil fuels in all areas. Its viability may also be affected by changing precipitation patterns and water supply.
- Biomass is a reliable renewable energy source that can be used on a large scale, for example in converted coal-fired power stations such as Drax in Yorkshire. However, it requires a constant supply of biomass, which in some cases has to be imported, contributing to greenhouse gas emissions. It may therefore not be a viable alternative to fossil fuels in all areas.
- Wind generates 6% of the UK's electricity, and large offshore windfarms can generate significant amounts of power. But the wind does not always blow, so they are unreliable as they cannot generate electricity all the time.
- Solar is a growing source of renewable energy in the UK, but it is not yet used on a large scale and provides only 0.4% of the UK's electricity needs. It needs quite intense sunlight to produce significant amounts of power, so although it may be a viable alternative to fossil fuels in some countries, it is not suitable for all.

1.3 This question is level marked. There are 3 extra marks available for spelling, punctuation and grammar. How to grade your answer:
Level 0: There is no relevant information. *[0 marks]*
Level 1: There is a basic view stated and a simple justification. *[1-3 marks]*
Level 2: There is a clear view stated and an adequate justification using at least one figure and other knowledge. *[4-6 marks]*
Level 3: There is a thorough evaluation of the effectiveness of each scheme at reducing the social, economic and environmental consequences of climate change, and a clear argument for a chosen scheme. The answer draws on evidence from several figures. *[7-9 marks]*
Make sure your spelling, punctuation and grammar is consistently correct, that your meaning is clear and that you use a range of geographical terms correctly *[0-3 marks]*.
You must use your own knowledge and information from Figures 1-6 to decide which of the schemes you think will best reduce the social, economic and environmental consequences of climate change. You will need to examine the pros and cons of each scheme and produce evidence to support your choice. Here are some points your answer may include:
- Schemes 1 and 2 in Figure 6 aim to reduce the effects of climate change by reducing the CO_2 emissions, which Figure 1 suggests contribute to global warming. The schemes may help to make the effects of climate change on people and the environment less severe, but do not directly help those affected.
- Scheme 3 reduces the effects of climate change by helping those worst affected, but doesn't help to reduce climate change itself.

- Scheme 1 aims to reduce emissions from cars, which would lead to a slower increase in atmospheric greenhouse gases and therefore reduced climate change. It is an international agreement, which means it is likely to reduce emissions in most countries around the world. However, it may make new vehicles more expensive, which may cause economic problems for poorer people and encourage people to keep using older, dirtier vehicles. It also only aims to reduce emissions from cars, not from other major sources.
- Scheme 2 aims to reduce carbon emissions from countries with a large carbon footprint, e.g. the USA, which has a carbon footprint of 17 tonnes per person, by encouraging people to change their behaviour. It aims to reduce emissions from a range of sources, such as homes and transport, and it targets a broader range of sources of emissions than Scheme 1, so it could deliver large reductions in carbon emissions. However, it relies on individuals to make changes, which they may be unable or unwilling to do. By targeting individuals it seems to ignore large sources of emissions, such as industry. It is also aimed at countries that already have a large carbon footprint, so it won't prevent developing countries from expanding their carbon footprints.
- Scheme 3 offers aid to those who are worst affected by climate change so they can overcome its effects. For example, droughts could reduce crop yields in affected areas, so food packages could be delivered to these areas to help to prevent starvation if crops failed. However, aid does not offer a long-term, sustainable solution to the problem. The scheme also makes no attempt to reduce climate change, it just reduces some of its effects. Without tackling the underlying causes, some effects may continue to get worse, and will therefore need ever-more aid or funding to mitigate their impacts. In addition, the scheme focuses only on people and makes no attempt to relieve the environmental effects of climate change.

Fieldwork

Page 240-241

1.1 Any two from: e.g. the ranging poles may not have been held straight, affecting the angles recorded *[1 mark]*. / The ranging poles may sink into the sand, affecting the angles recorded *[1 mark]*. / It can be difficult to take accurate readings with a clinometer *[1 mark]*. / It might be difficult to identify the low water mark *[1 mark]*. / The tide will be going in or out during the data collection, changing the point where measuring starts unless all profiles are taken at the same time by different groups *[1 mark]*. / The 5 m interval could include a break of slope, so the results wouldn't show the true profile *[1 mark]*.

1.2 E.g. she might have selected a part of the beach with no management strategy in place, and two parts with different strategies *[1 mark]*, so that she could compare them to learn how different strategies affect the cross-profile of the beach *[1 mark]*. / She might have chosen points at regular intervals along the beach *[1 mark]*, to investigate how the cross-profile changes along the shore *[1 mark]*.

Her decision might also have been affected by accessibility and safety concerns.

1.3 Any one from: e.g. the student could annotate the graph *[1 mark]*, so that there was more information about the beach features at each location *[1 mark]*. / The student could add photographs of each location *[1 mark]*, so that the features of the beach at each location could easily be seen *[1 mark]*. / The student could include a map showing the location of each of the profiles *[1 mark]*, so that they could be linked to other geographical features *[1 mark]*.

1.4 E.g. more cross profiles could have been measured *[1 mark]* at equal intervals along the beach *[1 mark]*.

2.1 Any one from: e.g. water hazards, such as drowning *[1 mark]* / weather hazards, for example getting too cold, too hot or sunburnt *[1 mark]* / potential for slips and falls *[1 mark]* / being hit by falling rocks *[1 mark]*.

2.2 This question is level marked. How to grade your answer:

Level 0: There is no relevant information. *[0 marks]*

Level 1: There is a basic description of at least one technique used and an attempt to support its use in the investigation. *[1-2 marks]*

Level 2: There is a detailed description of at least two techniques used and clear evidence to support their use in the investigation. *[3-4 marks]*

Here are some points your answer may include:
- Measures of average, e.g. mean, median or mode, can be used to summarise the data collected to make it easier to spot patterns and draw conclusions.
- Measures of spread, e.g. range or interquartile range, can be used to show how far the data is spread out or how consistent the results are. This can give an indication of the precision/repeatability of the data.
- Lines of best fit can be used to identify correlation between sets of data and to help draw conclusions about the relationship of one set of data to another.
- Percentage increase and decrease can be used to show how much something has changed over time. They are useful when comparing two data sets with different amounts of data in each, because a percentage shows a proportion rather than an absolute value.
- Calculating percentiles can tell you if a data point is very big or small compared to the rest of the data set.

Try to include specific details about why you used each technique or how it helped you to identify patterns in your data.

3.1 This question is level marked. How to grade your answer:

Level 0: There is no relevant information. *[0 marks]*

Level 1: There are a few points about the effectiveness of the data collection techniques used. *[1-2 marks]*

Level 2: There is a clear evaluation of the effectiveness of the data collection methods used and the answer attempts to come to a conclusion. *[3-4 marks]*

Level 3: There is a detailed evaluation of the effectiveness of the data collection methods used and the answer comes to a clear conclusion. *[5-6 marks]*

Here are some points your answer may include:
- An outline of the data sets collected and the conclusions that could be drawn. Whether these conclusions answered the original question.
- An outline of the limitations of the data collection methods used, and how they may have affected the validity of the conclusion.
- An overall conclusion about the effectiveness of the techniques used in answering the research question.

Acknowledgements

Photograph of Montserrat on page 7 © Dr. Richard Roscoe, Visuals Unlimited/Science Photo Library

Photograph of Montserrat damage on page 12 by Wailunip licensed under the Creative Commons Attribution-ShareAlike 2.5 Generic license. https://creativecommons.org/licenses/by-sa/2.5/deed.en

Photograph of Nepal earthquake damage on page 12 by Krish Dulal licensed under the Creative Commons Attribution-ShareAlike 4.0 International license. https://creativecommons.org/licenses/by-sa/4.0/deed.en

Satellite images on page 18 and 21: Jeff Schmaltz, MODIS Rapid Response Team, NASA/GSFC

Photograph of Slidell, Louisiana on page 23 © FEMA/Liz Roll

Data used to construct graphs of global temperature on pages 23 and 35 from NASA's Goddard Institute for Space Studies (GISS). © NASA/GISS

Map on page 26: Aqueduct Global Maps 2.1 Indicators. Constructing Decision-Relevant Global Water Risk Indicators by Francis Gassert, Paul Reig, Tien Shiao, Matt Luck (Research Scientist) ISciences LLC and Matt Landis (Research Scientist) ISciences LLC - April 2015. Licensed under a Creative Commons Attribution International 4.0 License (https://creativecommons.org/licenses/by/4.0/)

Graphs of rainfall and temperature, and sunshine hours on page 28 © Crown Copyright, the Met Office. Contains public sector information licensed under the Open Government Licence v3.0 - http://www.nationalarchives.gov.uk/doc/open-government-licence/version/3/

Photograph on p.30 © Rose and Trev Clough/ p.31 © John Douglas/ p.86 (top right) © Trevor Littlewood/ p.86 (top left) © Peter Styles/ p.86 (bottom left) © Bill Boaden/ p.86 (bottom right) © Peter Jeffery/ p.88 © Martyn Gorman/ p.89 (left) © Dudley Smith/ p.89 (right) © Colin Smith/ p.98 (Agriculture) © Roger Lombard/ p.98 (Development) © Lewis Clarke/ p.98 (Industry [left]) © Mike Faherty/ p.98 (Industry [right]) © David Dixon/ p.98 (Coastal Management) © David Dixon/ p.99 © Arthur C Harris/ p.101 (top) © Raymond Knapman/ p.101 (middle left) © Nick MacNeill/ p.101 (middle right) © Eugene Birchall/ p.101 (bottom) © Peter Trimming/ p.102 © Robin Webster/ p.103 (top) © N Chadwick/ p.103 (bottom left) © David Dixon/ p.103 (bottom right) © Maurice D Budden/ p.105 © Rob Farrow/ p.109 and p.124 © Bob Bowyer/ p.113 (top) © Greg Fitchett/ p.113 (middle left) © Roger Templeman/ p.113 (middle right) © Steve Daniels/ p.113 (bottom) © Rose and Trev Clough/ p.114 (top) © Stephen Craven/ p.114 (bottom left) © Andy Waddington/ p.114 (bottom right) © Peter Standing/ p.115 (top) © Rose and Trev Clough/ p.115 (bottom) © Andy Connor/ p.117 (top and bottom) © Rose and Trev Clough/ p.118 © Rose and Trev Clough/ p.122 (top) © Trevor Rickard/ p.122 (middle) © Steve Daniels/ p.122 (bottom) © Rod Allday/ p.128 © Gordon Brown/ p.130 (top) © John Smith/ p.130 (middle left) © Dudley Smith/ p.130 (middle right) © N Chadwick/ p.130 (bottom left) © Ivan Hall/ p.130 (bottom right) © Meirion/ p.132 © Katy Walters/ p.133 © Anthony Parkes/ p.134 (top) © Richard Webb/ p.134 (bottom) © John S Turner/ p.153 © Colin Smith/ p.154 © Philip Halling/ p.155 © Ken Brown/ p.158 © Robert Graham/ p.159 © Albert Bridge/ p.165 © Bob Jones/ p.170 © Christine Matthews/ p.174 © Helmut Zozmann/ p.203 © John Spivey/ p.204 © Walter Baxter/ p.208 © Jim Barton/ p.209 © David Anstiss/ p.215 © Octal/ p.228 © SuSan A Secretariat. Licensed for re-use under the Creative Commons Attribution-ShareAlike 2.0 Generic Licence. http://creativecommons.org/licenses/by-sa/2.0/

Data used to compile the temperature variation graph on page 36: based on Palaeogeography, Palaeoclimatol., Palaeoecol., 1 (1965) 13-37, H. H. Lamb, The early medieval warm epoch and its sequel, p25, Copyright © 1965, with permission from Elsevier.

Data on UK climate change on page 40 from Adapting to climate change UK Climate Projections, 2009. Contains public sector information licensed under the Open Government Licence v3.0. http://www.nationalarchives.gov.uk/doc/open-government-licence/version/3/

Data on sea levels on page 40 from Lowe, J. A., Howard, T. P., Pardaens, A., Tinker, J., Holt, J., Wakelin, S.,Milne, G., Leake, J. , Wolf, J., Horsburgh, K., Reeder, T. , Jenkins, G., Ridley, J. ,Dye, S., Bradley, S. (2009), UK Climate Projections science report: Marine and coastal projections. Met Office Hadley Centre, Exeter, UK.

Graphs on page 41 adapted from Figure SPM.6 Climate Change 2014: Synthesis Report. Contribution of Working Groups I, II and III to the Fifth Assessment Report of the Intergovernmental Panel on Climate Change [Core Writing Team, Pachauri, R.K. and Meyer, L. (eds.)]. IPCC, Geneva, Switzerland.

Sea level graph on page 43 adapted from Climate Change 2001: The Scientific Basis. Contribution of Working Group I to the Third Assessment Report of the Intergovernmental Panel on Climate Change. Figure 5. Cambridge University Press.

Graph on page 44 data source: Satellite observations. Credit: NASA National Snow and Ice Data Center Distributed Active Archive Center https://climate.nasa.gov/vital-signs/arctic-sea-ice/

Photograph of desert in Morocco on page 72 by Anderson sady; topographic map of the UK on page 86 and 88 by Captain Blood; photograph of Central Park, NYC on page 156 © Jean-Christophe BENOIST ; photograph of Bath on page 174 by David Iliff; all licensed under the Creative Commons Attribution-ShareAlike 3.0 Unported license. https://creativecommons.org/licenses/by-sa/3.0/deed.en

Geological maps of the UK on pages 87 and 91 contain British Geological Survey materials © NERC 2017

Graph of urban population on page 137: The World Bank: World Development Indicators and © Copyright 2016 United Nations Development Programme

Classification of countries by HDI on page 137 © Copyright United Nations Development Programme

Satellite image of Lagos on page 141: USGS/NASA Landsat

Map overlays showing extent of Lagos by 1920, 1960 and 1990 adapted from Planning, Anti-planning and the Infrastructure Crisis Facing Metropolitan Lagos, page 373, by Matthew Gandy, and Piecemeal Urbanisation at the Peripheries of Lagos, page 5, by Lindsay Sawyer.

Photograph of slum in Old Delhi on page 146 © iStock.com/BluesandViews

World Population Graph on page 147 based on the data from the United Nations, Department of Economic and Social Affairs.

Satellite image of London on page 152: image courtesy NASA/GSFC/MITI/ERSDAC/JAROS, and U.S./Japan ASTER Science Team.

Data on foreign-born residents in Newham and Kingston-upon-Thames on page 153; birth rates in 1964 on page 162; map of over 65s on page 162; data used to plot 2013 London population pyramid on page 163; working hours figures on page 166; media industry figures on page 168 and 173; wages in Huddersfield and London on page 169; average household income data on page 169; life expectancy in England data on page 169; ethnicity data on page 169; internet access data on page 169; FDI data on page 171; investment in infrastructure figure on page 171; graph of wheat yield on page 207; data on energy sources in 1950 on page 230; data used to compile graph of UK energy mix on page 230; data used to make pie charts showing UK energy sources in 1970 and 2014 on page 232 all contain public sector information licensed under the Open Government Licence v3.0. http://www.nationalarchives.gov.uk/doc/open-government-licence/version/3/

Photograph of wind turbines on page 156 © Hans Hillewaert / CC BY-SA 4.0

International migration data on page 152; graph of migration to/from London on page 159; data used to plot 2001 London population pyramid on page 163; ethnicity data on page 163; data used to construct pie chart on page 164; data on employment in the IT sector on page 165; UK R&D spending data on page 165; Burnley employment rate data on page 167; table of international migration into UK on page 175; data used to construct the Population Density of the UK map on page 218 all sourced from: Office for National Statistics Licenced under the Open Government Licence V.3.0. http://webarchive.nationalarchives.gov.uk/20160105160709/https://www.nationalarchives.gov.uk/doc/open-government-licence/version/3/

Data used to compile the UK average rainfall map on page 161 from the Manchester Metropolitan University.

Map of population density on page 161 adapted from the Office for National Statistics Licenced under the Open Government Licence v.3.0.

Land use map on page 161: Cole, B.; King, S.; Ogutu, B.; Palmer, D.; Smith, G.; Balzter, H. (2015). Corine land cover 2012 for the UK, Jersey and Guernsey. NERC Environmental Information Data Centre. http://doi.org/10.5285/32533dd6-7c1b-43e1-b892-e80d61a5ea1d. This resource is made available under the terms of the Open Government Licence.

Data used to construct 2001 population pyramid on page 162 source: Office for National Statistics licenced under the Open Government Licence v3.0. http://webarchive.nationalarchives.gov.uk/20160105160709/https://www.nationalarchives.gov.uk/doc/open-government-licence/version/3/

Data used to construct 2015 population pyramid on page 162 from Population Division, World Population Prospects, the 2015 revision, by Department of Economic and Social Affairs. © United Nations 2016. Accessed 23.06.2016. Reprinted with the permission of the United Nations.

Data used to compile the table on page 162 © Central Intelligence Agency

Data used to construct 1901 population pyramid on page 162 contains Parliamentary information licensed under the Open Parliament Licence v3.0. http://www.parliament.uk/site-information/copyright/open-parliament-licence/

Graph showing change in employment sectors on page 165 source: Office for National Statistics licensed under the Open Government Licence v.2.0. http://www.nationalarchives.gov.uk/doc/open-government-licence/version/2/

Data For imports and exports on page 166 from The Observatory of Economic Complexity by Alexander Simoes. Licensed under a Creative Commons Attribution-ShareAlike 3.0 Unported License.

Acknowledgements

Data on life expectancy in Scotland on page 169 © Crown Copyright. Data supplied by National Records of Scotland.

Photograph of Chadderton on page 174 by Jza84, and photograph of damaged building in Libya on page 184 by Al Jazeera English licensed under the Creative Commons Attribution 2.0 Generic license. https://creativecommons.org/licenses/by/2.0/deed.en

Data to construct map on page 178 from The World Bank: Country and Lending Groups

HDI data on page 178 from 2015 Human Development Report, United Nations Development Programme from hdr.undp.org. Licensed for re-use under the Creative Commons Attribution 3.0 IGO license (https://creativecommons.org/licenses/by/3.0/igo/)

Data used to compile a table (except HDI) on page 178 from The World Factbook. Washington, DC: Central Intelligence Agency, 2017.

Data used to construct quintiles diagram on page 182 sourced from The World Bank: World Development Indicators.

Data used to compile the table on page 183 (except GNI data); data used to compile table on page 184 © Central Intelligence Agency

GNI data in table on page 183 from The World Bank: Indicators.

Data on Nicaragua and the UK on page 183: © World Trade Organization 2016. http://stat.wto.org/CountryProfile/WSDBCountryPFReporter.aspx?Language=E

Photograph of Time Square on page 185 © iStock.com/dibrova

Data on tourism in Kenya on page 189 sourced from the World Bank: International tourism, number of arrivals: World Tourism Organization, Yearbook of Tourism Statistics, Compendium of Tourism Statistics and data files.

Kenya's HDI data on page 189 provided by the UNDP is copyrighted under the Creative Commons Attribution 3.0 IGO licence. http://creativecommons.org/licenses/by/3.0/igo/legalcode

Photograph of schoolchildren in Africa © iStock.com/africa924

Data on India's GDP and GNI per capita on page 191: the World Bank: India: World Bank national accounts data, and OECD National Accounts data files.

HDI data on page 191 from 2015 Human Development Report, United Nations Development Programme from hdr.undp.org. Licensed for re-use under the Creative Commons Attribution 3.0 IGO license (https://creativecommons.org/licenses/by/3.0/igo/)

Data on industrial employment in India on page 191 from the World Bank: Employment in industry (% of total employment): International Labour Organization, Key Indicators of the Labour Market database.

Data on service sector employment in India on page 191 from the World Bank: Employment in services (% of total employment): International Labour Organization, Key Indicators of the Labour Market database.

Data on enrolment in primary education on page 191 from UNESCO Institute for Statistics (UIS), http://uis.unesco.org

Data on life expectancy on page 192 from the World Bank: India: Life expectancy at birth, total (years): United Nations Population Division. World Population Prospects

Data on fertility rate in India on page 192 from the World Bank: India: Fertility rate, total (births per woman): United Nations Population Division. World Population Prospects

Data on urban populations on page 192 from the World Bank: India: Urban population (% of total): United Nations, World Urbanization Prospects.

Urban Population and Literacy rate data used to construct table on page 193 © Office of the Registrar General & Census Commissioner, India. HDI data © Copyright 2016 United Nations Development Programme.

Data on GDP per capita in Bihar and Maharastra on page 193 from statisticstimes.com.

Data on literacy rates for Indian women on page 193 from the World Bank: India: Literacy rate, adult female (% of females ages 15 and above): United Nations Educational, Scientific, and Cultural Organization (UNESCO) Institute for Statistics.

Article about aid project in Ghana on page 196 source: Department for International Development licensed under the Open Government Licence v3.0.

Graph on page 198 from World Population to 2300, by Department of Economic and Social Affairs, Population Division , © 2004 United Nations. Reprinted with the permission of the United Nations.

Map of global cereal production on page 200 © FAO 2015 Cereal production quantities by country 2012-2014 http://faostat3.fao.org/browse/Q/QC/E 11.3.2016 This is an adaptation of an original work by FAO.

Map of World Hunger Index on page 200 source: von Grebmer, K., J. Bernstein, A. de Waal, N. Prasai, S. Yin, and Y. Yohannes. 2015. 2015 Global Hunger Index: Armed Conflict and the Challenge of Hunger. "Bangladesh," "Malawi," and "Prevalence of Stunting in Children Under Five Years (%)." Figures. Bonn: Welthungerhilfe; Washington, DC: International Food Policy Research Institute; Concern Worldwide: Dublin. http://dx.doi.org/10.2499/9780896299641.

Photograph of refugees on page 202 by Magharebia and photograph of hand pump on page 204 by Vicki Francis/Department for International Development licensed under the Creative Commons Attribution 2.0 Generic license. https://creativecommons.org/licenses/by/2.0/deed.en

Graph of corn production in Canada and Zimbabwe on page 210 © FAO 2015 Corn production quantities in Canada and Zimbabwe 1960 - 2010 http://faostat3.fao.org/browse/Q/QC/E [16/03/16] This is an adaptation of an original work by FAO.

Map of global water scarcity on page 213 copyright 2014 World Resources Institute. This work is licensed under the Creative Commons Attribution 3.0 License. To view a copy of the license, visit http://creativecommons.org/licenses/by/3.0/ 1

Photograph of children collecting water in Kenya on page 220 © iStock.com/journalturk

Data used to construct energy production map on page 221 source: U.S. Energy Information Administration

Map of energy consumption per person (tonnes of oil equivalent) on p.221 and graph on history of crude oil prices on p.223 © BP Statistical Review of World Energy 2016

Data to create map on oil production on page 223 from OPEC Annual Statistical Bulletin 2016.

Data on oil consumption increase between 2014 and 2015 on page 224 source: U.S. Energy Information Administration (April 2017).

Pie chart on page 227 based on the data from a study by the government-funded Carbon Trust.

Data on oil production and products on page 232 source: U.S. Energy Information Administration (Jan 2017).

Graph of global temperature difference on page 236: figure 5.7 (c) from Masson-Delmotte, V., M. Schulz, A. Abe-Ouchi, J. Beer, A. Ganopolski, J.F. González Rouco, E. Jansen, K. Lambeck, J. Luterbacher, T. Naish, T. Osborn, B. Otto-Bliesner, T. Quinn, R. Ramesh, M. Rojas, X. Shao and A. Timmermann, 2013: Information from Paleoclimate Archives. In: Climate Change 2013: The Physical Science Basis. Contribution of Working Group I to the Fifth Assessment Report of the Intergovernmental Panel on Climate Change [Stocker, T.F., D. Qin, G.-K. Plattner, M. Tignor, S.K. Allen, J. Boschung, A. Nauels, Y. Xia, V. Bex and P.M. Midgley (eds.)]. Cambridge University Press, Cambridge, United Kingdom and New York, NY, USA.

Graph of CO_2 concentration on page 236: figure 6.11 from Ciais, P., C. Sabine, G. Bala, L. Bopp, V. Brovkin, J. Canadell, A. Chhabra, R. DeFries, J. Galloway, M. Heimann, C. Jones, C. Le Quere, R.B. Myneni, S. Piao and P. Thornton, 2013: Carbon and Other Biogeochemical Cycles. In: Climate Change 2013: The Physical Science Basis. Contribution of Working Group I to the Fifth Assessment Report of the Intergovernmental Panel on Climate Change [Stocker, T.F., D. Qin, G.-K. Plattner, M. Tignor, S.K. Allen, J.Boschung, A. Nauels, Y. Xia, V. Bex and P.M. Midgley (eds.)]. Cambridge University Press, Cambridge, United Kingdom and New York, NY, USA.

Graph of carbon footprint on page 236: The World Bank: CO_2 emissions (metric tons per capita): Carbon Dioxide Information Analysis Center, Environmental Sciences Division, Oak Ridge National Laboratory, Tennessee, United States

Data used to construct pie charts on page 236 source: U.S. Energy Information Administration.

Map extracts on pages 89, 90, 97, 105, 112, 129, 135 and 149 reproduced with permission by Ordnance Survey ® © Crown Copyright 2017 OS 100034841.

Maps on page 130 and 175 contain OS data © Crown copyright and database right (2017).

Map on page 233 by David Maliphant. Contains OS data © Crown copyright and database right (2017).

Index

Index